D1527016

Women in the Crossfire

WOMEN IN THE CROSSFIRE

Understanding and Ending Honor Killing

Robert Paul Churchill

OXFORD
UNIVERSITY PRESS

1-27-21
$ 90.00

OXFORD
UNIVERSITY PRESS

Oxford University Press is a department of the University of Oxford. It furthers
the University's objective of excellence in research, scholarship, and education
by publishing worldwide. Oxford is a registered trade mark of Oxford University
Press in the UK and certain other countries.

Published in the United States of America by Oxford University Press
198 Madison Avenue, New York, NY 10016, United States of America.

Library of Congress Cataloging-in-Publication Data
Names: Churchill, Robert Paul, author.
Title: Women in the crossfire : understanding and ending honor killing /
Robert Paul Churchill.
Description: New York, NY : Oxford University Press, 2018. |
Includes bibliographical references and index.
Identifiers: LCCN 2017053466 (print) | LCCN 2017056886 (ebook) |
ISBN 9780190468590 (online course) | ISBN 9780190468576 (updf) |
ISBN 9780190468583 (epub) | ISBN 9780190883409 (companion website) |
ISBN 9780190468569 (cloth : alk. paper)
Subjects: LCSH: Women—Violence against. | Honor killings. | Women's rights.
Classification: LCC HV6250.4.W65 (ebook) | LCC HV6250.4.W65 C577 2018 (print) |
DDC 362.88—dc23
LC record available at https://lccn.loc.gov/2017053466

Dedicated to the memory of my eighth great-grandmother
Martha Allen Carrier (1659–1692)
Hanged as a witch
August 19, 1692, in Salem, Massachusetts for
refusing to confess to crimes impossible to have committed and
sentenced by men unable to question the "realities" holding them in thrall.

CONTENTS

PREFACE

Honor killing is an age-old practice whereby a girl or woman, suspected of having behaved shamefully, is put to death by members of her own family. This is a confounding and shocking violation of human rights. Thus the major objective of *Women in the Crossfire* is to attain a comprehensive understanding of the "life-world" of those who practice honor killing and who inhabit what I call "honor–shame communities." Following efforts to acquire a detailed, empirical account of honor killing, including features commonly shared among honor killing incidents, I seek to clarify conceptions of honor and shame that underwrite commitments that make the psychology of honor killing possible.

People often do not comprehend the reasons why they engage in a specific practice, especially one as costly and counterintuitive as killing a member of one's own family. Consequently, special attention is given to the causal processes affording reasons for the practice, albeit unknown to those who accept honor killing. I pursue causal questions at the micro-level, that is, in terms of the psychological conditions enabling perpetrators to kill and in terms of interpersonal and social conditions that produce victims. Then I examine, at the macro-level, the development of the practice as a result of cultural evolution over centuries.

Of course, the desperate need for the more efficient and secure protection of potential victims of honor killing, as well as an end to the practice altogether, generates moral demands that knowledge be translated into action. Hence the second major objective is the hope that research, arguments, and explanations in this book will assist activist-reformers in forging effective ways of moving beyond outrage and helplessness to a sustainable end of honor killing. The final three chapters offer recommendations for emergency protective and preventative strategies and tactics. Much creative thinking will be required by those best positioned to initiate change, and other strategies and tactics might be judged more effective;

nevertheless, I will be content if this study serves to provoke and stimulate such thinking. Ultimately, the challenge will require a moral transformation across communities in which honor killing is presently accepted. This transformation will require, among other changes, acknowledging that living honorably can never require the sacrifice of female family members perceived to be wayward, as well as renouncing honor killing as an immoral and dysfunctional social practice.

Women become trapped in and subjected to terror and deadly violence as a consequence of the ways men vie with one another for honor and status within a form of extreme patriarchy. This is a repeating motif throughout the book. However, the title, *Women in the Crossfire*, is not meant to connote typical instances in which innocent civilians are caught in the crossfire between rebel snipers and a regime's soldiers. The girls and women studied here are not victims accidentally; that is, they are not in the wrong place at the wrong time, as civilians and bystanders might be during an armed insurrection or war. On the contrary, the hierarchical patriarchies in which honor killings occur sustain and replicate themselves through the systemic and structural victimization of women and girls. Women are permanent potential victims whose lives are disposable should men believe it necessary to kill to maintain their status as honorable men and to uphold the honor of the extended family, and through it, patriarchy itself.

Writing this book was extremely difficult: first, of course, because of the grim subject matter, but there were other reasons as well: much important empirical data and theory was either nonexistent or fragmentary, the research project required crossing disciplinary boundaries, and it was often difficult to develop or adapt methodologies adequate for the range of questions addressed. Initially, it appeared necessary to defend the integrity of this cross-cultural study from a range of possible critics (e.g., cultural and ethical relativists) who might consider it impossible, bound to misinterpret its non-Occidental subjects, or otherwise biased. Quite apart from the widespread consensus that cultural and ethical relativism are no longer theoretically viable, arguments in defense of the possibility and probity of the project would have had a narrow audience—appealing only to specialists interested in the long-standing Orientalism debate and issues relating to cultural studies, postcolonial issues, and cross-cultural interpretation.

Likewise, detailed and explicit explanations and justifications of the various methodologies employed have been deleted. Only brief comments on methodology have been retained and only when absolutely necessary. In addition to increasing the book's length, logical and epistemological issues relevant to methodology would distract readers from the main tasks of this book: providing the critical and comprehensive understanding of honor killing needed to serve as a springboard for effective protection, preventative measures, and an eventual moral transformation. This is the subject of greatest interest to the widest range of readers: activists and social reformers, educated and concerned citizens, and professionals in government, international organizations, and educational, health and medical, and legal services (among others), as well as academicians in many fields. Appealing to the widest audience—the change agents—is what knowledge of the subject requires, morally.

Each of the nine chapters begins with brief introductory comments on the subject of the chapter's sections. As readers need only to scan these introductions to discover their contents, no more need be said here. However, because coming to understand honor killing is far more cumulative a process than linear, readers will find useful cross-references in each section to related materials in other chapters' sections.

Finally, it must be emphasized that this is an exploratory study of honor killing, and its theoretical status necessarily relates to the moral and pragmatic needs for action. Those able to do so must apply protective and preventative strategies and tactics when greater good than harm will result and assess and improve techniques when possible, even in the absence of well-corroborated theoretical knowledge. *Women in the Crossfire* thus affirms the historical role of philosophy in initiating new and imaginative inquiries into subjects that will be later more fully and rigorously investigated in the behavioral, physical, social, and human sciences. Further research should yield results bearing probability and exactness sufficient to enable investigators to postulate genuinely (social) scientific hypotheses. The point at which such knowledge can be claimed to be sufficiently corroborated should come well after honor killing itself is in its death throes and, wherever possible, is the result of voluntarily choice on the part of its former practitioners.

Robert Paul Churchill
Westminster, Maryland
September 2017

ACKNOWLEDGMENTS

This book would not have been possible without the generous assistance and contributions of many persons. Despite her difficult life and premature death, my mother, Nancy, a stalwart champion for justice, imbued me with compassion for the less fortunate and respect for the equality of women. My wife, Eileen, read all of the drafts, making numerous helpful comments. Eileen's help with footnotes and the bibliography were godsends. My former student, Sarah Holmes, served as project manager for the empirical study in Chapter 2 and then accepted my offer to co-author the book. Unfortunately, Sarah's own plans resulted in her decision not to continue as co-author, but I will always be grateful for her research contributions, her insightful comments, and the camaraderie we enjoyed.

A University Facilitating Fund grant from George Washington University (GWU) for the summer of 2013 made it possible for me to begin research for this book. Likewise, a Columbian College Fellowship from GWU for the summer of 2014 enabled Sarah and me to complete our empirical research. Parts of the book were presented to my colleagues and in other forums at GWU, and I am especially grateful to David DeGrazia, Ingrid Creppell, Michèle Friend, Eric Saidel, and Tad Zawidski for their encouragement, helpful suggestions, and recommendations. As Michèle and I commuted long distances together to and from GWU, we had an unusual opportunity to discuss our respective research projects, and I benefited greatly from her prescient comments, hard questions, and patient listening.

Various papers and talks based on research for this book were offered at universities and professional societies. While it is not possible to recognize here all who made helpful comments, I would be remiss if I failed to recognize Joe Betz, Michael Brannigan, Duane Cady, Trudy Conway, Janet Donohoe, Joe Frank Jones, Barry Gans, Bill Gay, Andy Fitz-Gibbons, Fuat and Selin Gürsözlu, Gurjeer Kaur, Charlie Harvey, Ron Hirschbein, Hande Kesgin, Ray Kolcaba, Sanjay Lal, Wim Laven, Christian Matheis, Kate

Mukungu, José Orosco, Lani Roberts, Erin Stern, Jack Weir, and Jeremy Wisnewski.

I am extremely grateful to Lucy Randall, at Oxford University Press, for her enthusiasm about the project, her patience and helpful advice, as well as the expert and efficient help of Hannah Doyle and others at Oxford for enabling me to put *Women in the Crossfire* before the largest possible audience, and also for the expert and efficient efforts of Tharani Ramachandran, Sudha Ramprasath, and Joann "Annie" Woy at Newgen. co in copy-editing, formatting and producing the book. Smrita Jain has my gratitude for contributing the original art for the cover of the book. Many students offered unusual inspiration or served as research aides and otherwise buoyed my hopes that my efforts were intelligible and might be effective. Manali, who arrived at GWU with only one name, inspired me with her ability to overcome the most difficult of obstacles, as did Monica, for her courage in refusing an arranged marriage, leaving her home, and obtaining a restraining order against her parents. For my students Riad Alarian, Michelle Avrutin, Sarah Carson, Lauren Courtney, Nichole Cubbage, Rachel Gabriel, Rosalba Gleijeses, Victoria Goncalves, Cecelia Lee, Christina Ottati, Neerali Patel, and Jessie Rohrer, many, many thanks.

Reviewers for Oxford University Press, David Boersema, Allen Buchanan, and Andrew Fiala, made many challenging comments and offered extremely helpful suggestions. The responsibility for the final product is, of course, entirely my own. Finally, I must recognize Anthony Kwame Appiah whose *The Honor Code* first led me to believe honor killing might be overcome by a moral revolution and Morris Dees and Nicholas Kristof for the inspiration of their tireless struggles for freedom and justice on behalf of those victimized.

ABOUT THE COMPANION WEBSITE

A companion website housing the book's Glossary, Bibliography, and Name Index is available at http://www.oup.com/us/womeninthecrossfire.

Women in the Crossfire

CHAPTER 1

First Steps Toward Understanding Honor Killing

The oddity and complexity of honor killing make the phenomenon difficult to understand. Comprehension thus requires viewing the practice
from a number of disciplinary lens, as well as in increasing degrees of depth
and completion. For this reason, Section 1.1 offers a short, orienting overview of honor killing, offering brief accounts of sample incidents as well
as comments about a number of general features of honor killing and a
working definition of the practice. This initial account is intended to supply
scaffolding for the richer, more detailed discussions of honor killing in subsequent chapters.

The incidents, or cases, reviewed in Section 1.1 also reveal significant
differences between honor killing and other forms of extreme gender violence and crime. Section 1.2 argues that honor killings manifest distinctive characteristics and therefore should not be lumped together with
other crimes allegedly involving "honor," with other crimes specifically
targeting women, or with domestic violence or crimes of passion. Section
1.3 addresses two additional questions for an introduction: first, what is
the scale of honor killing as a global phenomenon, and is it declining or on
the rise? Second, is there public support for honor killing in areas in which
it is traditional? Section 1.4 considers whether or not there is any special
connection between honor killing and Islam.

The term "honor killing" is of relevantly recent vintage, having been introduced in 1978 by Ane Nauta, a Dutch-Turkish scholar at the University of Leiden.[1] This may have marked the first time honor killings were noted as a distinct type of gender violence and distinguished from the broader category of "crimes of honor"[2] (see Section 1.2). While the media rarely covered honor killings before 1990, Radhika Coomaraswamy, as United Nations Special Rapporteur on violence against women, and Jordanian journalist Rana Husseini were prominent early women's rights activists demanding an end to honor killing. Between 1993 and 2003, Coomaraswamy organized hearings and conferences, investigated conditions within UN member states, and campaigned tirelessly for women's rights.[3] Since 1994, Husseini has relentlessly reported on honor killings in Jordan's English-language newspaper, *The Jordan Times,* and lobbied for legal reforms. Husseini was among Jordanian feminists and rights advocates spearheading a women's movement for legal reform in Jordan, a campaign supported by Queen Rania Al Abdullah of Jordan.[4]

A series of terrible incidents continue to galvanize public concern. One receiving widespread attention was the murder of Samia Sarwar in Lahore, Pakistan, in 1999. Samia was shot at close range and in the head by Habid ur Rehman, acting at the behest of Samia Sarwar's parents. When Samia was shot, she was in the office of her lawyer, Hina Jilani, and just a few feet away. And the "crime" for which Samia was executed? She had left her abusive husband and sought counseling at a women's legal services center

---

1. Khalid Sohail, "Honour Killings of Women" on CHOWK at http://www.chowk.com/Views/Society/Honour-Killings-of-Women. January 25, accessed June 10, 2012. CHOWK is a website about current affairs in India and Pakistan. According to Tahira S. Khan in *Beyond Honour: A Historical Materialist Explanation of Honour Related Violence* (Oxford and Karachi: Oxford University Press, 2006), 3, the earliest study of honor killing in a Muslim society was by Mazhar ul Haq Khan from Pakistan and published in 1972 as *Purdah and Polygamy: A Study in the Social Pathology of Muslim Society* (Peshawar: Nasiram-e-Ilm-o-Traqiyat, 1972).

2. "Crimes of honor" and "honor-related violence" are generic terms referring to any crime or act of violence against women and girls presumably motivated by considerations of honor or traditional values. Thus, crimes of honor include abductions, forced marriages, rape, and dowry murders and a range of other attacks in addition to honor killings.

3. For an overview, see Radhika Coomaraswamy, "Preface: Violence Against Women and 'Crimes of Honour,'" in Lynn Welchman and Sara Hossain (eds.), *"Honour": Crimes, Paradigms, and Violence Against Women* (London and New York: Zed Books, 2005), xi–xiv, and notes with references to UN reports at xiv.

4. Rana Husseini's efforts are chronicled in her book, *Murder in the Name of Honor* (Oxford: Oneworld, 2009).

and shelter run by Jilani and her sister Asma Jahangir (at the time the UN Special Rapporteur on extrajudicial killing).

Samia's widely publicized execution, plus the "inability" of the Pakistani police to apprehend and prosecute Samia's publicly prominent family, raised a storm of controversy in Pakistan and widespread condemnation abroad. Jilani and women's rights activists persuaded Senator Iqbal Haider to introduce a resolution before parliament condemning honor killing. The resolution was roundly defeated. Several legislators rose in parliament to extol the virtues of Pakistani traditions and laud Rehman, the Sarwar family chauffeur and trigger man, as heroic for his sacrifice in upholding the Sarwar family's honor. (Rehman was shot to death in a gun battle with a shelter guard as he attempted to escape the scene of the shooting.) Samia's parents, obvious accomplices in her murder, were never arrested or charged. Jilani and Jahangir were denied an opportunity to participate in an investigation of the conspiracy to kill Samia and received death threats from a number of religious groups.[5]

Efforts in Pakistan to make honor killing a public criminal offense were long hampered by parliament's concessions to Muslim *shari'a* law that privatized the crime. Until passage of legislation in 2016, under *shari'a* provisions, a murderer could go free if his parents or family members forgave him for killing his sister, wife, or mother in the name of honor. While reforms in 2016 did recognize honor killing as a criminal offense, the victim's relatives retained the "right" to pardon a killer if the latter received a death sentence. However, it is dubious that tougher laws will lead to real changes.[6] The Human Rights Commission of Pakistan stated that some 1,100 incidents of honor killing had been reported for 2015–16, with at least another 1,000 unreported. Incidents reported in 2017 suggest that the rate of honor killings has not slackened. In one instance, in a frenzied attack in January 2017, Hayat Khan slit the throat of his 16-year-old sister Samaria in Karachi. "She used to talk to a boy over the telephone," said Hayat from his cell.[7]

On the other side of the globe, the 2002 execution of 16-year-old Heshu Yones by her father, Abdullah, is generally regarded as the first criminal

5. This account is based on Amir Jafri, *Honour Killing: Dilemma, Ritual Understanding* (Oxford: Oxford University Press, 2009), 1–3.

6. Kelly Chen and Sophia Saifi, "Pakistan Passes Legislation Against 'Honor Killing," CNN News, Oct. 8, 2016, www.cnn.com/201/10/06/asia/pakistan-anti-honor-killing-law/index.html, accessed July 6, 2017.

7. Amar Guiriro, "Pakistan Honour Killings Continue Despite Tough New Laws," ABC News, Jan. 11, 2017, www.abc.net.au/news/2017-01-11/why-honour-killings-continue-in-pakistan-despite-tough-new-laws/8173756, accessed July 6, 2017.

case actually tried as an honor killing in Great Britain, although not the first of its kind in Britain.[8] In the same year, Rahmi Sahindal killed his daughter Fadime in Uppsala, Sweden, by shooting her point blank in the head. Following a brutal beating at the hands of her brother and because of the inability of her family, who had lived in Sweden since 1984, to integrate into their new homeland, Fadime had addressed the Swedish parliament urging a better understanding of problems posed by cultures of honor.[9]

The public execution of Ghazala Khan in 2005 by her brother, Akhtar Abbas, and in front of a railway station in Denmark, was probably the first honor killing captured on film. It set a precedent in Europe as the first honor killing case in Europe in which the victim's male relatives, in addition to the actual killer, were charged with conspiracy to commit homicide.[10] Du'a Khalil Aswad, a student at the Fine Arts Institute in Bashiqa, Iraq, was pitilessly stoned and beaten to death before a cheering mob in 2007, in the first honor killing known to have been broadcast around the world on the Internet.[11] In the United States, the murder in October 2009 of Noor al-Maliki in Phoenix, Arizona, although certainly not the first honor killing in the United States, was the first case in the United States in which charges were brought against the perpetrator for an honor killing.

In 2001, Human Rights Watch (HRW) published a definition of honor killing that reads in part as follows: honor killings are "acts of vengeance, usually deaths, committed by male family members against female family members who are held to have brought dishonor upon the family."[12] The definition focuses on honor and the role of male family members as perpetrators and a female of the same family as a victim.[13] The definition also emphasizes a breach of honor by a female family member as motivating the vengeful killing; it suggests, as well, that the female's behavior has

8. Husseini, *Murder in the Name of Honor*, 158–61.

9. Unni Wikan, *In Honor of Fadime: Murder and Shame*, trans. by Anna Paterson (Chicago and London: University of Chicago Press, 2008).

10. Wikipedia, "Honor Killing of Ghazala Khan," http://www.ask.com/wiki/Honor_killing_of-Ghazala_Khan, accessed Mar. 15, 2013.

11. Nicholas D. Kristof and Sheryl WuDunn, *Half the Sky: Turning Oppression into Opportunity for Women Worldwide* (New York: Alfred A. Knopf), 82–84.

12. Human Rights Watch, "Integration of the Human Rights of Women and the Gender Perspective: Violence against Women and 'Honor' Crimes," www.hrw.org/en.news/2001/04/05, accessed Jan. 4, 2011.

13. Thus the term "honor *killings*" in the HRW definition is appropriate even when the practice does not always result in loss of life because killing is always the *goal* of such attacks. In relatively rare cases when victims survive an attempted honor killing, perpetrator(s) do not change their minds at the last moment or act to save them; rather, they are left for dead or manage to escape.

brought dishonor upon the family as a whole. A definition is not an explanation, of course, but this one suggests that, as a way of restoring honor,
honor killing became a *traditional social practice*—that is, a practice of long
historical standing that is generally condoned within the immediate community in which it occurs.

I begin with the HRW definition in this book because of its brevity, as
well as its benefits of neutrality and wide currency. It is free of implicit
judgment, a factor that could undermine objectivity and defeat efforts
to engage in rational, respectful dialogue with persons in areas in which
honor killings occur but still defend some version of moral relativism or
the "right" of a sociocultural group to determine its own values. A neutral definition should open up discourse about the nature and "function"
of honor killing. Secondly, this 2001 definition is now widely in circula-
tion, and the use of a well-known and straightforward definition makes
communicating with policymakers, scholars, activists, and others more
efficient.

Employing the HRW definition and reviewing a large number of reports
of honor killing makes it possible to formulate some key assumptions. In
the first place, the practice is a unique kind of homicide. Gideon Kressel
designates it as *sorocide-filiacide* to refer to the killing of sisters and daughters by other members of the birth, or natal, family of the victim.[14] The vast
majority of killers are men, usually fathers, brothers, uncles, or cousins,
but women (mothers, sisters, aunts, and grandmothers) sometimes kill as
well.[15] In a small number of cases, the actual "executioner" is not a family
member but someone ordered or hired to kill on behalf of the family, as in
the Sarwar case, or a more distant blood relative in a clan or tribe. Thus,
for example, the killer may be a husband if he is also a blood relative of the
victim, a not uncommon occurrence within groups that legitimate honor
killing,[16] or a mother-in-law within the same clan or tribe. In Pakistan and
India, some perpetrators are males ordered to kill by elders in a village
council (a *jirga* or *khap panchayat*) all of whom regard themselves as having

14. Gideon M. Kressel et al., "Sorocide-Filiacide—Homocide for Family Honor,"
Current Anthropology 22 (1981), 141–58.

15. Females kill most often when they have to act as the head of the household because they are widows or because the male patriarch is abroad working, in the military, imprisoned, or absent for some other reason. See Sections 2.1–2.2 for further
discussion.

16. The ideal marriage in such communities is between first cousins: the sons
and daughters of brothers. I return to the significance of first-cousin marriages in
Chapter 6. In general, the killing of a woman by a husband is not an honor killing
unless he is related to her by blood. See Section 1.2 for further discussion of this point.

a vested interest in restoring a family's honor and, thereby, the purity of the community.[17]

A second distinctive feature of honor killing is the claimed motivation or justification for the homicide. There is a clear link between the intent to kill a female alleged to have behaved dishonorably and the perceived need to restore the family's honor. Perpetrators claim that they restore family honor by "washing the honor with blood." This is, by and large, a sincere claim. Perpetrators are motivated by a desire to restore honor to their family, tribal group, or community and return to the status quo ante. States of agitation, humiliation, and rage in erstwhile perpetrators certainly produce false positives: that is, instances in which perpetrator(s) are *certain* the intended victim has behaved dishonorably when in fact she has not. Yet, however mistaken and unjustified, honor killings are marked by perpetrators' beliefs about the social "necessity" of washing sullied shame in blood. For this reason, murder to dispose of an unwanted daughter or wife or for any form of economic or personal gain disqualifies an incident from classification as an honor killing.[18]

Honor killings involve an explicit and socially sanctioned double standard. Women and girls are killed for alleged offenses that their brothers, fathers, cousins, and uncles may commit with impunity. A girl who is raped by a brother or uncle is very likely to be executed (if she cannot be discretely married off), although the rapist is not likely to be attacked for he brings no shame on his family. Likewise, if a male adulterer is attacked, then he is most likely to be attacked by the woman's husband or his relatives and as revenge. A revenge killing of a paramour is not made to "cleanse" family honor because the requirement arises only when a girl or woman behaves "dishonorably." On occasion, a girl or woman and her

---

17. A *jirga* is an all-male group of communal leaders in a Pakistani village or commune. Usually older men, they are tacitly accepted as decision makers for the community and their decisions regarding matters of propriety and honor are generally accepted as binding. A *khap panchayat* is the equivalent of a *jirga* in India. The latter's male members will be all Hindu or all Muslim and also will concern themselves with matters of caste, marriage, and class within the purview of honor.

18. In *Beyond Honour*, Tahira Khan maintains the thesis that most so-called honor killings, in Pakistan at least, are committed for selfish, self-interested reasons (e.g., material gain) rather than based on motives of honor as characterized here. When arrested, perpetrators make post hoc claims that they acted out of honor because this offers a more justifiable motive than does personal advantage, especially in countries where, until recently, honor killing was not a crime against the state. Khan provides many examples of self-interested murders colored by claims of "honor"; however, she does not demonstrate that all or even the majority of honor killings (even in Pakistan) are self-interested.

lover may be murdered together but usually only when they are caught in flagrante or in flight.

The dishonor in question is frequently related to perceptions of female sexual misconduct or assumptions that such misconduct has or will likely occur, although specific motives for honor killing include claims that a daughter has defied male authority, especially through wishing to marry a man not acceptable to the family or refusal to wed a partner selected by her father. However, even a cursory review of cases shows that defiance regarded as "warranting" death includes leaving the home without permission (even when a daughter is escaping persistent battery or fears death); reporting fears of family violence to authorities (at school, to police, or in women's shelters); or violating traditional norms expected of females with respect to dress, comportment, and behavior. Increasingly, pre-teens and teenage girls have been killed in immigrant communities, as well as in Muslim-majority countries, for becoming too "Westernized."

Fairly representative of two of the most commonly presented reasons for honor killings are evident in two incidents reported by David Ghanim. Eman Watta, a 23-year-old resident of the town of Edleb, Syria, had been divorced by her husband who suspected her of infidelity. He sent her to her parents' house "knowing full well," Ghanim says, "what her fate would be." Within days her brother slew her in the bathroom of their parents' home and then turned himself over to the police.[19] Faten Habash, a young Palestinian woman, was murdered by her father, who repeatedly beat her over the head with an iron bar. This occurred not long after she returned from a hospital where she had been treated for a broken pelvis and other injuries inflicted during earlier beatings. Faten's "crime" was her insistence on marrying a man her parents did not find suitable.[20]

As Section 1.2 more fully shows, the attitudes and emotional responses of families who commit honor killings have changed very little over time. Hence, Bouthaina Shaaban's account of the following childhood experience in Syria could well be contemporary: "I had just reached the police station . . . when I saw my classmate Aziz joyfully descending a hill in the centre of the village, waving a dagger dripping with blood and chanting, 'I've killed her and saved the family's honor!' He ran up to two policemen who were standing outside the station, handed them the dagger and said

19. David Ghanim, *Gender and Violence in the Middle East* (Westport, CT: Praeger, 2009), 46. For reasons discussed further in Section 1.3 and Chapters 2–3, it is common for perpetrators to turn themselves over to legal authorities but not because they believe they have committed a crime.
20. Ghanim, *Gender and Violence*, 46.

in a voice loud enough for everyone around to hear, 'I have killed my sister and have come to hand myself over for justice.' The three of them strolled slowly into the police station, chatting amicably."[21] Douglas Jehl reported similar attitudes in 1999 concerning a family's reaction to an honor killing. Jehl reports that it took 6 years for the al-Gaul family to hunt down their daughter Basa, who, divorced by her first husband, had secretly remarried. When Basa was found, her 16-year-old brother fatally shot her. In response to questioning, Basa's 18-year-old-sister, Amal, said, "Now we can walk with our heads held high." Basa's mother emphasized the return of the family to its rightful position of honor, mentioning in particular that she would once again receive the social calls she regarded as her due.[22]

Obviously, generalizations cannot be based on anecdotes; hence, the benefit of empirical studies reviewed in Chapter 2. In addition, as Section 1.3 suggests, although a deadly practice out of a dark past, honor killing shows no signs of abating in our globalized, postmillennial world.

1.2 THE DISTINCTIVENESS OF HONOR KILLING

One question likely to arise when attention turns to honor killing is this: Given the veritable global pandemic of gender violence, why focus on honor killing in particular, in contrast to gender violence more generally? Tens of millions of women die each year as a result of routine discrimination as well as from extreme gender violence. One way of estimating the global magnitude of this problem, now increasingly referred to as *femicide*,[23] is to update the research techniques pioneered by Amartya Sen. As long ago as 1990, Sen estimated that there may be as many as 100 million "missing women" worldwide as a result of gender discrimination. These are women who would be alive, given expected mortality rates, but who have "disappeared" as a result of birth selection (abortion) and of shorter

21. Bouthaina Shaaban, *Both Right and Left-Handed: Arab Women Talk About Their Lives* (London: The Women's Press, 1988), 3–5.
22. Douglas Jehl, "For Shame: A Special Report; Arab Honor's Price: A Woman's Blood," *New York Times,* June 20, 1999, www.nytimes.com/1999/06/20/world/for-shame-a-special-report-arab-honor-s-price-a-woman-s-blood.html, accessed July 7, 2001.
23. Jill Radford first defined "femicide" in 1992 as "the misogynous killing of women by men." See Jill Radford, "Introduction," in Jill Radford and Diana E. H. Russell (eds.), *Femicide: The Politics of Women Killing* (Buckingham, UK: Open University Press, 1992). In 2002, Nadera Shalhoub-Kervorkian broadened the term's scope in "Femicide and the Palestinian Criminal Justice System: Seeds of Change in the Context of State Building?" *Law & Society Review* 36, 3 (2002), 577–606.

periods of breast-feeding, poorer nutrition, and less health care than their male counterparts.[24]

In addition to this *everyday violence*, the numbers of girls and women who suffer overt and extreme violence is staggering. The World Health Organization (WHO) reports that domestic and sexual violence directly affects from 30% to 60% of women in most countries.[25] Nicholas Kristof reports that "Women worldwide ages 15 through 44 are more likely to die or be maimed because of male violence than because of cancer, malaria, war and traffic accidents combined."[26] In the United States alone, there is a reported rape every 6.2 minutes, and studies suggest that about 1 in 5 women will be sexually assaulted during her lifetime,[27] while "the more than 11,766 corpses from domestic-violence homicides since 9/11 exceed the number of deaths of victims on that day and all American soldiers killed in the 'war on terror.'"[28] In South Africa, an estimated 600,000 rapes occurred in 2012 alone.[29] To conclude just this sample list of gender violence, Gardiner Harris reports an estimate that "as many as 100,000 women are burned to death each year and another 125,000 die from violent injuries that are rarely reported as killings."[30] Thus, even by conservative estimates, violence against women, including sexual violence, is of staggering proportions. No part of the world is free from systemic violence against women.

It is an outrage that this preventable global pandemic of gender violence continues unabated. However, there is at present too little research to identify interventions that can be used equally well in responding to

24. Amartya Sen, "More Than 100 Million Women Are Missing," *The New York Review of Books*, Dec. 20, 1990. See also Ansley J. Coale, "Excess Female Mortality and the Balance of the Sexes in the Population: An Estimate of the Number of 'Missing Females,'" *Population and Development Review*, Sept. 17, 1991; Stephan Klasen and Claudia Wink, "'Missing Women': Revisiting the Debate," *Feminist Economics* 9 (Jan. 2003), 263–99.

25. Cited by Nicholas D. Kristof, in "Is Delhi So Different from Steubenville?" *The New York Times, Sunday Review*, Jan. 13, 2013, 10.

26. Kristof, "Is Delhi So Different," 10.

27. However, this famous "1 in 5" figure is subject to certain inaccuracies, including underreporting and controversy about what constitutes sexual assault. These are important issues worthy of further consideration; however, because the focus of this book is not rape in America, I include this statistic here only to illustrate the global nature of gender violence.

28. Rebecca Solnit, "A Rape a Minute, a Thousand Corpses a Year," *TomDispatch*, Jan. 24, 2013, http://readersupportednews.org/opinion2/273-40/15693-focus-a-rape-a-minute-a-thousand-corpses-a-year, accessed Jan. 25, 2013.

29. Solinit, "A Rape a Minute."

30. Gardiner Harris, "India's New Focus on Rape Shows Only the Surface of Women's Perils," *The New York Times International*, Jan. 13, 2013, 10.

threats of violence across the spectrum of female and gender vulnerability, especially considering the ways everyday and interpersonal violence is reinforced by systems of structural or institutional violence. In fact, a major lesson from Nicholas Kristof and Sheryl WuDunn's *Half the Sky* is that responses, if they are to have any chance of success, must be specifically tailored to address the local and particular cultural practices in which they are embedded. For instance, apart from some commonalities with respect to the legal and political responses to gender and sexual violence (e.g., insisting that the police, legislators, prosecutors, and judges respond to these crimes with the alacrity and seriousness they require), there is no special reason to suppose that a one-size-fits-all approach will be helpful. Indeed, given the complexities of honor killing, it is very likely that dowry murders, for example, will need to be approached in quite a different way, as will the sexual-slave trade, or practices of political rapes committed by higher status or higher caste men to humiliate and repress men of lower status or caste, or, again, genocidal rape (e.g., as occurred in Bosnia and the eastern Congo).

In Chapter 3, I show that, as a *social practice*, honor killing possesses its own particularity and density. Honor killing exists as a complex set of behaviors that acquire their purported purpose and meanings from the communities in which they occur and cannot exist without reinforcement from that sociocultural milieu.[31] Consequently, comprehending the complexities of honor killing poses significant challenges. Proposing recommended responses and interventions (see Chapters 7–9) is still more daunting. It stands to reason, therefore, that strategic guides and tactical reforms must be relevant to the specific and salient characteristics of honor killing as a unique form of gender violence. This remains true whether we seek short-term protective interventions and the leveraging of pressures for change from without (Chapter 7), or longer term transformative changes (Chapters 8–9).

Second, honor killing was chosen as the focus of study not only because it is an especially egregious violation of human rights but also because it is *confounding*. Some destructive or harmful practices exist because of a combination of false beliefs, a tradition of willful ignorance, and questionable motives. For instance, some combination of such factors underlies the practice of female genital mutilation (FGM). When ideology and discrimination, prejudice, or active animosity for designated "others" are added

---

31. For the reasons presented in Chapter 3, I refer to communities in which honor killings occur as honor–shame communities.

to this mix, the outcome can include extreme violence such as pogroms, lynching, ethnic "cleansing," or terrorism.

Honor killing is radically different in important ways. First, it is the killing by a family of one of its own members and, consequently, counterintuitive given a normal expectation that evolution would have endowed all fathers and brothers with a natural repugnance toward taking the lives of their own daughters, sisters, or mothers. Second, the misdeeds identified by perpetrators as justifying an execution are extremely common among human beings, but they are rarely judged by persons who are not members of honor-killing groups so serious as to deserve death. The death sentence seems so grossly disproportionate to the offense committed, especially when we consider (as discussed at greater length in Section 1.3 and Chapter 2) that allegations of dishonorable behavior are often based on *perceptions* rather than facts and that family members often are prodded to act as a result of hearsay or gossip.

A partial explanation of why males kill female family members can be found in perpetrators' frequent reports that the killings were a social "necessity" and of having been "compelled" to kill to restore family honor. Such responses raise a further question, however. The regular occurrence of honor killing testifies to the powerful grip of codes of honor and the culture of honor–shame communities (HSCs) in inducing men to kill. But, why then, should certain communal groups be so concerned about the errant behavior of disobediently fertile females and so alarmingly upset as to impose the normative requirement on members that misdeeds be followed by executions—and executions performed at the hands of the victim's family, no less? Is it possible that, as unlikely as it may seem today, honor killing once had a critical function within communities in which it occurred?

To ask this last question is to consider whether or not honor killing was one of a very few practices (infanticide being another) for which there was an adaptive advantage for closely knit and blood-related groups in encouraging members to adopt this practice. This is an issue I pursue in Chapter 6 in explaining why honor killing ever came into existence. This explanation will help explain why honor killing as a social practice continues to be discouragingly resilient despite modernizing and globalizing trends. Obviously, we cannot expect members of HSCs to know why they accept honor killing, any more, I suspect, than typical young men and women understand the causal factors underlying their own mating behavior. Nevertheless, perhaps the capacity of "outsiders" to attain "anthropologically" etic insights into the causes of honor killing will enable those best positioned to share these insights with denizens of HSCs so that these insights become emic as well and so that sustainable and transformative changes for the better can be made.[32]

I have been noting that perpetrators regard honor killings as required to "wash away shame"; their views are shared by those members of their communities who condone what they do. Many women in HSCs share such views, including many victims.[33] Now, why lump honor killings together with various types of criminal conduct under the general rubric of "honor crimes" or "honor-based violence" (HBV)? If there is a common denominator for such a category, then it is the real or apparent presence of references to "honor." For similar reasons, honor killings are sometimes confused with so-called crimes of passion, when a husband or lover claims to have acted to preserve his honor. Moreover, some even regard honor killing as a more extreme form of domestic violence or intimate partner violence (IPV), especially in regions where honor killings are well known to occur.

Some women's rights advocates point out that there is nothing "honorable" about honor killing but go on to argue that using the honor killing label perpetuates the notion that these killings reflect efforts to uphold honor. For such advocates, regarding honor killings as similar to domestic (IPV) deflates the "cultural defense" and enables us to see honor killings for what they are—criminal conduct. Admittedly, the notion of "honor killing" is rather oxymoronic for those whose primary conception of honor pertains to dispositions to behave nobly or virtuously, as generally understood within many Western cultural groups. Honor in such contexts has a meaning that is incompatible with "honor killing." The situation is quite different in what I am referring to as HSCs in which honor killing is a social practice. For members of such groups, honor killing is *not viewed as criminal*; on the contrary, wrongdoing has been rectified by the killing.

32. As used here, *emic* knowledge and interpretation exist within a culture as determined by its local customs and systems of belief and meaning. Emic knowledge is used to represent aspects of their culture by members of a specific group. By contrast, *etic* accounts are descriptions made by an out-group observer and usually are not available for those living within a culture. I extend the distinction between emic and etic knowledge to include awareness of the underlying *causes* of one's behaviors. For a useful discussion, see Thomas N. Headland, Kenneth L. Pike, and Marvin Harris (eds.), *Emics and Etics: The Insider/Outsider Debate* (Newbury Park: CA: Sage, 1991). The "Introduction" is available online at http://www-01.sil.org/~headland/ee.intro.html.

33. When victims do not share these views, it is often because they protest the claim that they have committed an offense by maintaining their innocence rather than by challenging group norms. However, some victims, such as those considered "too Westernized," do protest against or reject strict group norms.

Thus, in contexts in which honor killings occur, killing is not incompatible with honor.

Those who condone honor killings operate with conceptions of honor (discussed extensively in Sections 3.2–3.3) quite unlike those who think of honor in terms compatible with classical and Western ethical notions. Because many people in HSCs believe certain dishonorable actions warrant death, simply demanding they accept that "there is no honor in 'honor killing'" is roughly equivalent to the demand that they accept our (Western) normative standards. Perhaps this is a more reasonable expectation of immigrants wishing to integrate into the host country's sociocultural and legal system. However, the demand will have little purchase on those who choose to preserve their way of life against the incursion of alien legal and social systems.[34]

Other feminists and human rights advocates argue that putting honor killings into a broader category of criminal conduct avoids the impression that men who commit honor killings are especially cruel or barbaric, in contrast to men responsible for other types of criminal violence against women. Finally, still others maintain that assimilating honor killings into the HBV, IPV, or "crimes of passion" categories will lead to the development of more effective means of prevention and protection.[35]

My recommendation is that we distinguish, as far as possible, *factual* from *normative* and *strategic* considerations. In various ways, advocates of all three claims put normative and strategic considerations ahead of the facts. By contrast, my position is that getting the facts straight will yield the best platform for responding normatively and strategically to the problem. To be sure, many terms have judgmental and emotive connotations that cannot be eliminated. To describe an honor killing as an "atrocity" is to express the wrongness of the act as well as to describe its nature as unusual and aberrant behavior. However, this no more commits us to the view that perpetrators who kill for honor are inherently or incorrigibly barbaric and evil any more than the view that all Germans implicated in atrocities during the Holocaust or Serbians implicated in ethnic cleansing at Srebrenica were barbaric and evil.

34. My position will be revealed in Chapters 8–9 where, among other transformative changes, I argue for the *reframing* of honor to eliminate the notion that killing is honorable while retaining the values of honor for other aspects of communal life.

35. For authors representing these respective positions, see Aisha K. Gill, Carolyn Strange, and Karl Roberts (eds.), *"Honour" Killing and Violence: Theory, Policy and Practice* (Basingstoke, GB: Palgrave Macmillan, 2014); and Mohammad Mazher Idriss and Tahir Abbas (eds.), *Honour, Violence, Women and Islam* (Abingdon, UK, and New York: Routledge, 2011).

Turning to the third claim, the critical point is whether placing honor killings within one all-encompassing category would result in more efficient strategic ways of preventing honor killing and protecting potential victims. This is not an issue about the definition or analysis of a concept, however, but about its political uses. In a discussion of framing in Section 8.2, I recognize that classifying honor killings as one type of honor crime or IPV may be effective in certain European and North American countries where there have been long-standing women's rights movements combating domestic, intimate partner, and gender violence more generally. The adaptation of honor killings into broader categories of crimes against women is promising in such settings because common ground is more easily made between national feminist activists and women in immigrant communities and because of a national history of greater political responsiveness to women's security rights.

In most areas in which honor killings occur frequently, however, the history of women's rights activism is far less extensive, and the record of national debate and government responsiveness is, if not dismal, usually weak. In addition, as I argue in Section 8.2, pitching strategic efforts to end honor killing too broadly runs the risk of antagonizing members of HSCs who may experience broad-based opposition as an attack on their entire way of life, and reforms meant to end IPV might collide with religious prescriptions governing family life. Hence, a premature omnibus categorization will hinder activists' efforts to effectively protect potential victims and end honor killing. As honor killing is surely among the gravest of wrongs, it is critically important first to isolate it as a social practice from within the larger sociocultural milieu and to demarcate it as an archaic and dysfunctional practice that must be eliminated while assuring members of HSCs that expunging it will not rip apart a lifeworld they cannot imagine themselves (at least initially) doing without.

Many acts of gender violence, as typically occur with dowry murders, human sex trafficking, and *panchayat*-ordered rapes, are motivated by a desire for socioeconomic gain or to maintain caste or class privileges. Because of the widespread acceptance of honor killing as a practice in certain locales, crimes committed purely for self-interested reasons, such as the desire of a divorced man to avoid maintaining his wife or the desire to be rid of a first wife in order to remarry, lead murderers to accuse victims of having "brought shame" on them or their families and then attacking them. However, researchers must be alert to distinguish killings motivated by desires for socioeconomic or other personal gains from instances in which killings are plausibly motivated by concerns about obligation and expectations deriving from honor.[36]

While domestic violence, IPV, and spousal rape share with honor killing male violence against females, these acts seem motivated not by honor and shame but by insecurity, lack of respect for the wife or girlfriend, and, more generally, poor impulse control and inadequate problem-solving and emotional coping skills. Tragically, many perpetrators of honor killing also are batterers of spouses and abusers of daughters; however, incidents of honor killing have a particular "signature"—a combination of motive, intent, behavior, and rationalization—that sets them apart from domestic violence and IPV.

First, honor killing is almost always undertaken as an explicit *execution*, an outcome that is premeditated, planned, and usually enacted by an appointed executioner, whereas domestic violence and IPV is not, even when the latter may result in the death of the victim. Second, wife battery and IPV consist of violence targeted against a marriage or intimate partner, most frequently a wife abused by a husband.[37] Obviously, those terms do not apply to the most frequent class of perpetrators in honor killings, male members of the victim's natal family. Third, when genuine honor killings do occur, perpetrators, family members, communal witnesses, and even victim survivors refer to the motives, intentions, and actions of attackers as honor-oriented. However, this is not the way those intimately related in domestic violence and IPV, or others, think and speak about their actions.[38] Fourth, while perpetrators of domestic or partner abuse may regard their violence as justified, their attitudes and assessments are supported by other persons, primarily men, who are also disposed to commit such violence. Such persons could be said to belong to a particular "subculture" of sorts; however, so far as we know, they do not live within a group or a community that accepts their violence as traditional and as related to a code of honor critical for a way of life and dictating important forms of behavior.

36. Danielle Hoyek, Rafif Rida Sidawi, and Amira Abou Mrad, "Murders of Women in Lebanon: 'Crimes of Honour' Between Reality and the Law," "*Honour*," pp. 111–37, at 120.

37. National Domestic Violence Hotline, "Statistics," www.thehotline.org/resources/statistics, accessed Sept. 1, 2014.

38. According to Neil Blacklock, perpetrators of domestic violence "demonstrate a number of common factors (minimization, denial of responsibility, and a sense of entitlement . . .) that appear to be central to their abusive behavior." Honor, at least as understood here, simply does not enter into the domestic violence equation. See Neil Blacklock, "Domestic Violence: Working with Perpetrators, the Community and Its Institutions," *Advances in Psychiatric Treatment* 7, 1 (Jan. 2001), 65–72.

Another reason for resisting temptations to regard honor killing as just one kind of "honor crime" or "honor-based violence" is that, unlike honor killing, many so-called honor crimes do not, and are not intended to, end in death. For instance, in a number of sub-Saharan regions of Africa the following are traditional practices relating in various ways to local notions of honor: committing virgin girls, often under 10 years of age, to work as slaves in religious shrines; requiring a widowed woman to marry her husband's brother; and requiring a husband to purchase his wife in the system of bride price.[39]

It is also necessary to distinguish honor killings from politically motivated violence. The story of Malala Yousafzai is a particularly striking example of a political crime against women. When just 11, Malala gave a talk entitled "How Dare the Taliban Take Away My Basic Right to Education?" in Peshawar, Pakistan, after the Taliban started attacking girls' schools in the area. At around the same age she started blogging for BBC under a pseudonym. Incensed by her actions, the Taliban issued a death threat against her and paid a hit man to shoot her on her way home from school. Yousafzai, then 15, was fortunate enough to survive a serious gunshot wound to the head. Since then she has become the world's youngest recipient of the Nobel Peace Prize and continues to be a globally recognized activist for women and girls living under repression.[40]

Yousafzai's story is compelling, but the attack on her was not an attempted honor killing. The Taliban felt its political mission was threatened by her activism and not that its honor, or standing in a community, was jeopardized by a personal honor transgression committed by Yousafzai. The Taliban and the hired killer were not personally dishonored by Yousafzai's actions, and their execution plans were motivated not by honor but by politics. The same is true of the hundreds of women and girls who have been massacred by the Taliban in their schools,[41] as well as the thousands raped and sexually tortured for political causes in the Balkans and in Rwanda, Zimbabwe, and other African nations;[42] girls sexually violated by mandatory virginity

39. Nancy Kaymar Stafford, "Ending Honour Crimes in sub-Saharan Africa," in Idriss and Tahir Abbas (eds.), *Honour, Violence, Women and Islam*, 168–81.

40. "Malala Yousafzai Biography" (Biography.com, 2015), http://www.biography.com/people/malala-yousafzai-21362253, accessed Feb. 8, 2015. See also Malala Yousafazi (with Christina Lamb), *I Am Malala: The Girl Who Stood Up for Education and Was Shot by the Taliban* (New York: Little Brown and Company, 2013).

41. BBC News, "Pakistan Taliban: Peshawar School Attack Leaves 141 Dead," Dec. 16, 2014, http://www.bbc.com/news/world-asia-30491435, accessed Feb. 8, 2015.

42. IRIN News, "Zimbabwe: Focus on Rape as a Political Weapon," Apr. 8, 2013, http://www.irinnews.org/report/42985/zimbabwe-focus-on-rape-as-a-political-weapon, accessed Feb. 8, 2015.

tests in countries such as Egypt;[43] and those humiliated and abused for other political purposes.

It is important as well to distinguish honor killings from crimes of passion. The latter are occasionally confused with honor killings because both may involve women who are married or in intimate relationships. In addition, now that penal codes in many places have increased punishments, defendants who are arrested and tried for honor killings frequently attempt to reduce their culpability by asserting that they were overcome by a "fit" or "impulse" of passion. Unfortunately, "honor" and "passion" are used almost interchangeably in some penal codes, court proceedings, and press reports.[44] In addition, in countries such as Brazil, for example, "dishonor" is attached to the activity of married women outside the conjugal norms of society. Historically, wife-murderers in Brazil were absolved if they could prove they acted spontaneously in self-defense of their honor; in other words, when the victim was engaged in "an imminent aggression" against their honor.[45] Reviewing documentation on violence against women in Brazil for the 1991 Women's Rights Project of America Watch (WRP), Hillary Charlesworth found that the wife-murder defense of "honor" in trials for the murder of an allegedly unfaithful wife was successful in some regions in 80% of cases.[46]

I am not asserting that honor killings as defined in this chapter do not occur in Brazil or elsewhere in Latin America. Likewise, I am adamant in sharing the view that a "defense of honor" should never be available for wife-murderers in Brazil or elsewhere and defenses of "uncontrollable passion" only very rarely. Except in extremely rare circumstances, husbands, wives, fiancés, and fiancées always have options allowing for self-control, absenting one's self from the scene, breaking off and dissociation, moving out, separation, and divorce. Courts should accept a defense of "fit of passion" only when there is unimpeachable evidence that the defendant could not have done otherwise; that is, because of shock, trauma, or some other incapacitating condition, the defendant was deprived of choice.

43. Monia Ben Jemia, Laëtitia Sedou, and Marsha Scott. *Violence Against Women in the Context of Political Transformations and Economic Crisis in the Euro-Mediterranean Region: Trends and Recommendations Towards Equality and Justice.* (Copenhagen: Euro-Mediterranean Human Rights Network, 2014).

44. Khan, *Beyond Honour*, 40.

45. Celina Romany, "State Responsibility Goes Private: A Feminist Critique of the Public/Private Distinction in International Human Rights Law," in Rebecca J. Cook (ed.), *Human Rights of Women: National and International Perspectives* (Philadelphia: University of Pennsylvania Press, 1992), 85–115, 103.

46. Hillary Charlesworth, "What Are 'Women's International Human Rights'?" in Cook (ed.), *Human Rights of Women*, 58–84, 72.

Although rage is often expressed in the act of killing, honor killings do not usually occur when a married woman or girl and her paramour are discovered in flagrante, as might be expected in crimes of passion. Traps might be set to confirm rumors that a married woman or girl is involved with a man or boy, but such evidence is more often a prelude to the decision about the fate of the female. Insofar as there is spontaneity relating to executions, it pertains to opportunities to commit the execution, as in catching the victim unawares (e.g., when she is sleeping or drawing water from a well); or to killing the victim so as to attract public attention (e.g., when she ventures into a public square or street) and thereby openly demonstrating that one has "washed" the family honor.

Honor killings differ from crimes of passion in two additional ways. As Lama Abu-Odeh notes, crimes of passion involve a private relationship between a man and a woman, whereas honor killing involves a collective relationship between a solitary female (the victim) and all of the males related to her who are deeply engaged in defending their public image.[47] Abu-Odeh points out that, in crimes of passion, "female sexuality is not fetishized as the locus of reputation, but seen more as a libidinal goal and the locus of complicated human emotions." Thus, she adds, given that crimes of passion are between two people sexually involved with each other—whereas honor killing is not—crimes of passion are "less a matter of castrated masculinity and more of passionate jealousy."[48]

This points to yet a further difference. When death is due to an honor killing, the perpetrator is usually a blood relative of the victim—a father, brother, uncle, son—that is, a man with whom sexual interaction is prohibited both as social taboo and by religion. Hence a female's offense does not arouse jealousy, rivalry, or feelings of rejection associated with crimes of passion. The issue involves men's patriarchal power and control over women and the former's anger or fury, aroused as much by mulling over consequent male shame as by the allegedly forbidden (haram) behavior, rebellion, or defiance of the female purportedly under male control.[49]

Finally, the conceptual clarity and parsimonious use I recommend is even consistent with recognition of distinctive uses of "honor killing" when such uses are appropriately qualified. For example, Carolyn Strange

47. Lama Abu-Odeh, "Crimes of Honor and the Construction of Gender in Arab Societies," in Mai Yamani (ed.), Feminism and Islam: Legal and Literary Perspectives (New York: New York University Press, 1996), 155.
48. Abu-Odeh, "Crimes of Honor," 155.
49. Khan, Beyond Honour, 43.

calls attention to similarities between conceptions of honor still salient in the American South following the Civil War and honor killing (see Section 3.2).[50] David McConnell, author of *American Honor Killings*, also calls attention to honor killings committed by men born and raised in America in the late 20th century rather than among first- or second-generation immigrants.[51]

While it is important to look for possible similarities in the ways that conceptions of honor are enlisted to defend patriarchy or constructions of masculinity, Strange and McConnell discuss honor and violence in ways that are similar only in very limited respects to honor killings as defined and understood here. Strange discusses how descendants of early immigrant and Protestant whites resorted to honor to excuse the exercise of "pitiless violence," such as lynching to terrorize African Americans and reinforce racial segregation.[52] McConnell's subject is the killing of gay American men based on homophobic hatred and rage. But neither Strange nor McConnell discuss honor as a reason for the execution of *women*, neither presents perpetrator and victim *as members of the same family*, neither are perpetrators presented as feeling bound by honor to execute an alleged offender, and neither author presents honor killing as a practice involving communal expectations about conditions under which it is permissible to take life. Their writings on honor and violence are centered on *us versus them* mentalities among the perpetrators, not on the ways in which an individual's actions affect the family's position in society.

Because honor killing can be shown to refer to a specific and distinctive social practice that arose historically in certain regions of the world and continues today more or less in the same form, my recommendation is that authors such as Strange and McConnell not invite confusion by referring to the criminal activities they discuss as honor killings. If, however, they and others disagree, then reason requires at least the recognition of distinctively different conceptions of "honor killing." Here I will continue to use the term to refer exclusively to an ages-old practice originating in the deserts and high and arid mountain valleys of a vast region stretching from Morocco east and north of the Sahara through Egypt and throughout the Saudi peninsula, the Middle East, Afghanistan, Pakistan, and much of the rest of the Indian subcontinent (see Chapter 6).

---

50. Carolyn Strange, "Adjusting the Lens of Honour-Based Violence: Perspectives from Euro-American History," *"Honour" Killing and Violence*, 46–87.

51. David McConnell, *American Honor Killings: Desire and Rage Among Men* (New York: Akashic Books, 2013).

52. Strange, "Adjusting the Lens," 61.

Because honor killing has been studied only in the past few decades, it is not possible to identify trends or project possible increases or declines. Indeed, it is not even possible to know with certainty how many honor killings occur in any given year or even in any given country in a particular year. In 2000, the United Nations Population Fund estimated the annual number of honor killings to be approximately 5,000—a figure immediately assailed as too low.[53] Kristof and WuDunn estimate the actual number as closer to 6,000 yearly.[54] By contrast, women's rights activists working in the Middle East and Southwest Asia estimate that more than 20,000 honor killings occur throughout the world each year.[55]

The total remains unknown due to a lack of information on some countries and even entire regions. We know that honor killings occur in India and in Bangladesh, although numbers there are drastically underreported, and these killings probably occur in Malaysia and Myanmar, although reliable statistics are nonexistent. We have almost no information at all about possible honor killings in many parts of Africa, where honor killings are not officially reported and women's rights activists find it difficult to work; these include Algeria, Central Africa, Ethiopia, Djibouti, Mali, Niger, Somalia, and the Sudan, although we know honor killings do occur in Algeria and Somalia.[56] In addition, there are almost no figures at all for many other areas in Asia, including Indonesia, the most populous Muslim country in the world; Sri Lanka; and Russia, as well as virtually no data from republics of the former Soviet Union such as Azerbaijan, Kazakhstan, Turkmenistan, or from China and the Korean peninsula.[57] Finally, there are no or almost no figures from South America, although Brazil is one country

---

53. United Nations Population Fund (UNFP) 2000 Report, *The State of the World Population: Chapter 3: Ending Violence Against Women and Girls*, http://www.unfpa.org/swp/2000/english/press_kit/summary.html, accessed Jan. 14, 2011.

54. Kristof and WuDunn, *Half the Sky*, 82.

55. Among those insisting on this estimate are Diana Nammi, director of the London-based Iranian and Kurdish Women's Rights Organization (IKWRO), and Robert Fisk, a Beirut-based journalist who spent a year traveling and studying the practice. See Robert Fisk, "Invisible Massacre: The Crime Wave that Shames the World," *The Independent*, London, Sept. 7, 2010, www.independent.co.uk/Voices/Commentators/fisk/robert/robert-fisk-the-crime-wave-that-shames-the-world2077201.html, accessed Oct. 19, 2012.

56. Ayaan Hirsi Ali, *Infidel* (New York: Atria, 2007), 169, 210.

57. Honor killings are also reported from places such as South Korea, where they are less expected. See Andrea Parrot and Nina Cummings, *Forsaken Females: The Global Brutalization of Women* (Lanham, MD: Rowman and Littlefield, 2006), 174.

from which Coomaraswamy, as Special UN Rapporteur on violence against women, received communications.

In some areas, the practice is considered socially acceptable and noncriminal, either officially, as in Iran, or according to interpretations of *shari'a* or local, tribal "law," thus allowing potentially thousands of honor killings to "slip through the cracks" each year, never making their way to the ears of prosecutors, journalists, academicians, or nongovernmental organization (NGO) activists. In Iran, incidents are concealed from the independent press, and in Iraq, Egypt, and Morocco (and Pakistan until 2004) honor killings are treated largely as private family matters and reliable statistics are nonexistent.[58]

Even where honor killings are illegal and punishable by law, many governments are loath to release complete honor killing statistics for political reasons. Most states in the Middle East and North Africa do not attempt to gather official statistics or to publish information. Although approximately one-fifth of all honor killings probably occur in India, it was not until 2014 that police were required to list honor killings as a distinct category of crime rather than reported as regular homicides, but the recorded 251 honor killings for 2015 (up from 28 in 2014) indicate that Indian police are still wrongly categorizing or overlooking hundreds of cases.[59] Despite the European Union's pressure on the Turkish government to combat honor killings, Turkish officials have been reluctant to describe honor killings as human rights violations or even to publicize their own efforts.[60]

58. Husseini, *Murder in the Name of Honor*, 116.

59. Mirren Gidda, "Women Are Dying in Overseas Honor Killings, and No One Knows How Bad the Problem Is," *Newsweek*, May 3, 2017, www.newsweek.com/2017/05/12/hpnor-killings-violence-against-women-seeta-kaur-india-pakistan-593691.html, accessed June 14, 2017.

60. Studies indicate that, despite significant reforms of the Turkish Penal Code in 2004, Turkey still lacks "an institutionalized political will, and a coordinated comprehensive policy" to combat honor killing and violence against women. Both the UN Special Rapporteur on violence against women's mission to Turkey in 2006 and the Turkish General Directorate of Women's Status Report of 2008 cite the lack of comprehensive statistics and research as an impediment to increasingly effective implementation. See Pinar Ilkkaracan and Liz Ercevik Amado, "Legal Reforms on Violence Against Women in Turkey: Best Practices," in Moha Ennaji and Fatima Sadiqi (eds.), *Gender and Violence in the Middle East* (London and New York: Routledge, 2011), 189–99, 198. Leyla Pervizat explains that officials in the conservative Justice and Development Party (President Recep Erdogan's party) are silent in their public speeches about Turkish international initiatives on women's rights such as its initiation of a major resolution on crimes of honor at the 2004 UN General Assembly. Pervizat claims further that the Turkish government "cannot and will not alienate its own constituency" and that the government has "very traditional views regarding women." See Leyla Pervizat, "Lack

Honor killings occurring in Western nations are much more likely to garner media attention and public interest; of course, these crimes make up only a small share of the total. However, even in Western countries, many murders were not prosecuted or tried as honor killings, especially before honor killing was recognized as a distinctive crime. For instance, in June 2006, Great Britain's Scotland Yard announced it was reopening investigation of 109 possible honor killings between 1993 and 2003.[61] The same year in London, the Metropolitan Police Service announced that it was reviewing 117 murder cases over the previous decade to discover whether honor was a contributing factor.[62]

Evidence continues to suggest that the scale of the atrocity is probably well above the UN Population Fund's estimate and, in some areas, represents a significant proportion of unnatural deaths of women for any given year. For instance, in December 2004, Asma Jahangir, then UN Special Rapporteur on religious freedom, reported that approximately 400 so-called honor killings had been documented for that year in Afghanistan, although only 24 men had been arrested and each was given a light sentence.[63] Rana Husseini estimates that 400 honor killings occur each year in Yemen alone.[64]

In Pakistan, the Federal Minister of the Interior to the Pakistan Senate indicated that, between 1998 and 2003, some 4,101 people were known to be victims of crimes of honor.[65] However, the actual number for Pakistan alone may be closer to 2,000 annually. The Human Rights Commission of Pakistan reported more than 1,184 honor killings in Pakistan in 2015, but projected that almost as many had gone unreported.[66] In Turkey, a June 2008 report by the Prime Minister's Human Rights Directorate reported that, in Istanbul alone, there was one honor killing every week, and 1,000 over the previous five years. In Jordan, honor killings constitute 25% of

---

of Due Diligence: Judgments of Crimes of Honor in Turkey," in Idriss and Abbas (eds.), 142–53, 151.

61. Aisha K. Gill, "Reconfiguring 'Honour'-Based Violence as a Form of Gendered Violence," in *Honour, Violence, Women and Islam*, 218–31, 225.

62. Rana Husseini, "A Comparative Study of the Reform Work Conducted in Asia and Europe to Combat Violence and 'So-Called' Honour Murders," in *Honour, Violence, Women and Islam*, 154–67, 163.

63. Swedish Ministries of Justice and Foreign Affairs, "Report from the International Conference on Combating Patriarchal Violence Against Women—Focusing on Violence in the Name of Honour," Stockholm, Dec. 7–8, 2009, www.minmedia.minheder.nu/2011/05/konferonsrapporthedersvalid2009.pdf, accessed Oct. 21, 2016.

64. Husseini, *Murder in the Name of Honor*, 137.

65. Husseini, *Murder in the Name of Honor*, 112.

66. Guiriro, "Pakistan Honour Killings Continue."

annual homicides,[67] while it is suspected that 70% of all murders in the Palestinian territories are honor killings.[68]

By the beginning of the 21st century, women's and human rights activists were concerned that the incidence of honor killing was actually increasing. In 2000, Asma Jahangir, in her role as UN Rapporteur on extrajudicial, summary, or arbitrary executions released a report, "Honor Killings on the Rise Worldwide."[69] In 2007, a UN committee reported that honor killings were on the rise in Pakistan despite efforts to strengthen a law banning honor killings in 2004.[70] A recent study found that one in every five homicides in Pakistan is an honor killing.[71] Tahira Khan, in a review of statistical data published in 2006, declared: "One fact seems to be established: honor killings in Pakistan are on the rise. Similar observations are emerging from India, Turkey, Jordan, Egypt, and other countries."[72]

In 2011, Turkey's Justice Minister announced that murders of Turkish women had risen 1,400% in seven years, from 66 in 2002 to 953 in just the first seven months of 2009.[73] Statistics compiled by the Women's Center for Legal Aid and Counseling in Gaza and acquired from the office of the Palestinian Authority's Attorney General indicate that honor killings increased in Gaza. For instance, in a single year in Gaza and the West Bank, honor killings took a dramatic leap from 13 documented cases in 2012 to 27 in 2013.

Likewise, since 2000, honor killings appear to have increased within immigrant Muslim communities in Australia, Belgium, Canada, Denmark, Germany, Great Britain, Italy, the Netherlands, Norway, Sweden, and the United States. In 2008, Britain reported more than 1,700 victims of honor-related crimes (although, as noted in Section 1.2, not all so-called honor crimes are honor killings, and honor killings, as such, are not disaggregated in the statistics). In 2009, the European Parliamentary Assembly described

67. Mediterranean Women, "Rana Husseini Created a New Beat: Honor Crimes in Jordan," Mar. 5, 2005, http://www.mediterraneaneas.org/print.php3?id article=469, accessed Oct. 19, 20012.

68. Suzanne Ruggi, "Commodifying Honor in Female Sexuality: Honor Killing in Palestine," *Middle East Report* 28 (Spring 1998), 13.

69. Cited by Khan, *Beyond Honour*, 164. Note that Khan does not exclude so-called honor killings actually motivated by personal, material, or economic gains.

70. Sarah DiLorenzo, "UN Women's Rights Group Criticizes Pakistan for Honor Killing, Trafficking," *Associated Press*, June 9, 2007 and cited by Husseini, 113.

71. Robert Kiener, "Honor Killings: Can Murders of Women and Girls Be Stopped? *CQ Global Research* 5, 8 (2011), n. 16.

72. Khan, *Beyond Honour*, 163–64.

73. Kiener, "Honor Killings," n. 13. This claim is confirmed by sociologist Bingul Durbus, cited by Palash Ghosh, "Honour Killings: An Ancient Ritual in the Modern World," *International Business Times*, Jan. 30, 2012.

the outbreak of honor crimes in Europe as an "emergency." Resolution 1681 proclaimed, "the problem, far from diminishing, has worsened, including in Europe" and advised nations to create national action plans to combat violence against women in the name of "honor."[74]

Whatever the total number of yearly homicides due to honor killing in Europe and North America, we cannot rule out the possibility that increases, if real, merely reflect the larger proportions of immigrants from countries in which the tradition is strongest, such as Afghanistan, Iraq, Pakistan, Somalia, Syria, Turkey, and Yemen. We also cannot rule out the possibility that greater reporting and publicity are responsible for the appearance of a dramatic rise in rates and that there is little or no actual increase; nevertheless, the evidence—such as it is—supports the plausibility of estimates of incidents at the higher end of the range from 6,000 to 20,000.

Turning to public opinion surveys, we can see how extensively honor killing has been "normalized" within its traditional redoubts, as well as the extent to which the practice remains accepted even in countries such as Jordan and Turkey where there have been highly publicized national efforts to stiffen sentences. A 1999 study conducted in southeastern Turkey found that 74% of women surveyed believed their husbands would kill them if they had an affair.[75] According to a 2002 study conducted by Mohamed Awad, 99.2% of women interviewed in Egypt believed that a woman's honor lies in her virginity. By contrast, only 0.8% agreed that a woman's honor is based on her principles and values.[76] David Ghanim reports that, in 2008, a Syrian website devoted to women's issues asked participants to respond to the question, "Do you agree that your female relative should marry a man convicted of honor killing?" While 55.6% of the respondents said "no," an astonishing 41% answered "yes."[77] Since the question was posed on the Syrian Women's Observatory (SWO) website, the respondents, whatever their gender, were likely sympathetic to women's causes and may have been educated, given their computer literacy.

A July 2008 Turkish study by a team from Dicle University, undertaken in the predominantly Kurdish areas of Turkey, found that there was little if any social stigma attached to honor killing. The study also disputed

74. Kiener, "Honor Killings," n. 70.
75. Husseini, *Murder in the Name of Honor*, 145.
76. Husseini, *Murder in the Name of Honor*, 148.
77. Ghanim, *Gender and Violence*, 44. The Syrian Women's Observatory conducted the poll between January 16 and February 16, 2008. See http://www.nesasy.org, accessed June 19, 2013.

the view that honor killing is related to an archaic "feudal" social system among illiterate peasants. The report stated, "there are also perpetrators who are well-educated university graduates. Of all those surveyed, 60% are either high school or university graduates or at the very least literate."[78] Interviewing more than 850 teenagers in Jordan's capital city, Amman, in 2013, Manuel Eisner and Lana Ghuneim found that 46.1% of boys either "agreed" or "strongly agreed" with situations depicting honor killings. Among girls, 22.1% agreed with at least two honor-killing situations in the questionnaire.[79]

The largest study to date of beliefs and attitudes about honor killing among Muslims was conducted by the Pew Research Center and released in 2013.[80] The Pew data were collected in face-to-face interviews conducted in more than 80 languages with both men and women in large samples and relying on recognized sampling and interviewing methodology. Questions about honor killing were among a number of issues asked about Muslim views on moral, social, and religious subjects in the 23 countries surveyed.[81] At least half of respondents said honor killings are never justified when a women stands accused. Of all regions surveyed, support for honor killings of women was most extensive in North Africa, the Middle East, and in South Asia; in fact, only in two countries—Morocco (65%) and Tunisia (57%)—did a majority reject honor killings of accused women. In two countries—Afghanistan and Iraq—a majority of respondents (60% in both) reported that honor killings of women are often or sometimes justified. In addition, in 14 (60.9%) of the 23 countries surveyed, at least half of respondents stated that honor killings of women are sometimes justified, with the other half declaring they are never justified when a woman stands accused. In 15 (65.2%) of the 23 countries, at least half of respondents said honor killings are never justified when a man stands accused, while only in Afghanistan did a majority of respondents (59%) say that honor killings of men who allegedly engaged in pre- or extramarital sex are often or sometimes justified.

78. Murat Gezer, "Honor Killing Perpetrators Welcomed by Society, Study Reveals," *Today's Zaman*, July 2008, http://www.todayszaman.com, accessed June 20, 2013.

79. Laura Smith-Spark, "Third of Teens in Amman, Jordan, Condone Honor Killings, Study Says," June 20, 2013, Cable News Network, http://www.cnn.com/2013/06/20/world/meast/jordan-honor-crimes-study, accessed June 20, 2013.

80. Pew Research Center, "The World's Muslims: Religion, Politics and Society," Religion and Public Life Project, Apr. 30, 2013. The study is available at www.pewforum,org/2013/04/30/theworlds-Muslims-religion-politics-society.

81. Twenty of these countries have Muslim majorities; the other three—Bangladesh, Russia, and Thailand—have large Muslim minorities.

A couple of questions emerge from the Pew survey results. One concerns the separation of women's views from those of men; for instance, are women in Afghanistan and Iraq less inclined to support honor killings? Did interviewees distinguish adequately between honor killing and revenge killing of men? What the Pew research does show is the extent of support for honor killing in large areas. In addition, the polling results suggest that with vastly increasing populations, especially of younger people shown to be most likely to support honor killing as legitimate, killings are also likely to increase unless rigorous measures are taken to change public attitudes as well as to protect endangered girls and women.

Gurjeet Kaur's study of women in the state of Punjab in north India also suggests that development and modernization are not themselves promoters of women's and girls' welfare.[82] Despite the success of development in Punjab leading to its ranking among the top five Indian states in economic and health indicators, infrastructure development, and the Human Development Index, Punjab continues to be among the worst performing states on the Gender Development Index, with little or no change in traditional structural and cultural violence against women, including honor killing.

In addition, regimes in which honor killing remains unabated create unacceptable levels of psychological and structural violence, quite apart from the actual toll of victim suffering and death. It is also unacceptable that threats of such killings are a potent means of inducing terror and legitimating other forms of violence against millions of women who must be continually concerned that the slightest suspicion of unacceptable behavior could cost them their lives. Doubtless, honor killings effectively enforce repression within some of the most patriarchal systems in the world. Unni Wikan reports that, following the widely publicized murder of Fadime Sahindal in Sweden, Terrafam, an organization that helps immigrant girls in Sweden, received an unprecedented number of calls from girls more terrified than they were before the murder of the risks they would take "if they broke free." According to Wikan, Bermadita Nunez, the chair of Terrafam, reported, "'Everyone who has phoned us—we've had several hundred calls—has been afraid. No one sees any light at the end of the tunnel.'"[83]

---

82. Gurjeet Kaur, "The Status of Women in Punjab," paper presented at the Conference on the Global Status of Women and Girls, Christopher Newport University, Mar. 24–26, 2017.
83. Wikan, *In Honor of Fadime*, 32.

Honor killings also serve to reinforce male perceptions of what is required of them as masters of the household, as responsible for "their females," who, as "real men," must be seen by others as honorable. Mehmet, 14 and cousin of 16-year-old Sevda Gök, voluntarily fulfilled his "duty" by slitting open Sevda's throat like a sacrificial lamb. The scene selected for this shocking display was the town square, presumably chosen so that Sevda's bloody and gruesome death would have maximum effect. What was Sevda's "crime"? She had been repeatedly and brutally beaten because she protested after being told her schooling was ending, she had once gone to the market on her own, and she had been seen walking home from school with a boy. Terrified of further beatings and of her father's threats, Sevda ran away from home and stayed in an orphanage overnight.

"I cut her throat so that it may be a warning to others," said Mehmet proudly from his prison cell. Mehmet pronounced his dead cousin a "whore" and insisted steadfastly that strange boys had had their way with her, even after learning that a postmortem examination had proved Sevda to be a virgin. The larger meaning of Mehmet's warning, observed Turkish feminists studying the case, "is for other women who run away, for other men who are required to carry out honor murders, for those who are forced to witness the murder, for those of us who just count themselves lucky that such things have not happened to them."[84]

1.4 HONOR KILLING AND ISLAM

Although the rate of honor killing may be increasing, there is an upsurge in the willingness of women and activists to oppose the practice and risk reprisals. There is also an increasing willingness of elected officials to speak out and to support reforms. As one example, consider events in Palestine in 2013–14. Based on rumors of adultery, 32-year-old Rasha Abu Arra, a mother of six, was executed in Aqqaba, the West Bank, in November 2013. Following the execution, the mayor of the village reported, "[p]eople are outraged," while Rabiha Diab, the Minister of Women's Affairs in the West Bank said, "The entire society is incensed by the increase" of honor killings.[85] Earlier, the suspected honor killings of two teenage girls in Gaza led Hanan

---

84. Ayşe Düzkan and Filiz Koçali, "An Honor Killing: She Fled, Her Throat Was Cut," in Pinar Ilkkaracan (ed.), *Women and Sexuality in Muslim Societies* (Istanbul: Women for Women's Human Rights—New Ways, 2004), 381–87, 386.

85. Anne Marie O'Connor, "Anger Among Palestinians as Honor Killings Spike, *Washington Post*, March 4, 2014, A8.

Ashrawi, a top official with the Palestine Liberation Organization, to call for "maximum sentences" for those convicted of killing women.[86]

Yet, while there are encouraging signs in some areas, there are troubling questions about the politicization of the practice. Rhetoric suggests that ideals relating to honor, including honor killing as an appropriate reinforcement of women's traditional roles, are sometimes endorsed by radical and ultra-conservative clerics or are exploited for political purposes by fundamentalists and sectarians.[87] Traditional practices, including honor killing, are tempting subjects for arch-conservatives advocating "purification" processes necessary to reconstitute the political identity and solidarity of a "people." As Wikan has said, "Women are the symbols of . . . [the group's] solidarity and continuity. Women are trumpeted as the guardians of cultural identity. It follows that the cultural and/or national identity of the men must express itself in control of the women."[88] Consequently, conflicts threatening the political identity of a group or the masculinity of male guardians, such as the cycle of Palestinian–Israeli conflicts, might lead to increased efforts to enforce traditional models of proper feminine behavior.

It is well known that conditions for women greatly worsened under the Taliban in Afghanistan following the collapse of the Soviet invasion, and it is a reasonable concern that honor killings and other acts of gender violence will spike if the Taliban regains control following the 2015–16 reduction of US and NATO forces. Women also are more endangered in regions of Pakistan and North Africa, where movements associated or self-identifying with al-Qaeda, the Taliban, and the Islamic State in the Levant (ISIL or ISIS) are on the upsurge. As these radicalized movements place greater emphasis on traditional gender roles, there is concern that women will be increasingly threatened with honor killing in these regions.

Despite the encouraging examples at the beginning of this section, long-term trends in Gaza, Sinai, and the Israeli occupied territories suggest that the number of honor killings are rising. This is certainly an example of a volatile region in which honor has been associated with nationalistic and sectarian identity and aspirations. One chilling report from 2004 claimed that families expressing unwillingness to execute a female relative were

86. O'Connor, "Anger Among Palestinians," A8.

87. Marieme Hélie-Lucas refers to "Islamo-fascism" using Islam as a cover to create authoritarian states. See "Those Who Live Under 'Islamo-fascism,'" Secularism Is a Women's Issue (SIWI) Blob, Jan. 27, 2014, https:/www.siwi.org/article6768, accessed Feb. 16, 2015.

88. Wikan, In Honor of Fadime, 68.

informed that, unless they act, paramilitary operatives would carry out these "executions."[89] If such highly politicized and extrajudicial killings did occur, then they could not be regarded as honor killings.

Such concerns bring religion to the forefront. Honor killing and Islam are often seen as intertwined, but it makes little sense to claim that honor killing is a "Muslim problem" if that claim is meant to suggest that there is a causal connection between the Islamic faith and honor killing. Being a member of a Muslim community is neither a sufficient nor a necessary condition for being implicated in honor killing as a perpetrator, accomplice, or supporter. It is obviously not sufficient, for the vast majority of Muslims either oppose honor killing or have not and will never be implicated in honor killings. We also know that, until relatively recently, honor killing occurred in parts of Europe that were not Muslim, such as in Corsica, Greece, Sicily, and probably Sardinia and parts of Spain. Honor killing still occurs today within some Christian communities (of various sects), as well as within communities that are predominately of the Druze, Hindu, Jewish, Sikh, and Yazidi religions.[90]

The Pew Research Center's 2013 report on Muslim attitudes found *no* consistent linkages between attitudes of men and women about honor killing and religious observance or devotion. For instance, in most countries surveyed, Muslims who pray several times a day are just as likely as those who pray less often to say that honor killings are never justified. There also are no consistent differences in attitude by age or gender. However, in some countries surveyed, Muslims who support *shari'a* are *less likely* to say that honor killings of women and men are never justified.[91] These results are not inconsistent if, as I believe, support for *shari'a* reflects religious devotion much less than preferences for religious authoritarianism, strict observance of rules, and intolerance of both deviance and ambiguity. This is an inference reasonably drawn from dominant processes of training, socialization, and gender construction in communities that are both conservative and in which honor killing is most common (see Section 3.4). If I am correct, then, at most, one might infer an association between some forms of ultra-conservative Islam and such authoritarianism, strict rule observance, and intolerance, on the one hand, and support for honor killing, on the other.

---

89. Shahrzad Mojab, "The Particularity of 'Honour' and the Universality of 'Killing,'" in Shahrzad Mojab and Nahla Abdo (eds.), *Violence in the Name of Honour: Theoretical and Political Challenges* (Istanbul: Istanbul Bilgi University Press, 2004), 15–38.

90. See, e.g., Wikan, *In Honor of Fadime*, 70–88.

91. Pew Research Center, "The World's Muslims"; emphasis in the original.

Many Muslim clergy and officials are eager to dissociate honor killing from Islam. For example, Muzammil Siddiqi, Chairman of the Islamic Law Council of North America, states that "nothing in the Quran allows honor killings. They are totally un-Islamic and have nothing to do with the religion . . . never should a believer kill a believer. Take not life, which Allah hath made sacred, except by way of justice and law."[92] In 2007, Syria's Grand Mufti, Ahmen Badr al-Din Hassuon, condemned honor killing, noting, "He who kills on claims of honor is a killer and should be punished."[93] In the same year, Grand Ayatullah Shaykk Husayn Fadullah, who is associated with Hezbollah, used the occasion of International Women's Day to issue a *fatwa* binding on all Muslims. The *fatwa* prohibited all manner of violence against women including insults and decreed that an adult women does not require a guardian and that women may counter violence or sexual violence with violence or by other means.[94] In 2010, Lebanon's senior Shiite cleric called the practice of murdering a female relative for alleged sexual misconduct a "vicious phenomenon" and issued a *fatwa* forbidding honor killings.[95] Scholars and clerics representing the North American Fiqh Council and the Office for Interfaith and Community Alliance for the Islamic Society of America have made similar comments.

There are other cases where perpetrators use religious rhetoric to justify honor killings or where clerics speak out in support of the practice. However, in general, I agree with the conclusion reached by the research team directed by Filiz Kardam in Turkey who claimed that, overall, the relationship between religion and honor killing is "quite contradictory." The difficulty is that, over the past few hundred years, anecdotes, stories, and examples used to instruct about honorable behavior have become "highly wrapped in holy stories and religious instructions." Thus Kardam and her team were not surprised to find an Imam in Adana, Turkey, who presents a "perfect example" of the traditional patriarchal views that women must be strictly controlled. While many interviewees stated that religion dictates honor killings, many others claimed that Islam is against the practice: because as God has given us life, only God can take it away.[96]

---

92. Kiener, "Honor Killings," 190.

93. IRIN News, "Syria: Popular Campaign Takes Aim at 'Honour Killings,'" Feb. 15, 2011.

94. Sherifa Zuhur, "Strategy in the Battles over Her: Islamism and Secularism," in *Gender and Violence in the Middle East*, 153–74, 168.

95. Voice of America News, "Fatwa Against Honor Killings," Feb. 18, 2010.

96. Filiz Kardam, *The Dynamics of Honor Killings in Turkey: Prospects for Action* (Ankara, Turkey: United Nations Development Fund, 2012), 19, 42–44.

There is a general association, or overlay, between the density of enclaves in which HSCs exist and honor killing occurs and global regions that are predominantly Muslim. Obviously, this overlay appears to have some sort of geographical epicenter in the Saudi Arabian Peninsula since support for honor killing is weaker in certain regions that are farthest (e.g., Indonesia and Kazakhstan) from this epicenter.[97] This view is consistent with reports of some historians that Qays bin Asim, the ancient leader of the Al ash-Sheith family, a major branch of the large Banu Tamim tribe of Arabia, was the first to kill children on the basis of honor. According to legend, he is said to have murdered his daughters to prevent them from ever causing him any kind of dishonor.[98] However, perhaps honor killing had more than one point of origin. Sohail Akbar Warraich points to historical records suggesting that the practice originated among the Baloch tribes who are now a significant demographic group in Pakistan, but adds that the Pashtuns in Pakistan and Afghanistan claim an independent source for honor killing.[99]

Examples of honor killings in the Old Testament, the Roman Empire, and elsewhere also undercut claims that, insofar as honor killing depends on a specific conception of honor, honor-orientation is unique to the Arabic people or to any of the peoples of the Middle East, North Africa, or Southeast Asia.[100] The notion that one must protect his honor through violence has been a prominent theme in Western literature at least since people read and admired Homer's *Iliad*.

97. A scholar and blogger who identifies herself only as "hbd chick," where "hbd" stands for "human biological diversity," points out that the closer one gets to the "Arab expansion epicenter (the Arabian peninsula), the greater the enthusiasm for honor killing." Relying on the Pew Research Center's report of 2013, she notes that the difference between justification of honor killing of women versus honor killing of men is 47% in Jordan, 11% in Iraq, and 10% in Lebanon and Egypt, but she says, "at the edges of the caliphate" the differences are 0% for Turkey, 1% in Morocco, and only 3% in Pakistan. See www.hbdchick.com, accessed May 3, 2013.

98. Umm Rashid, "Honor Crimes and Muslims," www.islamicawakening.com, accessed Aug. 18, 2013.

99. Sohail Akbar Warraich, "'Honour Killings' and the Law in Pakistan," in Welchman and Hossain (ed.), "Honour," 78–110.

100. Honor killing is prescribed in the Old Testament in Deuteronomy (22:13–12), for instance, and in Numbers 31 as Moses orders it after the fall of Midian to the Israelites. Honor killing also appears to have been of concern in the biblical story of David's lust for Bathsheba and in the birth narrative of Jesus in the Gospel according to Matthew (1:18–19). It was encouraged in ancient Rome, where male family members who failed to take action against female adulterers were "actively persecuted." See Matthew A. Goldstein's "The Biological Roots of Heat-of-Passion Crimes and Honor Killings," in *Politics and Life Sciences* 21, 2 (Sept. 2002), 29. As Kiener notes, the Law of Mani in early India likewise prescribed death to adulterers and the self-immolation of widows (*suttee*) to prevent their further sexual activity, 194.

CHAPTER 2
Empirical Research on Honor Killing

In this chapter, I present, analyze, and discuss relevant quantitative and qualitative research on honor killings. My objective is to go well beyond the assumptions expressed in Chapter 1 and to extract from empirical research an account of honor killing sufficiently clear and robust to serve as grounds for the analyses, hypotheses, and tentative conclusions I draw in the remainder of this book, including, of course, my conjectures in Chapters 4–6 of the causes of the social practice, as well in Chapters 7–9 of recommended responses for prevention and protection.

I analyze a significant body of quantitative data accumulated with the assistance of my research aides, including, most importantly, an original study of honor killing incidents—the Churchill-Holmes study— published here for the first time. As emphasized in Section 1.2, honor killing is a social phenomenon and cannot be understood apart from the beliefs, intentions, motivations, and sociocultural norms of the persons for whom honor killing is an accepted reality. Therefore, I situate the quantitative data analyzed in the context of reported qualitative data resulting from extensive fieldwork undertaken by anthropologists and other researchers.

Section 2.1 offers a detailed presentation of the new quantitative investigation conducted for this project, including both the methodology of the study and our findings. In addition, Section 2.1 includes a comparison of the new Churchill-Holmes study with quantitative data from two other sources, professor Phyllis Chesler's published research and data collected by WikiIslam at its Honor Killing Index.[1] Section 2.2 presents an overview of important and useful prior empirical research that is both quantitative and qualitative in nature. These additional research findings are then assessed cumulatively with those discussed in Section 2.1.[2]

In Section 2.2, I interpret the research data, both quantitative and qualitative. Interpretation in this context consists primarily of inferring a number of generalizations from the research, designated as *central tendencies*. Central tendencies are claims to which I assign a very rough degree of probability based on study of the research data. The three categories are: *reasonably well supported, supported*, or *needs further study*, where the last category includes both claims unsupported by the data studied and for which there is no relevant data.

It will be obvious that claims or generalizations rated as *reasonably well supported* or as *supported* cannot be regarded as tested hypotheses. Available research data at present cannot provide the statistical accuracy to support such claims. All the same, claims so rated served as building blocks to guide further research and keep it on track. The speculative inferences of Chapters 4–8 depend on their probability. In particular, the central tendencies are critical in corroborating the most frequent, or typical, features of honor killing as a social practice and the sociocultural life-world of those who countenance the "normality" of honor killings (Chapter 3). In addition, they provide both guidance and constraints on accounts of the plausibility of the causes of honor killing in Chapters 4–6.

2.1 THE CHURCHILL-HOLMES STUDY AND OTHER DATA

The examination of cases, such as the incidents mentioned in Chapter 1, began to reveal what looked like general patterns, and my reading of

1. Phyllis Chesler, "Worldwide Trends in Honor Killing," *Middle East Quarterly* 17, no. 2 (Spring 2010), 3–11, also available at www.medforum.org/2646/worldwide-trends-in-honor-killing. The cases available at WikiIslam's Honor Killing Index (HKI) initially seemed promising, especially as they included cases from the non-English press. However, the data included fewer variables and therefore we used relatively few cases, and usually only those for which researchers also found an English language report. The HKI is accessible at Wikkiislam.net/Wiki/Honor_Killing_Index.

2. As indicated in the acknowledgments, my former student, Sarah E. Holmes, was co-principal investigator with me from July 2014 until December 2015 when, for personal reasons, she found it necessary to leave the project. I continue to use the pronoun "we" to refer to research Sarah and I conducted together, but use "I" to designate inferences drawn from this research in Section 2.2. Of course, I bear full responsibility for all claims made in the text, although Sarah's assistance was invaluable in Section 2.2 as well as with research for other parts of the book.

previously published studies—some discussed in Section 2.2—seemed to support general assumptions about the puzzling practice. However, we were motivated to create our own quantitative study principally for three reasons. First, my research assistant, Sarah Holmes, and I thought it critical to study a larger sample of incidents. Second, we wanted to examine data *ex post*, to consider it free from the influence of others' interpretations, so we could search for, identify, and track principal indicators and central tendencies in good faith.[3] Second, we were eager to look at primary- and secondary-source data, as well as both quantitative and qualitative data, to look for variables that may have been missed or discarded by other researchers.

In this section, I address the structure of our study and present the analytical findings. Some displays of data in charts and graphs offer comparisons with comparable data in one or more prior studies. An assessment of the results of comparative studies is presented in Section 2.2, where I consider the data—quantitative and qualitative—as a whole.

Methodology

We chose as most useful for our purposes a data search consistent with the tenets of Grounded Theory (GT). GT is especially helpful when raw data are highly ambiguous (e.g., it might report a case in which claims of honor were used as a defense for a murder driven by other considerations). Our research team, composed of the two principal investigators (PI) and (intermittent) student research assistants, located and reviewed hundreds of reports and narratives about honor killings from January 2012 through June 2014. We sought to obtain incident reports from historical records as well as cases represented within the past several decades.

---

3. For our purposes, the terms "principal indicators" and "central tendencies" designate markers for future research but are not intended to suggest specific quantifiable and predictive values. Principal indicators are the most important recurring variables consistently appearing across sets of quantitative data studied. Hence. a principal indicator designates a distinctive feature across honor killing incidents generally. For instance, being a female victim of kidnap is a principal indicator as it designates a higher risk of victimhood. By contrast, a central tendency is an identifiable trait or characteristic of honor killing or honor killing situations that has some probability based on our evaluation of the total evidence, qualitative as well as quantitative. We do not infer that a central tendency has a mathematical or statistical probability, however. Thus, for example, rather than saying it is a central tendency of honor killing that 69.3% of perpetrators are members of the victim's family of birth (see Table 2.1), we claim in Section 3.2 that the proposition that the perpetrator will be a member of the victim's family of birth is "reasonably well supported."

Sources searched included a large number of scholarly books, scholarly journal articles, English-language newspapers (including those published in places such as India, Jordan, and Pakistan), wire service reports, online databases such as the WikiIslam Honor Killing Index (HKI),[4] and the Honour Based Victim Awareness Network's online MEMINI (Remembrance) catalogue of honor crimes.[5]

Incident reports or narratives were flagged if they were described within the source material as an honor killing or met the Human Rights Watch definition, even if loosely. A data sheet was created for each honor killing incident and the researcher reading the particular report entered on the data sheet what appeared to be salient information. Data sheets included the source of the initial incident and as much of the following as possible: date of incident; location; nationality; ethnicity; religion; number of victims, ages, names, marital status; relationship(s) of perpetrator(s) to victim(s); names, ages, and total number of perpetrators; whether a perpetrator was the primary killer or took a secondary role; alleged honor offense; whether or not there was evidence for the allegation; reported facts about the victim (e.g., whether she was pregnant, left the home, had a boyfriend or lover, sought help, etc.); evidence of communal gossip or common knowledge of the alleged offense; perpetrator's stated motives; execution location and means used; reaction of perpetrator following the killing; and the roles of third parties: community members, social workers, doctors, village or communal leaders, police, and courts.

In keeping with GT, the next stage of our project was to review the data sheets with the objective of developing codes and the formation of concepts as needed. As might be expected, the information on many data sheets was incomplete, too vague, or ambiguous about an incident to be useful. Some questionable data sheets reviewed by a PI could be augmented by information from additional sources and were retained. However, data sheets with critically incomplete information were discarded along with data sheets for which the source was suspect or otherwise could not be confirmed. The culling process required discarding many recorded incidents and left us with 133 cases, well short of our target number of 200. At the same time, however, comparisons of the data sheets enabled us to standardize the codes for our study. These codes represent key distinctive points in the data and served as the bases for

4. See Wikiislam.net/wiki/Honor_Killing_Index, accessed repeatedly throughout the period of research.

5. Both sources were accessed repeatedly throughout the period of research. See, respectively, hbk awareness.com and www.memini.com.

further research. The codes are presented as categories in the tables and graphs presented in this book.

In coding our data and for the purposes of this section, we decided not to include data about the ethnicity, religion, or location of victims and perpetrators apart from the category of first- and second-generation immigrants into countries within Europe, North America, and Australia. From the outset, we knew that our sample would be too small to yield useful comparisons of these three dimensions. In addition, while it is predictable that a demographic of a certain ethnicity or religion located in a particular region will have a higher rate of honor killing than some other demographic groups, this fact alone does not yield information about how and why persons believe they ought to behave—that is, about the behavioral and cognitive components of honor killing. Yet it is precisely about the latter that information is required.

In addition, we decided not to include in this section data relating to third-party responses within the unofficial (e.g., tribal, communal, or caste) "legal" system or the state legal system: police, prosecutors, judges, and other legal authorities. We made this decision for two reasons. First, of readily accessible information about honor killing, the greatest amount pertained to legal and political responses, while there was a dearth of information about other dimensions of the problem. Second, and more important, my focus in this book is not on social and political responses, including legal, as they have occurred, but on what they *ought to be* and how they can be made more effective. Obviously, honor killings cannot be prevented and susceptible girls and women protected unless state legal and judicial responses, other extralegal and extracommunal interventions, and communal problem-solving become more effective. While empirical research on legal responses obviously has a bearing on making these methods more effective, legal approaches emphasize responses available within the formal legal system. By contrast, I seek to illuminate how changes in what happens outside formal legal systems but within honor–shame communities (HSCs) might result in what I call "moral transformations" (Chapter 8) that may end the practice of honor killing.

Reviews of the data sheets enabled us to form a few descriptive concepts needed to categorize the data in more useful ways. These concepts related to the alleged honor offense, perpetrators' motivations, and the means of execution. We found that there were a variety of ways of describing alleged responses that could be categorized as one or another of the "alleged honor offenses" exhibited by the categories under this subheading in Table 2.1. The category "other" designates the remaining offenses that could not be grouped into one of the main categories. Similar processes of collation,

Table 2.1 SUMMARY OF DATASET (N = 200)

Total victims	273	
Total perpetrators	356 (289 first-degree and 67 second-degree)[a]	
Earliest case	1919	
Latest case	2014	

Victim demographic information

Mean age	20.5 years (20 years, 6 months)	
Median age	19 years	
Minimum age	<1 (infant)	
Maximum age	55	
Known single	141	51.65%
Known married	96	35.16%
Unborn children	6	2.20%
Male victims	33	12.09%

Perpetrator information[b]

Perpetrator from natal family	199	69.6%
Perpetrator from marital family **or** boyfriend/lover's family	55	19.0%
Other perpetrator(s)	33	11.4%

Grouping information

Attacked alone	150	75.0%
Multiple victims	50	25.0%

Immigration status

Cases involving first- or second-generation immigrant families	51	25.5%

Alleged honor offenses

Unacceptable suitor	42	20.79%
Westernized	22	10.89%
Premarital sexual relations	20	9.90%
Interacted with a man or boy	19	9.41%
Raped	16	7.92%
Fled marital home	13	6.44%
Adultery	12	5.94%
Indecent behavior	12	5.94%
Divorced/sought divorce	11	5.5%
Refused arranged marriage	10	4.95%
Other[c]	25	12.4%

[a]First-degree designates a perpetrator who actually performed actions resulting in the death of the victim(s). Second-degree pertains to perpetrators who were responsible (e.g., the patriarch who orders the death) but did not actually execute a victim.

[b]These figures are imperfect. In some cases, a group of unknown size acted as perpetrator. In other cases, single perpetrators are effectively double counted. The latter occurs when a case involved more than one victim, and the perpetrator(s) had different relationships with each victim (for example, in a case involving the death of a daughter and her cousin, the perpetrator is coded twice, as "Father" and "Uncle.")

[c]Includes several categories that are poorly represented in the database: Fled family (natal) home (3%), unknown (2.5%), disobedience (2%), acted without father's permission (1.5%), accompanied by non-kin male (1%), rejected by husband (1%), homosexuality (1%), kidnapped (0.5%), prostitution (0.5%), and theft (0.5%)

comparison, and contrast enabled the PIs to develop appropriate concepts and, hence, tractable categories for "reasons/motivation for honor killing" and "means of execution." We found it necessary to disaggregate the category of "indecent behavior" by looking more carefully at the facts of cases and reclassifying. However, it was not possible to disaggregate "too Westernized" into useful categories because there were too many seemingly incompatibly different ways of being "too Westernized," and often more than one type of alleged misbehavior was regarded as evidence of being too Westernized.

We decided not to continue as quantitative measures the evidence of gossip, rumor mongering, and the like or common knowledge about an alleged offense. Statements about the effects of gossip and rumor, as well as statements to the effect that "the whole village knew" were common in incident reports. The difficulty, however, was that common knowledge (e.g., "everyone knew") was itself based on the reported presence of rumors and gossip, thus leaving us with only two categories: evidence of gossip and rumors (or hearsay) and no evidence of gossip and rumors (where "evidence" is based on the incident report).

Too often, it was not possible to determine whether gossip and rumors occurred before the attack on the victim and therefore might have had an effect on precipitating the attack or whether gossip and rumors peaked following attacks. Reports mentioning gossip and rumors often did not make this distinction. Moreover, the presence or absence of rumor and gossip generally was not included in news or official or nongovernmental organization (NGO) reports about incidents and usually could be found only in the smaller number of in-depth reports by anthropologists or other on-site observers or interviewers.

In addition, although torture is frequently mentioned in connection with honor killing, when culling the data sheets, we chose not to base a separate category on the concept of torture. Torture, as ordinarily understood, involves both the intention to cause excessive humiliation and pain or suffering as well the actual infliction of excessive pain and suffering. However, we found that while perpetrators were often frank, if not also proud about their motives or reasons for killing, few confessed to intentional torture. At best, one might attempt to infer from data about the means of execution those means that seem intended to cause excessive pain and suffering. However, the means of execution might be determined by deadly implements readily at hand, other circumstances, the desire of perpetrators to make death appear to be accidental (e.g., falling into a well) or a suicide (e.g., jumping from a bridge or rooftop), or the desire to destroy the evidence (e.g., burning the corpse or burying a victim alive). In addition, what qualifies as excessive humiliation or suffering is subject to differences of cultural perception as well as the vagaries of subjective interpretation. Finally, suffering is often a feature of the victim's knowledge of impending death—true for all but a very small number of victims in our dataset—and the time one is made to anticipate such a horrible ending—information that generally was not accessible. Nevertheless, as with gossip and rumor, we did not discard data about apparent torture; instead, I discuss these presumed aspects of honor killings in Section 2.2, where I consider qualitative interpretations of our data along with the research of others.

Finally, although we had hoped to track the number of "co-liable accusations"—that is, public accusations made by relatives against the patriarch of the female's family or against another male regarded as responsible for controlling her—we were unable to find sufficient information in the data sheets. As indicated in Chapter 3, in honor–shame cultures in which honor killing occurs public accusations of dishonor negatively affect all the blood relatives of the accused, or those regarded as "co-liable." Accusations also induce intense shame and therefore can be expected to galvanize those shamed (subsequent perpetrators) to remove the socially recognized "cause" of the shame, namely the female whose behavior is alleged to have been improper.

Indeed, Joseph Ginat found a co-liable accusation in all of the 14 instances resulting in death that he researched. However, it was absent in all but 3 of the 38 cases reported by Ginat in which alleged honor offenses were charged but no death resulted. Consequently, Ginat argued that the presence or absence of public co-liable accusations was very significant in the causal chain leading to the actual execution.[6] Unfortunately, the vast majority of instances accessible to us did not represent Ginat's thorough fieldwork, and we were left to assume that most of the authors, media outlets, NGOs, and officials who reported incidents either were not familiar enough with honor killings to include in reports the presence or absence of co-liable accusations, did not find evidence of them, or did not see them as relevant to the ways in which subsequent events developed. I do return to an assessment of the relevance of public co-liable accusations in Section 2.2, where I assess the qualitative aspects of our and others' research.

The final stage of gathering and processing incident reports required the selection of additional—not previously reviewed—instances of honor killing to reach our target number of 200. Given the concepts and categories

6. Joseph Ginat, *Blood Revenge: Family Honor, Mediation and Outcasting*, 2nd ed. (Brighton, UK: Sussex Academic Press, 1997), 129–97.

formulated and their refinement, this process moved more quickly than the selection of the initial 133 incidents. It was most important, however, not to force new reports into our preexisting categories; consequently, only the PIs selected and coded the final 67 instances. Our major challenge at this final stage was the absence in many incident reports of all the data categories of interest to us. Due to external constraints on our search (time, budget), we elected to add to our dataset incidents with information on at least 60–70% of our codes. Likewise, we continued to maintain data in categories we previously decided not to include in our quantitative calculations (e.g., gossip/rumors) in the hope that it might still be illuminating qualitatively.

Although the prior empirical research was certainly useful, we found that no single resource sufficiently captured the variables that we considered to be of interest. Therefore, from our bank of 200 incidents we abstracted the features presented in the following sections to examine and analyze. Due to the lack of available information, some countries where we suspect honor killings may occur are omitted entirely, and other regions are likely very underrepresented. We came to believe that raw data about geographical location and nationality have little or no bearing on the behavioral dynamics of honor killing; honor killing as a social practice has a rather remarkable consistency over time and from place to place.

More serious, even the most data-rich incidents tended to be missing some key pieces of information, such as victim age, incident date, community response, and response of local authorities to the honor killing. Moreover, because these incidents capture human behavior, some of our most interesting data—the perpetrator's motivation and the victim's alleged honor offense, for example—tend to be somewhat assumption-oriented. As we analyzed the data sheets, we found many reports of first-person statements about perpetrators' motives, but we also found recurring stock phrases used by community and family members to describe both alleged offenses and perpetrators' motives.

I emphasize our consistent efforts to avoid cherry picking incidents, and, indeed, we went into the project with as few preconceptions as possible about the statistical information that our dataset might eventually reveal. While we have done our best to ensure the integrity of each individual incident and the database, the data may reflect inaccuracies in the initial information from reports and narratives; the collection, annotation, and cataloging of the case studies was a human effort. Moreover, because we certainly do not claim the incidents in our dataset are representative of the "population" of honor killings, our findings should not be taken as proof of trends or central tendencies. Despite such shortcomings, however, we believe that there is important and interesting quantitative information to be gleaned from our dataset.[7]

Statistical Analyses

Within our dataset of 200 honor-killing incidents, there were 273 total victims and approximately 289 total first-degree perpetrators.[8] Of these victims, 30 (just under 11%) survived or escaped the attempted honor killing; the remaining 243 died during or shortly after the attack.

The dataset features cases from 28 countries and territories: Afghanistan, Algeria, Australia, Belgium, Canada, Denmark, Egypt, France, the Gaza Strip, Germany, India, Iran, Iraq, Israel, Italy, Jordan, Norway, Pakistan, Palestine (the Sinai and West Bank), Russia, Saudi Arabia, Sweden, Switzerland, Syria, Turkey, the United Kingdom, and the United States. Given that our dataset is not globally representative, we elected not to provide here a breakdown of incidents per country or region.

Alleged Honor Offense/Motivation for Honor Killing

We identified 18 categories of alleged honor offense, alphabetically listed as follows: (1) acted without father's permission; (2) adultery; (3) disobedience; (4) divorced or sought divorce; (5) fled family (natal) home; (6) fled marital home; (7) homosexuality; (8) indecent behavior; (9) illicit interaction with a boy or man; (10) kidnapped; (11) premarital sexual relations; (12) prostitution; (13) raped, including incestuous rape; (14) refused arranged marriage; (15) rejected by husband; (16) theft; (17) unacceptable suitor; and (18) too Westernized. These categories are discussed more thoroughly later in this section. Because some case studies lacked information about the victim's alleged honor offense, we added a final category, "unknown," to capture knowledge gaps.

It might be supposed that one could analyze the incident reports with an eye on actual honor offenses committed in contrast to those only

---

7. I am grateful to Sarah E. Holmes for the preparation of tables and charts in this chapter.

8. This number is approximate: some cases lacked sufficient detail about the perpetrator(s).

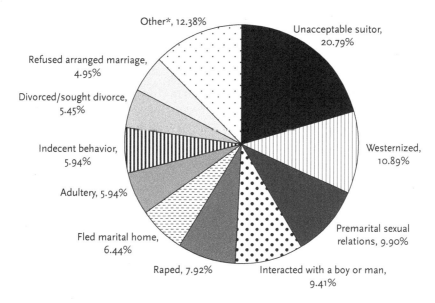

Figure 2.1 Categories of alleged honor offense, across full dataset.

* The "Other" category encompasses several categories that are poorly represented in the database: Fled family (natal) home (3%), unknown (2.5%), disobedience (2%), acted without father's permission (1.5%), rejected by husband (1%), homosexuality (1%), kidnapped (0.5%), prostitution (0.5%), and theft (0.5%).

alleged to have occurred, and we initially attempted to collect some rudimentary statistical information on this distinction since, in some instances, postmortem evidence demonstrates that the accused was innocent (e.g., that the victim was a virgin). However, executions are based on what perpetrators *believe* victims have done, sometimes as a result of mere gossip. As noted earlier, we consider information about rumor or gossip and its effects to be largely qualitative.

Note also that there is a significant gray area and overlap among the categories just presented (see Figure 2.1). For example, nearly every category could easily be lumped under "indecent behavior" for these activities are considered socially inappropriate in HSC.[9] Second, some case studies cited multiple allegations of honor offense; in those cases, we selected the category that was most specific and seemed to account for the largest share of the perceived insult to the family honor, given the relevance of the family's sociocultural beliefs and way of life. For these reasons, we consider

---

9. We were as specific as possible with our alleged misconduct categories, but in some ways "indecent behavior" remained a catch-all category for us. Incidences of "indecent behavior" included such differences as choosing to frequent the public square and town market, begging, and fraternization with individuals of different socioeconomic classes.

the information about our categories of alleged offenses to be largely qualitative rather than quantitative, and I reconsider these data in Section 2.2.

The three most common alleged honor offenses were unacceptable suitor (20.79% of cases fell into this category), Westernized (10.89%), and premarital sexual relations (9.90%). Examples of "unacceptable suitor" included wanting to accept a marriage proposal from a man with a more progressive background, marrying a man of unacceptable socioeconomic status and an unacceptable religious sect, and marrying interracially. Common complaints of "Westernized" included inappropriate dress and having European or North American boyfriends.

The "premarital sexual relations" category is self-explanatory, but among the most troubling components of the database only 12 (60%) of the 20 cases citing premarital sexual relations also contained details confirming that the victim had indeed engaged in premarital sex. At least 3 (37.5%) of the other 8 incidents in this category featured victims who, upon autopsy, were determined to be virgins. In total, 61 (30.5%) of the total cases in the database featured alleged honor offenses which were ultimately proved inaccurate or lacked confirmatory evidence. This tendency toward unsubstantiated allegations was also revealed in Gideon Kressel's 1970s quantitative study (see Section 2.2), in which only about 1 in 5 cases featured attacks backed up by explicit proof of an honor offense.

Our findings overlapped with those in a recent quantitative study conducted by Phyllis Chesler and analyses of the WikiIslam HKI. Common categories of alleged honor offense in the HKI include unacceptable boyfriend and/or expression of interest in marrying or cohabitating with an unsuitable partner (40% of cases in non-Muslim majority nations), too Westernized (36% of cases in non-Muslim majority nations), and illicit sexual relations (21.2% of cases in Muslim majority nations). Although Chesler divided motivations for honor killing into just two categories—too Western and sexual impropriety—both are reflected in our findings.

These similarities across large datasets warrant treating perceptions of illicit sexuality or intended illicit sexuality (broadly construed) as a principal indicator. This means that girls and women perceived as having engaged or intending to engage in such illicit activity are more likely to be attacked. Similarly, being perceived as too "Westernized," especially in non-Muslim majority countries, is a principal indicator because it, too, correlates with a higher probability of being attacked. To avoid belaboring these correlations, in the remainder of this section we simply discuss the relationships discovered, such as that between the victim and family members most likely to serve as executioner.

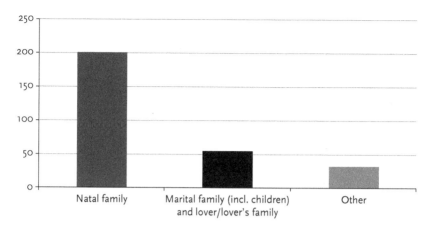

Figure 2.2 Perpetrator–victim relationships, across full dataset.

Perpetrator–Victim Relationships

Examining the relationship between perpetrator and victim was critical in corroborating the claim, incorporated in our acceptance of the Human Rights Watch definition, that honor killing involves the execution of the alleged offender by members of her own natal family. It is not surprising, therefore, that we found the overwhelming majority of perpetrators (69.6%) to have come from the victims' natal family. Far fewer, 19.0%, came from the victim's marital family or (in the case of unmarried victims) were his or her lover or other members of the lover's family.[10] Another 11.4% were categorized as "other," a group that included hired killers, community or tribal councils such as the *kap panchyats* of India or *jirgas* of Pakistan (see Section 1.2), and perpetrators classified as "unknown" due to lack of information. Except for the very small number designated as "unknown," all killers were known to family members of the victim (see Figure 2.2).

When we analyzed the available information with more granularity, we found that brothers were the most common perpetrators, accounting for 27.3% of overall perpetrators. Fathers were second most prevalent, at 19.4%, and lover's family members, or in-laws, accounted for 11.4%. As can be seen in Figure 2.3, all other perpetrator–victim relationships occurred relatively infrequently.

10. The distinction between natal family and marital family obscures the reality that many marital relations are also close relatives; for example, the husband of a victim might be a cousin and her father-in-law also her father's brother. See Sections 6.2–6.3 for a discussion of marital practices, especially first-cousin marriages, within honor–shame communities.

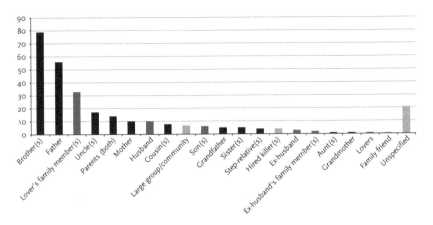

Figure 2.3 Specific perpetrator–victim relationships, across full dataset.

These findings were again supported by other quantitative studies. The HKI data also identified brothers and fathers as the most common perpetrators in honor killing cases, accounting for 37% and 23% of cases in Muslim majority nations, respectively, and 32% and 54% of cases in non-Muslim majority nations, respectively. In our study, brothers and fathers combined accounted for 46.7% of all perpetrators; in the HKI, they accounted for 60% of perpetrators in Muslim majority nations and 86% in non-Muslim majority nations. In Chesler's study, fathers were implicated in 37% of worldwide cases and 31% of cases in the "Muslim world" (Chesler's term). While our dataset shows slightly smaller figures for brothers (27.3%) and fathers (19.4%), a trend still seems evident: a woman is most likely to find herself at risk of honor killing from her father or male sibling(s).

We were curious to see the case studies involving brother(s) as perpetrator(s) broken down further, so we next reviewed the relative ages of brother/perpetrator and victim. The results were clear: among those cases where the relatives' ages were known, 69.4% involved brothers who were older than their victim(s), and 30.6% involved brothers known to be younger than their victim(s). Unfortunately, just over half of our case studies involving brother/perpetrators contained no details about the relative ages of those involved. Nonetheless, knowing that older brothers were more than twice as likely to commit an honor killing than their younger counterparts is critically important, and I return to this point in our more detailed assessment of the data in Section 2.2 as it suggests that a perpetrator's awareness of, and perception of, responsibility for the condition of the family's honor is a critical part of the honor killing process.

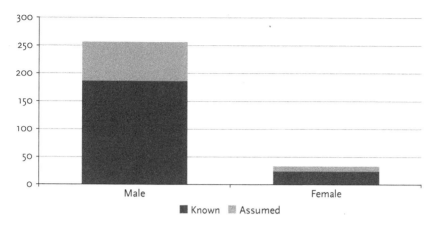

Figure 2.4 First-degree perpetrators by victim, across full dataset.
Note: Assumed figures calculated by obtaining gender percentages among perpetrators of known gender (88.52% [male] and 11.48% [female]) and multiplying number of perpetrators of unknown gender (80) by these percentages.

Finally, we evaluated the perpetrators' genders. We found that, among those perpetrators of known gender, 185 (88.5%) were male and 24 (11.5%) were female. Another 80 perpetrators were of unknown gender (usually because a name other than the family name was not given), but, using the previous calculations, we estimated that 71 of those were likely male and 9 female. These results underscore the premise, also noted by many others, that honor killing is in fact a crime committed by men against women. The relatively small number of honor killings committed by women can be explained by the ways in which women become enmeshed within the honor–shame culture (see Section 5.3) and feel themselves obligated to take the role of de facto head of the household when they are widows or the male head is unavailable (e.g., working abroad, fighting in the military, or imprisoned) (see Figure 2.4).

Victim Age

Another important set of variables to review were the ages of the victims (where known), to gain a better understanding of our "average" victim and to estimate key periods in a woman's life during which she may be at particular risk for honor killing. The youngest victim in the database—a victim of an attack on the mother—was still in the womb at the time (past the first trimester); the youngest born victim (carried by her mother while she fled) was almost 1 year old. The eldest victim was 55 years old. We

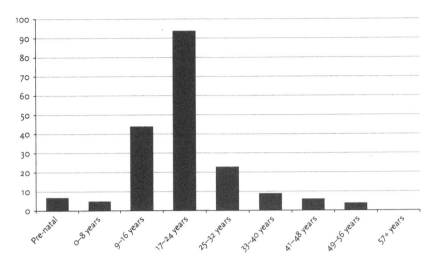

Figure 2.5 Distribution of victim ages, across full dataset.

calculated the mean (20.5 years) and median (19 years) figures from our dataset, then created a frequency array to examine into which age groups the victims fell.

As Figure 2.5 shows, most victims were between the ages of 9 and 32 at the time of the honor killing or attempted honor killing. The 17- to 24-year-old age range was most prominent, represented by 94 (49.0%) of the 192 victims of known age. This was followed by the 9- to 16-year-old age range, which included another 44 (22.9%) victims, and the 25- to 32-year-old age range, which included 23 (12%) victims. All other age ranges (prenatal, 0–8 years, 41–48 years, and 49–56 years) contained 10 or fewer victims. The age distribution of our dataset is relatively normal, with a slight positive skew. Of the total, 81.25% of observations are within one standard deviation (9.5 years) of the mean age (20.5)—only 36 observations (18.75%) were less than 11 years or greater than 30 years.

This distribution of victim ages closely matched that in the HKI (see Figure 2.6), but revealed an important distinction between our results and Chesler's. While our results and those in the HKI were relatively normal, Chesler's were bimodal. Without access to Chesler's data, it is difficult to say definitively what accounts for this discrepancy, but differences in data collection practices seem the most likely cause. We are confident in both the integrity of our collection efforts and the analysis and interpretation of our dataset.

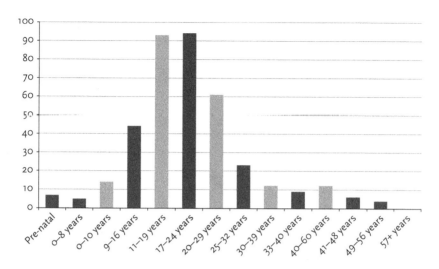

Figure 2.6 Comparison of victim age distribution in full Churchill-Holmes dataset and HKI dataset.

These findings reinforce our idea that women are at greatest risk for honor killing with the onset (often early) of puberty and throughout childbearing age.

Marital Status

We next evaluated victims' marital status. Unfortunately, a number of our case studies did not specify the victim's marital status, so we were only able to account for that status in 86.8% of the total victims. Of those, 59.5% were married and 40.5% were single at the time of the honor killing or attempted honor killing. Married victims appeared in our database approximately 50% more frequently than their single counterparts.

As Figure 2.7 shows, known married victims were more than twice as likely as their single counterparts to suffer execution (or attempted execution) at the hands of a marital family member, lover or lover's family member, or some combination thereof. Just over 10% of known single victims were killed by a marital family member, lover, or lover's family member, but more than 25% of known married victims died at the hand of such a perpetrator or perpetrators. However, the overwhelming majority of victims in all categories (known single, known married, and full dataset) were killed at the hands of members of their natal family.

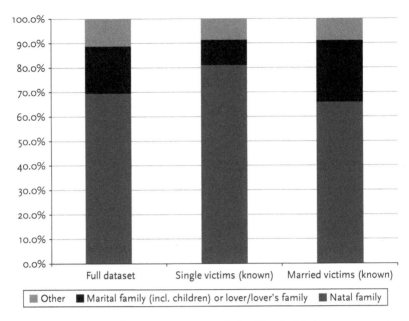

Figure 2.7 Comparison of perpetrator–victim relationships in full dataset among single victims and married victims.

Execution Circumstances

The means of execution is very often one of the most prominent features of reports of honor killing, partly because so many of these tragedies are reported by journalists as human interest stories. We identified 18 means of execution in the incidents: axing, beheading, blunt force, broken neck, burning, drowning, gunshot, hanging, live burial, poisoning, slit throat, stabbing, stoning, strangulation, suffocation, a fall (being thrown from a building or a bridge), and vehicular homicide (including being run over by a tractor). Some executions were designated as "forced suicides" without further specification of the means of death.

The three most common methods were gunshot (representing 32.3% of cases with known means of execution), stabbing (13.1%), and strangulation (12.7%). We noticed, in addition, the superfluity of methods of killing in many incidents. In other words, many victims (13.8%) were killed via multiple means (for example, a victim sustaining multiple stab wounds might also have been bludgeoned with a blunt instrument, either of which would have been sufficient for death). The other means of execution were relatively uncommon, each appearing 10 times or fewer in the database (Figure 2.8).

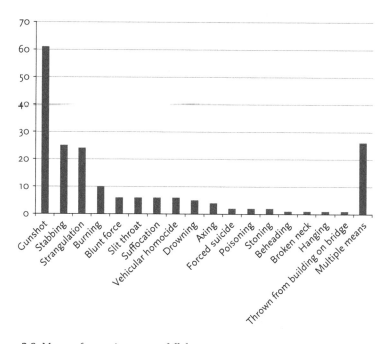

Figure 2.8 Means of execution, across full dataset.

In assessing the data, we were interested in the fact that many incidents involved methods of killing that inflicted excessive or drawn out suffering for victims. Chesler has reported that more than half of victims worldwide in her data were subjected to torture, and we estimated that approximately 41% of victims in the HKI dataset were tortured (43.6% in Muslim majority countries and 38.4% in non-Muslim majority countries). We were interested in whether anything like this pattern emerged in our Churchill-Holmes dataset. Moreover, while it seemed unlikely, we wanted to consider whether there was any suggested relationship between the means of execution and the marital status, age of victim, age of perpetrator, or category of alleged offense (motivation).

Public Versus Private

We also tracked the public versus private nature of the executions. We were interested in this distinction for two reasons. Private versus public became an important cue in our initial screening of honor killing cases, and, consequently, we initially believed that it might be important. A number of studies have emphasized that honor killing often occurs publicly and thus has a communicative or symbolic feature. Unfortunately, many reported incidents omitted this information or provided inadequate details for us to make a determination. Of the 139 case reports with known execution location, 75 (54%) happened in public areas and 64 (46%) occurred in private. In the following assessment section, I consider the possible relevance of the distinction between public versus private execution in relation to other variables measured. However, the significance of the public location of 54% of the total incidents must be understood as a qualitative inference from the data. The same is true, as noted later, about the frequently mentioned male "family council" issuing the decision to execute the alleged offender and what Joseph Ginat called the "co-liable accusation"—namely, a protestation publicly and by one or more prominent family member that the male person most responsible for the alleged female offender had not yet carried out the execution.

Immigration Status

Of the 200 Churchill-Holmes cases, 51 or 25.5% featured first- or second-generation immigrant families. This number should not be taken to suggest that approximately 1 in every 4 honor killings happens in an immigrant community; honor killings occurring in immigrant communities, especially those in Europe and North America, tend to gain more media attention and public interest than those that happen in countries of origin. However, we were interested to find that many of the statistics we calculated for the entire dataset held true when we isolated for those cases involving first- or second-generation immigrant families. For example, compare the perpetrator–victim relationship data in Figure 2.9.

While the relative proportions of natal family perpetrators to marital family perpetrators remained essentially constant in relation to other perpetrators, a more granular review revealed some key differences. In the complete dataset, brothers were the most common first-degree perpetrator, representing 27.3% of all perpetrators. When we controlled for immigration status, however, we found that fathers were the most common first-degree perpetrator, representing 27.0% of immigrant-status perpetrators. Brothers were second most common in this group, representing 24.3% of perpetrators. A more detailed breakdown and comparison is shown in Figure 2.10.

The most striking difference among immigrant groups, aside from the roles of brothers and fathers just discussed, is the increased incidence of ex-husbands or family members of ex-husbands acting as first-degree

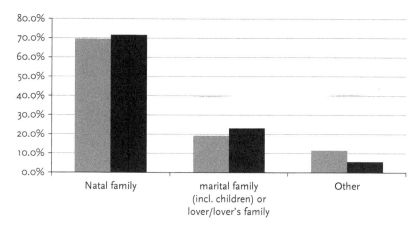

Figure 2.9 Comparison of perpetrator–victim relationships among full dataset and among first- and second-generation immigrants.

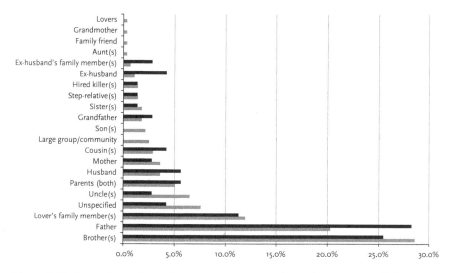

Figure 2.10 Comparison of specific perpetrator–victim relationships among full dataset and among first- and second-generation immigrants.

perpetrators. Across the entire dataset, these categories represented only 1.7% of the total perpetrators; among immigrant families, they represented 6.8%. There are several explanations for this striking difference; a possible explanation is that separation and divorce, or the expressions of wives' desires for such, may be more common in European and North American immigrant communities. This factor might combine with an increase in the pool of ex-husbands and in-laws as potential perpetrators, especially if members of the wife's family are not in the immigrant population or the marriage had been arranged among closely related families.

Ages and Marital Status

We found that the alleged honor offenses in the case studies involving first- or second-generation immigrant families differed from those in the full dataset. Eight of our original 18 categories of alleged honor offense did not appear at all in the immigrant cases: (1) accompanied by a non-kin male, (2) fled family (natal) home, (3) homosexual, (4) indecent behavior, (5) kidnapped, (6) prostitution, (7) raped, and (8) unknown. The most common complaint, unsurprisingly, was "Westernized"—21 (41.2%) of our cases cited this issue. The second most common complaint was "unacceptable suitor," representing 10 (19.6%) cases, followed by "refused arranged marriage" in 5 (9.8%) cases, "premarital sexual relations" in 3 (5.9%) cases, and "divorced or sought divorce" in 3 (5.9%) cases. The following categories: "interacted with a boy or man," "fled marital home," "adultery," "disobedience," "acted without father's permission," "rejected by husband," and "theft" were each featured in less than 4% of immigrant case studies (Figure 2.11).

In brief, the full database and the set of cases featuring first- or second-generation immigrants share many key indicators. The absence of whole categories of honor offense in immigrant communities seems best explained by the often drastic differences between countries of origin and the realities of host countries with respect to socioeconomic, political, and sociocultural conditions. A particular difference is the relatively greater freedom and independence of women in non-Muslim majority countries and contact with alternative social norms in schools, shopping malls, the media, among neighbors, and so forth.

The prevalence of honor killing within immigrant communities that share honor–shame orientations (see Chapter 3) is among the most important lessons gleaned from our database as it reveals that simple geographical separation from what we call HSCs in countries of origin is not enough to effectively prevent honor killings. In other words, HSCs are particularly resilient, and, in this global age, they no longer depend on geographic locale. Accordingly, honor killing as a social practice is not merely situational, but so deeply culturally ingrained that exposure to alternative ways of life is often not sufficient to inspire real change.

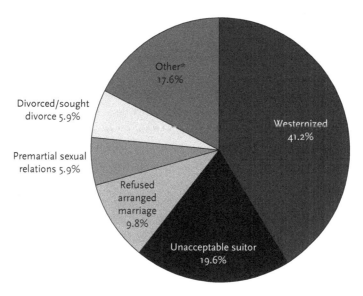

Figure 2.11 Categories of alleged honor offense among first- and second-generation immigrants.
* The "Other" category encompasses several poorly represented categories: interacted with a boy or man (3.9%), fled marital home (3.9%), adultery (2.0%), disobedience (2.0%), acted without father's permission (2.0%), rejected by husband (2.0%), and theft (2.0%).

2.2   RESEARCH ASSESSMENTS AND CENTRAL TENDENCIES

I present the results of my overall assessment of the research studies, quantitative and qualitative, as a series of generalizations about honor killings and the circumstances in which they occur. Note that the quantitative data reviewed in the previous section focused on principal indicators and the relationship between several variables, presented numerically as percentages and in charts and graphs. In interpreting the data, some inferences were drawn in Section 2.1, for instance, about perpetrators' relationships to victims and the likelihood of attacks on girls and women.

The generalizable claims I present in this section go beyond the interpretations in Section 2.1. My objective now is to bring into focus tentative generalizations inferred from *all of the data*, including qualitative data not previously discussed, as well as the quantitative data reviewed in Section 2.1.[11] As inferences about honor killings collectively,

11. In addition to Chesler, HKI, and WIC databases cited earlier, the major sources for qualitative and quantitative studies were the following: Minoo Alinia, *Honor and Violence Against Women in Iraqi Kurdistan* (New York: Palgrave Macmillan, 2008); Centre for Egyptian Women's Legal Assistance, "'Crimes of Honour' as Violence Against Women in Egypt," in Lynn Welchman and Sara Houssain (eds.), *"Honour"*

these generalizations are what earlier I called *central tendencies*. These central tendencies are thus claims, albeit speculative, about the likelihood or probability of certain tendencies or characteristics of honor killings generally.

I present these central tendencies in an easily understood list format. Note that the inferred central tendencies are organized into three categories by level of general inductive support: *reasonably well-supported claims, supported claims*, and *claims needing additional research*. I forbear from assigning degrees of inductive probability to each category (e.g., "reasonably well-supported'" versus "needing additional research") or even to the probability claims within each category. The restraint is reasonable. Recall that the principal indicators discussed in Section 2.1 were presented as relationships between variables (such as between illicit sexuality and likelihood of attack) within a dataset or as relationships common across datasets; however, as admitted earlier, the imprecision, or "fuzziness," of some of the descriptors (e.g., "too Westernized") made it difficult to be confident that we had found truly relevant factors. In this section, I move beyond principal indicators in the quantitative datasets to make general claims—central tendencies—about honor killing as a social practice. This move involves the logic of inductive reasoning that cannot be mathematically or statistically precise simply because central tendencies are conjectures about what all incidents of honor killing are likely to have in common, including future cases not studied or observed. Moreover, given the very partial and incomplete data, as well as a few apparent discrepancies, anything but extreme caution is inappropriate.

Crimes, Paradigms, and Violence Against Women (London and New York: Zed, 2005) 137–59; Ginat, *Blood Revenge*, 1997; Danielle Hoyek, Rafif Rida Sidawi, and Amira Abou Mrad, "Murders of Women in Lebanon: 'Crimes of Honour' Between Reality and the Law," in Welchman and Houssain (eds.), *"Honour,"* 111–36; Rana Husseini, *Murder in the Name of Honor* (Oxford: Oneworld, 2009); Filiz Kardam et al., *The Dynamics of Honor Killing in Turkey: Prospects for Action* (Ankara, Turkey: UN Population Fund, 2012) available at www.unfpa.org/sites/default/files/pub-pdf/honoukillings.pdf; Gideon M. Kressel, et al., "Sorocide/Filiacide: Homicide for Family Honour" and "Comments and Replies," *Current Anthropology* 22, no. 2 (April 1981) 141–58, available at http://www.jstor.org/stable/2742599; Ayse Onal, *Honour Killing: Stories of Men Who Kill* (London and Berkeley: SAQI, 2008); Nicole Pope, *Honor Killings in the Twenty-First Century* (New York: Palgrave Macmillan, 2012); Nadera Shalhoub-Kevorkian, "Researching Women's Victimization in Palestine: A Socio-Legal Analysis," in Welchman and Houssain (eds.), *"Honour,"* 160–80; Aida Touma-Sliman, "Culture, National Minority and the State: Working Against the 'Crime of Family Honour' Within the Palestinian Community in Israel," in Welchman and Houssain (eds.), *"Honour,"* 181–98; Unni Wikan, *In Honor of Fadime: Murder and Shame*, trans. by Anna Paterson (Chicago and London: University of Chicago Press, 2008).

The list of central tendencies thus reflects my educated and inductive inferences based on the information studied. In only some of the following generalizations do I find it helpful to cite percentages from the studies presented in Section 2.1, and I do so only for the sake of clarity. Four brief but important points must be made. First, some important claims here are inferred from what is *absent* from the body of evidence. For instance, in the Churchill-Holmes study, we did not collect data relating to honor offenses committed by men and boys followed by honor-motivated attacks on them. As noted in Section 1.1, there is a vicious double standard in communities in which honor killings occur, insofar as men and boys committing adultery, rape, or fornication are not made to suffer as women and girls are. The *absence* of comparable male victimization (except as a matter of revenge) is nevertheless an important inference, not only from the database, but from all materials studied.

Second, it was not possible to eliminate some influence from the broader understanding of honor and HSCs (see Chapter 3) that I acquired before the Churchill-Holmes dataset was compiled and we began to look at patterns.

Third, I follow the list of central tendencies with hypotheses that require further research but may frame future studies and analyses in this area. Both the first group of claims and the hypotheses for further research are organized by topic: HSCs, honor killing, victims, and perpetrators. Because these social phenomena happen "organically," there is some overlap between topics.

Fourth, it is important to remember that the research findings are generally not definitive due to four main limitations:

- There is no claim whatsoever that samples studied are representative of any general national, ethnic, or religious group, such as Sunni or Shi'a Muslims in Iraq. In addition, all the studies analyzed were based on samples involving actual or intended honor killings and drawn from available reports, including those of interviewees willing to respond to questions. Consequently, while the samples shed light on honor killing as a phenomenon, they cannot be taken as conclusively representative of the actual "population" of honor killings cases (e.g., including unreported cases) and certainly not of the general proclivities or tendencies of groups in which future honor killings may occur.
- While the case studies in the database present reports of honor killings known to have occurred or been attempted, as far as I know, there is no available data on how many honor "offenses" occur each year, what percentage are met with an actual or attempted honor killing, and what factors of the community or family—such as educational attainment,

social status, economic well-being, etc.—might cause that percentage to vary.

- Samples are underrepresented in areas for which reports of honor killings are less frequent (e.g., Bangladesh, Kuwait, Saudi Arabia) and for regions in which it is dangerous or difficult to acquire data (e.g., Afghanistan, Algeria, Iran, parts of Pakistan, Somalia, Syria). Information is overrepresented in the samples for some groups, especially Kurds in Iraq and Turkey; Bedouin in the Palestinian territories; and from some regions, such as Egypt, northern India, Jordan, and Pakistan, as well as immigrant communities in Western Europe and North America.
- Some of the qualitative data collected through the techniques of participatory observation or in-depth interviewing might have had unintentional and unforeseen effects on reports made by respondents and interviewees.

LIST OF CENTRAL TENDENCIES

Reasonably Well-Supported Claims
Honor–Shame Community Characteristics

- Honor is understood, in communities in which honor killings occur, as concerned especially with control of female sexuality and female bodies and behaviors, as well as the responsibility of male family members to maintain that control.
- Male honor requires that a male family member respond appropriately by "washing" the honor when a female in his family is alleged to have committed an honor offense. By contrast, male sexuality, except homosexuality (when publicly admitted as a sexual orientation), is not a matter of honor or dishonor.
- In cases where perpetrators and family members of victims and surviving victims are interviewed, interviewees provide overwhelming evidence of social pressure to kill; they feel almost under compulsion and that they cannot do otherwise.
- Interviews with witnesses of honor killings, persons who know or hear about them, or members of communities where they occur express overwhelming support for the need to uphold honor and the subordination of women to men.
- In general, honor killing is a cross-religious and cross-cultural as well as a cross-national, or international, type of crime.
- Honor killing follows a fundamental pattern. Despite differences from one locale to another, or of religion, ethnicity, and the like, the pattern

is sufficiently similar. We can reasonably expect that a person familiar with the practice in one area (e.g., Punjab) would recognize a description of the practice in another area (e.g., Iraq).

- Females bear the burden of a presumption of guilt: if there is gossip or rumors, or a girl or woman has not conformed to expectations (e.g., been outside alone), there is the general presumption of illegitimate intent or offensive behavior. There are no such burdens borne by males.

Honor Killing Characteristics

- The clear majority of incidents studied involve intentional efforts to "wash" family honor, despite the variety of more particular reasons given. While incidents studied might have included a small number of cases in which motives are ambiguous and "honor" might be used as a cover for personal profit or advantage or to obscure crimes of other kinds, attempts were made to avoid inclusion of such cases.
- Honor killings are intended to be lethal and usually are: only 11% of women and girls attacked escape or survive.
- Honor killings are almost always premeditated and display evidence of advanced planning, often following a discussion among men about what should be done and who must act (the so-called family council). The killing usually follows by at least a day or two the decision to execute the honor "offender." Only a few incidents involve apparent efforts to kill "preventively," that is, to prevent the harmful effects of gossip and shame.
- Documented evidence in many regions about police apprehension, arrest, and detention, and legal charges, trials, and prison sentences, and the like indicates that members of official state legal systems often accept community mores or regard honor killings as matters beyond legal concern. Reported police and official behavior often supports the widely held presumption that legal officials distort the mechanisms of the legal system to support local informal "justice" systems or strong public views. Recently, efforts to affect local behaviors and mores and to require official conformity with official legal standards have increased in some areas.

Honor Offenses

- All of the major quantitative studies demonstrate a general convergence on three primary categories of behaviors thought to violate honor: sexual impropriety (premarital and extramarital sex or a meeting with a male that suggests a sexual interest or intent), rebelling directly against patriarchal authority and its rules (having an unacceptable suitor, marrying against parents' or tribal wishes, resisting an arranged marriage, seeking divorce or fleeing the marital home), and becoming too Westernized.

- In immigrant communities, there are categories of honor offense not found in the countries of origin. In addition, being too Westernized is provided as a motive in far more cases in immigrant communities (41.2% compared to 13.1%). Alleged honor offenses are more likely to be seen as a product of the Western environment rather than a more specific transgression. Likewise, in immigrant communities, fewer categories of alleged honor offense are found than in those featuring country of origin communities (11 categories compared to 18).
- Whether or not a girl or woman is actually guilty of an honor offense is irrelevant in many incidents: in 30.5% of the cases in the Churchill-Holmes dataset the victim was innocent.
- The most important causal factors leading to a death are what others in the extended family and community believe, the pressure exerted by other family members, the peer and psychological pressures exerted on family members by the community, and the availability of alternative options to killing that also will be seen by members of the community as having "cleansed" the family honor.

Means of Execution

- While shootings are far and away the most frequent means of execution, there is a wide variety of ways of killing, and stabbing and strangulation occur frequently as well.
- Multiple means of execution are used in many incidents, even when there is only one perpetrator. In addition, there are many cases in which the use of a weapon is excessive, such as in multiple gunshot wounds or stabbings, reflecting "overkill" on the part of perpetrators.

Role of Gossip

- Public accusation of an honor violation, including gossip, and pressure from relatives and the community are among the most important causal elements leading to an honor killing.

- While it is difficult to measure the presence of gossip or rumor and its effects quantitatively, qualitative evidence indicates that gossip and rumor about an alleged offense is a significant factor in limiting options of families and precipitating an attack.

Victim Characteristics

- Females targeted for execution are usually single individuals, but in some cases multiple individuals are killed at the same time, typically because they are each perceived as responsible for behaving dishonorably or because they are seen as accomplices, enablers, or instigators of the primary victim's honor offense. Occasionally, an additional death results when a person is physically proximate to the principal target or, in the case of a fetus, expires with the killing of the mother.
- A significant number of victims of honor killings are innocent of charges made against them (e.g., postmortem exams show that many are virgins).
- Women and girls of all ages are at risk of attack, but victims are most often in the age range of 12–39 years. This age range coincides closely with the onset of female fertility and continues through the peak childbearing years.

Perpetrator Characteristics

- The majority of honor killings are committed by males in the birth, or natal, family of the victims. Even among husbands who kill, some are related by blood to the victim. Relatively small percentages of deaths result from unrelated perpetrators (hired killers) or are perpetrated by nonrelated husbands or in-laws.
- Some women (mothers, sisters, aunts) do commit honor killings, but the number is very small relative to the number of honor killings committed by male relations. When females are implicated, they are far more likely to be accomplices rather than primary perpetrators.
- The largest number of perpetrators are the brothers of victims; fathers are second. This strongly suggests (a) that some younger males looking forward to future positions of male dominance volunteer to be executioners, while others are pressured into performing the "necessary duty," and (b) there is considerable social pressure on patriarchs to fulfill their expected roles.

- In contrast to figures for the dataset overall (Churhill-Holmes, Chesler, and HKI), within immigrant groups in Europe and North America fathers were the most common first-degree or principal perpetrators.
- In immigrant groups, there is an increased incidence of ex-husbands or former in-laws acting as first-degree or principal perpetrators.
- Multiple perpetrators participate in a large proportion of honor killings, in approximately 40% of incidents in some studies.
- Despite the presence of multiple perpetrators in many cases, in most incidents there is a principal executioner who is either assigned to commit the killing, has volunteered, or self-incriminates as the responsible party.

Supported Claims

Honor–Shame Community Characteristics

- Although she is divorced or a widow, a woman's body and sexuality are still under the strict control of her family of birth, her former husband, or her in-laws.
- In the opinion of members of HSCs, divorce is not a sufficient punishment for the wife suspected of infidelity. The woman must be killed by members of her natal family or by a blood relation.

Honor Killing Characteristics

- Honor killing is predominantly a male-against-female crime. Family members very rarely attack men who engage in behaviors that are regarded as dishonorable by the family and community if such behaviors are done by a female.
- In general, the family of the girl or woman charged with an honor offense is obligated to redress the offense. If the alleged offender is married or betrothed, the male partner is not involved in redressing the matter as his honor has not been besmirched. Exceptions include divorced or widowed women who are seen as the "property" of or under the control of both the natal family and in-laws.
- All members of a family, extended family, clan, and even tribe are subject to shame by the dishonorable behavior of a single female member. All will be relieved of the shame only when the violation has been successfully redressed, as required by the honor code.
- Active efforts made by girls or females to protect themselves are typically regarded as further proof of guilt. Efforts of females to seek assistance

from sheiks, town officials, shelters, and others usually result in further public exposure, prolongation of shame for the family, and, often, an increased resolve to kill.

- Despite community support for such a robust and stringent view of what the honor code requires, interviews with perpetrators, surviving victims, and members of HSCs more generally reveal that the communities have very vague and abstract conceptions of honor and its meaning.
- Following a completed honor killing, public shaming of most families of victims ceases, and victims' families are accepted back into their communities and might resume their prior positions and roles within their respective communities.
- The motive to execute an "offender" as a means of reestablishing family honor is generally not lessened by knowledge that the "offender" herself has been a victim of an arranged marriage she opposes, of severe spousal abuse, of divorce or ejection from her marital home, of kidnap, or of rape, even when the rapist was a member of the immediate family or a blood relative.
- Majorities of mothers and sisters of victims' support or do not resist the decision to execute their relative.
- In a small number of cases, a family member spoke up on behalf of an honor "offender" and objected vehemently to a death penalty. The objector was a mother or sister in some instances, and, in some cases, the intervention was successful in preventing an attack.
- The data suggest that there is a correlation between a family's ability after the charge of an alleged honor offense to find a "solution" other than death and a family's ability to contain evidence of an honor offense and avoid exposure and gossip. Other factors contributing to avoiding the "necessity" of killing include social status, wealth (e.g., in having a girl married off), relative economic independence of the family (enabling the family to move), or power relations between the family's males and the community, clan, or tribe.

Victim Characteristics

- The likelihood of a single girl's death increases if she becomes pregnant and especially if there is gossip about the situation. Evidence of pregnancy of an unmarried woman (e.g., visiting a hospital for an abortion) also increases the likelihood of her death through honor killing.
- If a male is attacked, it most likely occurs when he is apprehended along with a female who has been charged with an honor offense, during flight

or in hiding, while eloping, or being surprised while engaging in "illicit" activity. Males of the female's family carry out the attack. It is generally not sufficient to "wash" family honor that only the male be killed; the "cleansing" is not complete until the female is killed. Most male deaths associated with the honor killing victim's death are not also honor killings. Rather, these deaths are inflicted as revenge, and the agent is not the female's or male's natal family, but usually the cuckolded husband.

Perpetrator Characteristics

- Whether all members of HSCs commonly regard females as the "property" of the men in their families, it is common for perpetrators and others interviewed to speak of the female and the self in terms of identity; that is, of the female victim as a "part" of the family or the perpetrator (e.g., "my flesh") as not possessing an independent stature.
- Perpetrators interviewed overwhelmingly express no guilt over their deeds but report instead that they have done the right thing, or they seem to be self-satisfied or prideful.
- Very few perpetrators express any sympathy for their victims or report missing them, although many continued to express anger about the "necessity" of killing and most expressed considerable sorrow for themselves.
- Perpetrators' views of the honor code and their commitment to honor generally do not change following their incarceration or conviction for killing the victim.
- Perpetrators tend to be supported by their families, are encouraged and protected by relatives and members of their communities, and are regarded highly by other prison inmates for killing the victim.
- Of incarcerated perpetrators interviewed, a majority believe their sentences have been unjust and regard themselves as the victims. Many in this group regard other factors (e.g., the media) or other persons (e.g., a boyfriend) as responsible for the outcome.

Torture and Excessive Force

- Perpetrators inflicted many deaths in torturous ways or in ways causing extensive pain, psychological and physical suffering, and with a callous disregard for the victims' plight. Perpetrators generally express satisfaction with the suffering imposed.

- In many instances, death is inflicted by more than one means or is excessive and reflects rage on the part of the perpetrator (e.g., desecration of the corpse, dozens of knife wounds).

Claims Needing Additional Research

Honor–Shame Community Characteristics

- Families residing in a community, or connected by blood ties with families in a community, are bound together by powerful norms of honor and are equally "liable" to be subjected to gossip or charges about a breach of honor by females of the family. No family, from *shaiks* (sheiks) to mere peasants, is free from shaming, severe criticism, and social isolation.
- Relationships between members of HSCs appear to be characterized by vigilance and a zero-sum approach when it comes to honor: a loss of one member's honor seems to confer a net increase of the honor of unrelated community members.

Honor Killing Characteristics

- Despite some evidence that the least educated, poorer persons who reside in remote areas or who emigrate to urban ghettoes or enclaves are more likely to commit honor killings, the practice is found within all social and economic classes. It also occurs among the highly educated, those in professional occupations, and the wealthy.
- Except for a married or divorced woman who was in, or alleged to be in, an extramarital or a postmarital relationship, there is no apparent ranking of the seriousness of honor offenses or of those who are most deserving of death.
- The likelihood of an honor killing decreases for a girl or young women who has been kidnapped or raped if a marriage can be arranged between her family and the family of the kidnapper or rapist, but it does not decrease when such arrangements cannot be made.
- In contrast to concerns about honor, the differences in family position relating to wealth, tribal and political connections, and status can have a significant impact on how the crisis of perceived dishonor is resolved. In general, wealth, tribal connections, and power and status (personal, familial, and tribal) correlate positively with the decreasing likelihood that the female "offender" will be condemned.

- If a family decides not to execute a female perceived to be an honor "offender," but to save and protect her instead, then usually that family will be expected to sever ties with the community and to emigrate. This is true even if the protective family has significant status in the community and is in a powerful tribe.
- Of all types of dishonorable conduct by females, the lowest rates of homicide are associated with elopement or kidnapping. Possibly elopement and kidnapping are compatible with a bargain between the two families to marry the couple. The likelihood of "resolution" through marriage is increased if the elopement can be disguised or kept secret.
- The likelihood of elopement or kidnapping leading to "resolution" through marriage is increased if the female's family is of high status or has wealth. If her family is poor, it will have difficulty demanding concessions from a wealthier family. However, if the male partner's family is much poorer than the female's, it is unlikely that an alliance will be made and, consequently, more likely that the female will be attacked. In all cases, "resolution" requires that the community does not shun or socially exclude the female's family.
- While distinctions between the public or private place of execution did not seem significant in the Churchill-Holmes study, other research strongly suggests that executions performed publicly have a significant symbolic or communicative dimension, demonstrating the communally "required" "washing" of honor with blood.
- Increased judicial penalization for executions is likely to have increased the number of executions occurring within private family homes or in remote or less frequented areas. This penalization might explain a rise in the number of juvenile male executioners who are subject to lesser punishment and the number of "forced suicides" (e.g., when a victim might be coerced to eat rat poison while the family is out).
- It is extremely difficult to calculate the proportion of alleged honor "offenses" resulting in honor killings or attempted honor killings because it is difficult to determine how many honor "offenses" may occur at any given time. Research indicates that the categories of "offense" are broad, and whether behavior is regarded as typifying a category is a matter of subjective judgment. In addition, in studying only cases in which an attack has taken place, researchers cannot determine whether community members might exercise discretion in deciding which "offenses" become the subject of rumor and then evolve to a charge of "dishonor."
- Public co-liable accusations, made by blood relatives against the male who is regarded as most responsible for an allegedly dishonorable girl

or woman, increase the likelihood that male family members will perpetrate an honor killing.

- A widow's risk of being a victim of honor killing greatly increases if there are allegations that a widow has fraternized with men other than those in her immediate natal family. It is also extremely difficult for divorced women to avoid death if they are alleged to have nonrelative male friends or lovers.
- A review of data across the quantitative studies does not corroborate Ginat's claim about the significance (i.e., necessity) of a co-liable accusation. In addition to the absence of evidence in many incidents, a small number of cases involved "preemptive" killings performed to prevent public shaming before such accusations could be made.
- Inconsistent findings are reported concerning the relationship between the number of honor killings and the size of the town or village in which they occur. The common supposition is that honor killings occur more frequently in rural areas with small communities and in urban areas in which enclaves of emigrants sharing values and similar worldviews persist. However, some data suggest that honor killings increase in frequency with the size of the town in which families live, even in nonurban areas.
- Despite many references to family meetings or councils held to decide the fate of alleged offenders and to designate perpetrators, including references within many cases in the Churchill-Holmes dataset, we did not find this variable to be significantly related to others measured in the research studies.

Victim Characteristics

- The number of reported honor killings of males who are charged with honor offenses (e.g., homosexuality, lewd behavior) is very small compared to the large numbers of reports of honor killings of females.
- Women who are married, widowed, or divorced are more likely to be executed than unmarried girls and women, except for the latter who are pregnant. Married and divorced women are more likely to be charged with extramarital or postmarital sexual relations, which is generally regarded as a more serious offense.
- So far, quantitative studies do not corroborate the claims from Kardam's qualitative study that accused women known to be married or divorced are twice as likely as single women to suffer execution at the hands of a marital partner, an in-law, or a lover.

Other Hypotheses to Consider

Honor–Shame Community Characteristics

- It would be helpful to know more about the social factors that encourage bystanders and community supporters to perceive death as a fitting or proportionate punishment for an honor offense. It is important to discover, as well, why confession and contrition by the accused is not accepted, why there are no rites of forgiveness or purification other than deadly violence, or why other known conflict resolution techniques are not employed.
- Comparative research should be conducted to discover whether HSCs exist in which honor killings rarely occur or not at all, and how and why these communities differ from those in which honor killings occur regularly.
- Further research through in-depth interviews or detailed investigation of cases is needed to determine the extent to which a public, co-liable accusation corresponds to a decision to attack a girl or women for an honor "offense."
- Comparative studies of HSC responses to alleged female "offenses" and male homosexuality are needed to indicate why common knowledge of the latter (based on a "don't ask, don't tell" consensus) so rarely results in a violent response.

Honor Killing Characteristics

- One hypothesis to check, if possible, is the claim that population density is irrelevant to the rate of honor killings; that it is rather the strength of communal ties and commitments to honor and prescribed forms of behavior that are most important.
- There is to date no attempt to chart the frequency of charges of dishonorable behavior (i.e., communal honor crises) per community and thus to consider their possible periodicity or possible correlations with major cultural, social, economic (e.g., a rise in unemployment), or political (e.g., greater instability) changes.

Victim Characteristics

- Narrative reports included in the Churchill-Holmes and from interview materials often suggest that "offenders" are typically more curious, adventuresome, determined, and bolder than their peers. Further research might indicate whether this is an impression based only on the fact that a trespass occurred or whether the likelihood of "going astray" or being attacked correlates with character difference(s) between conformists and nonconformists.

Reformative Measures

- There was too little data in the quantitative research on the effects of intervention by women's rights, human rights, NGOs, and other activist groups to predict when, how, or what kind of efforts to assist women or their families might have the most success. Given strong evidence that women's initial efforts to seek assistance from outside the family worsen the situation, then emergency interventions such as the provision of shelters and legal response must be bold and decisive. (See Section 7.1.)
- Given the resilience of honor killing as a social practice and the network of cultural norms grounding it, emergency and protective measures will not succeed in ending honor killing on their own. Protective interventions are likely to be regarded as foreign intrusions similar to the efforts of official state law to end honor killing through criminalization. It is necessary that change agents introduce long-term transformative measures that isolate honor killing as archaic and dysfunctional and help community members elect to bring the practice to an end. (See Chapter 8.)
- Although they are crimes by men against women, honor killings also represent a general communal commitment to maintenance of its time-honored practices. Most women within such communities share the attitudes, beliefs, and values of its men. Consequently, presumptions are likely mistaken that women in HSCs will readily ally with outside efforts to end honor killing.
- The "necessity" of honor killing is a recurrent theme in both the quantitative and qualitative studies, given social expectations and the lack of alternative means of "washing" the family honor. Although recommended strategies and tactics for a transformative end to honor killing are multiple and complex (Sections 8.2–8.3), it is critically important to enable community members to envision alternative lives for themselves that do not require honor killing, including imaginative ways of responding nonlethally to the "offenses" presently associated with the "need" to kill.
- Reformative strategies and tactics should focus on three major points: freeing community members from attaching honor to the killing of women; alleviating men and women from the burden of believing

it is still necessary—as a response to communal concern about an "offense"—to undergo the test of killing to demonstrate trustworthiness and loyalty to the group; and providing community members with adequate alternatives for resolving communal problems.

In concluding, I look ahead very briefly to the connections to be made between the empirical studies discussed in this chapter and the remainder of the book. In Chapter 3, I consider the ways in which honor killing is normalized as a social practice in what I describe as HSCs and how conceptions and norms regarding honor as the supreme communal value both shape a worldview and way of living that continue to exercise a powerful grip. Chapter 4 connects the norms of honor with child-rearing practices and socialization, including gender construction and identity formation. In addition, Chapter 5 explores the formation of warrior masculinity and the predisposition of males in HSCs to occupy roles as perpetrators in accepting obligations to violently uphold family honor. Chapter 5 illuminates the causes of honor killing at the micro-level in terms of agency. In Chapter 6, I offer a plausible explanation, at the macro-level, for the cultural evolution of herding and pastoralist groups into HSCs in which—despite appearances to the contrary—honor killing as a distinctive social practice endowed an adaptive advantage to groups practicing it. Referring to the "reformative measures" discussed earlier, I look to possible means for protection and prevention, which receive full and rich treatment in Chapters 7–9.

While the empirical research reviewed in this chapter and the central tendencies provide grounding for the entire enterprise, I do not often refer back to the principal indicators and central tendencies in the pages ahead. This is partly because of their generality, but more often because the arguments and explanations ahead require a careful logical handling of empirically dense and rich material from disciplines such as anthropology, psychology, and cultural evolution, and space does not allow for looking back and discussing how further research leads to the corroboration, refinement, or extension of the inferred central tendencies presented here. I do urge, however, that readers remember the lists of central tendencies in this section as a convenient reference point while reading ahead.

CHAPTER 3

The Social Realities of Honor

The extensive empirical analysis of honor killing in Chapter 2 indicates that *honor killing is a social practice*. This means that, despite some variations from incident to incident, critical roles and behaviors recur with regularity. Very complex, interpersonal, psychological, and social dynamics come to be unified and replicated in a sustained social practice. Section 3.1 illuminates what it means to call honor killing a social practice by analyzing the major features that constitute such practices.

Obviously, honor killing exists within communal groups that provide it with strong normative support. Perpetrators' anxiety to behave *honorably* and frequent claims that honor *requires* executions testify to dominant social norms and communal expectations. Section 3.2 analyzes conceptions of *honor* and *shame* critical for understanding both perpetrators' motives as well normative support for it.

Whereas Section 3.2 focuses on *sharaf*, the general honor concept, Section 3.3 examines *'ird*, or *'ard*, the conception of honor relating to sexuality, to women's chastity and men's responsibilities as the guardians of females. Section 3.4 takes up the constitutive features and dynamics of honor–shame communities (HSCs)—that is, the sociocultural groups within which honor killings occur most frequently. While throughout Sections 3.1–3.3, I will need to refer to HSCs before they are analyzed in Section 3.4, difficulty can be avoided, if, before Section 3.4, the term "honor–shame community" is understood as roughly synonymous with philosopher Kwame Anthony Appiah's notion of an "honor world."[1] For

---

1. Kwame Anthony Appiah, *The Honor Code: How Moral Revolutions Happen* (New York: W.W. Norton, 2010), 19–20, 61–62.

Appiah, the term "honor world" describes a group of people who acknowledge the same, usually unwritten, honor code and for whom honor norms are critically important in regulating behavior. Moreover, honor and dishonor or shame accorded to individuals depends on the extent to which these individuals exemplify the values of the collective.[2]

3.1   HONOR KILLING AS A SOCIAL PRACTICE

As noted in Section 2.1, one point of describing honor killing as a *social practice* is to emphasize that it is not free-standing: it cannot be completely abstracted from communities in which it occurs. Honor killing is both dependent on and helps to structure the larger sociocultural life of HSCs. Various social practices contribute to the whole life of a community by sharing various common forms of behavior and often cannot be easily "un-entwined." This is to be expected. Although the continuity of a social practice depends on its transmission across generations of a repertoire of linguistic and behavioral meanings, performances constituting one practice may partially constitute others, and various social practices may overlap or "nest" within a more extensive and complex life-world.[3]

Recall that the *central tendencies* of honor killing in Section 2.2 were identified based on the *frequency* of their presence across the dataset of incidents, even if they are also behavioral "elements" present in or contiguous with other social practices. We can also conceive of the *frequency* with which various central tendencies cluster together. Hence, what makes a social practice most distinctive is how a configuration of behavioral and belief components function together *intentionally* and *causally* in producing a distinctive outcome. For instance, a teenage daughter may be beaten repeatedly and even locked up before her alleged behavior is regarded as justifying her execution. While the components of the abusive behavior *prior to* the honor killing might overlap in significant ways with behaviors comprising the execution (perhaps she is bludgeoned to death), the motives and outcomes—both intended and causal—are distinct. In instances of abuse prior to the execution of daughters and sisters, parental (and possibly sibling) intentions and anticipated consequences are to correct, punish, and to

---

2. Appiah, *The Honor Code*, 61.
3. For instance, attending a friend or colleague's daughter's wedding ceremony and reception might simultaneously enact the witnessing of the wedding, a gift-giving exchange, and recommitment to one's own marital vows, as well as enjoyment of meeting new people and rebonding with friends through social conviviality.

deter. In the case of honor killing, the objective is to end a life and thereby restore family honor.[4]

In addition to honor killing and the widespread use of force to "discipline" wives and children, several logically distinct social practices frequently overlap in honor worlds. These include the *hijab*, or *veil*, covering a woman's hair, or the *burka* covering the entire body; consanguine (bloodline) patriarchy; shared family and tribal obligations to seek revenge; the sequestration of girls with the onset of puberty; arranged marriages; marriages between cousins (frequent); polygamous marriages (in some areas); male circumcision; female genital cutting ([FGC] in some areas), and child betrothal (in some areas). All of these social practices are knit together in the encompassing honor world by common norms of honor and shame as well as by communally shared expectations about the ways these practices are to be enacted (see Section 3.4). Despite these interlocking and mutually supportive practices, each exhibits a fairly unique configuration of behavioral and belief components, and, as noted earlier, each combination functions intentionally and causally to produce a *distinctive* type of outcome.

For the sake of convenience, let us now regard the central tendencies analyzed in Sections 2.1–2.2 as the *material conditions* of honor killing; that is, as the conditions that generally persist across a wide variety of instances. Our focus now shifts to the *formal conditions*, the conditions that establish honor killing as a distinctive social practice. A *social practice* should be understood in terms of several defining characteristics.[5] Altogether, there are five characteristics that honor killing possesses in common with social practices generally. In addition, there are two characteristics of honor killing that are shared only with some social practices. It is interesting from the perspective of the social sciences to consider the reasons why social practices have certain characteristics. However, because this is a study of honor killing and not social psychology or sociology, I list the seven characteristics and offer only very brief comments when necessary. Ultimately, the objective of understanding honor killing as a social practice is to appreciate why effectively ending it requires what, in Chapter 8, I call a *moral transformation*.

4. See Section 1.3 for my reasons for excluding from this analysis of honor killing so-called *honor crimes* in which suspected paramours are killed or in which perpetrators are not close blood relatives of the victims (e.g., husbands or in-laws).

5. Logicians refer to this method of definition as definition by limiting condition. See Robert Paul Churchill, *Becoming Logical: An Introduction to Logic* (New York: St. Martin's Press, 1986), 112–15.

1. *A social practice is a form of socially established and cooperative human activity with a fairly unique organization, or patterning, of behavioral components forming a recognizable unity.*

2. *The pattern of cooperative linguistic and physical components is causally related to a relatively distinctive outcome, end, or objective.* Note that the distinctiveness of outcome means that two or more social practices will not, *insofar as they are practices*, have the same outcome. We might think that two or more social practices might produce the same outcome, but only if we describe the outcome with misleading generality. For instance, one might claim that the practices of law, medicine, engineering, and others have the same objective of making money or earning a living. However, although many capable and skilled persons do earn good livings, a skilled lawyer or architect cannot improve health as does a physician as a practitioner. This demonstrates the need to distinguish between the primary purpose of a practice, qua practice, and subsidiary purposes, or, alternatively, between *external* ends such as making money and the *internal* end distinctive to the practice.[6]

3. *Standards of behavior appropriate and acceptable within the practice relate directly to our understanding of the point or purpose of the social practice.* It must be possible for those who value a social practice to distinguish clearly between persons who succeed in attaining the end or objective and competitors who fail. For complex, in highly developed practices, there may be different levels or degrees of success; for instance, winning the Olympic gold medal, in contrast to winning the silver or bronze. Whether or not differences between expertise, competence, and failure are coarse or finely grained, those who engage within a practice submit themselves to the normative standards for success within the practice.[7]

4. *Social practices are replicable patterns of linguistic and physical behavior passed down from one generation to the next through socialization and internalization.* Despite being a legacy of the past, honor killing continues to be resilient because the norms which dictate the required and expected behaviors remain robust and because the outcome—tragically—continues to be valued. Note that when behavioral norms remain powerful and outcomes valued, the behavioral components of a practice

---

6. See Alasdair McIntyre, *After Virtue: A Study in Moral Theory* (Notre Dame, IN: University of Notre Dame Press, 1981). However, my focus will be on practices that have no real "internal goods" regardless of how skillful or "virtuous" participation may be within the practice. Honor killing is among these, as is torture, stoning for adultery, FGM, and certain forms of terrorism.

7. McIntyre, *After Virtue*, 178.

and the ways they produce expected outcomes can undergo adaptation and cultural reinvention without a dissolution of the practice. Consider, for instance, that one effect of ratcheting up penal sentences in Turkey has been an increase in the number of juvenile males who kill, as well as the number of "forced suicides"; victims are increasingly left with poisons or nooses dangling over stools and told that, unless they take their own lives while the family is out, they will subsequently experience a more brutal form of execution.

5. *The outcome, or objective, of a social practice is valued by members of the sociocultural community for whom it is a meaningful practice, insofar as this outcome is a result brought about by engaging in the practice.* Although often a "regrettable necessity" for a family, many inhabitants of honor worlds regard executions of females suspected of violating the code as highly "desirable" or "necessary," and a family failing to discharge its "obligations" is severely criticized.

Moreover, the execution of the "offender" is valued *precisely because it is an outcome of the social practice* of which this expectation forms an important component and has become normative. Members of the HSC would not be satisfied, and might feel thwarted, if the dishonored female died of a medical emergency prior to the family execution or as a result of an automobile accident.[8] Note, as well, that the killing is not the only valued outcome of the practice. The execution also vindicates the honor code's prohibitions, and the willingness of blood relations to kill a family member graphically demonstrates the strength of their commitment to the honor code (see Sections 6.3–6.4). Generally, members of the community do not regard those who kill for honor as having committed murder; on the contrary, the wayward female committed the wrong and her family must kill her to set matters right.

6. *Honor killing shares with only some social practices the characteristic that participating within the practice is, for principal agents, nonelective or coerced.* "Nonelective" means that individuals experience their actions as compelled or obliged by irresistible social pressure, even when others are not literally coercing them. Unfortunate victims-to-be have no control over whatever rumors or gossip swirls around them, and a targeted female's natal family has little control over whatever shame befalls it. Once a female is marked as a target, her family experiences

8. For similar reasons, a young woman who manages to flee is often hunted down and executed even if this requires years of searching, often abroad; a designated male who refuses to kill is often threatened with death himself and, in some instances, actually executed.

what they routinely report as an almost irresistible pressure to act as expected.

The following comments are fairly representative of this sense of compulsion. "I did it to wash with her blood the family honor . . . and in response to the will of society that would not have had any mercy on me if I didn't," said a 25-year-old Palestinian man, explaining why he had hanged his sister. "Society taught us from childhood that blood is the only solution to wash the honor."[9] An anguished Palestinian woman who had put a plastic bag over her daughter's head and slit the girl's wrists, said, "I had to protect my children." The victim had brought shame upon the family because she had been raped and impregnated by a brother. "This is the only way I could protect my family's honor," added the mother.[10]

Other social practices requiring nonelective participation include soldiers responding obediently to officers' commands in battle, students obediently completing exams, and citizens dutifully filing income tax reports. Honor codes are especially notable for making demands on particular agents even when they themselves have done nothing to create personal responsibility.[11] Although fairly rare today, the idea that honor might make a person responsible for the conduct of another, although he himself has not acted dishonorably, was a common theme in past North Atlantic societies. As Appiah notes, a gentleman's defense of a lady's honor in Europe or North America in the 18th century might require that he fight a duel.[12]

7. *Honor killings share with some, but not most, social practices the general inability of persons to offer reasons for their participation in the practice except to reiterate that tradition, social custom, society, religion, or the like requires it.* Often perpetrators, family members, and approving neighbors express *cognitive certainty* about the morality of executing a person to "wash the

9. Yotam Feldner, "'Honor' Murders—Why the Perps Get Off Easy," *Middle East Quarterly* 7, no. 4 (Dec. 2000), 41–50.

10. Soraya Saraddi Nelson, "Culture of Death? Palestinian Girl's Murder Highlights Growing Number of 'Honor Killings,'" *Jewish World Review*, Nov. 18, 2003, http://www.jewishworldreview.com/1103/honor_killing.php3, accessed Aug. 9, 2016.

11. Appiah, *The Honor Code*, 19–20, 61–62.

12. Appiah, *The Honor Code*, 61–62. If one feels obligated to defend a lady's reputation, then he must impugn the honor of the man who has insulted her. Thus the intention of challenging the insulter to a duel is to force his hand. If the insulter apologizes or retracts his statement, then he is publicly exposed as a liar or an intemperate cur. However, if an apology or retraction is not forthcoming, then the duel must proceed. Once the challenge has been issued and an apology rejected, neither gentleman can refuse to take the field for to fail to fight is to increase the shame. Not only will the insult to the lady stand, but both gentlemen will be disgraced as cowards.

family honor with her blood," but this is combined oddly with an *inability to provide reasons for this moral certainty that reach beyond common clichés:* for example, "Tradition requires it," "It must be this way," "My people do this, and so I must do like they do," "It is the custom," "God wills it," and so on. Responses such as these beg the question, why does tradition, or custom, or religion require it?

When really pressed, some participants will refer to the prudential reasons for killing, as did the 25-year-old Palestinian male just quoted, or the negative consequences of failing to kill, as did the anguished mother. However, interlocutors find that their requests for the justification of the traditional social practice is perplexing, as indicated by the interviewee's long pauses, embarrassment, or disbelieving stares. *Moral dumbfounding* is the term coined for this sudden speechlessness despite feelings of certainty, or the inability to verbally offer moral reasons for what one seems to know intuitively.[13] Questions about a number of social practices elicit the same kind of moral dumbfounding: questions about FGM often elicit nothing more than appeals to tradition.[14] The same occurs when a member of an HSC is asked to justify the systematic discrimination against young girls.[15]

While honor killings studied in Chapter 2 were spread across five continents (Africa, Asia, Australia, Europe, North America), the seven characteristics discussed here help to explain why honor killings exhibit a highly consistent structure and pattern despite variations of time, place, and participants. Moreover, a successful execution, as occurring within *this practice,* is understood by community members as exemplifying *honorable* behavior. An honor code prescribes roles for the victim, male family members, and on-lookers, as well as justifies the killings; moreover, this code is also relevantly similar wherever there are HSCs.[16] This brings us to

13. Jonathan Haidt, *The Righteous Mind: Why Good People Are Divided by Politics and Religion* (New York: Vintage Books, 2010), 29.

14. See, for example, Juliette Minces, *The House of Obedience: Women in Arab Society* (London: Zed Books, 1982), 101.

15. Nawal El Saadawi, *The Hidden Face of Eve: Women in the Arab World*, new ed. trans. and ed. by Sherif Hetata (London and New York: Zed Books, 2007), 18.

16. Except for the Pasthun of Afghanistan and Pakistan and their code known as *Pasthunwalli,* there is no written honor code for communities in which honor killings occur. Rather, "code" as used here refers to a long-standing oral tradition consisting of proscribed and required behaviors. Membership in an honor world requires accepting the code, although most individuals are acculturated to accept the code unquestion-ingly. Because of its central importance, the honor code resists change and continues to regulate behavior despite geographic dispersal, and it continues to be fundamentally the same in all honor–shame communities.

an investigation of the conceptions of honor which organize much of life in HSCs, as well as its twin, shame, another value constantly in play when honor is at issue.

3.2 CONCEPTIONS OF HONOR AND SHAME

The meaning of "honor" is relative to cultural contexts as well as to values or standards and hence has a variable meaning.[17] In many modern North Atlantic communities, for example, honor is understood as a matter of personal integrity, as when a person strives to do what she believes to be good or right;[18] to act autonomously and authentically, as in being self-governing;[19] or to have self-respect, as in the sense of one's own dignity or worth, whether or not that person also receives social esteem.[20] By contrast, in HSCs, honor *is* social esteem, and honor depends almost entirely on how others view one.

In contemporary North Atlantic groups there is frequently a gap between "external" and "internal" components of honor and self-worth. External honors can be bestowed as accolades, awards, promotions, and so forth, but judging that the awardee is a person of honor is usually based on an affirmative "match" between external honors and inward character or moral integrity. This is why observers say that external bestowals, recognitions, and rewards should be "fitting"; that is, that the individual honored does indeed possess the qualities or have the merits for which she is honored. Of course, external awards and internal character may be misaligned: a person can be honored by others without being worthy of the honor or without subjectively feeling one merits the honor; likewise, one can, like Socrates, regard one's self as honorable, or as having moral integrity, without being recognized and respected by others.

By contrast, within honor worlds, there are generally no gaps between external appearances and subjective experiences. The external and internal components of honor are fused together in lived experience.[21] In such communities, being honored externally through the regard of others is at

---

17. Tahira S. Khan, *Beyond Honour: A Historical Materialist Explanation of Honour Related Violence* (Oxford: Oxford University Press, 2006), 42.

18. Paul G. Hiebert, *Anthropological Insights for Missionaries* (Grand Rapids, MI: Baker Book House, 1985), 212.

19. Gerda Lerner, *The Creation of Patriarchy* (New York: Oxford University Press, 1986), 80.

20. Unni Wikan, *In Honor of Fadime: Honor and Shame*, trans. Anna Paterson (Chicago and London: University of Chicago Press, 2008), 53.

21. Wikan, *In Honor of Fadime*, 54. Socrates sought to revolutionize many other moral concepts as well as honor. The predominant Greek conception of honor, *timē*, referred

the same time to be an honorable and moral person and results in one's subjective feelings of self-worth and esteem. Moreover, where distinctions between internal and external components of honor are rarely drawn, it becomes more difficult to appreciate *honor as moral integrity*. If a person regards her honor as a matter of moral integrity, then she will care far less about being respected than she does about knowing she is *worthy* of respect. Likewise, when honor is a matter of moral integrity, then the capacity of an individual "to have shame," that is, to know that she has not lived up to what she expects of herself, is one sign of a person worthy of honor.

This is why it makes sense in North Atlantic cultural groups to reproach one who is expected to act with integrity but who has taken a serious misstep by asking, "Have you no shame?" Such a question is, however, completely inappropriate among members of an HSC. A "shameless individual" in such a setting is not a person who has committed a significant breach of morality or good manners, but rather, a person who has not done anything dishonorable. A shameless individual in an honor world is commendable rather than blameworthy. In this setting, for a man who is seen as honorable by his peers, the proper response to the question, "Have you no shame?" is an equally simple, "Yes, I have done nothing dishonorable."

For inhabitants of HSCs, *honor concerns a person's worth in the eyes of others*. Social recognition is far more important than the individual's private sense of self.[22] Honor is also dependent on how others see the world around the individual and perceive his situation in relation to the social world. Honor is thus doubly relative. First, others must accord one a requisite minimal amount of esteem to be regarded a bona fide group member. Second, men ascertain or weigh their honor "on the scale of community perceptions."[23] An individual's honor is estimated based both on the community's valuation of his achievements or qualities and in terms of the perceived gap between the individual's and his neighbors' reputations in the community. An individual's, a family's, and even a tribe's honor is relative to that of potential competitors within the community or region.

Although an agent is often said to *have* honor in such a social world, honor cannot belong to individuals as a "quality," or disposition of character, and as apart from the appraisal of the social group. Honor is not *personal* and due a person apart from his or standing in a collectivity. In

---

to honor or respect attained through distinguishing feats such as winning a contest or a battle.

22. Wikan, *In Honor of Fadime*, 53.
23. Khan, *Beyond Honour*, 64.

this sense, honor *attaches to one* only insofar as one's identity within the collectivity is secure. *Thus, whether or not one is honorable depends on how the situation is interpreted.* One's honor is also always conditional for it depends not just—or even mostly—on what an individual does, but on how others *perceive* him or her.

Members of HSCs tend to be ever wary and watchful, alert for the possibility that their honor is shifting relative to others. One's reputation and family name are guarded zealously against prying eyes, idle tongues, and malicious intentions. At the same time, opportunities to take advantage of others' apparent losses are quickly exploited in order to bolster perceptions that one's own honor is rising and to challenge those whose esteem might seem to be rising more quickly than one's own. Gossip and rumor are the primary means by which possible shifts in a family's honor become known and are therefore critical in initiating "honor competitions." Unni Wikan, who spent years studying family life in a poor section of Cairo, says "Rumors are *social facts* that you have to deal with. It follows that protecting your private life is hugely important. You should *never* give people reason to gossip."[24]

Like honor, the reality of shame is "external" and depends on disclosure, also making it subject to what lies in the eyes of beholders.[25] Fear of humiliation can be endured if a misstep can be kept private, but once dishonor becomes a perceived "fact" to outsiders, an individual can be "cleansed" only by behaving in a manner communally accepted to restore honor. Families do their best to keep setbacks and misbehavior secret, and, as Wikan notes, "The situation is closed" (*mastwr ilhal*) is a standard Arabic reply to the question "How are you?" It translates as "Fine, thank you—my home and my family are screened from view."[26]

In addition, *self-worth* and even *identity* are dependent on a general social consensus that one is worthy of equal respect as a member of the community.[27] Indeed, without being esteemed as honorable one is in danger of losing one's sense of self—in effect, *one sees one's self as one appears to others.* The common usage of *wajh*, or "face," for honor signifies this mirroring relationship, for the face one presents to the world is precisely the same as

---

24. Wikan, *In Honor of Fadime*, 58 (emphasis added).
25. Wikan, *In Honor of Fadime*, 61.
26. Wikan, *In Honor of Fadime*, 58.
27. The tight connection between possessing honor and personal identity is borne out by Frank Henderson Stewart who points out that, among the Bedouin, a man's honor is looked upon as something constituting his recognizable person, not unlike visible features such as the nose, eyes, or an arm. See Frank Henderson Stewart, *Honor* (Chicago: University of Chicago Press, 1994), 143–44.

the face one sees in reflection. The *fusion* of the individual's self-worth and identity with social recognition accounts for the widespread remark among observers of "the anxiety to be honored and respected at all cost, and by whatever means."[28]

This complex interrelationship between social perception, honor, self-worth, and identity is not common only across HSCs; historically, one also finds similar combinations in many Western texts. For instance, William Shakespeare has the Roman Mark Antony profess, "If I lose mine honor, I lose myself."[29] Bertram Wyatt-Brown, speaking of the American ante-bellum South, says "the opinion of others [was] an indispensable part of personal identity and gauge of self-worth."[30] Further examples of this kind are easily found in literature and express the same notion as a proverb common in the Arabic world: "It is better to die with honor than to live in humiliation."[31]

Honor is seen as a matter of survival for most members of an honor world. Individuals literally report that without honor a man has nothing, that life is not worth living, and that dishonor is a living hell.[32] Research shows how severe the consequences of dishonor can be. Dishonor breaks social bonds: acquaintances and family alike may shun one. A person will be subjected to ridicule or jeers, become the butt of jokes in the community, or be spat upon. A dishonored family will find it difficult, if not impossible, to exchange children in marriage alliances; dishonored men may become un-employable, business partners may end cooperative enterprises, or one is likely to lose customers and might end up out of business. Generally, those morally "outcast" will not be physically attacked or have home or business burned down, but a family will often feel it necessary to leave the commu-nity; if not, they might be expelled or outcast.[33] While relatively rare, there are instances in which a man who refuses to vindicate the family honor is himself executed.

28. David Pryce-Jones, *The Closed Circle: An Interpretation of the Arabs* (New York: Harper & Row, 1989), 35.

29. Quoted in Andrew Bard Schmookler, *Out of Weakness: Healing the Wounds That Drive Us to War* (Toronto and New York: Bantam Books, 1988), 141.

30. Quoted in Schmookler, *Out of Weakness*, 133.

31. Quoted in Stewart, *Honor*, n. 1, 145.

32. Pryce-Jones, *The Closed Circle*, 35.

33. Philip Carl Salzman, *Culture and Conflict in the Middle East* (Amherst, NY: Humanity Books, 2008), 54; Emmanuel Marx, *Bedouin of the Negev* (Manchester: Manchester University Press, 1967), 182–83, 199–200; William Lancaster, *The Rwala Bedouin Today*, 2nd ed. (Prospect Heights, IL: Waveland, 1997), 46–47, 73, 76, 140; Joseph Ginat, *Blood Revenge: Family Honor, Mediation, and Outcasting*, 2nd ed. (Brighton, UK: Sussex Academic Press, 1997), ch. 4.

In sum, honor is in the eye of the beholding public, leaving the dishonored person with a very precarious sense of self. Studying a Berber people of North Africa known as the Kabyle, Pierre Bourdieu concluded that "the being and truth about a person is identical with the being and truth that others acknowledge in him."[34] This view of the self-concept as constituted by inputs from others' perceptions might be the fullest realization of Charles H. Cooley's theory of the "social self," according to which we share the judgment of other minds.[35] Referring to what he calls the "looking-glass self," Cooley says, "There is no sense of 'I,' as in pride or shame, without its correlative sense of you, or he, or they."[36] Cooley finds the formation of the "social self" to be the outcome of three operations of the imagination that together demonstrate the submergence of the self in collective perception and judgment. According to Cooley, one imagines how she appears to others, she imagines how others judge her, and she experiences a consequent "self-feeling" of pride or mortification.[37]

Cooley's account seems descriptively accurate when compared with reported "self-talk" in HSCs. Presumably, Cooley would concede that we also imagine that others have the expectations that we feel pride or mortification. Perhaps those processes attributed to the imagination may be the effects in part of empathy or even of "mirror neurons."[38] Whatever the contributions of imagination or empathy, I contend that these processes are tightly "bounded" by behavior regarded as permissible or impermissible within the community. Thus while group members may be acutely attuned to other's perceptions, they lack a broader repertoire of experiences, and hence they are unable to imagine possibilities outside the proscribed circle.

Shame has been discussed earlier in connection with honor. Here it is worth considering shame in some greater detail, especially insofar as it differs from guilt. When one perceives a loss of his honor, the communal expectation is that he will feel shame and experience himself as shamed. Whereas honor is a conditional state of being, shame is a *consequence* of perceiving one's self in a conditional state of diminution, or "disappearance." Insofar as shame is affective, or emotional, the more appropriate opposite of shame is not honor, but

34. Bourdieu, quoted in Schmookler, *Out of Weakness*, 133.
35. Charles H. Cooley, "The Social Self," in Talcott Parsons, Edward Sihls, Kaspar D. Naegele, and Jesse R. Pitts (ed.), *Theories of Society: Foundations of Modern Sociological Theory* (New York: Free Press, 1965), 822–29, 824.
36. Cooley, *The Social Self*, 824.
37. Cooley, *The Social Self*, 824.
38. Christian Keysers, "Mirror Neurons," *Current Biology* 19, no. 21 (2010), 971–73.

pride.[39] Paul Hiebert notes, "Shame is a reaction to other people's criticism, an acute personal chagrin at our failure to live up to our obligations and the expectations others have of us."[40] J. David Velleman adds that shame is primarily "a response to an injury to one's public standing as a 'self-presenting creature.'"[41] Both points appropriately emphasize the occurrence of shame as a reaction and response, although they also reflect the relativity of standards of honor.[42]

Shame differs from guilt in three important respects. First, whereas guilt can be relieved by confession, atonement, and the forgiveness of others, shame cannot be alleviated in these ways. In HSCs, one is said to "cleanse" or "wash" away the shame. The continually reiterated requirement that there be a "washing away" of shame (including the occasionally symbolic whitewashing of a home after an honor killing) suggests that intuitions about defilement or pollution, and the need for purification, are closely related to conceptions of shame.

Second, shame is ended only when communal peers once again see a person as honorable and whole, or restored. Communal expectations often require the forceful or violent removal of what has brought shame upon one's family and community (see Section 5.3). Some honor codes make readmission to fellowship contingent on ritual acts of violence against the self (e.g., suicide, as *seppuku* among the Japanese samurai) or violence against others (e.g., European practices of dueling and vendettas). Honor killing falls into this ritual "washing away," "excising," or "cutting off" category of violent actions for which supporting evidence is ample. For instance, a 22-year-old Jordanian woodcutter spoke with pride: "We do not consider this murder," said Wafik Abu Abesh, as his brother and sister nodded in agreement. "It was like cutting off a finger."[43] Likewise, an honor killer presented another fairly typical response: "It is better that one person dies than the whole family [dies] of shame and disgrace. It is like a box of apples. If you have one rotten apple, would you keep it or get rid of it? I just got rid of it."[44] Jordanian tribal leader Trad Fayez expressed

39. Unni Wikan, "Shame and Honour: A Contestable Pair," *Man* 19 (1984), 635–52; Gabrielle Taylor, *Deadly Vices* (Oxford: Oxford University Press, 1985), 70–90; Gideon M. Kressel, "More on Honour and Shame," *Man* 23 (1988), 167–70.

40. Hiebert, *Anthropological Insights*, 212.

41. J. David Velleman, "The Genesis of Shame," *Philosophy and Public Affairs* 20 (2001), 27–52, 37.

42. Vellman emphasizes feeling shame when "we are unable to control the persona we present to others" (58), whereas Hiebert is more attuned to perceptions of negative responses to living up to others' expectations.

43. Quoted in Khan, *Beyond Honour*, 53.

44. Rana Husseini, *Murder in the Name of Honor* (Oxford: Oneworld, 2009), 10.

a similar view about purity and expiation: "A woman is like an olive tree. When its branch catches woodworm, it has to be chopped off so that society stays clean and pure."[45]

A third difference between guilt and shame pertains to the distinction between perceptions and feelings versus objective evidence. It is notorious that witch hunts in the Middle Ages, tortures by the Spanish Inquisition, and disappearances under Argentine generals were intended as much to create the public *appearance* of guilt as to terrorize and eliminate possible opponents. However, guilt is more frequently associated than shame with *evidence* of an actual infraction or violation of a religious or moral rule or a law. This is perhaps why punishment seems more fitting following an official determination of guilt. Of course, we do speak often enough of other persons "making one feel guilty," an expression suggesting peer or social condemnation. At the same time, however, those who believe an individual should feel guilty for an alleged infraction usually accept that the correctness of their belief should be settled by examining the evidence.

By contrast, in most HSCs there is no *logical gap* between perceptions of an individual as dishonorable and ascriptions of shame. Shame follows perception and does not wait for proof of guilt; consequently, there is a closed circle going from social perceptions of a violation to worthlessness engendered in the perceived offender and back then to social condemnation. Shaming behavior also has a very strong performative component because the ways through which one is typically shamed—malicious rumors, mockery and ridicule, mimicking, joking at one's expense, shunning—are communicative acts that constitute, at least in part, the dishonoring of the shamed individual. These shaming behaviors (in contrast to the supposed shameful behavior of the transgressor, or *ayb*, in literary Arabic) are legitimated communal responses and often publicly pronounced and ritualized. As such, shaming behaviors partly consist of the punishment inflicted, although, as noted earlier, there are also expectations that shamed males will attempt to rectify the situation in a violent or forceful manner.

Some dynamics of shaming behavior are well illustrated in the following incident: Basma was divorced by her husband six years earlier and then she ran away and married another man. She attempted to remain in hiding due to her fear of her family. Her mother Um Tayser, carrying a gun, went looking for Basma. When she was found, Basma's 16-year-old brother shot her to death. Basma's 18-year-old sister, Amal, offered these comments: "We

45. Quoted by Husseini, *Murder*, 63.

were the most prominent family, with the best reputation. . . . Then we were disgraced. Even my brother and his family stopped talking to us. No one would even visit us. They would say only, 'You have to kill!' Now we can walk with our heads held high. Before my sister was killed, I had to walk with my eyes to the ground."[46]

It needs to be emphasized that in HSCs what other people believe has a far greater impact on an individual's behavior than what the individual himself believes. For this reason, one's liability to experience shame is only loosely connected with the individual's own knowledge that a female family member has or has not committed an infraction. If he knows his daughter or sister is innocent of charges, then he might protest against the public opinion of her and of himself as a failed guardian. However, as his shame increases with mounting communal pressure, he is likely to find it increasingly difficult to *feel* that her claim of innocence is true. As my study of cases for the Churchill-Holmes dataset indicates (Section 2.1), only in a few instances did a male family member protest communal condemnation of a daughter or sister.

By contrast, if one is not a member of a "shame culture" and one knows a close relative has not transgressed, then one is much more likely to continue to insist on her innocence and fight the accusation. Also, where guilt predominates in a culture and one has transgressed but the indiscretion remains undiscovered, one might well be inclined to think, "I should feel guilt regardless." In a "shame culture," however, infractions occurring secretly are far less likely to occasion feelings of shame. The attitude that "no one knows, so I am not shamed" is more likely to predominate.[47] Joseph Ginat, who spent years studying honor among the Bedouin in Palestine and the Israeli occupied territories, relates that a Bedouin judge and mediator put it this way: "Shame is not when one's daughter has illicit sexual relations; the shame is when it is public knowledge that she has had illicit sexual relations."[48]

The fact that the interior, subjective experience of shame depends on one's public image suggests that individuals can engage in wrongdoing carte blanche as long as they succeed in acting surreptitiously.[49] A person cannot bring shame upon himself, or "blacken" his own face, in the absence

46. Douglas Jehl, "For Shame, Arab Honor's Price: A Woman's Blood," *New York Times*, Aug. 6, 1999, summarized in Khan, *Beyond Honour*, 12.

47. Anonymous, "The Arab Mind: Part IX," posted April 16, 2008 on the blog *Shrinkwrapped. A Psychoanalyst Attempts to Understand the World*, http://shrinkwrapped. blogs.com/blog/2008/02/The-arab-mind-1.html, accessed June 15, 2012.

48. Quoted in Ginat, *Blood Revenge*, 130.

49. *Shrinkwrapped*, Part IX.

of public awareness. However, one must be continually vigilant lest others find out. It is extremely difficult to avoid the public eye altogether in closely knit communities, and surmises, impressions, and inferences can turn as deadly as actual observations.

Moreover, quick and unpredictable shifts of public perception usually add to the deterrent effects of wrongdoing in communities in which everyone seems to know everyone else's business. "Rumors and gossip are likely to spread like wildfire based on another's perception of the slightest misstep."[50] As Raphael Patai points out, it is necessary that one "always be aware of the imperative of *wajh* ('face'); under all circumstances a man must beware of allowing his 'face' to be 'blackened'; he must always endeavor to 'whiten his face,' as well as the face of the group to which he belongs. Cost what it may, one must defend one's public image. Any injury done to a man's honor must be revenged, or else he becomes permanently dishonored."[51] Abu-Rabia writes: the "fact that individuals are controlled by public threats to their personal reputation and honor is what transforms Bedouin and Arab societies into 'shame cultures.'"[52] The consensus in the literature supports this claim, but it is especially true of HSCs in which honor killings occur.

3.3 HONOR AS *SHARAF* AND AS *'IRD*

So far, the discussion of honor has focused on the ways conceptions of honor in HSCs are based on public perception. It is now necessary for a finer grained analysis to distinguish between two *gendered* conceptions of honor. The broad, general conception of honor discussed in Section 3.2 applies primarily to the behavior of men, while a more restricted conception of honor pertains primarily to female *sexual* comportment and to male control of female sexuality. Honor, as discussed in Section 3.2, is known variously as *sharaf*, or *izzat*, or occasionally *wajh* ("face") in literary Arabic; as *ghairat* in the Hindi, Punjabi, Sindh, and Urdu languages of India, Pakistan, and parts of Afghanistan; as *namus* or *namoos* in Kurdish, Persian/Farsi, and Turkish; as *manum* in Tamil, in southern India, and Sri Lanka; as *onore* and *omertā* in Italian (especially in Sicily, Apulia, Calabria, and Campania); as *nderi*

---

50. Khan, *Beyond Honour*, 58.

51. Raphael Patai, *The Arab Mind*, rev. ed. (Tucson, AZ: Recovery Resources Press, 2007), 96.

52. Aref Abu-Rabia, "Family Honor Killings: Between Custom and State Laws," *The Open Psychology Journal* 4 (2011) (Suppl. 1–M4), 34–44, 35.

in Albanian; and as *machismo* ("manliness") in many Spanish-speaking communities.

Sharaf is multidimensional in three important ways. First, a man's honor is subject to change: it can increase or decrease; likewise, it can be lost and then regained. Second, a man's *sharaf* is always relative to social perceptions of others' honor, thus leading to frequent *"sharaf* honor competitions" (discussed more fully in Sections 4.3–4.4). Third, the bases for social recognition among men are variable and wide in latitude. Traits such as assertiveness, strength, courage, tenacity, endurance, and capability—when associated with male dominance—increase *sharaf*. So, too, do many of the means for maintaining one's independence, freedom, and equality: wealth and business success; control of one's household; plural wives and many progeny; lineage (especially real or alleged descent from the Prophet); influence over others, such as through a reputation for piety, wisdom (associated with age), generosity, wit, and slyness; or a leadership role, such as that of sheik.

The emphasis on male honor in the secondary literature often stresses contestation and domination. For instance, Philip Carl Salzman claims, "Subordination of any kind results in a loss of honor, and a sense of shame."[53] As the Arabic proverb puts it, "'He who rules over you, emasculates you.'"[54] Victory validates manhood and confers honor, while defeat is symbolic castration and shames the defeated. "In the Middle East, in confrontations great and small, there is no virtue in being a victim. . . . Domination gives honor; submission gives shame."[55]

Because honor as *sharaf* is primarily masculine, *sharaf* is generally not ascribed to women, and certainly never in virtue of feminine traits. Rather, women may share in or participate in the *sharaf* of their menfolk, more or less as *stakeholders*. For this reason Wikan speaks of an individual in this broader category as "someone who manages a share of the tribal honor."[56] All members of an HSC likewise participate as stakeholders in the *sharaf* earned through and among male members, just as they participate in dishonor through male failures to live up to what the honor code requires.

While *sharaf* is a broad and variable conception of honor, at its core there is a much more inflexible notion of honor, and although not all HSCs mark this distinction linguistically, the core aspect of *sharaf*-honor

53. Salzman, *Culture and Conflict*, 106.
54. Quoted by Gideon M. Kressel, *Ascendancy Through Aggression: The Anatomy of a Blood Feud Among Urbanized Bedouins* (Weisbanden, Germany: Harrasowitz, 1996), 104.
55. Kressel, *Ascendancy*, 106.
56. Wikan, *In Honor of Fadime*, 16.

is known in literary Arabic as *'ird,* or *'ard.* Both *sharaf* and *'ird* provide critically important norms, but *'ird,* as the more restrictive core, connotes stricter obligations and duties. The most important duty *'ird* imposes on males consists of *wilaya* (in literary Arabic), or protection and guardianship of females in one's charge. Honor as *'ird* also requires that a male discipline a female who defies his authority and show his willingness to take effective measures should allegations arise about females of the family. Moreover, *'ird* requires that the family remedy the situation on its own. It would be a flagrant violation of honor and a cause of further shame should the family attempt to solve the problem by appealing to authorities or organizations outside the community.

The relationship between *sharaf* and *'ird* can be illuminated by reference to Frank Henderson Stewart's distinction between horizontal honor and vertical honor. As Stewart points out, *horizontal honor* concerns the right to respect as an equal.[57] *Vertical honor* refers to a right to special or particular respect enjoyed by those who are superior, either due to higher rank or individual or group achievement (e.g., winning a competition or performing a daring feat). On this view, *sharaf* can be vertical in a way in which *'ird* cannot.[58] For instance, should a man's power or influence increase, his *sharaf* increases commensurately, just as it would through great acts of hospitality, or bravery, or through renowned wisdom or religiosity. By contrast, *'ird* is horizontal; it can be lost and possibly regained, but one cannot have a greater degree of *'ird.* A poor man of lowly status is unlikely to enjoy the same measure of *sharaf* as a relatively wealthy tribesman, but as long as his *'ird* is unsullied, he will enjoy equal standing in the community and hence enjoy the same horizontal honor. Thus by keeping his family's *'ird* 'clean,' a man maintains his esteem and identity as respectable. Moreover, a man risks losing his *'ird*—and through it the loss of his *sharaf* as well—*only if he does not respond appropriately,* in the eyes of the community, to a real or alleged violation of *'ird* on the part of a female family member. Thus, when it comes to *'ird,* a man cannot be responsible for a loss of honor by any action on his part, except through omission.

Unlike *sharaf,* both men and women participate in *'ird,* either through maintaining *'ird* or destroying it.[59] By contrast with men, however, female

57. Stewart, *Honor,* 148.
58. Stewart, *Honor,* 148.
59. There is some disagreement on this point. Stewart claims that "'*ird* referred exclusively to a single kind of honor, the one that is allotted to all and only the men in the community" (1994, 143). By contrast, other authorities such as Abou-Zeid and Antoun refer without question to a woman's *'ird.* See Ahmed Abou-Zeid, "Honour and Shame Among the Bedouins of Egypt," in J. G. Peristiany (ed.), *Honour and Shame: The Values of Mediterranean Society* (Chicago: Chicago University Press, 1966), 243–59; and

'ird is entirely *one dimensional* and *static*. *'Ird* for women is understood as consisting in absolute chastity, modesty, and obedience in keeping with the traditional 'code' of the HSC. (However, as evidence in Sections 2.1– 2 shows, the code is distressingly more elastic than its defenders claim, making it difficult even for the most intentionally compliant women to be sure they are observing its stringencies.) A female's *'ird* is fixed at her birth and as a consequence of her sex; it cannot be increased through virtuous behavior on her part. *'Ird* requires that women under a man's control must be "intact."[60] Nawal El Saadawi puts this point literally in saying that a man's *'ird* is safe "as long as the female members of his family keep their hymens intact."[61] In addition, a woman's honor is generally conceived to have an all-or-nothing stature; it cannot be lost by degrees, but only all at once and as a consequence of conduct perceived as shameful. Once a woman has lost her honor, it can never be regained by or for her.

This is another of a number of treacherous double standards regarding male and female honor and behavior. For whereas a woman can never regain lost *'ird*, as Stewart points out, *'ird* is "reflexive" for the male family members shamed by her conduct.[62] By "reflexive" Stewart means that the original act—the disgraceful behavior of a female—does not itself destroy a male's honor irretrievably; *it is only by not responding appropriately to the female's loss of 'ird that one's 'ird will be damaged.*[63] Women, then, are also responsible for maintaining the family's honor. From an observer's perspective, it might well be asked, why have members of HSCs created a social practice in which some of the most precious social goods, the *'ird* of men and their families, are invested in those young females who are viewed as fragile vessels and likely to disappoint expectations? This is a question to which I return in Sections 4.4 and 5.4.

The problem of ensuring unsullied *'ird* does not end after an arranged marriage or with the traditional presentation of a blood-spotted bed sheet, where this expectation persists. Should the daughter or sister be divorced,

---

Richard T. Antoun, "On the Modesty of Women in the Arab Muslim Villages: A Study in the Accommodation of Traditions," *American Anthropologist* 70, no. 4 (Aug. 1968), 671–97.

60. The Italian word for "intact," *intatta*, is still used to describe a virgin.
61. El Saadawi, *The Hidden Faces of Eve*, 31.
62. Stewart, *Honor*, 83, 64–71.
63. As I touch only on the aspects of *'ird* and *sharaf* most important for this study, I gloss over Stewart's point that there are occasions on which *'ird* can be reflexive for women as well. For instance, a women insulted by other women will experience diminished *'ird* but only if she does not respond appropriately—that is, by successfully rebutting—the attacks on her *'ird*. Thus a woman's *'ird* can be reflexive within relatively narrow limits; if gossip succeeds in impugning her reputation for sexual continence, then she cannot redeem her *'ird*.

or should she leave a husband, even if her spouse is abusive, or should she be suspected of an affair (among other possible causes) then the family's *'ird* is tarnished and their faces 'blackened.' As noted in Sections 1.1–1.2, those especially affected are *agnates* of the individual who committed the transgression; that is, they share kinship linkage based on blood. Honor is regarded as being *transitive*. Males most closely related—father, brothers, paternal grandfather, paternal uncles, and paternal cousins—will be most adversely affected and most eager to find a "solution."[64] This is especially true because collective, or associative, responsibility and *co-liability* predominate in HSCs.

Co-liability means close kin-blood relatives will automatically ally with one another if one becomes implicated in a conflict.[65] The obverse of this principle is equally true; namely, blame incurred by anyone in the kin-blood network is automatically shared by those genealogically closest. Many in the community will also see themselves as negatively affected because intermarriage within HSCs is extensive and because of the very strong group identity (see Section 3.4). Members of the collective all have a stake in shared honor—family, clan, and tribe. If one of them is dishonored, so are they all.

The significance of *'ird* cannot be overemphasized, and not just because *sharaf* can be "trumped" by *'ird*: once *'ird* is irretrievably lost, one has lost everything and no increase in *sharaf* can compensate for the loss of *'ird*.[66] The connection between *'ird*-honor and female sexuality permeates consciousness in an obsessive way. Rana Husseini speaks of the view of the hymen as a "small piece of quasi-mythical flesh,"[67] and writer Mouland Feraoun aptly notes that, for many men in the Arabic world, "their honor [is] buried in the vagina as if it [is] a treasure more precious than life."[68] Feraoun's comment is hardly an exaggeration. Journalist Douglas Jehl reports on the answer an Egyptian writer received when, as a schoolboy, the latter asked a male teacher: "What is honor?"

"His biology teacher put it to the class, but went on to answer it himself after turning to a poster showing the female genital apparatus and pointing

64. Due to the common practice of arranged marriages between paternal first cousins, the youthful age of most brides, expectations that brides produce male heirs, the male spouses' privileges of sex-on-demand, along with the absence of birth control, the "family" is often quite large.

65. Salzman, *Culture and Conflict*, 12–13.

66. Feldner, "'Honor' Murder."

67. As quoted by Jane Fonda in the "Foreword" of Rana Husseini, *Murder in the Name of Honor*, x.

68. Quoted in Schmookler, *Out of Weakness*, 167.

to the vaginal opening: 'Here is the site of the family honor!'"[69] Lama Abu-Odeh relates the issue directly to masculine identity when she answers the question, "What is it to be an Arab man?" by saying, "In Arab culture, a man is that person whose sister's virginity is a social question for him." [70]

In HSCs, a man's honor as *'ird* is more closely linked with females in his family than with his own behavior or that of his brothers, father, or uncles. Indeed, a man's sexual improprieties are not themselves a cause of his loss of *'ird*. As El Saadawi notes, a man may be a sexual predator of the worst caliber and yet be regarded as an honorable man provided his womenfolk can protect their genital organs.[71] A brother who rapes a sister or a father who rapes a daughter generally will not suffer a loss of *'ird*, although a rape may have consequences that diminish his *sharaf* (e.g., another family may reject overtures about an arranged marriage or he may be sent away for a time).

Illicit sexual conduct by a young girl can have many forms: an unknown boy's picture is seen on a Facebook page, a girl is seen where she is not expected to be, she leaves home without permission, or returns home too late, or offers a confidence which is betrayed by a friend. In general, however, when illicit sexual conduct has occurred, is planned, or suspected, the male partner can very easily be discovered, either through the ever-vigilant eyes and ears of the "watchdog" community or through the very common beatings, which often border on torture, administered to the girl. Yet reprisals made against supposed paramours are surprisingly infrequent; although, when they do occur, it is most often when the two are caught in hiding or trying to escape. This extremely harsh and rigid double standard was first mentioned in Section 1.2, where honor killings were distinguished from revenge murders of paramours. I postpone until Sections 6.2–6.4 a fuller explanation of why men are far less frequently victims of honor killing because this subject requires understanding the function of honor killing as the practice evolved culturally. Until then, suffice it to say that the killing of males involved in illicit love affairs cannot serve the symbolic, ritual, and social functions of honor killing.

When an impropriety is suspected, it is as if a singular idea dominates collective minds: simply because she is a female, the girl or woman is

---

69. Quoted in Douglas Jehl, "For Shame, Arab Honor's Price," July 26, 1999. Husseini relates a very similar story in *Murder in the Name of Honor*, 148–49.
70. Lama Abu-Odeh, "Crimes of Honor and the Construction of Gender in Arab Societies," in Mai Yamani (ed.), *Feminism and Islam: Legal and Literary Perspectives* (New York: New York University Press, 1996), 363–80, 373.
71. El Saadawi, *The Hidden Faces of Eve*, 47–48.

always to blame. This assumption prevails even when the accused has been kidnapped, raped, or a victim of incest by a member of her own family. This *predetermination of blame* arises, as I show in Sections 4.2–4.4, both from the systemic and absolute conviction that female lives are worth less than those of males and from the indelible sociocultural perception of the *danger* posed by the feminine principle. Women are the source of *fitna*, or chaos, in the world, and no matter how carefully men shield themselves from feminine seduction, they must count themselves fortunate if they are not overcome by it.

In Chapters 4 and 5, I explore in detail the formation of what I call the *warrior personality type* to understand why males in HSCs adhere with great tenacity to the conceptions of honor elucidated here. I also explore the inculcation of cultural honor values through socialization, as well as why males become so anxiously "eager" to fulfill the requirements of honor.

In concluding this chapter, I consider the structure and function of the communities which support honor codes and which sanction honor killing as a social practice.

3.4 HONOR–SHAME COMMUNITIES

What distinguishes the tightly bound collectivities I have been calling HSCs from other groups? I propose the following as a working definition: *An HSC is a collectivity of interdependent persons who self-describe as members of the same group and who share a collective acceptance of honor, shame, the importance of an implicit but unwritten honor code, and the legitimacy of honor killings in appropriate circumstances.* Note that this provisional definition might be regarded more properly as a definition of *an honor killing HSC* because the provisional definition (in italics) says that HSCs are those that legitimize honor killing. In fact, however, there are very similar communities with honor codes and the same norms of honor and shame but whose members *do not* share collective beliefs about the justification of honor killing. (See Section 8.3 for examples.) As long as this caveat is kept in mind, using the provisional definition just given will greatly simplify the task ahead.

HSCs as understood here are presented as abstractions, but the concept is more than merely heuristic. Empirical research going well beyond the scope of this study would be required to determine the extent to which the model discussed here matches actual communities in areas in which honor killings occur. A good beginning could be made by first cataloguing the sites where this happens most frequently (e.g., Bamian, Ghor, and Nuristan provinces in Afghanistan; Haryana, Rajasthan, and Utter Pradesh states in India; Basra in Iraq, and Erbil and Sulaimaniyah in Iraqi Kurdistan; Baluchistan, Khaipur district, Peshawar, Punjab, Swat Valley, and Sindh province in Pakistan; and Batman, Diyarbakir, and Mardin provinces in southeast Turkey). However, I am not concerned with the locales of most frequent executions "for honor," but rather at how HSCs continue to exert such powerful influence over their members.

A good place to begin is to consider how HSCs came into being. In her book on honor killing, Tahira Khan emphasizes groups of people "who lived together in the same area for quite some time and whom have developed a sense of sharing happiness and sorrow together and who watch each other daily."[72] Even pastoral and nomadic groups who must move their flocks with seasonal changes maintain a single community by traveling together in closely knit clans or tribal groups, intermarrying, and depending for cultural identity on ties with the regions offering forage for their herds. Khan emphasizes the solidarity arising from common descent, a shared history, and a sense of destiny, as well as shared daily experiences and a shared repertoire of folk tales, jokes, cultural idioms, styles of dress, dialect, cuisine, and modes of expression. Common descent or consanguinity is critical: in addition to having been close neighbors since childhood, most, if not all such groups will be connected by blood or intermarriage. Khan's point about watching each other daily is critical as well for it addresses the need to continually recalibrate shared norms through reassurance about the appropriateness of one's behavior and through raising an alarm about behavior that is deemed inappropriate and potentially dangerous.

The collectivity is interdependent physically and psychologically. The group consists of one's familiars upon whom one can hope to call for assistance despite constant tussles to gain dominance or avoid subordination. Group members supply each other's needs through exchanges or cooperate with each other to bring animals to market and share necessities such as wells or pasturage while vigilantly guarding group assets against encroachment from outsiders. Group members often share close consanguinity, as a clan or a tribal grouping, for it is from within the group that parents ordinarily find marriage partners for sons and daughters. Indeed, in most HSCs throughout the Arabic "world," as well as in Afghanistan and Pakistan, the ideal marriage is between paternal first cousins (i.e., a father's son or daughter married to a brother's child). Entry and exit into the community is limited. Generally, entry is only by birth to parents within the

---

72. Khan, *Beyond Honour*, 58. Khan does not employ a definition of an honor–shame community, but I infer that the groups she describes are honor–shame communities as discussed in this section.

community, and exit is usually by death. The importance of close blood relations means that adoptions are generally unheard of in HSCs. (See Sections 6.2–6.4 for a discussion of these communal features in the context of cultural evolution.)

The physical organization of HSCs may be that of a rural village in a tribal area, seasonal encampments on grazing ranges, a neighborhood in a larger town, a district in an urban center, a diaspora or immigrant community in a foreign land, or even a densely inhabited street or sector of a town or city. Postmodern technology and global travel have gone far to substitute the need for geographical proximity with interpersonal and psychological "nearness" for the continual self-maintenance of a community: email, instant messaging, texting, and social media, enable families to stay in touch and to negotiate, while rapid transportation enables a family or clan to assemble quickly should a crisis arise. Thus some HSCs have become transcontinental. Case studies show that members of a Kurdish immigrant group in Stockholm or London, or Iraqi immigrants in Phoenix, have not integrated well into host countries' cultures and remain culturally dependent on mores and relatives in the "homeland." This is often true despite long years lived abroad or even after accepting citizenship of the adopted countries. Likewise, studies indicate that crises affecting honor can lead even far-flung families to quickly assemble and to plan "solutions."

In 2003, the Swedish organization Kvinnofoum began a project financed by seven European countries and the European Commission. As a response to rising rates of honor-related violence within European immigrant communities, the project sought to raise awareness among immigrant men from countries with HSCs about conceptions, standards, and best practices widely accepted in Europe for resolving domestic disputes. Men participated in discussion groups, and efforts were made to teach them how to engage nonviolently with family members and resolve domestic disputes by employing techniques for nonviolent conflict resolution. Says Khan about the disappointing outcome: "This multi-state project is proof of the unchanging rigid attitude of Muslim men against women, no matter in which advanced country they have been living as citizens and no matter for how many decades they have lived in a different culture."[73]

What makes cultural commitments so resilient that, despite efforts at integration, it remains difficult to broaden the space for reflectivity within a shared or "common psyche," as Khan puts it? Lama Abu-Odeh points

---

73. Khan, *Beyond Honour*, 22. See also http://www.qweb.kvinnofoum.se/, accessed Aug. 14, 2013.

to "the primordial idea of the integration of the individual in the group where one becomes deeply sensitive to and threatened by public opinion."[74] Reading Abu-Odeh, one is reminded of the tight fit between the integration of the individual and the significance of honor and shame discussed in Sections 3.1–3.3, as well as the "looking-glass self" and the ways in which commonalities are reinforced by "everyone's watching everyone else."

Life within HSCs seems to defy a distinction, well-established in cross-cultural psychology, between collectivist and individualist cultures.[75] Collectivist cultures emphasize harmony, interdependence, conformity, and putting the needs of the group ahead of individual accomplishment. In contrast, individualistic cultures emphasize autonomy, personal achievement, political freedom, and the needs and rights of the individual. As Robert Sapolsky notes, these cultural differences have testable biological correlates which extend to differences in perception and the processing of information, as well as to dopamine receptors in the cortex associated with novelty-seeking, extroversion, and impulsivity.[76] Significantly, however, members of HSCs display some collectivist characteristics typically associated with honor–shame cultures in East Asia, but otherwise exhibit greater affinities with individualist cultures.

Khan's emphasis on a "common psyche" and my account of shame and the dependence on peers for self-esteem highlight characteristics generally associated with collectivist orientations. In part, HSCs are entities constituted by what Carol Gould calls "individuals-in-relations" who stand "in internal relations to each other such that they became the individuals they are in and through such relations."[77] It is still common for individuals to define themselves by their lineage—that is, in context. For instance, in *Infidel*, the Muslim apostate, Ayaan Hirsi Ali, says that as a five-year-old Somali she was instructed to answer the question, "Who are you?" by providing her lineage and "count[ing] my forefathers back for three hundred years." She adds, "Osman Mahamud is the name of my father's sub-clan, and thus my own. It is where I belong, who I am."[78]

74. Lama Abu-Odeh, "Crimes of Honor," 153.

75. Robert M. Sapolsky, *Behave: The Biology of Humans at Our Best and Worst* (New York: Penguin, 2017), 273–91.

76. Sapolsky, *Behave*, 274–82.

77. Carol C. Gould, "Group Rights and Social Ontology," in David Boersema (ed.), *The Philosophy of Human Rights: Theory and Practice* (Boulder, CO: Westview, 2011), 106–12, 107–08.

78. Ayaan Hirsi Ali, *Infidel* (New York and London: Atria/Simon & Schuster, 2007), 3. As she later flees an arranged marriage and seeks refuge in the Netherlands, Hirsi Ali rejects efforts to define herself in terms of tribe, clan, subclan, and family.

In addition, HSCs are highly collectivist in terms of both collective social actions and what Edward Hall calls "high-context communication."[79] Collective social actions are actions undertaken by individuals who see their actions—and are seen by others—as representing the collectivity. Collective social actions depend on what Raimo Tuomela calls "we-acceptances."[80] First, all persons believe that others within the collectivity accept the same beliefs, attitudes, values, and dispositions; and second, each person believes every other participant in the collectivity also accepts these beliefs, attitudes, values, and dispositions *as their own*. Thus, while there is never complete homogeneity in any group, cooperation in HSCs presupposes a more or less continual consensus of we-acceptances undergirding certain traditional social practices. Because these actions are performed with reference to legitimizing we-acceptances, agents regard them as communally authorized. Thus, for example, shaming behaviors, including the gossiping and shunning that precede honor killings, are collective social actions.

Hall's distinction between low-context and high-context communicative frameworks also has direct relevance to we-acceptances and collective social actions. Contrary to the amount of information in a communicative string (i.e., spoken or written sentence), *high-context* refers to what can remain *unexpressed* because human receivers are primed by the communicative context to interpret meaning. Thus, as Hall puts it, "HC [high content] transactions featured preprogrammed information that is in the receiver and in the setting, with only minimal information in the transmitted message."[81] Where contexts may be more variable and identities less shaped or bounded by collectivities, low-context communication becomes more typical. In such cases, transmitted messages must contain more information to compensate for what is missing from the context.

It is beyond dispute that high-context communications are common in HSCs. Khan refers to "the honour killings and community attitude among the Balochi tribes," where, on occasion, "an allegation or taunt by the neighbor or fellow tribesman is enough to spur a man into killing his wife, sister, or mother."[82] Similar assumptions about what "remained unexpressed" led to deaths in other areas as well; for instance, in February 2007, a taxi driver

79. Edward T. Hall, *Beyond Culture* (New York: Doubleday, 1976) and *The Dance of Life* (New York: Doubleday, 1983),

80. Raimo Tuomela, *The Philosophy of Social Practices: A Collective Acceptance View* (Cambridge and New York: Cambridge University Press, 2002), 136.

81. Hall, *Beyond Culture*, 101.

82. This is a quotation of text from Khan, *Beyond Honour*, 61, who is referring to a story by Manzoor Kohiyar, *Daily News*, Karachi, Nov. 9, 1995.

in Dubai in the United Arab Emirates shot to death his 22-year-old married sister after he received an anonymous call suggesting she was having an extramarital affair.[83] Another jarring incident occurred in October 2012, when a Pakistani couple killed their 15-year-old daughter simply because she turned to look at a boy driving by on a motorcycle. Tragically, her protested innocence, "I didn't do it on purpose. I won't look again" was ignored.[84]

Where collective social actions change little over time, core symbols (e.g., the *hijab*) tend to be definite and fixed, norms tend to be rigid, and the psychic spaces in which individuals negotiate and experiment with emergent self-identities are relatively circumscribed. Groups may find it relatively easy to adapt to changes as long as they do not threaten core we-acceptances and norms. For instance, women may be permitted to work outside the immediate community, wear blue jeans, and use cell phones as long as identity traits and fundamental norms are not challenged. These continuities illuminate the persistence of HSCs as well as the discouraging outcome of the Kvinnofoum project mentioned earlier. Only something like such a dialectic between forming individual identities and replicating group identity can explain why—at present—there is little margin for imagining alternative perspectives.

At the same time, however, some characteristics of members of HSCs do not fit the binary collectivist–individualist distinction. As we have seen, the actual *ideals* of *sharaf* honor are highly individualistic, especially the emphases placed on self-assertion, equality, and self-reliance. It is not known why the culture of HSCs is a hybrid between collectivism and individualism. However, a likely surmise is that whether or not members of HSCs are presently pastoralists, farmers, or reside in urban areas, their ancestors were pastoralists and herders. Significantly, research suggests that collectivist and individualist orientations arose from the evolution of "eco-cultures," or the ways people worked to produce food staples. Herding and the farming of grains (especially wheat) promoted autonomy and self-reliance, in contrast to the greater need for cooperation, conformity, and interdependence of groups primarily dependent on the cultivation of rice or fishing.[85]

83. United Arab Emirate News Dubai, "Dubai: Man Killed Sister for 'Honour,'" *7 Days in Dubai*, www.7daysindubai/en/2007/02/09/, accessed Jun. 12, 2014.

84. BBC News Asia at www.bbc.co.uk/news/world-asia-20202686?print=true, accessed Nov. 4, 2012.

85. Ayse K. Uskul, Shinobu Kitayama, and Richard E. Nesbitt, "Ecocultural Basis of Cognition: Farmers and Fishermen Are More Holistic Than Herders," *Proceedings of the Natural Academy of Science (PNAS)* 105, no. 25 (June 24, 2008), 8552–56; Thomas Talheim et al., "Large-Scale Psychological Differences Within China Explained by Rice Versus Wheat Agriculture, *Science* 344 (May 9, 2014), 603–08.

Having reached this understanding of honor killing as a social practice and the conscious we-acceptances and collective social actions of HSCs members, we are well poised for further inquiry. It is now clear why HSC members can defend age-old we-acceptances about the "necessity" of honor killing. The next steps begin by asking: why *those* we-acceptances about the execution of "dishonored" women and girls? And how can we account for the social and epistemic "invisibility" of the true reasons why honor killing exists? This brings us to causal explanations to be explored in the next three chapters, beginning with Chapter 4 where we examine acculturation promoting personality traits that are independent, controlling, and domineering, as well as persons eager to be admired, honored, and to avoid shame.

CHAPTER 4

Socialization, Gender, and Violence-Prone Personality

This is the first of three chapters in which I explore *why* honor killings occur. Chapters 4 and 5 together investigate causation in terms of micro-processes; that is, in terms of the motives, intentions, and beliefs of perpetrators, victims, and sympathizers. Thus, these chapters focus on the psychology of honor killing in terms of agent-centric *reasons* or *reason-explanations* for key agents' behaviors. My objective is to explain how agents come to have certain motives and shared we-acceptances; in addition, I explain how a personality capable of overcoming aversion to killing is formed.

Obviously, the formation of a personality type with violent motives is shaped in large part by child-rearing and parental practices, as well as by adverse life conditions. In this chapter, I examine a variety of socializing and situational factors that causally contribute to what I characterize as a *violence-prone personality* (VPP). One with such a personality construct is predisposed to act violently, even to kill, in the appropriate circumstances. In Section 5.1, I investigate further by demonstrating the connection between VPPs and *warrior masculinity*, which paradoxically requires both the exaltation of women and their victimization.

Because of complexities encountered in researching, Section 4.1 must begin with several preliminary points about methodology as well as conceptual and logical issues. Section 4.2 presents the first part of coming of age in honor–shame communities (HSCs); that is, significant events from birth through early adolescence. Section 4.3 offers important background on challenges faced by boys from circumcision up to early adulthood. In both sections, the emphasis is on the causal effects of child-rearing, parental responsiveness or indifference, and other salient socializing processes which contribute to male identity and a VPP. The effects of these causes are discussed in Section 4.4. I postpone commentary on the victimization of women until Section 5.2.

4.1 CONCEPTUAL, LOGICAL, AND METHODOLOGICAL ISSUES

The first methodological issue concerns what we can reasonably expect this investigation to produce. First, we cannot expect to discover deductively certain connections between the violence-proneness of individuals and attempted honor killings. Unfortunately, we can know who perpetrators are only after the fact, that is, after an attack has occurred. Also, because executions occur within a social practice, an honor killing is multicausal. Hence, reasoning must be *inductive* and reflect unavoidable indeterminacy. At most, we can learn only why and how individuals become *liable* to kill, with "liable" understood as *prepared* to kill, assuming would-be perpetrators and others in the HSC believe they are acting as socially expected and in circumstances as described in Chapters 1–3. Obviously, it does not follow that an agent who is liable to act in a certain way will necessarily do so.

Second, I shall not attempt to forecast where individuals liable to be perpetrators are most likely to be concentrated—other than generally living in HSCs, as indicated in Section 3.4—or even what proportion of males might be susceptible to these liabilities. Instead, my present efforts have two foci. While Sections 3.2–3.3 addressed many elements of honor and peer pressure relevant to culture, my first focus here is to make a finer grained analysis of socialization through interpersonal relationships, beginning with childbirth. This task is necessary for the second: sketching a *hypothetical model* of males most likely to acquire what I characterize as a *violence-prone personality*. Males with a VPP have a high probability, I believe, of undergoing what, following Bonnie Mann, I call a *shame-to-violence conversion* and becoming actual perpetrators.[1] The shame-to-violence conversion is discussed in Section 5.1, where I develop a model of personality type I will call the *warrior personality*.

Understanding the connections between a VPP and warrior masculinity will require attention to male gender identity and its contrast with the

---

1. I adopt the concept of the shame-to-power conversion from Bonnie Mann, *Sovereign Masculinity: Gender Lessons from the War on Terror* (New York and London: Oxford University Press, 2014), 108–36. I accept full responsibility for the interpretation and use I make of Mann's concept.

feminine, as well as the complex ways in which the upbringing and socialization of children and adolescents become intertwined in the development of VPP. Insofar as the presence in HSCs of primed perpetrators is a *necessary condition* for honor killing, then it obviously behooves us to give this development careful attention, with a view toward the ways this "construction" might be modified or transformed.

Discussion of warrior masculinity requires analysis of the highly controversial and contested conceptions of *sex* and *gender*. Until recently, sex was regarded primarily as a biological outcome as indicated in part by genitalia, whereas "gender" usually referred to a socially constructed identity; that is, socially enforced expectations about the proper behaviors of the two sexes, corresponding to men and women. It is now known that binary distinctions cannot accommodate the complex reality: gender identity is molded biologically as well as socially, and there may be gender fluidity due either to biological or social factors.[2] Moreover, a person's genitalia may not align with his or her sexual orientation, which itself is strongly influenced biologically.[3]

However, traditional HSCs do not recognize possible variations among sexual orientation and gender identity. With rare exceptions, one's sex at birth determines one's gender, and vice versa.[4] There is also one pattern of socialization for boys, or males, and a radically different pattern for girls, or females. In addition, because my objective here is not to criticize simplistic binary distinctions but to emphasize the drastically negative consequences of the formation of a type of masculine identity, I shall proceed *as if* the

2. In an insightful passage, Bonnie Mann writes: "How does someone who has a pussy operate in a cultural milieu saturated with the fear of being called one? How does the unrelenting misogyny that underwrites that fear underwrite the life of a woman who is a soldier? . . . Does the woman bomber pilot even have a pussy, when she drops her payload, in the sense that men fear having one? I don't think so. But in the barracks as . . . the recently released film *The Invisible War* shows definitively . . . she apparently gets it back." See *Sovereign Masculinity*, 99.

3. "Special Issue: Gender Revolution," *National Geographic* 231, no. 1 (Jan. 2017), 6–8.

4. The ability of recognized gender to determine sex, as well as vice versa, is manifest in the unusual Balkan tradition of the sworn virgin, or *virgjinesha* (in Albanian), who takes a vow of perpetual chastity, wears men's clothing, and engages in traditional male activities. See Mildred Dickemann, "The Balkan Sworn Virgin," in Stephen O. Murray and Will Roscoe (eds.), *Islamic Homosexualities: Culture, History, and Literature* (New York and London: New York University Press, 1997), 197–203. In addition, in a few areas, as in one part of Oman, three genders appear to be accepted: men, women, and *xanith*. The xanith usually appear to be biologically male but identify themselves as women, dress as women, and are generally accepted in women's activities, but they are regarded by men as homosexual prostitutes. See Unni Wikan, *Behind the Veil in Arabia: Women in Oman* (Baltimore and London: The Johns Hopkins University Press, 1982), 168–86.

expectations of members of HSCs were accurate; that is, as if biological sex (i.e., genitalia) at birth determines the proper gender category, although gender has to be "completed" through socialization.

Thus, for the HSCs I discuss, "masculinity," "masculinities," and "manliness" are gender terms referring to sociocultural expectations for male behavior. "Manhood refers to the state of an achieved manliness as an adult male, in the sense that such a state must be continuously maintained in the eyes of other men."[5] What counts as a "real man" is an individual with a man's genitalia *and* whose values, skills, bodily presentation, and behavioral scripts live up to conventional ideals in HSCs. Judith Butler's view of gender as largely *performative* is useful in this context; as Butler says, "gender is manufactured through a sustained set of acts, posited through the gendered stylization of the body . . . What men in these cultures take to be internal, biological features of the self are actually anticipated and produced through certain bodily acts."[6] In "becoming a man," an individual links his own self-awareness with other men exhibiting socioculturally defined masculine behavior. Females are similarly initiated into femininity, socialized to embrace norms and behaviors that society accepts as womanly.

Suad Joseph in *Intimate Selving in Arab Families* and Maleeha Aslam in *Gender-Based Explosions* demonstrate how well Butler's notion of gender as performative can be adapted for cross-cultural analyses and, in particular, to Aslam's helpful distinctions between different types of Islamic and Muslim masculinities.[7] Aslam notes that, although Muslim men often justify their "hyper-masculinized and predominately aggressive and oppressive personalities" by appealing to religious texts and narratives, there is nothing inherently Islamic about the dominant "hegemonic and aggressive Muslim masculinity."[8]

Aslam is primarily concerned with one subtype, namely, militant-jihadist masculinity, which she finds most likely to be involved in terrorism. By contrast, my concern is with a form of masculinity that is particularly authoritarian, dominant, and aggressive. It is masculinity of the latter

---

5. Herbert Sussman, *Masculine Identities: The History and Meanings of Manliness* (Santa Barbara, CA: Praeger, 2012), 1.

6. Judith Butler, *Gender Trouble: Feminism and the Subversion of Identity* (New York: Routledge, 1990), xv.

7. For Joseph's discussion of gender, see Suad Joseph, "Introduction: Theories and Dynamics of Gender, Self, and Identity in Arab Families," in Suad Joseph (ed.), *Intimate Selving in Arab Families: Gender, Self, and Identity* (Syracuse: Syracuse University Press, 1999), 1–15. For Aslam's discussion of gender and Islamic and Muslim masculinities, see Maleeha Aslam, *Gender-Based Explosions: The Nexus Between Muslim Masculinities, Jihadist Islamism and Terrorism* (Tokyo and New York: United Nations University Press, 2012), 73–143.

8. Aslam, *Gender-Based Explosions*, 91.

type that, in Section 5.1, I analyze as warrior masculinity.[9] Whereas warrior masculinity today finds its most pervasive performance within HSCs, it can also be found in cultures of machismo in Mexico and Brazil and elsewhere, including the United States Marine Corps. As Herbert Sussman notes, "the warrior code is remarkably uniform over history and across cultures."[10] Indeed, as noted in Sections 3.2–3.3, wherever honor–shame cultures predominate, a man's actions and his sense of personal worth will depend on the opinions of his peers and the threat of exclusion from the community. Examples of men enacting warrior masculinity are numerous, ranging from the Homeric warriors of the *Iliad*, the ancient Spartans, the Vikings, and the samurai of feudal Japan right up to the Gurkhas of Nepal, the Rajputs of northern India, the Yanomamo of Brazil, the Pashtuns of northeast Pakistan, and the Kurdish *peshmerga*.[11]

As Sections 3.2–3.3 indicate, when masculine identity becomes inextricably entwined with honor, "social death" results from betraying the honor code's most stringent requirements. Before turning to a causal analysis of warrior masculinity in Chapter 5, we must attempt to clarify the causal pathways between child-rearing and socialization in HSCs and the result: namely, males willing and able to execute female family members. Obviously, perpetrating an honor killing is as extreme a masculine performance as we are likely to find. It is equally obvious that the capacities for such a performance cannot arise *sui generis*. Hence, the sociocultural and causative antecedents making possible these deadly performances must be present in the formation of dispositions and experiences shaping the development of attitudes, emotions, and, indeed, the "brain architecture" of males, hence making them able to perform, when expected, as slayers of daughters, sisters, mothers, aunts, and female cousins.[12] The

9. While I am not aware of studies attempting to correlate characteristics of honor killers and militant jihadists, Aslam's study indicates that we should expect similarities between the two groups. Honor killings do occur among peoples—e.g., Bedouin Arabs, Kurds, Pashtuns, Somalis, and Yemenis—from whom militant jihadists have been recruited.

10. Sussman, *Masculine Identities*, 16.

11. See, for instance, Kwame Anthony Appiah, *The Honor Code: How Moral Revolutions Happen* (New York and London: W. W. Norton, 2010); James Bowman, *Honor: A History* (New York: Encounter Books, 2006); Raewyn W. Connell, *Masculinities*, 2nd. ed. (Berkeley and Los Angeles: University of California Press, 2005); Mann, *Sovereign Masculinity*; Richard E. Nisbett and Dov Cohen, *Culture of Honor: The Psychology of Violence in the South* (Boulder: Westview, 1991); and Sussman, *Masculine Identities*, 16.

12. The term "brain architecture" is defined by Harvard University's Center on the Developing Child to refer to the way inherited genes and experience work together to construct brain circuitry and brain pathways, especially in the amygdala, hippocampus, and prefrontal cortex that continue to develop from infancy through adolescence and

main objectives of Sections 4.2–4.4 can be summarized as involving two steps: first, examining the hardships and stresses males typically experience in coming of age in HSCs; second, considering how the consequences of growing up under adversity contribute to VPP. The latter provides critical potential for warrior masculinity and the shame-to-violence conversion.

Note that I cannot claim to have found all the important links in the construction of VPP. Even if certain negative developmental experiences do produce VPP, not all men possessing this personality type, or even warrior masculinity, are would-be killers. At most, VPP and warrior masculinity represent the *potential* for honor killing. Although having this combination constitutes a necessary condition for honor killing, it is not *sufficient* on its own. Also necessary are honor–shame cultures with expectations about proper male responses to suspected female dishonor, peer pressure, and the prior existence of honor killing as a culturally evolved social practice (Chapter 6). Without these contributing causes, actual performances of the deed would not be *called forth* or *triggered*.

Furthermore, consider what it *means* to say that VPP and warrior masculinity are a conjointly necessary condition for honor killing. As noted, not all males in HSCs with such personality constructs will become honor killers; moreover, it is possible that some honor killing perpetrators will not have a VPP profile or warrior masculinity. However, my causal claim is not meant to generalize over all males with VPP and warrior masculinity; rather, the causal claim is about the relationship between two "populations." One population concerns the total number of honor killing attacks (fatalities and nonfatalities); the other population is made up of males "primed" because they do have these personality constructs. In other words, my causal hypothesis is that the relationship between these two populations, understood as the *rate of honor-killing attacks,* would not be as strong, or as high, as it is unless a significant proportion of the male population was primed to be perpetrators because of their VPP and warrior masculinity.[13]

My causal hypothesis is restricted to the population of primed perpetrators, but others in HSCs also have VPPs and abet executioners. Hence, it is reasonable to ask what proportion of members of HSCs must have suffered such aversive socialization—been so traumatized and

that have lifelong consequences. See www.developingchild.harvard.edu/science/key-concepts/brain-architecture, accessed July 20, 2017.

13. The logic of the causal connection is analogous to the causal connection between smoking and lung cancers. Some heavy smokers never contract cancer while some nonsmokers do get cancer. Yet, the rate of lung cancers among smokers is much higher than it is for nonsmokers.

blighted—in order for VPP and warrior masculinity to be implicated in honor killing? There is clearly no way to know, and so statistical percentages of primed males cannot be associated with numbers of incidents. However, as I indicate in Section 5.4, research in network theory suggests that, for any given community, the numbers of "dedicated avengers," or persons likely to be willing to commit or insist on honor killing, need not be large. I complete the argument for the VPP as a necessary component of warrior masculinity in Section 4.4.

I devote Section 5.1 to completing the model of warrior masculinity as a critical micro-cause for honor killing. The shame-to-power conversion and subsequent executions cannot exist except for flights from shame and within cultural groups where violence is the socially accepted way of responding to shame. In fact, when honor codes prevail socially, then experiences of shame can be "cleansed," and thus transformed, only through violence defined by the code as redemptive. Consequently, a vicious circle of sorts occurs: socialization must equip males with domineering, aggressive, and violent inclinations whose behaviors continue to perpetuate VPP. Likewise, social groups depending on honor and shame to maintain social order must rely on the constant production of shame, resulting in violent masculine performances taking culturally prescribed forms.

One final methodological issue remains to be considered before turning to childhood socialization. Much empirical evidence available for analysis can be said to have an unavoidable "patchwork quilt" quality. Moreover, questions arise about the generalizability and cross-cultural "transportation" of research findings. "Patchwork quilt" is a metaphor for the absence of much systematic cross-cultural work in the "Arabic world" (in which the first cross-national study of parenting did not take place until 2006) as well as in the Middle East and South Asia.[14] Consequently, particular research findings have to be "patched" together—some from Egypt, from Morocco, from the Palestinians, etc.—to form anything resembling a composite picture.

In addition, discussions of the universality versus cultural relativity of certain dispositions and traits have been fraught with controversy. Many anthropologist, including Donald Brown, emphasize human universals; by contrast, Joseph Henrich and his colleagues renew support for claims about cultural relativity, demonstrating that cultural differences can even

---

14. The "Arabic world," a term often occurring in the literature, is used here to designate both a geopolitical and interpsychic space of language, literary, and cultural influence.

affect sensory processing.[15] The co-evolutionary processes through which human brains produce culture—which, in turn, shapes brains—is extremely complex. That is why both sides of the debate are right depending on what is selected and where one splices into the co-evolutionary process.[16] Most important for our purposes are cross-cultural similarities that have been given robust support. As noted in Section 3.4, one is the East Asian–Western collectivist–individualist dichotomy, and another pertains to the links among ecology, mode of production, and culture. As Robert Sapolsky points out, anthropologists have long noted similarities among descendants of pastoralist peoples inhabiting dry, hardscrabble, wide-open landscapes and who are without the benefits of a centralized government and the rule of law[17] (Chapter 6). Certain similarities exist in culture as well as in individual behavioral traits, especially among young men in HSCs in the Arabic world and subcultures of honor in America, especially in the South.[18]

As Sapolsky observes, "childhood is the time when cultures inculcate individuals into further propagating their culture."[19] In the case of the perpetuation of VPPs, most important are repetitions of the burdens and trials of coming of age that prevent children from developing fully. The VPP type has transgenerational resiliency and differs little among cultures of honor. It would be absurd to attempt here to capture the diversity of child-rearing practices among millions of Muslims or all of the different ways males and females experience growing into adolescence. But such large-scale description goes far beyond my objectives. My purpose is to focus on a selective demographic that continues to live by stringent norms of honor and with the social practice of honor killing. Obviously, dividing lines between this demographic and others may defy absolute clarity. Yet, despite fuzziness at the margins, the replication of culture at the center remains robust in HSCs.

Consider the significance of an observation about gender made by Mai Ghoussoub and Emma Sinclair-Webb. In many areas of the Arabic

---

15. See respectively, Donald Brown, *Human Universals* (New York: McGraw-Hill, 1991); and Joseph Heinrich, Steven J. Heine, and Ara Norenzayan, "The Weirdest People in the World," *Behavioral and Brain Sciences* 33, no. 2/3 (2010), 1–75.

16. For an overview of the range of complexities, see Robert M. Sapolsky, *Behave: The Biology of Humans at Our Best and Worst* (New York: Penguin, 2017), 266–327.

17. Sapolsky, *Behave*, 273–83.

18. Nisbett and Cohen, *Culture of Honor*, 1–24, 86–94; Sapolsky, *Behave*, 282–91; and Bertram Wyatt-Brown, *Southern Honor: Ethics and Behavior in the Old South* (Oxford and New York: Oxford University Press, 2007), 3–87.

19. Sapolsky, *Behave*, 336.

world, women are increasingly seen in what were formerly exclusive "male domains," such as markets, offices, the streets, buses, and venues like beaches and theaters, and they are often seen wearing Western attire. Due to print and electronic media, these modern images, including women expressing nontraditional ideas, are readily available even in the most conservative and rural areas. Nevertheless, as Ghoussoub and Sinclair-Webb assert, "When it comes to gender relations, men's perceptions still follow ancient imprints of inherited memories regarding masculinity and femininity."[20] The point is that cultural transmissions of "ancient imprints of inherited memories" continue to bind—and often to complicate—the lives of even the most "liberated" women in major metropolitan areas. By analogy, there are prominent and compelling "ancient imprints of inherited memories" concerning proper parent–child relationships, child-rearing practices, and "ideal" feminine and masculine performances that remain common across cultures of shame and honor.

4.2 EARLY CHALLENGES OF COMING OF AGE

This section offers a basic overview of coming of age for both sexes, emphasizing childhood experiences most important for gender identity and the formation of personality. Particular emphasis will be on young males, given their susceptibility for VPP and for warrior masculinity as adults. Hence, there is a particular focus on experiences that contribute to the hypothetical model of VPP as explained in Section 4.1, as well as on the dynamics creating female identity considered in Section 5.1.[21] There is no comprehensive monograph or textbook on children and youth in the Middle East and North Africa. Thus, although this model is based on relevant research, the patchwork quality of the overview is unavoidable. Fortunately, some important research conducted in the West has been replicated in studies of subjects in the Arabic world, the Middle East, or South Asia. In addition, I rely on similarities between socialization in HSCs and in other honor cultures when appropriate.

---

20. Mai Ghoussoub and Emma Sinclair-Webb (eds.), *Imagined Masculinities: Male Identity and Culture in the Modern Middle East*, 2nd ed. (London: Saqi Books, 2006), 230.

21. The concept of a violence-prone personality is not intended to imply that an agent with VPP will act aggressively or violently without an environmental stimulus or trigger. See Section 7.3 for a brief discussion of a general theory of aggression. The point is thus that a set of triggering events is sufficient to elicit violence in an agent with VPP but usually not sufficient to elicit violence in an agent without VPP.

Associations between sex and gender begin at birth, as well as discrimination against the girl child. A boy's birth is celebrated as proof that the parents are meeting family and communal expectations; the husband is demonstrating his virility and the wife is fulfilling her responsibility by producing a male heir.[22] A girl's birth is generally not a welcome event and may be the occasion for mourning. However, all infants are said to experience close bodily contact with mothers or female caretakers at least for the first year or so. Some sources assert that babies are generally indulged and nursed on demand and "are never allowed to cry more than a few seconds without being pacified, usually with the breast."[23] This may reflect an ideal standard rather than reality, however, for according to UNICEF data for 2016, mothers breastfeeding in the first six months range from a high of 53.1% in Iran to lows of 11.1% in Kuwait and 8.5% in Tunisia, with an average of 27.5% for the 15 countries in the Middle East and North Africa (MENA) and 64.9% in India and 37.7% in Pakistan.[24] Children are usually toilet trained by the end of the first year, presumably because frequent bodily contact enables caretakers to sense when babies are about to urinate or defecate.[25]

Daily childcare is almost always considered women's work and unworthy of men's attention.[26] This is true even when men are at home, and mothers permitted to work are expected to make necessary arrangements for childcare, often requiring the aid of daughters or enlisting female relatives, as well as paying for care, when necessary, out of their own wages.[27] Childcare is reported to be characterized by early maternal affection and physical comforting, especially for sons, interspersed with threats, slaps,

22. Raphael Patai, *The Arab Mind*, rev. ed. (Tucson: Recovery Resources, 2002), 33.

23. Susan Schaefer Davis, "Growing Up in Morocco," in Donna Lee Bowen and Evelyn A. Early (eds.), *Everyday Life in the Muslim Middle East*, 2nd ed. (Bloomington: Indiana University Press, 2002), pp. 24–35, 26. See also Suad Joseph and Afsāna Iaqmūbādī (eds.), *Encyclopedia of Women and Islamic Cultures: Family, Body, Sexuality*, Vol. 3 (Leiden: Brill, 2006), 78.

24. UNICEF, "Infant and Young Child Feeding: Global Database," Updated October, 2016, https://data.unicef,org/topic/nutrition/infant-and-young-child-feeding/, accessed July 23, 2017.

25. Davis, "Growing up in Morocco," 28; Joseph and Iaqmūbādī, *Encyclopedia*, 78.

26. David Ghanim, *Gender Violence in the Middle East* (Westport: Praeger, 2009), 94.

27. Homa Hoodfar relates an incident in which Mahmoud and his wife, Mona, were arguing about the injury of the youngest son who had fallen down the stairs while Mona was not at home. Mahmoud, who had been at home when the toddler fell, was angry with Mona and accused her of not taking care of her responsibilities. Mahmoud also rejected Hoodfar's suggestion that, because he had been at home while his wife was shopping for food, he should have kept an eye on the child. See Homa Hoodfar, *Between Marriage and the Market: Intimate Politics and Survival in Cairo* (Berkeley and Los Angeles: University of California Press, 1997), 174.

and beatings as the child grows. Similar patterns of abrupt parental shifts appear common across honor cultures. Umma Saliah recalls from her childhood in Pakistan that it was "the norm to be smacked by your parents, extended relatives and anyone else that [*sic.*] happened to be around and in a bad mood."[28] Bertram Wyatt-Brown also reports that, in the antebellum South, parents "were prone to sudden anger, and slapped their children harshly."[29]

Parents and guardians are unlikely to reason or participate in discussions with children; they are far more likely to lecture and to issue orders. Children are expected to obey their parents, especially the father's orders, without question. For much of the child's early life, the father is absent, either at work, searching for work, or otherwise in the company of adult males. He is likely to be remote psychologically and to be seen by young children as a powerful and imposing figure as they observe their mother and other household members, including adult siblings and in-laws, obeying his commands. The relatively small time the father interacts with his children is likely to alternate between affection and praise and indifference or stern, sometimes violent, punishment. Children learn it is often best to avoid approaching a father with a question or request and to have their mother intercede for them. Because members of the extended family are expected to assist in rearing children, and many neighbors are also relatives, discipline is generalized, with many adults presuming the right to mete out verbal threats and physical punishment.

One reported aspect of close physical contact between mothers, females, and sons involves fondling the boy's genitals. While unknown how widespread this frank sexual play is, it is said to occur without embarrassment and to have symbolic and educational value. Raphael Patai reports that a common practice with a crying infant is to pick him up and sooth him by handling his genitals. Other female relatives, visitors, and older siblings, will play with the penis of the boy, both to calm him and to make him smile.[30] Ipek Ilkkaracan and Gülşah Seral report that it is common in

28. Umma Saliah, "An Islamic Perspective on Child-Rearing and Discipline," *New York Times*, Parenting Blogs, Jan. 12, 2011, https://parenting.blogs.nytimes.com/2011/01/12/an-islamic-view-of-parenting/?_r=0, accessed July 23, 2017.

29. Wyatt-Brown, *Southern Honor*, 142.

30. Patai, *The Arab Mind*, 34; see also Hamad Ammar, *Growing Up in an Egyptian Village* (London: Routledge and Kegan Paul, 1954), 120; and Horace M. Miner and George de Vos, *Oasis and Casbah: Algerian Culture and Personality in Change* (Ann Arbor: University of Michigan, 1960), 58.

Turkey for young boys to be told to proudly show their penises to relatives and neighbors.[31]

Ilkkaracan and Seral add that touching the boy's penis is a significant part of gendered sexuality. This point is also emphasized by Fatima Mernissi based on her knowledge of child-rearing in Morocco: "His penis, *htewta* ('little penis'), is the object of a veritable cult on the part of the women rearing him. Little sisters, aunts, maids, and mothers often attract the little boy's attention to his *htewta* and try to teach him to pronounce the word. . . . One of the common games played by adult females is to get him to understand the connection between *sidi* ('master') and the *htewta*. *Hada sidhum* ('this is their master') say the women, pointing to the child's penis. They try to make him repeat the sentence while pointing to his own penis. The kissing of the child's penis is a normal gesture for a female relative who has not seen him since his birth. *Tbarkallah 'ala-r-Rajal* ('God protect the man'), she may whisper."[32]

The sexual "education" of little girls is equally explicit but does not engender in them anything approximating a little boy's "phallic pride." "Little girls are told in detail about the vagina and the uterus, and about the penis's destructive effects on these two parts of women's bodies."[33] Parents, older siblings, even relatives warn the girl, when she is still allowed to play outside, that it is shameful to expose, even by mistake, a quick glimpse of her underwear.[34] She confronts "a series of continuous warnings about things that are supposed to be harmful, forbidden, shameful, or outlawed by religion."[35] Worries about the little girl's body combine with other messages. Girls continue to be hugged and told that they are pretty, but receive far less attention than boys, especially when weaning begins or between the first and second year. "Small girls do not cry or demand attention to show they resent being slighted, but just sit quietly and observe."[36] Thus, as Magda M. Al-Nowaihi puts it, "the

---

31. Ipek Ilkkaracan and Gülşah Seral, "Sexual Pleasure as a Woman's Human Right: Experiences from a Grassroots Training Program in Turkey," in Pinar Ilkkaracan (ed.), *Women and Sexuality in Muslim Societies* (Istanbul: Women for Women's Human Rights, 2000), 187–96, 187.

32. Fatima Mernissi, *Beyond the Veil: Male-Female Dynamics in Modern Muslim Society*, rev. ed. (Bloomington and Indianapolis: Indiana University Press, 1987), 162.

33. Mernissi, *Beyond the Veil*, 161.

34. Ilkkanarcan and Seral, "Sexual Pleasure," 187.

35. See Ghanim, *Gender Violence*, 72–74; and Nawal El Saadawi, *The Hidden Face of Eve: Women in the Arab World*, trans. and ed. by Sherif Hetata (London and New York: Zed, 2007), 10–11.

36. Davis, "Growing up in Morocco," 29.

child is keenly aware of men and women as two different categories of being."[37]

Gender differences become increasingly pronounced from the age of three or four years. Even when very young, girls run errands, wash dishes, sweep, and care for younger siblings. Childhood ends very quickly for most girls. As Davis reports, "it is not unusual to see a five-year-old carrying a one-year-old on her back."[38] When not required for housework, little girls are usually allowed to play outdoors, although they will be expected to stay within ear-shot of the home or under the watchful eye of a brother. Also, girls may be forbidden to engage in more vigorous activities such as riding bicycles, running, or jumping, as these might risk tearing the hymen.

Increasing restrictions on girls' behavior accelerates until, near menarche, they are completely secluded and permitted to leave the home only with permission and with a *wadi*, or male guardian. The institution of daughter-maids depends mostly on female preteens and teenagers. Girls of this age learn to do all the basic household tasks of washing, cleaning, cooking, and childcare and, in addition, are accompanied by brothers or male cousins while running errands.[39] Girls are thought to be marriageable when they reach menarche, but they will remain in the family until, after an arranged marriage, they move to the husband's home.[40]

Typically, boys are not asked to perform household chores except to run errands and to display authority, as in answering the doorbell and representing the household when the father is not present. Even young boys are encouraged to make demands of older sisters and to discipline them, including hitting, while sisters are not allowed to retaliate. Boys take pleasure in their superiority and in serving as sisters' guardians. "Spoiled" and mischievous behavior including tantrums are often tolerated from young boys while almost never from girls.[41] "Consequently," Maleeha Aslam

37. Magda M. Al-Nowaihi, "Constructions of Masculinity in Two Egyptian Novels," in Suad Joseph (ed.), *Intimate Selving*, 235–63, 252.

38. Davis, "Growing up in Morocco," 30.

39. Davis, "Growing up in Morocco," 31.

40. Mernissi reports that in a 1987 survey of rural Moroccans, the ideal age for the marriage of females was thought to be 13. Fifty percent of girls are married before they reach puberty, and another 37 percent are married during the first two years following puberty. See Mernissi, *Beyond the Veil*, 101.

41. An anthropologist relates the following example involving Metin, a young boy; Emine, his sister; and Hatjie, their mother: "Metin began to tease Emine and some other visiting women, pushing them and running away. Hatjie smiled at him indulgently and continued her knitting. Metin approached the television, looking back to see who was watching. On top of the television was an embroidered cloth under small ceramic statues of horses and dogs and a cheap vase. Metin grasped the cloth and yelled 'Look!' Hatjie looked up from her knitting and uttered a half-hearted admonition: 'Don't.' She

reports, "a boy child begins to feel extraordinary early in life. The illusion of . . . being more capable . . . [than] his sisters is artificially created."[42]

Encouraged to play in neighborhood streets and alleys, boys soon learn to be assertive, prideful, and tough. Soccer is a great favorite for boys from age 6 to 12 and usually the only organized form of play. Boys commonly rough-house, play pranks, and attempt to establish themselves in the neighborhood's pecking order. Davis reports, "Another common game involves a gang of boys each trying to kick one another in the pants."[43] Davis adds that boys' play commonly expresses aggression, and notes, "they behave irresponsibly, sometimes even destructively, but are not blamed."[44] Generally allowed to come and go freely, boys often run wild well into their teens. Yet, despite developing potency and a desire for greater influence, male teens will continue to chafe under the control of fathers and elders. Parental permissiveness is not to be equated with a son's independence.

Indulging boys as "holy terrors" is not based solely on the boy's privileged status or the mother's internalized bias against her own gender. Studies of family life in other honor societies emphasize the ambivalence and frequent bitterness of mothers due to the "incompleteness arising from the role assigned her," and thus necessary repression was "hidden in outward shows of affection, a denial to the self as well as to the object of the manipulative love. . . . "[45] Moreover, sheltering such deep feelings from themselves, many mothers were no more in touch with their feelings than were the boys they raised; boys whose tantrums indicated that they could not control their impulses or feelings.[46] There is certainly no reason to believe mothers in HSCs are any less ambivalent and conflicted.

Children of both sexes are taught the importance of honor and of shame, 'ayb, or 'aib, and of 'hshim (a shameful act), from an early age, with increasing emphasis as children mature. 'Ayab means "Show some shame!"

---

looked back at her knitting as, with a flourish, Metin pulled the cloth and the statues onto the floor, whooping. The women laughed. The statues and the broken vase lay on the floor until the next morning when Emine picked them up as she was sweeping the house." See Jenny B. White, "Two Weddings," in Bowen and Early (eds.), *Everyday Life*, 63–77, 68. See also Davis, "Growing Up in Morocco," in Bowen and Early, 24–35, 29.

42. Aslam, *Gender-Based Explosions*, 117.

43. Davis, "Growing Up in Morocco," 31.

44. Davis, "Growing Up in Morocco," 31; Davis adds the following anecdote: "People used to warn us never to allow children in our house because 'they have not yet "become responsible" and might steal something.' We assumed the warning applied to children under seven, as was in fact correct for girls; the boys they referred to were up to fifteen and evidently not yet held responsible for theft." See Davis, 34.

45. Wyatt-Brown, *Southern Honor*, 171.

46. Wyatt-Brown, *Southern Honor*, 174, 152.

or "Behave!" when spoken as a command, and the objective of inculcating *'ayb* is to develop *mu'addabla*: polite, disciplined behavior that conforms to the values of the group.[47] *'Ayab* is also closely related to *'qal*, or*'qel*, which means "to develop a mind," or to show maturity and social responsibility.[48] However, the self-control and suppression of impulse expected of preteen and teen girls is not required of boys; as Davis notes, "The last thing one would expect of boys at this age is that they would have *'qel*."[49]

Clearly, gendered notions of *'ayb* are combined with different gender expectations. In addition, what is *'ayb* pertains to what is publicly regarded as *shameful* within the community and *what others presume to know you to have done* (Sections 3.2–3.3). Hence, whatever is likely to bring shame onto the family is prohibited. Jean Said Makdisi remembers from her Lebanese childhood that "the most important thing in the world was how people regarded them: *shu biquoulou al-nas?* (What will people say?)"[50] This admonition is a constant refrain. In addition, it is common for parents to see their children as extensions of themselves. Others often give parents credit for their children's successes and much of the blame for their failures.[51] Parents and elders will attempt to "instruct" by making negative comparisons of a child with others and will shame children before other family members, friends and peers, and strangers.[52]

Shaming is purportedly employed in child-rearing as an aversive technique. Shamed for unwanted behavior, presumably a child will avoid doing whatever will shame her in the future. However, the effects of shaming are global rather than specific; shaming calls into question the value of one's existence, and, hence, shaming teaches a child to do whatever is necessary to avoid rejection. A shamed child learns not to feel guilty for specific behavior, not to confess and be forgiven, but to avoid detection and humiliation.[53] If a child feels "bad" about stealing, for example, this is probably not because stealing is *wrong in itself*, but because he has been caught or fears being caught and hence suffering humiliation. The effectiveness of shame as social control, even for an otherwise unruly boy, was revealed, according

---

47. Joseph and Iaqmūbādī, *Encyclopedia*, 78.
48. Davis, "Growing Up in Morocco," 30–33.
49. Davis, "Growing Up in Morocco," 32.
50. Jean Said Makdisi, "Teta, Mother, and I," in Joseph (ed.), 25–52, 48.
51. ArabiCare, www.arabicare.org.aus/about/culture=traditions/140-child-rearing-practices, accessed July 27, 2017.
52. See, e.g., Margaret Nydell, *Understanding Arabs: A Contemporary Guide to Arab Society* (Boston and London: Intercultural Press, 2012), 63–72; Joseph and Iaqmūbādī, *Encyclopedia*, 78.
53. Wyatt-Brown, *Southern Honor*, 155; and Helen B. Lewis, *Shame and Guilt in Neurosis* (Madison, CT: International Universities Press, 1971), 41–42.

to Davis, in a class of preschool children in a village. "Because a child would not behave in response to directions or even slaps, the teacher stood him in the corner for a few minutes. That he cried as if his heart were broken is not understandable unless one realizes the impact of being publicly shamed."[54]

Demands to avoid *'ayb* require keeping family problems and indiscretions hidden from prying eyes and communal gossip. This code of silence is so pervasive and powerful that even a boy or young man's mother is rarely mentioned by name; instead, one refers to a mother as *Umm*, "mother," plus the name of her eldest son, as in "Umm Ahmed." It is an insult for a nonrelative to refer to a person's mother by name.[55] At the same time, however, an emphasis on appearances means that discipline is often inconsistent. Parents may threaten the most severe punishment but not carry it out when disobedient behavior does not bring anticipated shame down on their heads. Likewise, parents may punish to relieve their own feelings of shame,[56] or even when they *anticipate* others will perceive a child's behavior as shameful, yet inconsistently fail to condemn the same behavior in the future if negative public comments do not follow its commission.

Despite demands to avoid *'ayb*, males are not encouraged to develop impulse control or capacities for independent judgment and critical thinking which are important for autonomy and self-reliance. As Sana Al-Khayyat reports, "Children are not taught to think for themselves, or to develop their creativity and individuality." She adds: "Later on they tend to blame other people for what goes wrong in their lives."[57] One possible further consequence is a form of delayed adolescence.[58] For instance, in Egypt, in contrast to the expected adolescent project of becoming self-reliant and preparing for separation from the family, males are preoccupied with learning how to exploit social networks and refining their skills for dominating others.[59]

54. Davis, "Growing Up in Morocco," 30.
55. A UN Women's Rights initiative titled "Give Mom Back Her Name" was begun on Mother's Day 2015 in Cairo, Egypt. It was directed at getting boys and young men to publicly identify themselves as the sons of their mothers by speaking her name publicly. A video clip produced by Mohammed Naciri, the UN Woman Regional Director, in cooperation with BBNO Dubai, was widely circulated on YouTube, showing some males complying with the request, often with beaming mothers, but others refusing. See http://www.egyptianstreets.com/2015/03/22/why-do-egyptian-men-refuse-to-reveal-their-mothers-name/
56. Wyatt-Brown (*Southern Honor*) says at 151 "the advantage of the shaming method was its satisfaction for the wielder of power not the moral training it supposedly gave the young."
57. Sana Al-Khayyat, *Honour and Shame: Women in Modern Iraq* (London: Saqi, 1990), 54.
58. Ghanim, *Gender Violence*, 192–93.
59. Barbara S. Mensich et al., "Gender Role Attitudes Among Egyptian Adolescents," *Studies in Family Planning* 34, no. 1 (2003), 10.

Lili Mottaghi reports that while up to 70% of youth in Egypt say that *wasta*, or connections and favoritism, are forms of corruption, roughly the same percentage seek such connections to acquire higher paying, higher status, and more secure jobs in the public sector.[60]

The picture of parental permissiveness regarding boys and male adolescents contrasts starkly with the actual severity of threats and punishments. Discipline, or *adab*, begins very early in life, and threats and physical blows punctuate the young boy's seemingly idyllic relationship with his mother. As noted, a mother's cuddling and indulgence of her son is often punctuated by angry scorn, slaps, swats, and more. After the ritual circumcision and continuing through adolescence, punishment of boys becomes increasingly prominent and severe as training for the trials expected in life. Cross-cultural studies establish strong associations between harsh socialization and the incidence of violence among adults.[61] This is especially true in cultures of honor where parenting practices, or "parenting styles," tend to be authoritarian or a combination of authoritarian and permissive.[62] Diane Baumrind's pioneering work on identifying different parenting styles[63] has been well-corroborated by studies in North America and Europe, and while there are far fewer relevant studies in Arabic or South Asian cultures, two research teams claim Baumrind's typology is valid for "Arab cultures."[64]

Authoritative parenting styles are thought to have the best consequences for developing healthy children. Such authoritative parenting sets clear and consistent expectations and is responsive and supportive; it emphasizes using reason, listening to the child, offering praise and forgiving rather than punishment. Authoritative parenting correlates positively with

60. Lili Mottaghi, "The Problem of Unemployment in the Middle East and North Africa Explained in Three Charts," World Bank Blogs, Aug. 25, 2014, blogs.worldbank. org/arabvoices/problem-unemployment-explained-middle-east-and-north-africa-three-charts, accessed July 26, 2017.

61. Bruce M. Knauft et al., "Violence and Sociality in Human Evolution," *Current Anthropology* 32, no. 4 (1991), 391–428; and Marc Howard Ross, "A Cross-Cultural Theory of Political Conflict and Violence," *Political Psychology* 7, no. 3 (1986), 427–69.

62. Nisbett and Cohen, *Culture of Honor*, 32–35; Sapolsky, *Behave*, 203–07.

63. Diane Baumrind, "Child Care Practices Antedating Three Patterns of Preschool Behavior," *Genetic Psychology Monographs* 75, no. 1 (1967), 43–88; and Diane Baumrind, *Early Socialization and the Discipline Controversy* (Morristown, NJ: General Learning Press, 1975).

64. Nuba Abudabbeh, "Arab Families: An Overview," in Monica McGolderick, Joe Giardano, and John K. Pearce (ed.), *Ethnicity and Family Therapy* (New York: Guilford Press, 1996), 333–46; Marwan A. Dwairy et al., "Parenting Styles in Arab Cultures: A First Cross-Regional Study," *Journal of Cross-Cultural Psychology* 37, no. 3 (2006), 230–47.

high self-esteem, self-confidence, security, and curiosity in children and adolescents, and correlates negatively with anxiety, aggression, and behavioral problems.[65] *Authoritarian* parenting requires that rules be rigidly followed, but demands are often arbitrary and reasons or justifications are rarely offered; parents rely on punishment, and the child's emotional needs get low priorities. "Permissive parents" set few demands or expectations, or, alternatively, they set high demands but are largely nonresponsive or indifferent.[66] Moreover, each particular parenting style has significant developmental outcomes for children, beyond producing adults who employ the same parenting style.

Children from "authoritarian homes" are more likely to exhibit anxiety and aggression, to have lower self-esteem, and to become involved in behavioral problems.[67] While drastically understudied, evidence suggests that the most common parenting style in the Arabic world, and hence in many HSCs, is authoritarian.[68] In 2006, Marwan Dwairy led an important study of 2,843 Arabic adolescents in eight Arabic-speaking countries.[69] Researchers used variants of the Baumrind typology: *inconsistent* (combining authoritarian and permissive), *controlling* (authoritarian and authoritative), and *flexible* (authoritative and permissive.) While results support the investigators' main prediction—namely, that there are significant differences in parenting styles across Arab societies—results also revealed that 60.5% of adolescents experienced either inconsistent or controlling parenting styles compared to 39.5% for flexible. Researchers found that the inconsistent style had the least beneficial outcomes for child

65. John R. Buri et al., "Effects of Parental Authoritarianism and Authoritativeness on Self-Esteem, Personality and Personality," *Personality and Social Psychology Bulletin* 14, no. 2 (1988), 271–82; and David A. Reitman and Joan Asseff, "Parenting Practices and Their Relation to Anxiety in Young Adulthood," *Journal of Anxiety Disorders* 24, no. 6 (2010), 565–72.

66. See Sapolsky, *Behave*, 203; and Radha J. Horton-Parker, "Teaching Children to Care: Engendering Proscocial Behavior Through Humanistic Parenting," *Journal of Humanistic Education and Development* 37, no. 2 (1998), 66–77.

67. Diane Baumrind, "The Influence of Parenting Style on Adolescent Competence and Substance Use," *Journal of Early Adolescence* 11, no. 2 (1991), 56–90; and Fred Rothbaum and John R. Weisz, "Parental Caregiving and Child Externalizing Behavior in Nonclinical Samples: A Meta-Analysis," *Psychology Bulletin* 116, no. 1 (1994), 55–74.

68. Adnan Hammad et al., *Guide to Arab Culture: Health Care Delivery to the Arab American Community*. ACCESS Community Health Center: Health Research Unit (1999); Abudabbeh, "Arab Families"; Rashi Garg et al., "Parenting Style and Academic Achievement for East Indian and Canadian Adolescents," *Journal of Contemporary Family Studies* 36, no. 4 (2005), 653–61; Saigeetha Jambunathan and Kenneth Counselman, "Parenting Attitudes of Asian Indian Mothers Living in the United States and in India," *Early Child Development and Care* 172 (2002), 657–62.

69. Dwairy et al., "Parenting Styles in Arab Cultures."

development. In addition, adolescents raised in "inconsistent homes" were lower in connectedness with parents (were more rebellious), and many more suffered from a variety of mental disorders. As a further and important result, researchers found that socioeconomic status, parental educational level, and urbanization were not significantly related to parenting styles.[70] Parenting styles did differ markedly relative to the gender of the adolescent, however, as male adolescents experienced a higher level of authoritarianism than their female counterparts.[71]

I discuss in Section 4.4 the difficulties children and adolescents encounter in coping with authoritarian and inconsistent parenting, as well as maternal ambivalence, insofar as these influence the development of VPP and warrior masculinity. Of course, authoritarian and inconsistent parenting styles do not necessarily entail psychological or physical abuse. Yet, in the traditional areas of North Africa, the Middle East, and South Asia, the incidence and severity of beatings administered to children is a subject of serious concern, and there appears to be no enforced or socially accepted conception of child or spousal abuse in many regions.

Often parents insult, curse, and threaten children, as traditional punishment includes intimidation, or *takhjil* (to incite fear and shame), and corporal punishment ranges from swatting, slapping, and spanking to beatings with hands, fists, and objects. Hamad Anmar, commenting on his own Egyptian village, reports that children were socialized through "techniques of fear" added to the effects of shaming; consequently, children resorted to lies and deception of all sorts.[72] Even when children and adolescents personally escape the worst forms of humiliation and abuse, they are almost certain to have witnessed the depreciation, humiliation, and abuse of others. Much of this begins within the family. As Ghanim points out, divorce threats are often "part of the daily drama" among parents as unions are based on contracts and not "love matches."[73] A majority of men and women expect that husbands and fathers will rely on the

70. Dwairy et al., "Parenting Styles in Arab Cultures"; see also Majedh F. Abu Al Rub, *Parenting Styles Used with Preschool Children Among Arab Immigrant Parents in a US Context*, PhD Dissertation, Summer 2013, Colorado State University. Available at www.digitool.library.colostate.edu///exlibris, accessed Jul. 15, 2015.

71. This difference was possibly related to the gender of the parent as well, for in a separate study of 321 Palestinian-Arab adolescents conducted in 2004, Dwairy suggested that the strongest influences on parenting were the cultural context and the gender of the disciplining parent. See Marwan A. Dwairy, "Parenting Styles and Psychological Adjustment of Arab Adolescents," *Transcultural Psychiatry* 41, no. 2 (2004), 233–52.

72. Quoted in David Pryce-Jones, *The Closed Circle: An Interpretation of the Arabs* (New York: Harper and Row, 1989), 42.

73. Ghanim, *Gender Violence*, 186.

religiously sanctioned right of men to physically discipline women *(ta'deeb)*. Sadly, children are socialized to accept all of this as normal behavior.

In cultural groups reluctant to divulge information to outsiders, it is extremely difficult to obtain accurate numbers about serious physical abuse or taboo subjects such as incest and sexual abuse. However, studies suggest that the number of children victimized or exposed to severe violence is alarming. Noting that the severity of punishment coincides with the conservativism of a community, Robin Grille reveals that the Department of Public Works in Alexandria found that 25% of Egyptian children suffered from various injuries such as concussions, fractures, and even permanent disability.[74] In various surveys, up to 95% of the women in Afghanistan, as well as in Bahrain, reported being abused, as did 70–90% of the women in Pakistan, while 80% of women in rural Egypt reported abuse. In one survey in Turkey, 97% of women suffered physical or psychological abuse, as did 63% of female university students in Qatar, more than 40% of female respondents in Yemen, and approximately 33% in Lebanon.[75] Sociologists at a 2000 conference funded by the Ford Foundation claimed that 50% of Lebanese women had been victims of rape, incest, or sexual abuse and estimated that as many as 70% of Moroccan women might have suffered such abuse.[76] A study released in 2013 reported that 53.3% of Bedouin women surveyed had been sexually abused at least once, and 89.6% disclosed physical abuse.[77]

---

74. Robin Grille, *Parenting for a Peaceful World*, 2nd ed. (Avlon Beach, Australia: Vox Cordis Press, 2013), 141–56.

75. See, respectively (for Afghanistan), Anne E. Brodsky, "Violence Against Afghan Women: Tradition, Religion, Conflict, and War," in Moha Ennaji and Fatima Sadiqi (eds.), *Gender and Violence in the Middle East* (London and New York: Routledge, 2011), 115–37, 120; (for Bahrain), "A Study in Bahrain: 95% Admit That Women Are Abused," *Al-Sharq al-Awsat*, Mar. 20, 2006 [cited in Ghanim, *Gender Violence*, 26]; (for Pakistan), Andrea Parrot and Nina Cummings, *Forsaken Females: The Global Brutalization of Women* (Lanham, MD: Rowman and Littlefield, 2006), 153; (for rural Egypt), Parrot and Cummings, 42; (for Turkey), OMTC (World Organization Against Torture), "Violence Against Women in Turkey," 2003 Report, http://www.omtc.org/pdf/VAW/Publications/2003/Eng_2003_09_Turkey.pdf; (for Qatar), "Beating Your Maid Is Normal in Qatar BUT Also Beating Female Family Members Is Part of Being Qatari," *Gulf Times*, Jan. 26, 2005; (for Yemen), "Statistics Prove That Violence Against Women Is a Yemeni and Global Problem, *Yemen Observer*, Dec. 2, 2007, http://www.yobserver.com/reports/printer_10013357.html; (for Lebanon), Syrian Women's Observatory, "Breaking the Walls of Silence with a Taboo Issue: A Third of Lebanese Women Are Abused," Dec. 27, 2007, http://www.nesay.org/index2.php?option=com_context&task=view&id=5307

76. Reported in Tahira S. Khan, *Beyond Honour: A Historical Materialist Explanation of Honour Related Violence* (Oxford and New York: Oxford University Press, 2006), 16.

77. Salman Elbedour et al., "The Scope of Sexual, Physical, and Psychological Abuse in a Bedouin-Arab Community of Female Adolescents: The Interplay of Racism,

Undertaking a research study in Cairo, Nawal El Saadawi estimated incest involving female children to be as high as 45% in uneducated families and 33.7% in educated families.[78] According to a study of the National Council for Social Research, there are approximately 20,000 cases of rape in Egypt every year, and 60% of these rapes are incestuous.[79] Hasan Mujtuba reports from a study conducted in Karachi, Pakistan, that "every ninth or tenth boy in school or at local *madrassas* or even at work, is sexually molested." Mujtuba adds that a sociologist who works with abused children reports that a victim "never reports this to his parents out of fear that they will blame him rather than a perpetrator."[80] Again, while many boys and girls will not be subjected to sexual abuse, or even physical abuse, they cannot help but know it is always a potential danger.

Brutal punishment can induce trauma and lead to identification with the aggressor, as discussed in Section 4.4. However, even nontraumatic corporal punishment has significance for the formation of VPP and, ultimately, the capacity of males to assume the role of perpetrators in honor killings. Imitation is itself a powerful basis for learning, and researchers have confirmed that merely observing aggression is sufficient to evoke aggressive behavior in young children.[81] Social learning theory also explains why physical punishment, contrary to classical learning theory, begets aggression rather than extinguishing it. The punitive behavior modeled by parents has a great communicative and cognitive impact on the child. As Jeffrey Goldstein summarizes, "the child is likely to learn not to suppress his aggression but to use it to influence the behavior of others."[82]

Growing boys will be aware of the strictures on the way sisters handle themselves, as well as the inconsistencies between notions that women exist to serve men versus the idea that women must avoid whatever might entice men. They will be increasingly aware of the incongruity between the reality of females consigned to a life of drudgery versus idealized visions of

Urbanization, Polygamy, Family Honor, and the Social Marginalization of Women," *Child Abuse and Neglect* 30, no. 3 (2006), 215–29.

78. El Saadawi, *The Hidden Face of Eve*, 31. Saadawi conducted her study in 1973–1974. She reports that, according to the Kinsey study, the comparable rate of incest in the United States in 1953 was 24%.

79. Cited in Ghanim, *Gender Violence*, 30.

80. Hasan Mujtuba, "The Other Side of Midnight: Pakistani Male Prostitutes," in Murray and Roscoe (eds.), *Islamic Homosexualities*, 267–74, 271.

81. Albert Bandura and Richard H. Walters, *Social Learning and Personality* (Lincoln: University of Nebraska Press, 1962).

82. Jeffrey H. Goldstein, *Aggression and Crimes of Violence*, 2nd ed. (New York: Oxford University Press, 1986), 37.

women as beguiling virgins.[83] Hence the awakening of sexual urges creates complications. Boys are likely to know that sexual desire is regarded as natural and that older males regard sexual predation as a prerequisite of masculinity. Inculcation of this masculine orientation may begin well before puberty. For instance, Suad Joseph reports the behavior of two Lebanese middle-class siblings at a social event: "The boy was advancing toward his younger sister. With roars of approval and great laughter the men and women in the room . . . shouted, '*bi hajim, bi hajim*' (he attacks, he attacks). The little boy, appearing somewhat confused, accelerated the behavior. . . . Such occasions were prime times for learning culturally appropriate sexual behavior."[84]

In emulating their fathers, younger males seek to take charge of sisters and mothers, who often defer to the son's control.[85] While there is little research on sexuality in brother–sister relationships, Joseph's fieldwork "indicates that the brother–sister relationship was sexually charged."[86] Joseph emphasizes the ways eroticization of brother–sister relationships arise from the dual roles of young men as their sisters' *partners* as well as protectors.[87] Joseph's fieldwork took place in Lebanon, but if similarly idealized relationships exist in HSCs, then there must be considerable tension between the strictly defined and separate roles for siblings and the desire for greater intimacy. It is hardly surprising, therefore, that sexually repressed males become preoccupied with symbols or ideals of "virginity," "purity," and "honor."[88]

The sexuality of the "pure virgin" of male desire is instantiated in one's sisters whose chastity and loyalty it is his honor to defend. When researching acculturation in the Middle East, one need not go far before

83. Ayaan Hirsi Ali in *Infidel* (New York: Atria, 2008) at 110 writes that as a teen she learned: "Even when all women had been covered up completely from head to toe . . . this was not enough. High heels tapped and could trigger in men the image of a woman's legs; to avoid sin, women must wear flat shoes that make no noise. Next came perfume: using any kind of pleasant fragrance, even perfumed soap and shampoo, would distract the minds of men from Allah's worship and cause them to fantasize about sinning. The safest way to cause no harm to anyone seemed to avoid contact with any man at all times and just stay in the house. A man's sinful erotic thoughts were always the fault of the woman who enticed them."

84. Joseph, *Intimate Selving*, 132.

85. Joseph, *Intimate Selving*, 133, n. 73.

86. Joseph, *Intimate Selving*, 131, n. 68.

87. Joseph comments on brothers and sisters walking arm in arm in the streets, grooming themselves for each other, commenting on each other's presentation, approving of each other's self-presentation, dancing together, and even sexual play-acting. See Joseph, *Intimate Selving*, 130.

88. Mernissi, *Beyond the Veil*, 160.

coming across the oft-told story (in Section 3.3) of a teacher pulling down a chart of female anatomy, pointing to the vagina, and declaring with all seriousness, "this is where honor lies."[89] Writing about Palestinian Arabs, Rob Baum avers, "Arab female sexuality is a category as dangerously loaded as the politics of Arab dis/possession." Women's bodies, Baum adds, are "depositories of vanquished hopes, oases from the repression of Palestinian rights."[90] As Mernissi notes, if in early childhood the boy believed society, as he knew it, was "organized to satisfy his sexual wishes," as he grows older he becomes aware that "sexual deprivation is systematically organized."[91] Mernissi adds that male sexuality is allowed no outward, licit expression. Speaking of the complexities Muslim boys must negotiate, Aslam asserts that it is inevitable that they suffer an "unhealthy and almost retarded fixation with the female body."[92]

Boys soon learn about one common sexual outlet: male-with-male sex. There is no shame in the use of another male to gratify lust if one is the active partner (the inserter) and if one's private behavior is not subjected to public criticism. As Michel Foucault argues, in the West, there has been a shift from same-sex activity as a set of specific acts to the view that homoerotic desire is a totalizing, determining basis of a specific type of man and of a specific type of identity.[93] This shift has not occurred in HSCs, however. In general, homosexuality is not defined by choice of the object of desire (e.g., an attractive boy) but as the rejection of masculine responsibilities (i.e., refusing to marry and to procreate).[94] Hence, sexual gratification with another male is not regarded as "homosexuality."

Despite the commonality of male-with-male sex, every boy must resist becoming the "boy on the bottom"; as Stephen Murray emphasizes, he risks losing his name, his honor, and perhaps more "if others know it and are known to know."[95] This is not likely to happen, however, for the decisive line is not between what is kept secret and the act known by many, but

89. One such report is made by Egyptian journalist Abeer Allam as reported in Douglas Jehl, "For Shame, A Special Report; Arab Honor's Price: A Woman's Blood," *New York Times*, June 20, 1999, www.polyzine,com/arabmomen.html, accessed Apr. 29, 2013.

90. Rob K. Baum, "Chasing Horses, Eating Arabs," in Lahoucine Ouzgane (ed.) *Islamic Masculinities* (London and New York: Zed Books, 2006), 105–22, 113 and 108.

91. Mernissi, *Beyond the Veil*, 162.

92. Aslam, *Gender-Based Explosions*, 116.

93. Michel Foucault, *The History of Sexuality: Vol. I: An Introduction* (New York: Vintage, 1990), 43.

94. Stephen O. Murray, "The Will Not to Know: Islamic Accommodations of Male Homosexuality," in Murray and Roscoe, *Islamic Homosexualities*, 14–54, 41.

95. Murray, "The Will Not to Know," quoting German Islamist Arno Schmidt, 17.

between talking behind one's back and saying it in one's presence, between a shared "secret" and public knowledge. As long as nobody draws public attention to something everybody knows, one ignores what might disrupt important social relations.[96]

The danger, instead, is that once sexually abused, the unfortunate boy "attracts the bachelors of the community like a pot of honey draws flies." It will be unthinkable for a boy once "breached" to refuse, and even if he does, he is likely to be subjected by force. One researcher notes that first-born sons succeed more often in avoiding being (ab)used, but "many younger brothers viewed it as inevitable."[97] In matters of male-with-male relationships, as with everything else, the assault on a man's masculinity occasions a severe psychological wound.[98] Moreover, because some males penetrate other males less for sexual gratification than to humiliate perceived opponents, the active role in homosexual relations is widely associated with brutal aggression.[99] Even a boy's youthful peers will take pleasure in his humiliation: in part because they can flaunt their masculinity in contrast to his enforced passivity and feminization, but also because his victimization enables them to escape a similar fate.[100]

4.3 ENTRY INTO A MAN'S WORLD

Two coming-of-age processes are especially important for male preadolescents and teens in HSCs: fuller entry into a "man's world" following circumcision and the boy's life-long relationship with his mother. Circumcision is expected of all Muslim males. By contrast, female

96. Reviewing literature on male sexuality in Oman, Morocco, Pakistan, Turkey, and Yemen, Murray, "The Will Not to Know," notes on page 17 that a sexually abused boy is expected to grow up as a heterosexual adult, in which case, Murray adds, "no one, not even those who remember it from personal experience, will mention his pre-adult sexual behavior in his presence (and probably not at all). His male honor depends on his conduct as an adult," 32.

97. Arno Schmidt, quoted by Murray, "The Will Not to Know," 20.

98. As indicated in Section 5.1, the severest threat to masculinity, and especially warrior masculinity, is to be feminized; that is, forced to assume the position of a woman.

99. Jim Wafer, "Muhammad and Male Homosexuality," in Murray and Roscoe, *Islamic Homosexualities*, 87–96, 91.

100. Fatima Mernissi says of Moroccan villages, "Most young men are resentful of being forced into sexual practices they abhor. They dream of getting married . . . [but] those suffering most from unemployment are from fifteen to twenty-four years old. When looking for a job for the first time, 83 percent of this group cannot find one. The young men resent the fact that older men who have more money monopolize and marry most of the young girls." See Mernissi, *Beyond the Veil*, 101.

circumcision is far less common in MENA and South Asia, although still common among many sub-Saharan Muslim peoples. Male circumcision generally occurs sometime between ages 5 and 13, with greatest frequency at the upper end of this range. Among educated parents in urban centers, the ritual is increasingly performed on two- to three-week-old infants in hospitals, but in more rural and conservative communities the incision is still performed as a ritual on prepubescent boys. As much a norm in the Muslim world as burial after death, circumcision is widely believed to decrease sensitivity to sexually exciting stimuli and is thus required if one is to have a chance at attaining *tahara*, or a state of purity. This religious-cultural ritual often is the boy's first decisive step in entering the man's world.[101]

The actual circumcision is typically proceeded by a procession and a celebratory feast and followed by congratulations and small gifts offered to the initiate; however, the psychological effects of the actual incision vary. Boys whose parents do not prepare sons with understanding and encouragement often feel humiliated and betrayed.[102] For a boy who recollects early physical comfort and admiration from his mother, the painful procedure altering his penis will stand in sharp contrast with prior admiration and protectiveness of his genitals. If the boy does know in advance, then he has probably been told that circumcision will be the first major test of his manliness. "The boys are expected to act brave and pretend they do not feel any pain during incision. Mothers place additional pressure on boys by insisting they uphold their parentage by keeping a brave face during the ritual."[103] If judged to have passed the test without shame, the boy has crossed the threshold of manhood: he has been through a trial involving acute physical pain while demonstrating courage. This is supposedly a life-long lesson that physical suffering, if met with strong will, heightens one's social acceptance and honor.[104]

Following circumcision, fathers become more powerful and decisive forces in boys' lives. Pierre Bourdieu refers to circumcision as a rite of

101. Abdel Wahab A. Bouhdiba and Abdu Khal, "Festivities of Violence: Circumcision and the Making of Men," in Ghoussoub and Sinclair-Webb, *Imagined Masculinities*, 19–31; and Aslam, *Gender-Based Explosions*, 110–11.

102. Davis, "Growing Up in Morocco," 30–33. On one occasion Davis attended, "the five-year-old boy cried heartbrokenly, a cry that suggested more than physical pain.... One of my bigger regrets was that I did not interview this child in the next few days....When I finally did ask him, about six months later, all he said was '*wellit sghrir*' ('I became small')." Davis, 33.

103. Aslam, *Gender-Based Explosions*, 110.

104. Ghoussoub and Sinclair-Webb, *Imagined Masculinities*, 21.

separation; its aim is "to emancipate the boy from his mother and to ensure his gradual masculinization."[105] While mothers see to nurturing the child, the common "folk mores" require than the father "develop[s] the boy's character." This refers to the process of instilling 'qal continuing throughout adolescence.[106] Training in 'ayb now focuses on protecting and supervising females in the family and exhibiting loyalty to the family, clan, and tribe. In addition, boys must be "broken" of expectations that they will get their way while others serve them, a bitter lesson given mothers' treatment of sons as young princes. The father's socialization is often harsh.[107] For Bourdieu, this "psychosomatic work" administered to boys consists of "stripping them of everything female which may remain in them."[108]

Senior kinsmen will insist on extreme respect and deference, and this must be manifested in strict obedience. Adolescents will be required to repress disappointment and anger. Because there is no customary point at which a young man leaves home to start his own life, young men may continue to experience life as frustrating. No male is regarded as truly an adult man until he marries, but marriage will usually depend on the wealth and efforts of his parents. Yet, even if married, an adult man will not achieve manhood until he fathers a child and perhaps not until it is a male child. Moreover, grown men, even if married, continue under the father's tutelage, especially if they continue living under the same roof. As Philip Carl Salzman notes, frustration "does not go away; it is stored and builds. . . . [B]uilt-up anger and fury can be transmitted to the legitimate targets, and be released, resulting in the pleasure of release."[109]

Repression and resulting aggression may account for Davis's observations in Morocco, such as her remark, "perhaps the most outstanding characteristic of late adolescence is the fact that boys are literally terrors."[110] As Davis notes, "Teenage males often abuse both sisters and mothers, who are hurt but tolerate their behavior. . . . One young man of our acquaintance was very sharp with female members of his family (he was brusque or silent with his father) and occasionally threw plates of food on the floor when he was especially irritated."[111] Yet, consistently blocked and frustrated by

105. Pierre Bourdieu, *Masculine Domination*, trans. Richard Nice (Stanford: Stanford University Press, 2002), 25.

106. Patai, *The Arab Mind*, 35.

107. Patai, *The Arab Mind*, 36.

108. Bourdieu, *Masculine Domination*, 27.

109. Philip Carl Salzman, *Culture and Conflict in the Middle East* (Amherst, NY: Humanity, 2008), 102–3.

110. Davis, "Growing up in Morocco," 31.

111. Davis, "Growing up in Morocco," 35.

males of greater power and status, younger males learn to identify with the power of elders. Salzman emphasizes that while internalizing loyalty to father and his kinship group, socialization does not include efforts to develop empathy. As Salzman says, "The question of whether 'my group' is right or wrong never comes up, because there are no external criteria that one is meant to judge it by. Rather, 'my group' is always right, because it is my group always."[112]

It is against competitors in his own age range that the youth seeks to assert himself, often with the assistance of family and clan. Hence Salzman's emphasis on "*sharaf* honor competition" and the "keen self-interest in rank competition, and the ways in which different groups may be tending to rise or fall."[113] Ernest Gellner wrote of rural Moroccan society that it "was agonistic—a tournament of wills . . . if Moroccan society has any chief guiding principles, it is probably that one genuinely possesses only what one has the ability to defend, whether it be the land, water, women, trade partners, or personal authority."[114] Salzman adds, "Ultimately public opinion is the judge, so observers from the public are also actors as communicators and judges. . . . Gaining strength and proving one's competitors' weaker raises one's rank. Deliberate strategies and tactics are employed to advance one's group. . . . Undermining other groups directly, either through neutralizing or attracting allies of other groups, or even seducing their women, are not unknown (although the latter is not well documented)."[115] The most basic principle governing conflict situations is to side with the genealogically closer versus those genealogically more distant. This is expressed in the ubiquitous Arab saying: "I against my brother, my brothers and I against our cousins; my brothers and cousins and I against the world."[116]

In the earlier stages of the painful transformation into manhood, boys may feel tempted to run back to their mothers and seek solace among those whose task is, so they think, comforting and indulging them.[117] Of course, becoming "a man" requires accepting that needing mothers is shameful; weak boys will be reminded, in no uncertain terms, that all things soft, caring, and feminine must be put behind them, and they will internalize the harshness of the authoritarian father. The result of this process is what

112. Salzman, *Culture and Conflict*, 103.
113. Salzman, *Culture and Conflict* 120.
114. Ernest Gellner, *Muslim Society* (Cambridge and New York: Cambridge University Press, 1985), 135–36.
115. Salzman, *Culture and Conflict*, 127–29.
116. Salzman, *Culture and Conflict*, 61.
117. Patai, *The Arab Mind*, 36.

Bertram Wyatt-Brown calls "primal honor," or the valorization of sacrifice, discipline, and violence as "morally purifying."[118] As I discuss further in Section 5.1, this socialization also results in a rupture between the feminine "world" of the compassionate, tender, loving mother and the male "world" of responsibility, competition, strife, and vigilance. A similar split occurs within the psyche of the male adolescent. Whereas nurturing love and intimacy had once been readily available, his very neediness now constitutes a terrible vulnerability for his mother possesses the terrible ability to unmask and shame him before other men.[119] Moreover, future emotional and sexual intimacy will be available only if he succeeds as the culturally demanded "man," although, paradoxically, such success will cost him the denial and repression of all that is feminine in his own personality.

Ambiguity and ambivalence in the mother–son relationship actually increases throughout adolescence and early manhood into a close and conflicted life-long tie. Further discussion of the contradictory effects of this relationship is postponed until Section 5.3. There the effects of a mother–son–wife triangle will be revealed as increasing the risks that females will be victimized by those with VPPs.

4.4 DEVELOPMENTAL INFLUENCES ON VIOLENCE-PRONE PERSONALITIES

This section offers a finer grained look at the ways coming of age and entry into a man's world promote VPPs and warrior masculinity. We must begin by calling attention to environmental effects that disturb development and that are well beyond the control of parents, caregivers, and educators. Many communities in the MENA area suffer from extreme poverty, high rates of unemployment, and considerable political instability and violence. A UNICEF report in 2017 indicates that in 11 MENA countries poverty continues to severely impact at least 29 million children or about 1 in every 4. These children are deprived of life necessities including nutritional food, adequate housing, safe water, quality health care, and basic education.[120] Many people live in abject poverty; percentages of those in the Arab world making less that $1.25 a day increased from 4.1% to 7.4% between 2010

118. Wyatt-Brown, *Southern Honor*, 34, 39, and 40. He adds, "If men believed these notions to be true, in some measure they were self-fulfilling."
119. Wyatt-Brown, *Southern Honor*, 52.
120. UNICEF Press Release, Rabat, Morocco, May 15, 2017, https://www.unicef.org/media/media_95964.html, accessed July 28, 2017.

and 2012. Moreover, World Bank statistics show that the number of people living below the poverty line was 26% in Egypt, 28% in Iraq, and 54.5% in Yemen, while in Gaza the per capita income in 2015 was 31% lower than it was in 1994.[121] These dreary socioeconomic conditions are not likely to improve soon as the unemployment rate for male youth (15–24 years) across the MENA region is 30% (30% of whom are university graduates), reaching a high of 60% for males in their 20s in Gaza;[122] moreover, much work is seasonal, in the informal sector of self-employment, and subject to frequent income fluctuations (e.g., up to 75% of recent labor entrants in Egypt).[123] Unemployment among young females seeking work is persistently high and often much higher than male unemployment; for instance, it is 50% in Jordan and Yemen and 65% in Egypt.[124]

These debilitating economic and social conditions are causes of acute and chronic stress that undermine caregivers' efforts even when the latter have the best of intentions. Stress is typically associated with the "fight or flight" response: perceptions of threat cause physiological reactions throughout the sympathetic nervous system, preparing us to fight or to flee. Familiar effects include a pounding heart, rapid respiration, focused concentration, and the energizing, or tensing, of the muscles. These effects occur as a cascade of hormonal steroids, known as the glucocorticoids and produced by the adrenal cortex, flush through the body. Perceived psychological threats (e.g., a perceived assault on one's status), whether or not they are likely, can trigger "fight or flight" stress responses. Temporary stress responses, even when acute, are not harmful. However, chronic stress responses produce toxic levels of hormonal steroids, such as cortisol, that have seriously harmful effects. Increases in heart disease, diabetes, high blood pressure, substance abuse, mental illness, suicide, and domestic violence are all consequences of chronic stress as well as of a depressed immune system and impaired capacities for attention, decision-making, and impulse control.[125] The debilitating effects of chronic stress result from

121. Adel Abdel Ghafar and Firas Masri, "The Persistence of Poverty in the Arab World," Brookings Institute, Feb. 28, 2016, https://www.brrokings.edu/opinions/the-persitence-of-poverty-in-the-arab-world/, accessed July 28, 2017.

122. William Booth and Hazem Balousha, "Trapped, Jobless and Bored: Gaza's Wasted Generation," New York Times, Aug. 7, 2017.

123. Richard Samani and Saadia Zahidi, "The Future of Jobs and Skills in the Middle East and North Africa," World Economic Forum, May 2017, www.weforum.org/docs/WEF_EGW_FOJ_MENA.pdf, accessed Jul7 27, 2017.

124. Mottaghi, World Bank Blogs, 2014.

125. Sapolsky, Behave, 125–27, 143, 437; and David Bornstein, "Protecting Children from Toxic Stress," New York Times Blogs, Oct. 30, 2013, https://opinionator.blogs.nytimes.com/2013/10/30/protecting-children-from-toxic-stress, accessed July 28, 2017.

difficulty in returning to homeostasis; hence the long-term effects of the glucocorticoids on the brain and other organ systems.

There are several ways in which chronic stress undermines parenting, aside from the greater likelihood of loss of the parent through disease, substance abuse, suicide, or family violence. Studies show that an individual can reduce his own stress or frustration through aggression against those weaker and more vulnerable, particularly wives and children.[126] Hence, chronic stress can brutalize fathers and older brothers who develop a habit of reducing the effects of their own stress by victimizing defenseless family members. Even when such brutality does not become habitual, parents suffering chronic stress are liable to sudden, apparently inexplicable explosions of rage. The glucocorticoids deactivate the prefrontal cortex and amplify fear in the amygdala, thus making it far more difficult for an individual to control herself.[127] It is not surprising then, that a child's tantrum, disobedience, or even an inopportune request for affection can trigger in parents their own feelings of helplessness and terror. Even parents escaping the worst effects of stress might experience depression and anxiety, causing them to be preoccupied, self-centered, lacking in empathy, and often indifferent to children. When children's typical behaviors increase parental anxieties or evoke parents' fears of inadequacy, then necessary responsiveness and support will be in short supply.

Supportive relationships with caring adults as early in life as possible can prevent or reverse the damaging effects of chronic stress in children. While the "blueprints" for brain circuits are genetic, these circuits cannot be completed and reinforced except through repeated interactions between the infant, child, and caretakers. Because of its plasticity, the brain is "built" and "rebuilt" through social interactions and experience. As Michael Vaughn writes: "early childhood relationships provide the neurobiological template and secure base for later cognitive, social, and emotional regulation capacity and are key in opening up learning potential."[128]

A necessary part of the developmental process is "serve and return" interaction between children and their caregivers and others in the family. "Serve and return" refers to an interactional pattern whereby a young child's signals and needs are met by appropriate and sensitive responses

126. The frustration-aggression, or neo-associationist, hypothesis promoted by Leonard Berkowitz has received robust corroboration. See Leonard Berkowitz, "Frustration-Aggression Hypothesis: Examination and Reformulation," *Psychological Bulletin* 106 (1989), 59–73; Sapolsky, *Behave*, 17.

127. Center for the Developing Child, accessed July 30, 2017.

128. Michael G. Vaughn, Matt DeLisi, and Holly C. Matto, *Human Behavior: A Cell to Society Approach* (Hoboken, NJ: Wiley, 2014), 161.

from caregivers.[129] For instance, when an infant babbles, gestures, or cries and an adult responds appropriately with eye contact, soothing words, or a hug, neural connections are built and strengthened in a child's brain that support development of communication and social skills.

Because genes and experience work together to construct brain architecture, learning how to cope with adversity is an important part of healthy child development. When a child's stress response system is activated within an environment of supportive relationships with adults, the physiological effects of stress are buffered and can be brought back down to baseline. The result is the development of a healthy response system. However, if the stress response is extreme and prolonged, and responsive caregiving is unavailable or parents are themselves contributing to the causes of stress, then the child's brain architecture—its circuitry and structures—will be damaged or weakened, with life-long consequences. Children are especially vulnerable to a toxic stress response; that is, to an excessive activation of stress response systems in the brain and body that derail healthy development. This vulnerability is multiplied when parental care is unavailable, care is highly unpredictable or inconsistent, and "correction" relies extensively on authoritarianism, bodily punishment, and shaming.[130] Under such circumstances, prolonged stress responses qualify as *toxic stress*.[131]

Toxic stress has severely negative effects on the amygdala and hippocampus, both of which develop early in life, and on the prefrontal cortex, which continues to mature throughout adolescence. The amygdala triggers emotional responses, and elevated levels of cortisol caused by stress generate immature responses to a widening range of perceived threats. As the center of short-term memory, a hippocampus saturated with stress hormones becomes programed to connect fear and anxiety with contexts in which threatening events were perceived, thus inhibiting learning, curiosity, and tolerance. The prefrontal cortex is the center for executive function that normally regulates emotion and thoughts leading

129. Center for the Developing Child, accessed July 30, 2017.

130. Persistent shaming is in itself sufficient to induce toxic stress. See Rebecca Eanes, "The Toxic Effects of Shaming Children," Positive Parenting Blog, July 23, 2015. www.positive-parents.org/2015/07/the-toxic-effects-of-shaming-children.html, accessed Aug. 8, 2017.

131. Toxic stress can be understood as the excessive and prolonged activation of the stress response systems in the body and brain, such as huge quantities of neurotoxic cortisol, that impair the development of neural connections in areas of the prefrontal cortex dedicated to higher order skills and the functioning of the amygdala and hippocampus and other organ systems, thus increasing risks of stress-related diseases as well as cognitive and emotional impairment well into the adult years. Center on the Developing Child, accessed July 23, 2017.

to action. Neurotoxic levels of glucocorticoids, especially cortisol, impair the prefrontal cortex's abilities to inhibit impulse control and aggression. These high levels also depress higher cognition, sensitivity, and empathy. According to Robin Grille, at their worse, the destructive effects of toxic stress are likely to produce "nervous systems that characterize remorseless fighters, and individuals hard-wired for hair-trigger violence."[132]

The cyclical replication, generation after generation, of persons inadequately prepared to assume the roles of responsive parents and caregivers is among the most tragic of destructive cycles occurring within HSCs. In addition to toxic stress and its damaging effects on learning, behavior, and health across the life span, childhood and adolescent experiences reviewed in Sections 4.2–4.3 make the young vulnerable to two other negative outcomes with life-long effects: traumatic bonding and negative attachment. Together with the persistent effects of toxic stress, these two dysfunctional outcomes are especially relevant for the formation of VPP and warrior masculinity.

Parenting and socialization for some male children will be so unpredictable, brutal, and traumatic as to result in traumatic bonding with their aggressors. Such bonding occurs as a result of ongoing cycles of abuse in which the intermittent reinforcement of punishment and reward results, paradoxically, in powerful emotional bonds with the victim's abusers.[133] Although the claim appears exaggerated, Patai characterizes the formation of the typical male personality in *The Arab Mind* as identification with the aggressor.[134] Traumatic bonding, also known as the "Stockholm syndrome," occurs because the victim perceives identification with the abuser as the only means of gaining safety.

The aggressor's highly unpredictable alteration of terrifying treatment and humiliation with kinder, friendly approaches makes it difficult for the victim to anticipate what will happen next. Moreover, the abuser's inconsistent behavior is combined with behaviors perceived by the victim as indicating that the abuser is not completely in control of the situation. For instance, the abuser may communicate that the victim's misbehavior makes him (the abuser) punish painfully and thus that ending the suffering

---

132. Grille, *Parenting for a Peaceful World*, 431.
133. Donald G. Dutton and Susan L. Painter, "Traumatic Bonding: The Development of Emotional Attachment in Battered Women and Other Relationships of Intermittent Abuse," *Victimology: An International Journal* 6, no. 4 (1981), 139–55; Nathalie De Fabrique, Stephen J. Romano, Gregory M. Vecchi, and Vincent B. Van Hasselt, "Understanding Stockholm Syndrome," *FBI Law Enforcement Bulletin* 76, no. 4 (2007), 111–5.
134. Patai, *The Arab Mind*, 36.

is "up to the victim." The result can be bonding in which the victim adopts the abuser's values, identifies with the latter's grievances, and emulates his behavior, even turning abusively on others. Such bonds have been found to be resistant to change and sometimes result in renewed cycles of violence, with former victims defending the abuse they had suffered.

In turning to attachment theory, a further dysfunctional outcome can be identified. According to John Bowlby, there is a biological basis for the child's propensity to seek an "attachment figure," a caregiver, to provide security when the child perceives a threat or experiences discomfort. The child's "attachment behavior" reflects the child's strategy for responding to a caregiving figure who is perceived to succeed or fail at removing the threat or discomfort.[135] Empirical research strongly justifies assumptions that there are a small number of basic attachment patterns and that these attachment patterns are cross-culturally valid.[136] Bowlby and his followers identified three basic forms of attachment: *secure* (readiness to be close to the caregiver, comfort about depending on him or her, and absence of worry over his leaving), *avoidant* (discomfort about intimacy and getting close, mistrust of the caregiver), and *anxious-ambivalent* (perception of caregiver as too distant and unloving and likely to leave the child).[137] Subsequent research has produced a fourth category known as "disorganized attachment" (a complete breakdown in the attachment process because of a child's inability to organize a coherent strategy for interpreting caregiver responses).[138]

In addition, Bowlby claimed that attachment theory "contains within it a theory of motivation," and he spoke of an "attachment control system" that serves as a "central feature of personality functioning throughout life."[139] Subsequent research has shown that Bowlby was correct insofar as threats to bonding that occur early in life contribute to the "unfolding of maladaptive behavior throughout the life course."[140] Researchers in the new science

135. John Bowlby, *A Secure Base: Parent-Child Attachment and Healthy Human Development* (New York: Basic Books, 1988); Vivian Prior and Danya Glaser, *Understanding Attachment and Attachment Disorders: Theory and Evidence* (London and Philadelphia: Jessica Kingsley, 2006).

136. See, e.g., Minna Lyons et al., "Patterns of Parental Warmth, Attachment, and Narcissism in the United Arab Emirates and the United Kingdom," *Individual Differences Research* 11, no. 4 (2013), 149–58.

137. Robert A. Baron and Donn Byrne, *Social Psychology: Understanding Human Interaction*, 7th ed. (Boston: Allyn and Bacon, 1994), 342.

138. Marinus H. Van Ijzebdoorn, Carlos Schuengel, and Marian J. Bakermans-Kanenburg, "Disorganized Attachment in Early Childhood: Meta-Analysis of Precursors, Concomitants, and Sequelae," *Development and Psychopathology* 11, no. 2 (1999), 225–50.

139. Bowlby, *A Secure Base*, 62.

140. Vaughn et al., *Human Behavior*, 49.

of interpersonal neurobiology hypothesize that attachment schema store memories that connect the orbitofrontal cortex and the amygdala, thereby regulating arousal, attention, and affect.[141] In this way, early attachment strategies continue to influence future brain developments and interpersonal relationships. As with toxic stress, negative attachment schemas correlate significantly with higher rates of physical and emotional illness as well as with violent behavior and problem behaviors from adolescence through adulthood.[142]

Children suffering from negative attachment typically adopt either of two modes of coping. One behavioral strategy is to become inhibited and withdrawn and to react to stress in a hide-and-freeze way. This usually involves complete compliance with the parents' demands at the cost of disowning one's own needs. Such a so-called *dove profile* combined with almost compulsive service is the pattern particularly common for young females socialized in HSCs (as described in Sections 5.2–5.3). More common among young males, I believe, is what Bowlby calls an "uneasy compromise," whereby the child oscillates reluctantly between compliance with parental demands and angry self-assertiveness.[143] Such children adopt a "hawk profile" and are prone to respond to interpersonal interactions as stressful events, adopting a flight-or-fight manner; they are likely to have high activity levels and to be impulsive, demanding, and combative, or alternatively, withdrawn and sullen. Because of poor impulse control and combative temperaments, such children are at risk for acting-out or externalizing inappropriate behaviors.[144]

Hawk profile males become largely emotionally self-sufficient or seek affection only from those with whom it is safe to bond (i.e., a group of peers, or "band of brothers," all having more or less the same developmental wounds). As Bowlby notes, "the picture such a person presents [as an adult] is one of assertive independence and emotional self-sufficiency. On no account is he going to be beholden to anyone, and, insofar as he enters into relationships at all, he makes sure he retains control."[145] Yet,

141. Louis Cozolino, *The Neuroscience of Psychotherapy: Building and Rebuilding the Human Brain* (New York: Norton Books, 2002).

142. Vaughn et al., *Human Behavior*, 59, 161.

143. John Bowlby, *Separation: Anxiety and Anger* (New York: Basic Books, 1973), Vol. II, 318. A third strategy involves the child adhering to his own viewpoint even at the risk of continued parental punishment. This strategy is less likely, I believe, when parental dissatisfaction can be exceptionally severe and hence dangerous, and where, as in HSCs, the child has little possibility of finding a substitute security figure because of conformity over expectations for proper behavior.

144. Vaughn et al., *Human Behavior*, 56.

145. Bowlby, *A Secure Base*, 50–51.

despite dependence on the regard of others, such males will tend to be egocentric in the sense Jean Piaget offered as "understanding and feeling everything through the medium of himself."[146] The attention of others, especially praise, is needed to compensate for the absence of an internalized representation of "care-taking" due to inadequate parenting.

The ego-centric and self-preoccupied child is a survivor of "scenes and experiences in which parents have treated children in ways the children find too unbearable to think about or remember."[147] Egocentrism is also a function of the child's need to focus vigilantly on information relevant to the self, excluding or shutting out a large part of the information reaching him. These individuals are, consequently, "high-self monitors" insofar as they regulate their behavior on the basis of external cues and the reactions of others, but also are strongly "self-focused"; that is, he is likely to minimize discrepancies between his self-concept and his actual behavior.[148] Again, due to the parents' own modeling of their self-obsession and little concern for the child's own needs or feelings, the child is likely to be emotionally detached and exhibit little empathy for those outside the band of brothers.[149]

For our purposes, we must emphasize the ways in which certain effects of traumatic bonding and negative attachment replicate or reinforce the outcomes of toxic stress. Where socialization processes make these outcomes abundant, as we must suspect for HSCs, then those communities will be burdened by an oversupply of individuals who are angry and resentful, insensitive, and potentially violent and who have impoverished capacities for impulse control, logical reasoning, and empathy. These are the traits of VPPs.

Let us imagine that traumatic bonding does not occur, nurturing parents enable children to form positive attachments, and the family protects children from many of the worst effects of stress. Even given these assumptions, we cannot suppose an HSC free from the effects of toxic stress. The unfortunate reality is that socialization within HSCs is fundamentally based on shaming, and it is doubtful that persistent shaming can have effects that are not toxic. As demonstrated in Chapter 3, to be shamed is to have the value of one's existence called into question; shame can induce psychological pain and even evoke terror of abandonment or

146. Jean Piaget (1935/1965) cited by Vamik Volkan, *Bloodlines: From Ethnic Pride to Ethnic Terrorism* (Boulder, CO: Westview Press, 1997), 136.
147. Bowlby, *A Secure Base*, 113.
148. Baron and Byrne, *Social Psychology*, 189–93.
149. See Volkan, *Bloodlines*, 101–35.

disintegration of the self. Hence, where shaming predominates, it is dubious that negative attachment and toxic stress can be averted.[150]

What are the expected consequences for a young man who has suffered the toxic stress of shaming? Following the work of clinical psychologists, Bonnie Mann speaks of "scene[s] of shame."[151] Briefly, a scene of shame combines two features: one consists of a cluster of mental, affective, and somatic stimuli (e.g., images, affects, desires, bodily states) that have become "bound" with shame. As Mann says, "If a child is habitually shamed for showing fear, feeling fear will become bound to shame. If a child is repeatedly shamed for expressing sexual excitement, sexuality will be a region land-mined with shame. If a child is regularly shamed for needing to be touched in a tender way, longing to be so touched will be shameful."[152] After persistent exposure, stimuli become operative on a prereflective but subconscious level but make automatic linkages with self-referential representations (e.g., from being called a "pussy"). The second feature of a "scene of shame" consists of a rapid succession of affective and cognitive states: feelings of shame give way to fear/terror, then rage, the activation of stored memories, rules for interpretation, and, finally, scripts for action.[153]

For the sake of illustration, consider a college-aged male watching a TV report about suffering children in war-ravaged Syria. While watching, he feels himself on the verge of tears (the stimulus), but representations of weeping have become bound with the shamefulness of infantile and feminine behavior. In turn, feelings of shame automatically elicit memories of being teased, mocked, and ridiculed and accompanying fearful states. Without knowing why, the TV viewer feels angry with himself, or the TV network, or women or children in the room; he abruptly gets up, changes the channel, switches off the TV, or leaves while repressing his feelings.

Obviously, this formulaic scenario presumes learned gender discrimination and the comparative worthlessness of "acting like a girl." The point, however, is that, although thoroughly internalized (as in my example) the process is the end-product of shaming that imposes control through a significant definition of the "proper" self and from without. A young man who has been shamed every time when those more powerful have regarded him as acting, feeling, or looking feminine will find the stimulus—whatever

---

150. Robin Grille and Beth McGregor, "'Good' Children—At What Price? The Secret Cost of Shame," *Our Emotional Health* Blog. www.our-emotional-health.com/articles/shame.pdf, accessed July 15, 2017; Rebecca Eanes, "The Toxic Effects of Shaming Children."
151. Mann, *Sovereign Masculinity*, 115.
152. Mann, *Sovereign Masculinity*, 114–15.
153. Mann, *Sovereign Masculinity*, 115, as reinterpreted here.

arouses "shameful" images, feelings, and the like—extremely threatening. Moreover, if our subject has been taught to believe that the only appropriate way to respond to shame is to turn off or shut down the stimulus, and he has come to believe that violent self-assertion is an appropriate expression of manhood, then it is hardly surprising that he will respond with anger and aggression when someone characterizes him as "a crybaby" or "a little girl."

It follows from this discussion that many predominant patterns of child-rearing, aversive training, educating for manhood, and socialization produce consequences highly dangerous for girls and women in communities for which norms of honor make aggression against females permissible, if not actually mandatory. It is not yet possible to know details about how combinations of deleterious processes increase the probability that males will be perpetrators. Finer grained causal analyses cannot be made. We are thus left with multivariate and distal causal factors that are nevertheless critical in shaping the characters of males most capable of fulfilling roles of willing executioners, thus making it easier for them to be "recruited" into the practice of honor killing.

CHAPTER 5

Warrior Masculinity and Female Victimization

This is the second of three chapters that focus on microcausal processes to explain *why* honor killings occur. Here I complete an analysis of honor killing in terms of agent-centric *reasons, reason-explanations* for the psychology of key agents.[1] We saw in Chapter 4 that child-rearing and coming of age often involve harshness and much humiliation and shame in terms of interpersonal relationships and socioeconomic conditions. Children and youth so raised will be vulnerable to toxic stress, traumatic bonding, negative attachment, and binding shame, all distal causes for what I call a violence-prone personality (VPP). Section 5.1 completes the microcausal analysis by showing how VPP is shaped into warrior masculinity in contexts where functioning as a true and honorable male requires systematic degradation of femininity and violent behavior. The transition from VPP to perpetrator is made through what I call the *shame-to-power conversion*.

While Section 5.1 completes an account of the causal contribution of perpetrators, Section 5.2 considers the causal contribution, if any, of others in honor–shame communities (HSCs). Section 5.2 is divided into three parts looking at the behaviors and traits of potential victims, at

---

1. Of course, the reasons why a potential perpetrator might commit an honor killing are not reasons we can expect members of honor–shame communities (HSCs) to understand. Until the moral transformation discussed in Chapters 8–9 is well under way, HSC members will understand their support in terms of "reasons" furnished by the norms and traditions of their own communities.

other female family members as perpetrators or supporters, and at general community members as facilitators. Section 5.3 investigates three conflictual "arrangements" in the organized life of HSCs that produce what I call *sure-fail mechanisms*. Tragically, the operation of the latter continually increases the risks that females will become victims of honor killing. Section 5.4 relies on social network theory and research on other social dynamics to assess the relative causal contributions of a key group who are not perpetrators but more than mere supporters and, hence, individuals I call *ardent avengers*.

5.1 WARRIOR MASCULINITY AND THE SHAME-TO-POWER CONVERSION

In Chapter 4, I made the case that males socialized in HSCs were particularly liable to develop VPPs which renders one likely to respond violently when one experiences intense shame. What I refer to as a model of "warrior masculinity" consists of a masculine identity construct that idealizes personal power and invulnerability. Section 5.4 ends with a simple scenario illustrating how easily anger and violence can follow shame. I continue to make use of Bonnie Mann's concept of the "shame-to-power conversion" to complete the model.[2] The model shows how shame reactions become embodied and include semi-automatic behavioral scripts for deflecting or shielding the self from shame. In addition, because many learned scripts for warding off shame require violence and self-vindication, they in turn reinforce warrior masculinity.

The connection of shame with fear of abandonment and self-disintegration helps explain why shame becomes embodied in a powerful way. Neurologists can observe the distinctive signature of shame—its imprints in the human body—and distinguish it from the effects of guilt.[3] Research on adolescents demonstrates an interrelationship among narcissism (an effect of negative attachment), shame, self-esteem, and aggression.[4] Most intriguing, recent research demonstrates that being ostracized (an extreme example of shaming) activates the same regions of the brain that are associated with physical pain. Moreover, excluded

2. Bonnie Mann, *Sovereign Masculinity: Gender Lessons from the War on Terror* (Oxford and New York: Oxford University Press, 2014), 108–36. I bear full responsibility for the use I make of Mann's analysis.

3. Michael G. Vaughn, Matt DeLisi, and Holly C. Matto, *Human Behavior: A Cell to Society Approach* (Hoboken, NJ: John Willy & Sons, 2014), 69.

4. Vaughn et al., *Human Behavior*, 144.

individuals will engage in desperate attempts to avoid "social pain" and regain attention from those who have snubbed them.[5]

The presence in the body of shame, Mann notes, is accompanied by bodily impulses to hide, to bury the face in one's hands, to hang one's head, slump over, drop one's eyelids, and cast one's glance downward. "The body collapses away from visibility."[6] Blood rushes from the viscera to the body surface, hence the frequently observed reddening or blushing, the sinking-heart or empty-pit sensations. Physiologically, shame produces a lower heart rate, increased skin temperature, and depressed respiration.[7] Silvan Tompkins writes, "the humiliated one . . . feels himself naked, defeated, alienated, and lacking in dignity and worth."[8] Louis Cozolino summarizes the effects of prolonged and unrelieved shame succinctly: "Alienated/isolated shame-ridden people die."[9] This is death via emotional starvation.

Because shame becomes embodied, *gender performances* are critical in efforts to alleviate shame. Gender requires not just the "proper" attitudes, beliefs, and behavioral scripts, but even the specifics for poise, posture, stance, and gait (i.e., for males: standing tall, looking one in the eye, holding up one's head, not letting them see you sweat, etc.). This extends to self-presentation, and, as Maleeha Aslam notes, in many Muslim regions men devote much attention to an appropriate body image. Facial and bodily hair are considered essential, and clean-shaven men are ridiculed for being soft-skinned; moreover, in many areas no "beautification" is expected of men, even on wedding days.[10]

Mann speaks of the masculine ideal of the "I can" or "can-do" body: "a body-in-the-midst-of-doing, immersed in its own action. The habit body undergirds and guarantees most of our skilled, coordinated, physical doing."[11] The male can-do body enables a man to act without deliberation or even conscious thought, drawing instead on the conditioned, skilled,

5. Kipling D. Williams and Steve A. Nida, "Ostracism: Consequences and Coping," *Current Directions in Psychological Science* 21 (2011), 71–5.
6. Mann, *Sovereign Masculinity*, 109.
7. Vaughn et al., *Human Behavior*, 69.
8. Silvan Tompkins, *Shame and Its Sisters: A Silvan Tompkins Reader*, ed. by Eve Kosofsky Sedgewick and Adam Frank (Durham, NC: Duke University Press, 1995), 133.
9. Quoted in Vaughn et al., *Human Behavior*, 161.
10. Maleeha Aslam, *Gender-Based Explosions: The Nexus Between Muslim Masculinities, Jihadist Islamism and Terrorism* (Tokyo and New York: United Nations, 2014), 167. For a fascinating history of ideals of masculinity and concern over gender appearance and performance in colonial Egypt, see Wilson Chacko Jacob, *Working Out Egypt: Effendi Masculinity and Subject Formation in Colonial Modernity, 1870–1940* (Durham, NC: Duke University Press, 2011).
11. Mann, *Sovereign Masculinity*, 131.

habituated, in-the-present body.[12] Acting *through* the can-do body offers the ultimate affirmation of personal agency and control (I am as I do) and masks all doubt and uncertainty. As Mann adds, to be like a man is "to act without hesitation, fear, compassion, thoughtfulness, awareness of one's inner life, or softness, that is, 'not be a pussy.' "[13]

Across all HSCs (and indeed in many other places), men perceive themselves as active, self-directed agents, and it is an insult to ask whether they really know what they are doing, where they are going, or whether they can "face it" or "take it."[14] Women, imbued with cultural norms, reinforce pressures for performance and "can be found teasing or mocking shy men and, ironically, even embarrassing such men by comparing them with women."[15] Writing about the Pukhtun (Pashtun) of Pakistan and southeast Afghanistan, Aslam notes that girls, like boys, are diligently educated in the principles and values of *Pukhtunwali* (*Pashthunwali*), the explicit code of Pukhtun honor. Girls and women are at times more strictly observant of the code; for instance, "women 'demand' that their men take appropriate revenge [for offenses] and the latter have no alternative but to follow instructions or else face *paighor* (taunts of cowardice)."[16]

The ideals of Arabic masculinity, or *rajulah* (*rajūlah*), Aslam claims, are brave deeds, risk-taking, fearlessness, assertiveness, willfulness, vigilance, and the willingness to defend the honor of home and community, as well as to uphold cultural definitions of gender-specific propriety.[17] Where the Bedouin heritage continues to be strong, such as in eastern Morocco, "heroic acts of both feuding and sexual potency" are memorialized and sung in front of admiring crowds, "making such events communal celebrations."[18] Of those she studied, Aslam says, "A Pukhtun sees himself as completely independent and takes orders from no one."[19] She adds, "they can go to any extent, even at the cost of their lives, to maintain their ego or 'stand

12. Mann, *Sovereign Masculinity*, 131.

13. Mann, *Sovereign Masculinity*, 109.

14. Aslam, *Gender-Based Explosions*, 114; David D. Gilmore, *Manhood in the Making: Cultural Concepts of Masculinity* (New Haven, CT and London: Yale University Press, 1990), 75–76.

15. Aslam, *Gender-Based Explosions*, 114.

16. Aslam, *Gender-Based Explosions*, 169.

17. Aslam, *Gender-Based Explosions*, 119; see also Lila Abu-Lughod, *Veiled Sentiments: Honor and Poetry in a Bedouin Society* (London: University of California Press, 1986); Gilmore, *Manhood in the Making*, esp. 40; and Julie Peteet, "Male Gender and Rituals of Resistance in the Palestinian Intifida: A Cultural Politics of Violence," in Mai Ghoussoub and Emma Sinclair-Webb (eds.), *Imagined Masculinities: Male Identity and Culture in the Middle East* (London, Saqi, 2006), 103–26.

18. Aslam, *Gender-Based Explosions*, 119.

19. Aslam, *Gender-Based Explosions*, 173.

by their word.' An honorable man is expected to do everything 'by taking risks.'" Moreover, they are "defensive of their identity and will not allow any damage to it—a threat they see as worse than death."[20] The Pukhtun honor code imposes the responsibility to take revenge (*badal*), and Aslam relates that they possess a good sense of "revenge historiography," adding: "Continuing a protracted hostility against the enemy in a no-win situation is closely seated [sic] in Pukhtunwali, which gives less significance to winning and more to 'not losing.' "[21]

Aslam frankly proclaims: "Pukhtun culture is largely egocentric." Ghanim makes a similarly bold but more general claim about the "highly exaggerated and inflated male ego."[22] The term "narcissism"—a clinical construct—is rarely evident in histories of the Arabic world. However, reading extensively the literature on traditional ideals of masculinity, one is struck by frequent mention of personalities and behaviors easily described as egocentric and narcissistic. For instance, David Pryce-Jones writes, in part, "Whoever judges that honor is due him must demand it. . . . A power broker must lay claims to a heroic past and strike attitudes accordingly, ascribing nobility to himself."[23]

Patai, drawing on studies by Egyptians Hāmid Ammār and Sādiq Jalāl al-'Azam, writes of the "*fahlawi* personality," said to be the "modal" personality type for men in Egypt.[24] *Fahlawiī* derives from the Persian word for a sharp-witted, clever person. Predominant features of the *fahlawi* personality, Patai says, are self-assertion, exaggerated self-presentation, and a persistent tendency to demonstrate one's superiority along with attempts to dominate situations.[25] In this context, to have a quick wit (*nukta*) is to be able to cover up or make light of a problem and to generate the appearance that one can take what an adversary dishes out and then top it.[26] "Self-assertion leads to the inclination to disparage, insinuate, and slander, to

20. Aslam, *Gender-Based Explosions*, 169–70; Gilmore, *Manhood in the Making*, 221.
21. Aslam, *Gender-Based Explosions*, 175.
22. Aslam, *Gender-Based Explosions*, 175; David Ghanim, *Gender and Violence in the Middle East* (Westport, CT: Praeger, 2006), 10, 208–10.
23. David Pryce-Jones, *The Closed Circle: An Interpretation of the Arabs* (New York: Harper and Row, 1989), 40.
24. Raphael Patai, *The Arab Mind*, rev. ed. (Tucson, AZ: Recovery Resources Press, 2007), 114.
25. Patai, *The Arab Mind*, 115.
26. An interesting comment recorded by Aslam suggests that the *fahlawi* personality may be more general. This Pakistani respondent said of his contemporaries: "Pakistani men have an imprint in their psychology. 'If I am a real man . . . I can make anything possible.' You start talking to a man and he will say: 'No problem—this can be done. No problem, I will do this now; no problem, consider this one done.' This is an ideal man according to Pakistani psychology. The fact is that *he cannot do anything* because of the circumstances surrounding him. When he fails, he starts indulging in whatever

belittle the value of others and their activities, and to scorn them; he who practices these arts is greatly admired and esteemed. The favorite character of Egyptian folklore, *Guhā (Jūhā)*, personifies and illustrates this negative side of the self-assertive personality."[27]

These observations converge on what one should expect: a product of negative attachment (see Sections 4.3–4.4) and adolescent experiences of continued shame, stress, and frustration. Research in the West demonstrates correlations among narcissism (as self-centeredness), shame, troubled self-esteem, and aggression.[28] The greater individuals' exposure to shame in social interactions, the greater their tendencies to become angry and engage in aggression.[29] (By contrast, similar connections were not observed between exposure to guilt and anger or aggression.[30]) Likewise, researchers find that narcissism is significantly correlated with anger, hostility, and both verbal and physical aggression.[31] In one particular study, narcissists were found to have fewer internalized negative emotions (i.e., they reported high self-esteem) but to be highly sensitive about social rejection and to respond with aggression to individuals who reject them, as well as to innocent third parties.[32] Finally, research suggests that narcissism as a personality disorder correlates significantly with defensive masculinity.[33]

As gaps between clinical psychiatry and behavioral and developmental psychology continue to close, researchers are finding that many

---

else is possible for him . . . be it smoking, dacoity, crime, murder, etc. Once they start indulging in something, they go right to the end as then it becomes a test of their manhood. They never quit halfway as that makes them *na-mard* [eunuch]." Aslam, *Gender-Based Explosions*, 204 (emphasis in original).

27. Patai, *The Arab Mind*, 115.

28. Vaughn et al., *Human Behavior*, 144.

29. See, e.g., David W. Harder and Susan J. Lewis, "The Assessment of Shame and Guilt," in James N. Butcher and Charles D. Spielberger (eds.), *Advances in Personality Assessment*, vol. 6 (Hillsdale, NJ: Earlbaum, 1986), 89–114; June Price Tangney et al., "Shamed into Anger? The Relation of Shame and Guilt to Anger and Self-Reported Aggression," *Journal of Personality and Social Psychology* 62 (1992), 669–75.

30. Robert A. Baron and Donn Bryne, *Social Psychology: Understanding Human Interaction*, 7th ed. (Boston and London: Allyn and Bacon, 1944), 64–65.

31. M. Brent Donnellan et al., "Low Self-Esteem Is Related to Aggression, Anti-Social Behavior and Delinquency," *Psychological Science* 16, 4 (2005), 328–35.

32. Jean M. Twenge and W. Keith Campbell, "Isn't It Fun to Get the Respect That We're Going to Deserve? Narcissism, Social Rejection, and Aggression," *Personality and Social Psychology Bulletin* 29 (2003), 261–72.

33. Adrian Furnham and Geoff Trickey, "Sex Differences on the Dark Side Traits," *Personality and Individual Differences* 50, 4 (2011), 514–22, reporting on a study of a sample of more than 18,000 British adults. See also Marco Del Giudice, Tom Booth, and Paul Irwing, "The Distance Between Mars and Venus: Measuring Global Sex Differences in Personality," *PLoS ONE* 7, 1 (2012), E-Journal, wwwncbi.nim.nih.gov/pmc/articles/PMC3251566, accessed Aug. 8, 2015.

psychological disorders share a common core. This core includes heightened assertiveness, high interpersonal antagonism, hostility, impulsivity, and, especially, the absence of negative self-directed affect. High levels of negative emotion are deflected outward due to the inability to accommodate negative self-representations within rudimentary and ideal ego elements.[34] Given this common core, it is very likely that, in men, narcissism and VPP are closely related, *assuming* that research on Western subjects applies to members of HSCs.[35] Certainly narcissistic personality traits are commonly thought to result from the same causes as VPP (Sections 4.3–4.4) and hence it is reasonable to be concerned about the possible overrepresentation of narcissists and VPP in communities that kill for honor.[36]

In fact, narcissism is a common male self-presentation in social groups for whom honor is prized and in which VPPs abound. As Andrew Schmookler points out, honor is highly valued in sociocultural groups where security and affection are scarce and self-worth tenuous.[37] In such hostile environments, or "psychic economies of scarcity," where, Schmookler adds, "the principle is the uncharitable rule—'Do unto others before they do unto you'—the symptoms of narcissism are most likely to be regarded as virtues and they are given a more glowing name, specifically: honor."[38] For Schmookler and others studying narcissism, a psychic economy of scarcity results in large part from the continual need of the narcissist to devalue other persons.

The urge to humiliate and hurt others arises from the narcissist's and VPP's (henceforth N-VPP) own past humiliations. Having deeply experienced his own vulnerability and possibly the violation of his own personal boundaries, the N-VPP will find passivity to be anxiety-provoking either because he is more easily a target of others' taunts, insults, and jibes or because inactivity conjures up memory images of past

34. Donald R. Lynam and Thomas A. Widiger, "Using a General Model of Personality to Identify the Basic Elements of Psychopathology," *Journal of Personality Disorder* 21 (2007), 160–78.

35. The question whether narcissism is a "personality disorder" and therefore "dysfunctional" is not a clinical psychiatric issue in this study. Hence it is irrelevant that narcissistic men in HSCs generally do not experience their behavior as aberrant and are not seen by their peers as dysfunctional. The approach taken here involves morality and reasoning. From this perspective, narcissism is highly suspect insofar as it contributes to the behavior of perpetrators.

36. While it is obviously not possible to estimate the proportion of males who have this (or a similarly) dangerous personality construct, in Section 5.4 we see why this is less important than it may seem.

37. Andrew Bard Schmookler, *Out of Weakness: Healing the Wounds That Drive Us to War* (New York: Bantam, 1988), 102–19.

38. Schmookler, *Out of Weakness*, 103.

wounds.[39] In a can-do warrior ethos, the fear of passivity and victimization outweighs even the values placed on courage and the discipline of the will. Being wary and suspicious, such persons adopt aggression as a kind of "armor" to cover the vulnerable core. Hence, by reverting to the can-do body, the N-VPP defends against anxiety; he expresses his entitlement to power and status; he seeks to outdo others and dominate them.[40] This point is succinctly put by Schmookler: "If I am the object of fear, then I need not be afraid."[41]

Moreover, already scarred by wounds, the warrior is eager to redress grievances; he is looking for a fight.[42] Conflict situations provide opportunities for "transference," that is, efforts to feel positive about one's self through belittling others. As Schmookler says, "the role the narcissist needs for others is the role he refuses to play himself—the role of the worthless one, the loser."[43] The pains of "losers" enables the N-VPP to feel good about the self, however momentarily. A further strategy is for such individuals to identify with others having a similar need for "specialness" and to mutually enhance self-esteem through becoming a clique or a tightly knit "band of brothers."

The brittleness of self, dependent on besting others and obtaining the regard of "those who count" explains why honor is so important. There is no complete self except insofar as others perceive one's success in maintaining the shield of honor. Pierre Bourdieu's point, quoted in Section 3.2, is exact: "the being and truth about a person is identical with the being and truth that others acknowledge in him."[44] It is through the "mirror in other's eyes" that the N-VPP with warrior masculinity sees himself.[45] Moreover, rage is typically this man's response to his perception that others have betrayed and wounded him. (Notably, almost all interviewed honor killers perceive themselves as the "real" victims.)

Vigilance will be the long-term result of the child's learning to be wary of impending parental violence and seeking to evade punishment. Rage is

39. Vamik Volkan, *Bloodlines: From Ethnic Pride to Ethnic Terrorism* (Boulder, CO: Westview, 1997), 162.

40. Volkan, *Bloodlines*, 161.

41. Schmookler, *Out of Weakness*, 71. See also, Elsa Ronnington, *Identifying and Understanding the Narcissistic Personality* (New York and Oxford: Oxford University Press, 2005), 86–87.

42. Schmookler, *Out of Weakness*, 129.

43. Schmookler, *Out of Weakness*, 102.

44. Pierre Bourdieu, "The Sentiments of Honour in Kabyle Society," in J. G. Peristiany (ed.), *Honour and Shame: The Values of Mediterranean Society* (Chicago: University of Chicago Press, 1966), 212.

45. Schmookler, *Out of Weakness*, 133.

an infantile reaction to shame, even to the smallest measures of disrespect, insofar as these reinvoke impressions of complete vulnerability. Hence, rage has no genuine problem-solving purpose; it exists instead to ward off threats of shame or end painful emotions. Rage is often disproportionate to its presumed cause, as reflected in the frequency of "overkill" and the humiliation and torture inflicted on honor killing victims (see Section 2.2.). Rage also lies close to the surface; a susceptible individual can be accommodating, friendly, and even charming one moment but savagely hostile the next.[46] When rage breaks out, it is often characterized by a loss of self-control, characterized by shouting, factual distortion, and groundless accusations—reflecting the agent's impaired impulse control and cognitive abilities.

Men socialized to find warrior masculinity alluring internalize scripts for "appropriate" performances. For instance, consider two men relaxing together with friends when one begins to make jokes. The joking comes too close for comfort for one when another male makes a jocular reference to the first man's wife. The man so degraded—as he sees himself—must negate the insult, especially if listeners appear amused. He might, if he is quick-witted, respond in kind and earn a larger laugh, or he might demand that the joker "take it back" or make some threatening gesture, such as drawing a knife. If the first man responds as desired, then this response "wipes out" the insult. The alternatives of escalating threats and then violence are also scripted.

A man will gain a reputation for being tough, and hence honorable, if he is likely to react violently to slurs, thus deterring challenges from others. Few others will be able to "prove" anything dishonorable against him. This is basically the same *pattern* a Pukhtun "warrior" exhibits when he regards himself as insulted; according to Aslam: "These are the moments when masculinity is invoked with great hopes: a test of the extent of a man's individual sense of honour, virtue, and chivalry."[47] No aggrieved Pukhtun is expected to rely on reason (*aql*) at such a moment; rather, he is expected to take out the sword (*tura*), brandish it, and make his countercharge. Usually that will confirm his courageous nature, and "the council of elders is expected to be rational and pacify the fearless and spontaneous man."[48]

---

46. David Thomas, *Narcissism: Behind the Mask* (Brighton: Book Guild Press, 2010).
47. Aslam, *Gender-Based Explosions*, 171
48. Aslam, *Gender-Based Explosions*, 171. Compare this account with Pieter Spierenburg, *A History of Murder: Personal Violence in Europe from the Middle Ages to the Present* (Cambridge and Malden: Polity Press, 2008), 9.

Rage is most often directed against culturally designated inferiors, such as uppity women and out-group members who fail to keep in their place, as well as against those whose approval is sought but not offered. Suppressed rage is a major source of enmity in marital relations, and it accounts for much abrasive and rebellious behavior among teenagers. Recall, for instance, Davis's account (Section 4.2) of teenage boys who smash dishes and throw things in the house, and consider the aftermath of an honor killing in Şanlıurfa, Turkey. In this case, a girl, Kadriye, had been raped by a cousin and killed by her older brother. Although honor killing victims often are not buried and mothers usually do not weep in public, an observer reported seeing Kadriye's mother visiting her daughter's grave. The mother began to cry, and, "at that moment her younger son (9 or 10 years old) warned the mother by kicking her and saying, 'Why do you cry after all? Cry for our brother who is in jail, rather than that whore.'"[49]

Those acceding to warrior masculinity often engage in grandiose fantasies about their entitlement to dominate women and other inferiors. Louise Archer reports that British Muslim boys she studied expressed confidence about dominating family females that was incongruent with the facts.[50] The boys stated that they "policed" and kept "their women under surveillance." They also reported that young Muslim women are "not allowed to continue their education," "have no choices in terms of future marriage," and "are forced to stay at home performing domestic chores for their families."[51] However, these boys were reluctant to acknowledge that their claims were contrary to reality for the majority of Muslim girls and women in Britain and accepted the truth only when pressed.

Prem Chowdhry suggests a positive correlation between a man's suffering a great gap between his ego ideals and reality, on one hand, and his vengeful insistence on traditional honor, on the other.[52] Undertaken in Haryana state in India, Chowdhry's study shows that young and unemployed males are most enthusiastic about sanctions against the "polluting effects" of breaking traditional marriage taboos within the same *gotra* or

49. Feliz Kardam et al., *The Dynamics of Honor Killing in Turkey: Prospects for Action* (Ankara, Turkey: United Nations Population Fund, 2006), 41, available at www.unfpa. org/sites/default/files/pub-pdf/honourkillings.pdf.

50. Louise Archer, "Muslim Adolescents in Europe," in Márta Fülöp and Alisdair Ross (eds.), *Growing Up in Europe Today: Developing Identities Among Adolescents* (London: Trentham Books, 2005), 55–70.

51. Archer, "Muslim Adolescents in Europe," 67–68.

52. Prem Chowdhry, "Crisis of Masculinity in Haryana: The Unmarried, the Unemployed and the Aged," *Economic and Political Weekly* 44, 49 (Sep. 2005), 5189–98.

violating caste, class, and status boundaries.[53] Likewise, in discussing what she calls "emasculated masculinity," Aslam finds that when patriarchal norms come under direct pressure, "men become more dominating, violent and abusive toward their women."[54]

As we would expect, factors creating acute and chronic stress dramatically increase frustration and aggression (see Section 4.3). Hence, the correlations Prem Chowdhry found can easily be explained by the frustration-aggression hypothesis. This is certainly true, but it is hardly surprising that disillusioned males who have N-VPPs are strongly attracted to opportunities for violent "self-redemption." In her study of 118 males (although in Pakistan and not India), Aslam found "a positive correlation between masculine constructions and the tendency to opt for militant-jihadist Islamism, currently often subsumed under terrorism."[55] Many men interviewed saw a connection between masculinity and jihad: "it provides them with an ample field of expression for authenticating the masculine gender."[56] Men made comments such as these: "men want to pose themselves as 'heroes' and they want to do all such activities that would make them look like a hero"; "they are brainwashed into believing that they will have *houri* [angelic virgins] in the afterlife"; and "[t]he test of manhood is not in training as a suicide bomber, but in *actually completing the deed.* Once they get involved in such activities they cannot escape [even if they realize it is futile] . . . they *complete the task to die as a man*."[57] Aslam herself adds: "there is ample evidence that anything involving action, war, militancy, rebellion and even bombing has a certain masculine charm, as most perceive it as somewhat heroic, *even if fallacious*."[58]

In addition to attraction to the shame-to-violence-conversion, those with N-VPP and warrior masculinity suffer from a form of codependency,[59] as incompatible as that may seem. We can infer from Sections 4.2–4.3

---

53. *Gotra* is a Hindu term for "clan" and it refers to a group, all of whom are descended from the same male ancestor. Endogamous marriage within the same *gotra* is prohibited by custom and regarded as incest.

54. Aslam, *Gender-Based Explosions*, 122–23. For a similar study of Palestinians, see Alean Al-Krenawi, Rachel Lev-Wiesel, and Mahmud A. Sehwail, "Psychological Symptomology Among Palestinian Male and Female Adolescents Living Under Political Violence 2004–2005," *Community Mental Health Journal* 43, 1 (2007), 49–56.

55. Aslam, *Gender-Based Explosions*, 209.

56. Aslam, *Gender-Based Explosions*, 234.

57. Aslam, *Gender-Based Explosions*, 209–11 (emphasis in original).

58. Aslam, *Gender-Based Explosions*, 210 (emphasis added).

59. The term refers to dependence on the approval of one or more persons such that the codependent person is excessively preoccupied with the needs and interests of these others in ways that go well beyond normal limits. See Anonymous, *Co-Dependents Anonymous, Inc.*, 2nd ed. (Phoenix: Co-Dependents Anonymous, Inc., 1995).

that *young women* in HSCs are prone to codependency due to "narcissistic abuse," a specific form of psychological abuse perpetrated by narcissistic parents who require a child to give up her own needs and feelings in order to feed parental needs for esteem.[60] The underlying condition of all codependency is that one's "own self-worth and value are dependent on the perception and behavior of others."[61] For this reason, psychiatrists recognize persons who are jointly narcissistic and codependent.[62]

For similar reasons, despite their defensiveness and reliance on the can-do body, individuals with warrior masculinity are highly codependent. They need others to maintain their perceptions (or illusions) that they are honorable as well as indispensable. These elements are expressed in intense homoerotic bonding with other males who possess similar traits, as well as service or self-sacrifice for the group.[63] Such men are known to die willingly to protect their "unit," tribe, or nation. Such men are often found in military service. As Bonnie Mann notes, "the point of basic training in the military is to convert devalued selves, through a process of punishing, to a valued collective fraternal self, to satisfy the urge for passionate belonging."[64] Herbert Sussman adds about the US Marine Corps that "being a Marine is a way of being. A man does not merely join the Corps, he *becomes* a Marine. . . . Once a Marine, always a Marine is a proud motto of the Corps. A man is a Marine . . . [it] is a totalizing life-long identity." [65]

Commitment to one's band of brothers is expected to be complete. This "male love" is, Sussman claims, "the *sine quo non* of the warrior and the basis of the intense loyalty, even to the death, felt toward fellow warriors." There is obviously another necessary condition for this intense bonding, and Aslam identifies it pithily: "Shame is the glue that holds the 'man-making' process together."[66] If a band of warriors has not undergone similar

60. James I. Kepner, *Body Process: A Gestalt Approach to Working with the Body in Psychotherapy* (London: Taylor and Francis, 2014).

61. Michael C. Graham, *Facts of Life: Ten Issues of Contentment* (Parker, CO: Outskirts Press, 2014), 12–67.

62. See Kepner, *Body Process*, 73; and Martin S. Bergmann, *Understanding Dissidence and Controversy in the History of Psychoanalysis* (Bloomington, IN: Open Books Press, 2004), 162.

63. J. Glenn Gray, in *The Warriors: Reflections on Men in Battle* 2nd Rev. ed. (Lincoln, NE: Bison Books, 1998), 59–95, and Herbert L. Sussman, in *Masculine Identities: The History and Meaning of Manliness* (Santa Barbara, CA: Praeger, 2012) at 33 recognize this homoerotic bonding as a genuine form of love that competes with other types of love, especially the erotic or romantic love of a man for a woman. Sussman notes that there is no special term for this form of love other than "brotherhood." Gray regards it as a special type of friendship.

64. Mann, *Sovereign Masculinity*, 133.

65. Sussman, *Masculine Identities*, 33.

66. Aslam, *Gender-Based Explosions*, 133.

processes of coming of age, marked by a psychic economy of scarcity, then codependency must be produced or intensified, such as takes place in boot camp. As boys, Spartans and samurai initiates left their families to live in communal all-male societies, a practice also followed among the Mamūlks in the *devshirme* system of the Ottoman Empire, and even in many *madrassas* today.

One significant consequence of mutual codependency is the need to preserve the boundaries of the group and, hence, of the self. Extreme violence may be the result of perceived threats to these boundaries. Writing on ethnic conflict, Vamik Volkan notes that when anxiety about identity increases, bonded group members are liable to shared anxiety and may consider a violently destructive response to the perceived threat rather than endure continued anxiety.[67] Hence, Volkan claims, violence, even war, caused by the fear of losing one's psychological boundaries can be regarded, rather ironically, as *curative* in the sense that the aggressive group attempts to *cleanse itself* of the externalized threat of contamination.[68] I follow Volkan's analysis of the externalization and projection of the group's shared but unwanted, or "bad," and the lingering concern that these bad and contaminating elements might return.

In this connection, note the obvious analogy between the group fear of contamination and the language used to explain and justify honor killing, replete with references to contamination: "impurity," "pollution," "filth," "rot," "spoil," "taint," as well as "washing" and "cleansing," etc. Note in Sections 3.2–3.3 that sexual purity and lineage honor—the purity of bloodlines—were important for an extended family or clan's *sharaf*.[69] The immodest woman, as the seed of corruption, must be "'extirpated from the 'body.'"[70] And "a woman shamed is like rotting flesh . . . if it is not cut away, it will consume the body. What I mean [a Pakistani merchant says] is that the whole family will be tainted if she is not killed."[71]

The psychological process known as *projection* is important. First, it is the primary means by which group members bond, and, second, it helps

67. Volkan, *Bloodlines*, 111–15.

68. Of course, the aggression against the "foe" is "curative" only from the perspective of the party perceiving a threat to identity. See Volkan, *Bloodlines*, 115 (emphasis added).

69. Samira Haj, "Palestinian Women and Patriarchal Relations," *Signs: Journal of Women in Culture* 7, 4 (1992), 761–78.

70. Richard T. Antoun, "On the Modesty of Women in Arab Muslim Villages: A Study in the Accommodation of Traditions," *American Anthropologist* 70 (1968), 571–697.

71. Quoted in James Emery, "Reputation Is Everything: Honor Killing Among the Palestinians," *World and I* (May 2003), www.worldandI.com/newhome/public/2003/may01/pub.asp, accessed Aug. 18, 2013.

to explain the negation and "outcasting" of feminine qualities and, paradoxically, the safekeeping of these qualities in devalued women. Hence a group's efforts to defend its boundaries helps explain increasing honor killings within HSCs in this era of globalization, especially within urban immigrant centers. The more stressful circumstances become, then the more preoccupied group members are with maintaining boundaries, including reenacting ritualistic patterns associated with group norms, values, and identities.[72] Studies of immigrant enclaves from Muslim majority countries strongly suggest that grown men are, as expected, more prone to "identity crises" than are their wives or children.[73]

Bonnie Mann reminds us that "real men" must avoid any connections with traits associated with images of "wimps," "sissies," "little girls," "pussies," and "faggots."[74] All of this involves "border maintenance" (a term Mann does not use), as can readily be observed by the obsessive need of erstwhile "real men" to "keep the cultural space saturated with contrasting images of . . . those who haven't shed relations to these names."[75] As Mann points out, a gender commitment can be viscerally held as "anchoring one's sense of belonging to a community and to a world," and, Mann adds, "one is unmoored if it is undone." A man may be "lost to himself" if his identity is shattered.[76]

Powerful anxieties about boundary maintenance relate to the traditional male fear of women as the cause of *fitna*, or chaos and evil. As Tahira Khan puts it, "uncontrolled female sexuality is thought to create disorder in Muslim society called *fitna* (evil) and imbalance in the Muslim family called *nushaz* (rebellion)." Connections between *fitna* in the public sphere and *nushaz* in private are causally reversible as well, for Khan adds, "*Nushaz* in the bedroom was presumed to bring *fitna* (disorder, evil) into the public sphere at the larger level."[77] Suruchi Thapar Björkert reports that pervasive concerns over the Hindu equivalent of *fitna* have led politicians in India to generate "pseudo-scientific smokescreens" to block reforms.[78] Opposing

72. Volkan, *Bloodlines*, 11.
73. Freshteh Abmadeh Lewin, "Identity Crisis and Integration: The Divergent Attitudes of Iranian Men and Women Towards Integration in Sweden," *International Migration* 39, 3 (2001), 123.
74. Mann, *Sovereign Masculinity*, 115.
75. Mann, *Sovereign Masculinity*, 115.
76. Mann, *Sovereign Masculinity*, 8–9.
77. Tahira S. Khan, *Beyond Honour: A Historical Materialist Explanation of Honour Related Violence* (Oxford and Karachi: Oxford University Press 2006), 95.
78. Suruchi Thapar Björkert, "'If There Were No Khaps [. . .] Everything Will Go Haywire . . .'" in Aisha K. Gill, Carolyn Strange, and Karl Roberts (eds.), *"Honour" Killing and Violence: Theory, Policy, and Practice* (London and New York: Palgrave Macmillan, 2014), 168–89.

reforms of the Hindu Marriage Act that would recognize "love matches," Chief Minister of Haryana, Bhupindar Hooda, and Member of Parliament, Naveen Jindal, seized on the notion that same-*gotra* marriages would lead to "genetic disorders."[79] Naresh Kayden, convener of the Kadyan *khap panchayats*, proposed that, without conservative restrictions imposed by *khaps*, "the crime rate would be twenty times of what it is now. Young boys and girls will start marrying in the same *gotra*, they will play loud music, girls will wear skimpy clothes—everything will go haywire."[80] The illogic of this reasoning states that a woman who refuses to obey the rules dictated by her communal *khap* is like a bacillus, and the immorality she unleashes will spread like a plague until everyone is infected.

Boundaries are critically important because they protect the self from all of those qualities that would betray a "real man" by undermining his reliance on the can-do body and, hence, his invulnerability. For those with highly abstracted ego ideals, and especially for those codependent on others, it is dangerous to own feelings and representations inconsistent with this pastiche of a self. Consequently, troubling and unacceptable ideas, feelings, and images are first repressed and then defensively projected onto other persons or objects deemed suitable for the embodiment of these representations. Likewise, representations of the better, or "good," aspects of the self will be projected and identified with persons, objects, or symbols with which the person identifies.[81]

Projection is a universal psychodynamic process in the formation of self and group identity.[82] For instance, as the child learns to appreciate cleanliness, psychologically speaking, he disowns his waste and begins to see it as dirty and disgusting.[83] Volkan introduces the concept of culturally defined "reservoirs" for both good, idealized elements and negative, rejected elements. Parents and other elders have psychologically invested in these reservoirs, and they socialize children to choose them as well.[84] As Volkan notes, for instance, when a group insists that an enemy's darker skin color and different smell indicates that "it" is contaminating, the group is rejecting the enemy as if it were feces.[85] Rising generations can be

79. Bjökert, "If There Were No Khaps," 171.
80. Quoted in Björkert, "If There Were No Khaps," 171.
81. Michael Jacobs, *Psychodynamic Counselling in Action* (Santa Barbara: Sage Publications, 2006), 109; Thomas Pitt-Aikens and Alice Thomas Ellis, *Loss of the Good Authority: The Cause of Delinquency* (New York: Viking, 1989), 120; and Hanna Segal, *Klein* (New York: Fontana Books, 1979), 116–19.
82. Volkan, *Bloodlines*, 87–89.
83. Volkan, *Bloodlines*, 113.
84. Volkan, *Bloodlines* 93.
85. Volkan, *Bloodlines* 113.

socialized to use designated reservoirs across generations; consequently, "transgenerational transmission" refers to the cultural continuity of a proper symbolic and ritual reservoir into which future generations continue to project and thereby invest, including such things as the *dishdasha* (male robe), swords, guns, and even rituals and institutions such as circumcision and honor killing.[86]

A serious difficulty, however, is that reservoirs for idealized elements must be kept safe against the possibility that projected negative elements "boomerang back" and contaminate the senders.[87] For instance, homoerotic warrior masculinity is also likely, quite paradoxically, to have strong homophobic strains. The possibility of passive receptivity must be projected as negative by those with warrior masculinity, otherwise there lurks contamination of dominant manliness through *"pleasure taken in being dominated for another's pleasure."*[88] Thus it is necessary for those with warrior masculinity to conceive of such pleasure as masochistic and feminine pleasure in sexual intercourse. Yet, even the possibility of such pleasure entering consciousness can represent the "boomeranging" of what is projected externally, and the fear that others could even think this of one can induce "homosexual panic," leading to a redoubling of efforts to repress such thoughts and project the unwanted fragments onto group-defined reservoirs of stereotypically weak and feminine men.[89]

Men with fragile identities will invest more attention, psychologically, as well as time and effort, in cultivating positive reservoirs of manliness. One example pertains to the significance of weapons for warrior masculinity and the fact that the intentional drawing of blood by a man, whether at a male circumcision, as an act of revenge, in warfare, or in an honor killing, is always "clean," unlike the blood of women in menstruation or childbirth.[90] Swords, knives, and firearms are widely associated with men in honor-shame cultures. For instance, in Pukhtun subculture, it is considered honorable for men to be able to use weapons skillfully, and "almost all men know how to fire a weapon as if it were second nature."[91] Weapons symbolically represent equality among warriors and the

---

86. Volkan, *Bloodlines* 43.
87. Volkan, *Bloodlines* 105.
88. Volkan, *Bloodlines* 105 (emphasis added).
89. Sussman, *Masculine Identities*, 150; see also Eve Kosofsky Sedgwick, *Epistemology of the Closet* (Berkeley: University of California Press, 1990), 185.
90. Women do not choose to lose blood; its loss *happens to them* either as the course of nature or victimization but not through "clean" agentic behavior, either by drawing blood or taking risks on others' behalf.
91. Aslam, *Gender-Based Explosions*, 167.

ability of the warrior to stand his ground. Weapons are carried wherever a man goes; he can never know when his honor might be challenged, and the weapon's presence will be apparent when even the slightest ambiguity arises. As one of Aslam's respondents related: "'Boy children are taught how to use a pistol at a very young age. This is very common all over Pakistan, especially in Peshawar. Handling weapons is not something very special for men in that sense. *They consider it as a part of their body and women stay away from it.*'"[92]

A similar point is made in *Love My Rifle More than You* by Kayla Williams, an American intelligence specialist deployed to Iraq in 2003. She offers a clear interpretation of the symbolic power of firing the rifle. "If the violent act is, among other things, a way of relocating the capacity to be violent (always) elsewhere, it produces the appearance that the subject who enacts the violence [fires the weapon] is impermeable to violence. The accomplishment of this appearance becomes the aim of violence."[93] The weapon is, as both Williams's and the Pakistani's comments illustrate, far more than a useful instrument: it is an extension of the can-do male body, that is, "a body-in-the midst-of-doing, *immersed* in its own action."[94] Of course one man's violence, or a group's, can be overcome by greater violence, but such a defeat is never a matter for shame. The Pukhtun, for example, "believe in a fair and tough fight,"[95] and a fight is always fair if one has the opportunity to defend one's self and die like a man.

Masculine warriors construct the feminine "other" in almost complete opposition to ideal male existence. Enemies and subordinates are also gendered as feminine.[96] Homosexual rape and castration, as they occurred in Bosnia and Kosovo, or by Col. Gaddafi's forces in Libya, are intended to terrorize through feminizing men.[97] Mann begins *Sovereign Masculinity* by relating the internment of a young Iraqi male, Dhia al-Shweiri.[98] Al-Shweiri claimed his torture and humiliation at the hands of US operatives at Abu Ghraib prison had been far worse than the torture (electroshock and strapedo) he had suffered under Saddam Hussain. "They were trying to humiliate us, break our pride. We are men: It's ok if they beat me. Beatings

92. Aslam, *Gender-Based Explosions*, 211 (emphasis added).
93. Kayla Williams and Michael E. Staub, *Love My Rifle More than You: Young and Female in the U.S. Army* (New York: W.W. Norton, 2005), 178.
94. Mann, *Sovereign Masculinity*, 90–91 (emphasis in original).
95. Aslam, *Gender-Based Explosions*, 169.
96. Joshua S. Goldstein, *War and Gender: How Gender Shapes the War System and Vice Versa*, 2nd ed. (Cambridge: Cambridge University Press, 2003), 333–56.
97. Joshua Goldstein, 356; Aslam, *Gender-Based Explosions*, 135.
98. Mann, *Sovereign Masculinity*, ix.

don't hurt us, it's just a blow. But no one would want their manhood shattered . . . they wanted us to feel as though we were women, the way women feel and this is the worst insult, to feel like a woman."[99] This worst form of torture imaginable, al-Shweiri added, was what made him decide to fight against US interests.

It is hardly surprising that warrior masculinity is built on profound contempt for womanliness, as Mann says. As explained in Sections 4.2–4.4, when initiated into the world of dominant men and exposed to unremitting competition and increased risks of humiliation, young men must also disown and banish from conscious awareness all that had previously been "feminine" in their personalities: softness, receptivity, and permeability. Hence, the shame-making attributes of the "mamma's boy," "sissy," "wimp," "wuss," or "pussy" and any admission of bodily or psychological vulnerability, need to be repressed and projected into highly abstracted representations of femininity and the female body. Because being womanly exemplifies being oppressed and exploited, the warrior male's boundary maintenance requires his hardening himself and contributing to female oppression while simultaneously repressing his own fragile self-worth, his slavish aspirations to belong, and a codependency that makes him exploitable by anyone able to control those needs.

We are able to appreciate how repression and projection, as well as the construction of reservoirs for both "good" and "bad" representations, relate to the shame-to-power conversion. At one point Mann says, "The shamed one's shame *converts* to rage, hostility, contempt, aggression; these reactions are just that, *shame reactions*."[100] Recall, however, that the most primitive effects of shame in the body are to hide or turn away from others, to collapse inward. Hence, the lashing out, the pushing away, the fighting back, are a secondary and defensive formation. In order for the successful conversion of shame to violence, a designated target must exist. Thus Mann speaks correctly of the "aspirational conversion of shame to power,"[101] and this is, in my view, what it means to live with warrior masculinity: young men are continually socialized to aspire to attain a "heroic" state of imagined infallibility and invulnerability and to force women to "absorb" their projected negative qualities.

---

99. Mann, *Sovereign Masculinity*, ix–x. Mann is drawing from Scheherizade Faramarzi, "Former Prisoner Prefers Saddam's Torture to US Abuse," Common Dreams.org, May 3, 2004, http://www.commondreams,org/cgi-bin/printcgi?file=/headlines04/04/0503-02.htm.

100. Mann, *Sovereign Masculinity*, 116 (emphasis in original).

101. Mann, *Sovereign Masculinity*, 135.

Previously, we noted evidence for links between shame-proneness and aggression. Recall that, unlike apprehensions of guilt, shame involves global negative evaluations of the self, rather than just the specific actions one has performed.[102] The cause of shame is a failure more than an error; it is a defect in the self. As Robert Baron and Donn Byrne put it succinctly: "it is the tendency of shame-prone persons to shred their own egos that underlies their greater proclivity for aggression."[103] The conversion of shame to rage begins very early in life and persists because it does not require constant processing: after childhood, intense shame induces a time collapse and evokes early representations of the dissolution of the self, and, hence, shame remains powerfully inhospitable. Now shamed, an individual undergoes the threat of regression and the reinvocation of unbearable fears, and, as we have seen, he projects these negative representations outward onto others. As with Volkan's account of projection, the shame-to-power conversion is perversely redemptive: as Mann claims, "it saves the degraded self, restores him to his world, secures him from the threat of abandonment."[104] Ultimately, masculine bodily action and being-in-charge is meant to supply its own justification: "'a manly man stands for stubborn insistence on himself' . . . To be manly is in fact to 'justify the way you do things,'"[105] for anything else is unmanly and, consequently, foolish, pathetic, and for little girls.

In ending this section, the dangerous ambiguity of the male construction of women must be emphasized. Women are gendered to bear two liabilities. To be female is to be *invested* with family honor, or *'ird*, and its associations with sexual purity, but not to be *entrusted* with it. In fact, girls and women are constant causes of male anxiety. For, contrary to investing their honor into something that can be kept safe, males contradictorily construct females as dangerous and uncontrollable. Not only are women weak and irrational, but these contradictory "creatures" are also constructed— through male projection—as possessing insatiable desires and the wily skills to seduce any man.[106] This is obviously an irrational process for there

---

102. June Price Tangney, "Assessing Individual Differences in Proneness to Shame and Guilt: Development of the Self-Conscious Affect and Attribution Inventory," *Journal of Personality and Social Psychology* 59 (1990), 102–11.

103. Baron and Byrne, *Social Psychology*, 465.

104. Mann, *Sovereign Masculinity*, 117.

105. Mann, *Sovereign Masculinity*, 180, drawing on Harvey Mansfield, as indicated by scare quotes. See Harvey Mansfield, *Manliness* (New: Yale University Press, 2006).

106. As one example of this fear, Mernissi relates the well-known fable in Moroccan folk culture of Aisha Kandisha, "a repugnant female demon." Mernissi adds, "She is repugnant precisely because she is libidinous. She has pendulous breasts and lips and her favourite pastime is to assault them [men] in the streets and in dark places, to induce them to have sexual intercourse with her, and ultimately to penetrate their bodies and

is no sense in assigning to women the responsibility for maintaining family honor when, by men's expectations, women are so ill-prepared to succeed.

This Janus-like construction of femininity is an almost unavoidable consequence of traditional upbringing and socialization, at least for many men with N-VPP propensities. Yet one wonders whether this maximal challenge—maintaining intact the family honor by ensuring the purity of family females—is itself a product of warrior construction. In Schmookler's view, despite having abjured their feminine qualities, men are aware that they cannot live without these life-giving resources. "The woman embodies, for the warrior, the core of life . . . she is the part of the world that is being fought for: she is the interior, the living energies that the lifeless armor protects. . . . It is with her that the warrior has a chance to embrace the life that grim necessity in a hostile world has forced him to deny in himself."[107]

Yet, given this psychological dependence on the feminine other, warrior males in honor cultures live with the constant anxiety of losing control of this highly abstracted and double-faced creature. Hence, in this psychic reality, one finds the deepest meaning of the sequestering of women; control of their movements; and imposition of the veil, *chador*, and *burqa*. Lama Abu-Odeh captures this point in a memorable way: "As he is busy cementing the blocks of 'his' women's walls (hymens, in the expanded sense), he is also, simultaneously bumping into other walls elsewhere (that is, those cemented by other men) . . . think of it graphically. Men throw their arms in their women's faces, asking them to stay away, and looking at other men warningly, they say, 'Don't you dare.' But that's not all that's going on. As they send their warning looks to each other, they are also trying to steal a look, a touch, a rub of other men's women."[108]

5.2 VICTIMIZATION AS A WAY OF LIFE

It may seem surprising that, in a book dedicated to ending the persecution of women, I emphasize the socialization of boys, male adolescents, and the development of VPP, narcissism, and warrior masculinity. I do not devote similar space to the hardships of girls coming of age, in part because

---

stay with them forever." See Fatima Mernissi, *Beyond the Veil: Male-Female Dynamics in Modern Muslim Society* rev. ed. (Bloomington, IN: Indiana University Press, 1987), 42.

107. Schmookler, *Out of Weakness*, 107.

108. Lama Abu-Odeh, "Crimes of Honor and the Construction of Gender in Arab Societies," in Pinar Ilkkaracan (ed.), *Women in Muslim Societies* (Istanbul: Women for Women's Human Rights—New Ways, 2004), 363–80, 373.

a number of exceptional studies do emphasize women's experiences[109] and in part because the critical formation of N-VPP perpetrators has been understudied. Most important, since the availability of a cohort of willing and able perpetrators is a *necessary* condition for honor killing, the focus on males in Chapter 4 and Section 5.1 is indispensable.

Is it possible that some women are socialized to become victims of honor killing or somehow contribute to the tragic social practice, apart from the ways all women are socialized as potential victims? Women do support honor codes, and some actively encourage executions. In addition, recall from Sections 2.1–2.2 that, on occasion, women have been perpetrators. At the same time, however, because honor norms require that males kill, female executioners remain the exception and usually act as surrogates for unavailable males. Yet, is there some overlooked way in which victims, other women, and community members increase the likelihood that particular individuals will be targeted? Answers to this question are subdivided into three parts. In the first of the following three subsections, I consider the possibilities of the "selection" of certain females for victimization based on certain traits or personal qualities that might differentiate some females from others. In the second subsection, I briefly consider the roles of mothers and other women in the natal family, both as perpetrators and supporters of the practice. Finally, in the third subsection, I consider what role general community members play in facilitating honor killing.

Behaviors or Traits of Potential Victims

In thinking about prospective victims, I distinguish between *social* behavioral traits and *personal* attributes, although this distinction is far from exact. Personal attributes consist of individuating characteristics such as temperament, personality, and personal hopes, desires, and fears, as well as obvious features such as height, eye and hair color, and bodily shape. Social behavioral traits consist of empirically observable roles or behaviors defined by communal norms and we-acceptances. Thus the latter are communally constructed: as I demonstrate, almost all of these traits are *imposed* on victims by the HSC (Sections 2.1–2.2). Certainly, victims behave "dishonorably," but only in the eyes of the communal group, and everything

109. See the Bibliography for works by Lila Abu-Lughod, Abdul Wahab Al Bouhadiba, Kecia Ali, Yvonne Yazbeck Haddad and John L. Esposito, David Ghanim, Deniz Kandiyoti, Nikki R. Keddie, Nikki R. Keddie and Lois Beck, Sana Khayyat, Fatima Mernissi, Juliette Minces, Nawal El-Saadawi, and Bouthania Shaaban.

else that does or does not befall them results from relatively fixed social meanings and behaviors beyond the victims' control. For instance, a female is more likely to be attacked if she is subjected to extensive gossip and if she is pregnant (Section 2.2). A female is less likely to be attacked if her family has considerable social capital and is able to demand concessions from a male paramour's family. (In one incident, the extended family of a rapist paid the victim's extended family "not to see" the violation.)

Are there are any other socially constructed traits that select certain females for victimhood? Researchers in the field of victimology refer to "revictimization" as a pattern whereby victims of abuse or crime have a statistically higher probability of being victimized again.[110] A person might be revictimized shortly after the first offense or, if abused as a child, revictimized as an adult years later. Risk factors are often environmental and cannot be easily mitigated by victims (e.g., residing where crime is high or having parents or partners with VPPs or with drug or alcohol addictions). Some sexually and physically abused children form inappropriate, maladaptive beliefs and behaviors that persist into adulthood. A common pattern involves victims who come to believe abuse is normal and who learn to expect it, thus unconsciously seeking it in the relationships they enter. This is one of a number of types of codependency.[111]

A second possible basis for revictimization is learned helplessness, similar to the "dove" response to childhood stress and negative attachment (Section 4.4). Finding themselves in abusive situations they have no hope of escaping, especially when abused by caregivers, children might regress to a primitive "freeze" posture analogous to death-feigning in other animals. Persistent helplessness continues well into adulthood, and some victimizers might be able to pick up subtle cues and be attracted to those easier to victimize. Learned helplessness makes for pliant targets since such victims exert little effort to fight back, resist, or even cry out. Afterward, victims often rely on psychological mechanisms, such as *just world thinking*, to explain away the suffering or minimize the significance of what happened to them.[112]

It is extremely distressing to think that previously victimized girls and women might be more liable to become victims of honor killings. The fact

110. David Finkelhor, Richard K. Ormond, and Heather A. Turner, "Re-Victimization Patterns in a National Longitudinal Sample of Children and Youth," *Child Abuse and Neglect* 31, 5 (2007), 479–502.

111. Terri L. Messmann and Patricia J. Long, "Child Sexual Abuse and Its Relationship to Revictimization in Adult Women," *Clinical Psychology Review* 16, 5 (1996), 397–420.

112. Sarah Wheeler, Angela S. Book, and Kimberley Costello, "Psychopathic Traits and Principles of Victim Vulnerability," *Criminal Justice and Behavior* 35, 6 (2009), 635–48.

that kidnapping, rape, and incest are regarded as violations of honor *by victims* suggests that revictimization may be common in HSCs. Given the prevalence of psychological and physical abuse across HSCs, a relatively large proportion of female victims of honor killing are likely to have suffered some form of prior victimization simply because shaming, beatings, and stress are so common for the entire female demographic. Hence, while it is possible that prior victimization is relevant to the likelihood of being a subsequent victim of honor killing, it remains questionable that it is a distinguishing "marker." In other words, because so many girls and women have been subjected to prior abuse, that fact alone does not help us know who might be victimized in the future.

Because many in HSCs believe honor killing has a deterrent effect, it might be supposed that girls or young women who persist in disobeying are more likely to be targeted. Some incidents do suggest this possibility; however, an equal number seem to have resulted in execution after a first offense, often on rather trivial grounds. In sum, at present, there is insufficient evidence that the typical victim differs in terms of social behavioral traits from the general but susceptible (of childbearing age) female population in HSCs, including the much smaller proportion of alleged violators/victims who were protected by relatives or the unknown proportion who committed "violations" but were not attacked. One might obviously object that, except in the least justifiable cases (e.g., looking at a boy on a motorbike or dancing gleefully in the rain), every victim chose to commit a violation of an honor code. To which I reply, yes, but the objection begs the question. It does not help us determine *before the alleged violation* whether or not there was differential selection; that is, why some females who disobey or infringe an honor code will be victimized and why some who did *not* disobey will be victimized (approximately the 30.5% of those charged but innocent) *in contrast* to those not victimized.

This leads to the intriguing question whether certain females possess personal attributes that make them more likely to be selected. Incident reports often describe the appearance, attitudes, temperament, or personality of victims.[113] Anecdotal evidence suggests victims were less inclined, as a whole, to toe the line and comply with authoritarian demands and were more adventurous and rebellious. Similar claims appear regularly in the secondary literature. For instance, Mustafa Hijazi says honor killing is

---

113. Holmes and I did not code for such characteristics in gathering objective data for Chapter 2, however, because such features, related by friends, family members, neighbors, or journalists, are likely to be deeply subjective and extremely difficult to verify.

"an act of reclaiming and deterring a woman who has tried to live for herself . . . an act of putting her back in her place as a tool that is owned by the clan."[114] Minoo Alinia makes a similar point, averring that for "women who will no longer be controlled by threats and beatings . . . murder becomes the only way to protect the system."[115]

A 30-year-old woman interviewed in Şanliarfa, Turkey added: "if one surrenders, then she is honorable; if you don't comply with, if you argue back . . . then you are dishonorable. If you have a free soul, you cannot be honorable."[116] The same is said about defying tradition due to being in love: as another informant from Turkey says, "in a tribe, you are not allowed to love. If a girl loves someone they will kill her, they will not let her live."[117] Alinia notes: "A child must not be produced based on individual desire. It is the family that decides with whom women should produce children."[118] Khan adds with equal bluntness: "marriage and reproduction belongs to the group that seeks to reproduce itself."[119]

There are thus possible grounds for a highly speculative hypothesis that girls in HSCs who are not completely socialized (and often reported by parents as troublesome) or who are more curious, independent-minded, adventurous, or otherwise stand out also bear greater risks of becoming victims. (As for "standing out," those reviewing photographs of victims continually remark on how many are beautiful or striking; but then we must ask: Were only photos of good-looking and striking victims publicized?) Are less obedient girls and those most curious and adventurous—freer spirits—being systematically or disproportionately eliminated? Given general adversity in HSCs to nonconformity and the need for bound group identity, it is interesting to speculate whether members have a motivational bias for eliminating females who challenge these boundaries. Perhaps, it might be suggested, the elimination of females with certain personal characteristics is in some way functional for the social group, apart (presumably) from we-acceptances about the supposed "benefits" of killing some to deter future honor violators.

---

114. Mustafa Hijazi, "Social Backwardness" [in Arabic], quoted and translated by Danielle Hoyek, Rafif Rida Sidawi, and Amir Abu Mrad in "Murder of Women in Lebanon: 'Crimes of Honour,'" in Lynn Welchman and Sara Hossain (eds.), *"Honour": Crimes, Paradigms, and Violence Against Women* (London and New York: Zed, 2005), 110–36, 132.

115. Minoo Alinia, *Honor and Violence Against Women in Iraqi Kurdistan* (New York: Palgrave Macmillan, 2013), 72.

116. Interviewee quoted in Filiz Kardam et al., *The Dynamics of Honor Killing*, 7.

117. Interviewee quoted in Kardam, *The Dynamics of Honor Killing*, 19.

118. Alinia, *Honor and Violence Against Women in Iraqi Kurdistan*, 130.

119. Khan, *Beyond Honour*, 36.

As interesting as such speculations are, there is not yet sufficient empirical data to either corroborate or dismiss them. There is no way of reliably knowing antecedently whether victims differed in possessing nonconforming or other unusual personal qualities. Given that many reports and annotations of honor killings are made by feminist and women's human rights groups, adjectives such as "free spirit" or "adventurous" may be used emotively and prescriptively in solidarity with victims. Usage of such terms may be analytical as well: anyone defying unjust traditions in HSCs might automatically qualify as brave and adventurous. It is also possible that females who are more curious, independent-minded, and adventurous might be more likely to take risks than timid peers. And perhaps it is the misfortune of risk-takers to be found out or spied on in circumstances that provoke gossip. If such possibilities are facts, they could explain why a greater proportion of victims are adventurous; but it would not show that members of HSCs are intentionally selecting such girls to be framed, or falsely accused, and then eliminated.

Even if there is some function fulfilled by systemic selection and sacrifice (Section 6.1), it does not follow that members of HSCs are consciously aware of it. Scapegoating theories have been proposed to explain increases in prejudice and violence against minority groups during times of economic hardship or decline, such as the lynching of blacks in the American South or ethnic conflicts in Eastern Europe.[120] As previously noted, females from families with considerable social capital, including wealth, are less likely to be attacked than females in families with less social capital. However, an HSC is a remarkably homogeneous group, excluding outsiders virtually by definition. Thus, although rife with *sharaf* competitions, there are not distinctive ethnic, racial, or religious minorities to be scapegoated. Moreover, scapegoating is most likely to occur when a group has experienced difficult and prolonged stress, for example, due to an economic downturn or military conflict or occupation. Even anecdotal reports (in the absence of reliable studies) that honor killings increase in areas of political and military conflict (e.g., Afghanistan, Gaza, Iraq, Syria, and Yemen) do not suggest a pattern apart from the presence of extreme stress.

As I noted, some evidence suggests an increasing global incidence of honor killing (Section 1.3). However, it seems far more likely that

---

120. See Carl Iver Hovland and Robert R. Sears, "Minor Studies of Aggression: VI Correlation of Lynching with Economic Indices," *Journal of Psychology: Interdisciplinary and Applied* 9 (1940), 301–10; Edwin Poppe, "Effects of Changes in GNP and Perceived Group Characteristics on National and Ethnic Stereotypes in Central and Eastern Europe," *Journal of Applied Psychology* 31, 8 (2001), 1689–709.

increasing incidents in areas of severe dislocation do not result from scape-goating per se but are secondary consequences of the deleterious effects of increased insecurity and psychic scarcity on warrior masculinity. This result is suggested by Aslam's study of Pakistani men: men undergoing such life challenges are likely to be even more vigilant, aggressive, and vengeful (Section 5.1). In addition, given the fact that many strictures of life in HSCs are contrary to normal human desires and impulses while others require inconsistent behavior patterns (points stressed in a following subsection and Section 5.3), it seems, sadly enough, that at least some women have difficulty conforming to these exigencies and end up as victims by accident if not as a matter of course. What requires explanation, then, is not some scapegoating process, but why these contradictory social patterns should have arisen and why they persist.

Female Family Members as Perpetrators and Supporters

Sections 2.1–2.2 provide data culled from the Churchill-Holmes study and other major empirical findings about the participation of women in honor killing. Do any of the mothers who are not complicit actively resist or protest the decisions to kill? At present, it is not possible to answer this question because case studies usually do not include in-depth information about the prior behavior of family members (other than the victim) unless they participate actively in the murder. In Ayse Onal's in-depth interviews, of the 8 (out of 10) narrative accounts in which mothers' attitudes and actions are known, half supported the execution (sometimes vehemently) and half objected, and, in one case, an objecting mother was herself shot.[121]

What contribution do women make, if any, to sustaining honor killing? Given the extensive socialization of women since childhood, it would be surprising if a larger number did openly oppose and resist honor killings. Women's compliance can be expected to be brutally enforced through beatings and threats of death. Moreover, patriarchy is extremely successful in effecting women's own internalization of the construction of femininity and cultural norms. As Catriona Mackenzie elaborates, "Oppression works best when the process of naturalizing oppression actually structures both

---

121. Ayse Onal, *Honour Killing: Stories of Men Who Kill* (London: Saqi, 2008). In one instance, a mother had her husband, who opposed the execution, physically restrained and demanded that her son kill her daughter. In the case in which the objecting mother was herself shot, it appears her husband-killer suspected her of complicity in his daughter's "sins."

the oppresseds' beliefs about themselves and their modes of relation to the world, that is, when the oppressed constrain their own possibilities, while believing that these possibilities are constrained by some natural, inescapable facts about themselves. In other words, the hallmark of oppression is its invisibility to the oppressed."[122]

Bourdieu, who developed the concept of "symbolic violence," says domination is "the product of an incessant (and therefore ahistorical) labor of reproduction." Repeatedly inculcated through multitudinous acts of instruction, imitation, repetition, correction, and repression, women's cognition of their subordination is "doxic acceptance"; it does not need to be thought about, and, in this sense "'makes' the symbolic violence which it undergoes."[123] As Georges Tarabishi notes, "She will internalize oppression and end up becoming her own oppressor."[124] Ghanim adds that, "in order to make sense of violence, suffering, and subjugation," women will rely upon the dominant system of social values they have internalized "that form the basis for their subordination and oppression as their own traditions."[125]

It is therefore a tragic consequence of women's common experiences of suffering and subordination that they do not generate solidarity in opposition to male gender violence. Unfortunately, therefore, insofar as women can exercise agency at all, it is primarily exercised through active roles in enforcing patriarchal control over other subordinated women.[126] Women also enforce patriarchal control through the institutionalization of the mother-in-law as a patriarchal "office" intervening in the lives of other women (e.g., arranging marriages) and policing their behavior through spying and gossiping.

It is not surprising, therefore, that even though many women suffer from gender violence, many, if not most, also idealize violence. As Ghanim points out, "men who are perceived to be attractive and desirable by women are those who are violent."[127] He adds, "it is perceived to be humiliating for women to not be married to a real man. Yet, a real man, in the patriarchal

122. Catriona MacKenzie, "A Certain Lack of Symmetry: Beauvoir on Autonomous Agency and Women's Embodiment," in Ruth Evans (ed.), *Simone de Beauvoir's The Second Sex: New Interdisciplinary Essays* (Manchester: Manchester University Press, 1998), 135–36.

123. Bourdieu, *Masculine Domination*, 42, 34.

124. Georges Tarabishi, *Women Against Her Sex: A Critique of Nawal el-Saadawi* (London: Saqi, 1989), 38.

125. Ghanim, *Gender and Violence in the Middle East*, 124.

126. Ghanim, *Gender and Violence in the Middle East*, 101–02.

127. Ghanim, *Gender and Violence in the Middle East*, 118.

context, is highly masculine, authoritarian, and expects servitude from women. The opposite type of man is considered by women themselves to be feminine."[128] The internalization of cultural norms also explains the otherwise surprising results of opinion polls among women, such as the report that 42% of young Qatari women condone the use of violence and abuse against their gender, believing that abused women deserve physical abuse.[129]

The critical meaning of *female* is, first, not being male, and second, keeping the family's honor safe. As one interviewee said, "When honor is lost the girl has no meaning."[130] Ghanim adds that the girl is "a burden, a reminder of bad luck, a boy that was not born. . . . Her birth is a transgression, and therefore, the girl is despised and rejected."[131] Although this sentiment is not universal in even the most tradition-bound communities, Ghanim finds the way a mother treats her daughter and responds to her plight "remarkable considering the mother herself has suffered from the very same social consequences her entire life."[132] The birth of the unwanted and unwelcome daughter occasions the mother's guilt, sorrow, and shame and reawakens her own feelings of being degraded, unacceptable, and hopeless. Resentment toward her own brutal treatment is involuntarily and subconsciously projected onto her daughter.

In this way, as Ghanim notes, the social mediation of the mother's role is the negation of her daughter's free will: "She will force her daughter . . . to surrender to the very same gender system that she herself has surrendered to, and in this way she will make sense of her own suffering . . . as the inevitable destiny of all women."[133] As paradoxical as it may seem, the "patriarchal bargain" for a mother's suppression and suffering is her own elevation to an authoritarian position as a mother-in-law.[134] Reporting about the 35 years she observed life in an Iranian village, Erika Friedl writes: "Older married women remember without fondness the days when they worked 'like servants' in their in-laws' house, enduring hard work, unwanted sex, insufficient food, and many pregnancies while still in their teens."[135] Should

---

128. Ghanim, *Gender and Violence in the Middle East*, 118.
129. Cited by Ghanim, *Gender and Violence in the Middle East*, 31, n. 44.
130. Cited in Kardam, *The Dynamics of Honor Killing*, 18.
131. Ghanim, *Gender and Violence in the Middle East*, 70.
132. Ghanim, *Gender and Violence in the Middle East*, 144.
133. Ghanim, *Gender and Violence in the Middle East*, 144–45.
134. Ghanim, *Gender and Violence in the Middle East*, 149–64.
135. Erika Friedl, "Sources of Female Power in Iran," in Mahnaz Afkhami and Erika Friedl (eds.), *In the Eye of the Storm: Women in Post-Revolutionary Iran* (London: I. B. Tauris, 1994), 151–88, 163.

there arise a publicly known and serious conflict between the males of the family and an allegedly wayward female, it is hardly surprising a mother will side with males in the family and against her daughter, just as, Ghanim notes, the mother-in-law's opposition to her daughter-in-law is a "betrayal of the oppressed in favor of the oppressor."[136] Sympathy and solidarity sufficient to challenge the patriarchal and tradition-bound system continue to be in tragically short supply, even among the oppressed.

General Community Members as Facilitators

Turning to roles of nonfamily members in the community, we can expect that significant numbers applaud or support honor killings.[137] There are two reasons for this support: first, they obviously regard honor as indispensable to their way of life, and, second, they believe such executions deter further breaches of the honor code. A failure to execute will be seen as undermining the honor code and threatening the collectively shared identity; moreover, if the deterrent effect is not promoted, then an onlooker must believe that he and his own family will face a greater chance of being in this dreaded predicament.

People are often confused about the real causes for their actions and sometimes are confused about the actual reasons for acting in one way rather than another.[138] Assertions about the need to cleanse honor with blood are often repeated but never actually explained[139] (Section 2.2). Claims about the importance and meaning of honor are exceptionally abstract and often reflect dumbfounding. Certain truths are "known" viscerally: "It seems to be something they just know and feel in their bones."[140] In my view, this is exactly what one should expect when representations of honor and purity serve subconsciously as reservoirs for good projections (Section 5.1). Because the process of projection is subconscious, it achieves its effect through shortcutting rational processing or even conscious awareness. I am interested in exploring other possible mechanisms leading

136. Ghanim, *Gender and Violence in the Middle East*, 155.
137. See Section 4.5 for a finer grained analysis of "significant numbers."
138. Jonathan Haidt, *The Righteous Mind: Why Good People Are Divided by Politics and Religion* (New York: Vintage, 2012), 32–83.
139. Phrases such as "cleanse honor with blood" serve as metaphors or frames that serve to activate neural pathways by bypassing conscious awareness. See George Lakoff, *The Political Mind: Why You Can't Understand 21st Century Politics with an 18th Century Brain* (New York: Viking, 2008), 12–13, 25, 232.
140. Alinia, *Honor and Violence Against Women in Iraqi Kurdistan*, 64.

community members to support honor killing in ways that they do not or cannot consciously grasp.

One point to notice is that where honor has zero-sum attributes and there are keen *sharaf* competitions, it can be expected that envy and resentment will flourish. "Honor is the cultural currency in which the ordinary people . . . trade, and often one person's honorable gain is another's loss."[141] Indeed, envy appears to be a necessary condition for honor–shame cultures precisely because envy, as a form of distress, is the "symptom . . . of the human tendency to evaluate one's well-being comparatively, by assessing how well one is doing in comparison with others."[142] Thinking that their own self-worth is diminished by others' success, they desire that rivals lose benefits they do not possess. In addition, studies involving brain scans show that envy is correlated with *schadenfreude*, the feelings of pleasure or joy at another's misfortune or loss.[143] Honor-hungry individuals often present an aura of high self-regard which masks low esteem, and studies show that people with lower self-esteem are more likely to experience *schadenfreude* than are those with higher self-esteem[144] (Sections 4.3–4.4 and 5.1).

Moreover, studies show that envy and resentment may be motives for "mobbing"; that is, concerted efforts to create a hostile environment— through innuendo, rumor, and public discrediting—directed at isolating and compromising a target.[145] Mobbing has been studied primarily within the workplace and occurs most frequently when working relations are dysfunctional. People prone to mobbing, like bullies, have inflated but fragile egos, and, because the mobbing-prone think too highly of themselves, they are frequently envious of others who deflect praise and admiration away from themselves, thus robbing them of what they regard as their just due. Hence it is not surprising to discover that organizational scientists regard mobbing victims as generally more qualified or better performers than those who attack them.

Something very similar to mobbing appears to occur in HSCs. The alleged violator's family is hounded with rumors, gossip, slurs, and hostile

141. Bowman, *Honor*, 19

142. Justin D'Arms, "Envy," in *Stanford Encyclopedia of Philosophy* (Winter 2013 Edition), Edward N. Zalta (ed.), http://platostanford.edu/archives/win2013/entries/envy, accessed Jul. 23, 2015.

143. Hidehiko Takahashi et al., "When Your Gain Is My Pain and Your Pain Is My Gain: Neural Coordinates of Envy and Schadenfreude," *Science* 323 (2009), 937–39.

144. Warren St. John, "Sorrow So Sweet: A Guilty Pleasure in Another's Woe," *New York Times*, Aug. 24, 2002.

145. Noa Davenport, Ruth D. Schwartz, and Gail Pursell Elliot, *Mobbing: Emotional Abuse in the American Workplace*, 3rd ed. (Ames, IA: Civil Society Publishing, 2005).

comments; they may be spat on, socially isolated, and their homes may be attacked with graffiti and broken windows. Note, however, that in such cases the subsequent victim is not the object of mobbing; rather, *her family* is targeted. If gossip might count as a form of mobbing, what characteristics or patterns relating to a family's position, such as sudden changes in wealth or status, might make families likely targets of mobbing? But such evidence is simply absent at present. Rather than some specific trait or characteristic of a potential victim or family, the present picture is one of pervasive one-upmanship, rampant domination, aggression, and a winner–loser mentality. Given conditions of psychic scarcity, when one stands to gain by another's fall, then few can resist the temptation to make an impression by passing along particularly damning gossip or turning another's troubles to one's own advantage if possible.

5.3 SURE-FAIL MECHANISMS AND THE PRODUCTION OF VICTIMS

Given the presence of honor killing as an established social practice and males primed to assume roles within it, the rather regular (and possibly increasing) supply of victims most probably results from a combination of social expectations which are too stringent to be followed with uniformity, plus tensions caused by sociocultural contradictions within the collectivity. In effect, sociocultural contradictions generate *sure-fail mechanisms* that systematically and regularly operate (and are continually reconstituted) to make victims available. Here, I briefly discuss the most prominent sure-fail mechanisms.

If systemic victimization results from a dysfunctional social system, then no questions about scapegoating need arise. Instead, the interesting question is why dysfunctional systems evolved culturally and why they persist (Chapter 6). In addition, there is no need to postulate particular characteristics of female victims making them more liable for selection. Instead, potential victims encounter a perfect storm of sorts. They possess desires, temptations, and inhibitions, not just normal for their sociocultural groups, but also probably *exacerbated* by life in HSCs. In effect, social relations are constructed in ways that make it difficult for women to avoid condemnation. For instance, the unnatural segregation of the sexes and male predation generate tensions: a girl is raped, or she is discovered (or alleged to have been discovered) with a boy; perhaps lovers or former friends betray her, or she is the victim of grudge informers, or the target of enemies of her family. These factors, plus various other conditions (gossip, pressure on the family, the absence of resources to protect, the inability of the family to ally its real or feared loss of face, or even a lack of imaginative alternatives) and the presence of a willing perpetrator conspire to complete the tragedy.

The first of the sure-fail mechanisms has been discussed (Section 5.1) and thus can be summarized briefly. This is the multiply contradictory construction of femininity in HSCs, as well as in much of the larger Arab world. "Woman" of male imagination and gender construction is, because of her contradictory construction, an impossible creature. Yet this contradictory construction is disastrous because, however much energy men invest in fantasies, they cannot do away with the insidious, underlying distrust of women. Living with wills so clearly in conflict with themselves strongly suggests that men in HSCs would renounce this contradictory construction if they could only see it for what it really is. Yet this is one more instance in which human beings are benighted. Moreover, the readiness to condemn women exists a priori, as is shown by the fact that it is always the girl or women who is to blame for an infraction, even in the event of rape, kidnapping, or a husband's decision to divorce his spouse. In effect, the cultural prejudice against women and girls is so overwhelming that there is a standing presumption of guilt, and females must prove their innocence— although, once allegations have spread, even efforts to argue for one's innocence usually fall on deaf ears.[146]

A second sure-fail mechanism has its origins in the contradiction between strictly regulating sexuality and enforcing these rules through shame. As explained in Chapter 3, shame requires actual or expected public exposure, but, as with homosexual relations, behaviors remaining hidden from others and unmentioned are not subject to shame and hence encounter few inhibitions. The same is true of sexual relations between men and women, although normatively taboo. Patai notes, "In private everything is allowed; there all the inhibitions are shrugged off. The knowledge that nobody sees what is being done, and that therefore anything can be done with impunity, breaks through the repressions and inhibitions."[147]

It certainly does not help that everyone accepts, as a rationale for strict prohibitions, the view that a man and woman left on their own will inevitably have sex. This amounts in many cases to a self-fulfilling prophecy

---

146. In many Muslim majority countries where honor killings occur, it is common for unmarried girls to be examined for evidence of intact hymens. However, many girls who pass such tests are attacked anyway because of the perception that it is dishonorable for the family to have felt the need for such an exam in the first place.

147. Patai, *The Arab Mind*, 147.

for, as Patai notes, boys and girls raised to believe that only what is seen by others counts "will behave accordingly." Patai adds, "Thus sex is both prohibited, and therefore feared, and desired, and therefore sought after. Both fear and desire are experienced with considerable intensity, which can be taken as an indication of the intensity of the childhood repression of the sexual interest."[148]

Patai also notes that accidental encounters between a man (or several men) and a woman are likely to result in rape or sexual abuse if the attackers expect anonymity.[149] Virility and dominance are associated with manliness and, hence, sexual predation is accepted as an expression of manliness (Sections 4.2–4.3). The tensions resulting from this double standard are greatly magnified by two systemic sociocultural phenomena. Given the hardships of coming of age, many men entering early adulthood will have developed what is called a "fast living style"; that is, they will be motivated to marry early and start a family while still young.[150] However, men who have developed this life orientation confront a situation in which employment is scarce; they are unable to support a wife and family; and, worse, the access to women is tightly controlled.

As if this is not enough, some norms and attitudes encourage efforts to gain sexual access through fornication, adultery, or rape, or by "poaching" (i.e., kidnapping or elopement).[151] Evolutionary psychologists speak colloquially of male mating strategies in terms of "cads versus dads."[152] Men typically allocate their reproductive energies along a continuum representing competition against other males with the "dad" strategy at one end and the "cad" strategy at the other. The "dad" strategy generally prevails when most men have opportunities to woo women for themselves and then settle down to invest in their children. A system of monogamous match-ups requires a setting in which women are relatively plentiful and must be wooed (women exercise choice), and, in addition, no male hierarchy induces an artificial scarcity of potential brides.

---

148. Patai, *The Arab Mind*, 148–49.

149. Patai, *The Arab Mind*, 149.

150. Barbara Hagenah Brumbach, Aurelio José Figueredo, and Bruce J. Ellis, "Effects of Harsh and Unpredictable Environments in Adolescence on Development of Life History Strategies," *Human Nature* 20, 1 (2009), 25–51.

151. In many areas in which honor killing is most frequent, requiring an abductor to marrying a kidnapped girl was a culturally accepted "solution" to the problem of kidnapping and, until recent decades, often legal as well.

152. Steven Pinker, *The Better Angels of Our Nature: Why Violence Has Declined* (New York: Penguin, 2011), 105.

If, however, there is a nonegalitarian skewing of available mates, or life conditions make settling down hazardous, then a male's optimal reproductive strategy is to be a "cad." Unless men incur risks, they are not likely to be able to reproduce. Thus the "cad" strategy prevails if, in order to have access to women, men must do so illicitly (i.e., through seduction, adultery, kidnap, or rape). Of course, the patriarchal strictures of HSCs artificially induce female scarcity: polygamy or multiple marriages (up to four wives) is allowed for more mature and successful men; young and unmarried women are segregated and controlled; arranged marriages often match young, fertile girls with older men; and widowed or divorced women are not permitted to remarry. These communities "breed" all of the conditions that select for "cad" mating strategies.

Nor is this all. The efforts of men who control females to retain superiority reinforces warrior masculinity and increasing social, but repressed, hostility. Meanwhile, because of sex-selective abortions, infant mortality rates, infanticide (in areas of India), and inadequate prenatal and child health care, the disproportion between males and females continues to grow everywhere throughout South and East Asia, the Middle East, and North Africa (except Morocco, Tunisia, and Turkey). The disproportion between males and females as of 2015 reached 115 males per 100 females in Egypt and rose in the Arabian Peninsula to a high of 274 males per 100 females in the United Arab Emirates.[153]

If male domination of women and sexual taboos actually do increase the probability of sexual attack and hence likely victimization, the constitution of marriage as a social institution presents a third contradictory contribution. If romantic love is viewed as a menace, then "love matches" will be relatively rare; because girls and boys cannot date or meet socially outside family gatherings, problems of relating to the opposite sex will be compounded by the "absence of modes of relatedness other than genital encounter."[154] Ghanim notes that "pre-marriage experiences socialize both men and women to perceive the other sex as different, unequal and even acrimonious," and he adds, "it is simply not conceivable that marriage will provide a way to escape the fate of the couple's earlier relationships."[155] Ghanim asserts that most couples are destined to have "loveless, dull, and dysfunctional marriages," and he agrees that the entire structure of society "conspires against the prospect of a loving relationship between the

153. Julia Smirnova and Weiyi Cai, "See Where Women Outnumber Men Around the World (and Why)," *Washington Post*, Aug. 21, 2015, A8.
154. Mernissi, *Beyond the Veil*, 145.
155. Ghanim, *Gender and Violence in the Middle East*, 165.

couple."[156] Fatima Mernissi adds: "Marriage institutionalizes the Oedipal split between love and sex in a man's life. He is encouraged to love a woman with whom he cannot have sexual intercourse, his mother; he is discouraged from lavishing his affection on the woman with whom he does engage in sexual intercourse, his wife."[157] In effect, Mernissi believes, marriage *is* conflict.[158]

Men and women bring irreconcilable objectives to marriage. As a contractual relationship for the primary benefit of others, partners are often incompatible. The wife is a captive who, following her virtual rape and communal celebration of the end of her virginity, is consigned to produce sons, to provide sex for her husband on demand, and to be a domestic servant for her growing family, at least until she becomes a mother-in-law.[159] Because the marriage replicates the victim–victimizer relationship, her husband will be the target of hostility and revenge.[160] Wives will capitalize on the resentments of children, especially sons, toward fathers; too many wives will be guileful, crafty, cunning, and devious; they will attempt to manipulate their husbands' sexuality; and they will use gossip, intrigue, and ridicule, especially as it may depreciate his virility.[161]

For their part, men bring to the relationship all of the unresolved sexual and emotional needs resulting from childhood and adolescent hardships. After all, a man's wife symbolizes "the perpetually unavailable woman" he has long dreamed of possessing. Yet, since warrior masculinity considers attachment to a woman to be a weakness and prohibits "feminized" feelings, the psychological task of denial is constant, and intimacy remains dangerous.[162] Fulfilling his masculine role through dominating

---

156. Ghanim, *Gender and Violence in the Middle East*, 107; Mernissi, cited by Ghanim in *Gender and Violence in the Middle East*, 149.

157. Mernissi, *Beyond the Veil*, 122.

158. Mernissi, *Beyond the Veil*, 108.

159. Ghanim correctly notes that marriage in such circumstances is public and not private: "it is the offering of a private body for the service of the public sphere and the community." Ghanim, *Gender and Violence in the Middle East*, 166.

160. "Wherever there is inequality, there is also dishonesty, subterfuge, hypocrisy, and a wish, whether acknowledged or not, for revenge." Fatima Mernissi, "Virginity and Patriarchy," *Women's Studies International Forum* 5, 2 (1982), 183–91,188.

161. Ghanim, *Gender and Violence in the Middle East*, 128; Nikki R. Keddie and Lois Beck, "Introduction," in Keddie and Beck (eds.), *Women in the Muslim World*, 19; Juliette Minces, *The House of Obedience: Women in Arab Society* (London: Zed, 1982), 44; and Abu-Lughod, "The Romance of Resistance: Tracing Transformations of Power through Bedouin Women," in Peggy Reeves Sanday and Ruth Gallagher Goodenough (eds.), *Beyond the Second Sex: New Directions in the Anthropology of Gender* (Philadelphia: University of Pennsylvania Press, 1990), 323.

162. Virginia Goldner et al., "Love and Violence: Gender Paradoxes in Volatile Attachments," *Family Process* 29, 4 (1990), 343–64.

his wife undermines the possibility of genuine, psychological intimacy. Paradoxically, as Ghanim notes, men expect respect, recognition, and support in addition to legitimation of their superiority in marriage, but by maintaining the inferiority of the very same persons from whom they seek recognition and affection.[163] Altogether, then, unless a pairing comes with fortuitous good fortune or both partners possess exceptional qualities of sympathy, tolerance, resilience, and understanding, marriages are destined to recapitulate the social oppression of women and will offer partners little refuge from the psychological stresses of life. Given the proclivity of many men when frustrated to rely on psychological and physical violence to force compliance, and the ability to divorce a wife through verbal repudiation, it is understandable that some women, approaching desperation, might seek contact with another man or that unwanted women will be cast aside as divorcees and left as easy prey for womanless cads.

Recall that the primary reason for this section concerned the availability of victims of honor killing. We can now conclude, I believe, that a possibly sufficient explanation for the continuing availability of victims is to be found as "fallout" from the efforts of fallible humans to negotiate three major contradictory social relations that produce sure-fail mechanisms. First, there is the contradictory construction of the female gender; second, the contradiction between sexual taboos and social dynamics driving male sexual predation; and third, the institution of marital arrangements designed for failure. Because of the normal operation of these sure-fail mechanisms, it is not necessary to hypothesize some additional scapegoating function or to assume that girls and women who are victimized differ in significant ways from those who are not.

5.4 FURTHER CAUSAL FACTORS: DEDICATED AVENGERS AND SPIRALS OF SILENCE

Obviously, perpetrators' roles are necessary since otherwise there would be no honor killings. However, possessing warrior masculinity is not in itself sufficient for killing and probably not always necessary either. Some males may kill although they do not have a warrior masculine personality profile; perhaps some find social expectations and pressures somehow inescapable. This section focuses on the possible causal contributions of two types of agents not yet considered: first, agents who occupy influential positions

---

163. Ghanim, *Gender and Violence in the Middle East*, 157.

and whom I call *dedicated avengers*, and second, those who, despite indifference or even opposition to honor killing, nevertheless remain caught in *spirals of silence*. While agents of these two types exert peer pressure on males who become killers, what requires explanation are the social dynamics that enable them to have an outsized influence.

Recall a question that arose about the proportion of the male population suffering a significantly adverse developmental process in order for warrior masculinity to prevail (Sections 4.4 and 5.1). I hold that warrior masculinity represents an expression of a VPP syndrome and that this personality syndrome is causally necessary for honor killing. Recall that this is an explanation of the rate of honor killing: it means that the number or frequency of honor killing incidents would not be as great as they now are unless a cohort of men in HSCs were psychologically willing and able to carry out executions, to pressure others to conform, and to punish by shaming those men who object or fail to cleanse honor with blood. I shall use the term *dedicated avengers* to refer to men who might not themselves kill, but who otherwise fit this description.

In the absence of a cohort of dedicated avengers, it might still be difficult to understand why female violations of honor would lead to the finality of death. Even granting visceral prejudice against women, it ought to be odd that men so willingly waste female life. Men ought to be sufficiently self-interested in the reproductive benefits of girls and wives or the economic advantages of retaining unwanted daughters (e.g., through trade to remote tribes, marriage, labor, or sale as prostitutes).[164] Thus it is important to ask whether a cohort of dedicated avengers really exists. There is certainly anecdotal evidence for justified belief in the reality of social pressure exerted by ardent avengers. Such evidence is reported by persons who resist fulfilling roles as perpetrators. For instance, one perpetrator claimed he had fled to avoid killing, but his relatives found him and telephoned him continuously, saying, "if you don't come and kill, we'll come there to kill you." Further evidence comes from frequent comments about the extent of public pressure, as in the interviewee who replied to Kardam's team "they kill so that a whole tribe from age 7 to 70 will not be deported."[165]

Given the mere awareness of the presence of ardent avengers, it is probable that some executions result from dynamics very similar to

---

164. In Chapter 6, I present a cultural evolutionary account of the origins of honor killing as a social practice. The existence of the social practice is a necessary condition for honor killing, but only distally causal; the existence of the practice does not explain why any particular execution occurs.

165. Both quotations are from Kardam, *Dynamics of Honor Killing in Turkey*, 47.

self-fulfilling prophecies: family members (usually males) *perceive* their honor under attack, *perceive* that gossip or allegations constitute an indictment against a family member, *imagine* that the consequences of failing to cleanse the family honor will be unbearable, and, finally, are *unable to conceive* of alternatives other than executions. Kardam pointedly says that the "most important point is the fact that an exaggerated interpretation of the power of social pressure may end up legitimizing the perpetrators of honor crimes."[166]

Finally, dedicated avengers are likely to make common cause with those whose motives cannot be sanctioned through the norms of honor. While careful to select for the Churchill-Holmes database only instances in which the expressed motives were about honor, there are sure to have been some in which elements of self-interest remain behind the scenes. In the end, given the "fog of hysteria" surrounding highly charged events in honor–shame cultures, it is sometimes difficult to disentangle motives based on a concern for honor versus those that are driven by self-interest, and especially when others pose as motivated by honor when they are really self-interested.[167]

By applying network theory and other sociological research, we can explain why even a relatively small number of dedicated avengers can have an outsized effect. Behavioral scientists regard social networks as theoretical constructs useful for studying relationships between individuals within groups regarding the distribution of information, interactions, and influence. Social networks have been found to be self-organizing and complex and to have emergent properties; at the same time, networks exhibit coherent patterns that characterize the system as a whole. Whatever the ultimate explanation of causal influence, or *transitivity*, within them, social networks "want us to do things,"[168] although they are hardly sentient. They are able to mimic the intentionality of agents. Mathematical models of flocks of birds, schools of fish, or bee colonies reveal that, while there

---

166. Kardam, *Dynamics of Honor Killing in Turkey* 47, although Kardam also adds on the same page that an emphasis on social pressure was more common among men and women interviewed, including professionals, who were close witnesses of honor killings.

167. A terrible case of this kind in Ayse Onal's *Honour Killing*, 201–33 takes place in the Turkish district of Brussels. Suspicions about a daughter, Emriye, end with the murder of a different daughter, Ulviye, so that the perpetrator can evade discovery of his rape of Emriye.

168. Scott Stossel, "'You and Your Friend's Friend's Friends,' Review of *Connected*, by Nicholas Christakis and James H. Fowler," Sunday Book Review, *The New York Times*, Oct. 4, 2009, www.nytime.com/2009/10/04/books/review/Stosell-t.html?page wanted=all&_r=o, accessed Aug. 21, 2015.

is no central controlling director telling animals when and how to move, collective intelligence somehow emerges so that the flock, school, or colony exhibits highly coordinated activity. Nicholas Christakis and James Fowler maintain that network science is exposing the same "super-organism" aspects of human collectives. Further research shows that a person's position in a social network is partially heritable and that central features of social networks may have evolved with social cooperation.[169]

As early as 1969, in the so-called *small world* experiment, Stanley Milgram sought to examine the average length of a path in a social network in the United States. Milgram found that, on average, individuals are separated by no more than five or six other persons.[170] Subsequent pioneering research by Christarkis and Fowler has established what has come to be known as the "three degrees of influence" rule about human behavior in social networks. The "three degrees" rule predicts that each person's individual social influence can stretch roughly three degrees—from an individual to a friend's friend's friend—before it fades away.[171]

The "three degrees" rule has now been well corroborated experimentally. Christarkis and Fowler were able to demonstrate that the mechanism holds true for a variety of diverse attributes including obesity, smoking, happiness, and risk perception; moreover, other investigators have found strong evidence for a causal process—*behavioral contagion*—although it is still less well-know *why* the process exists than that it does. A controversial experiment demonstrating behavioral contagion was conducted in 2014 on 669,000 users of the social media platform Facebook by filtering positive or negative content from their news feeds.[172] A massive study of 61 million voters in 2012 was able to demonstrate the spread of voting behavior up to two degrees of separation.[173]

---

169. James H. Fowler, Christopher T. Dawes, and Nicholas A. Christakis, "Model of Genetic Variation in Human Social Networks," *Proceedings of the National Academy of Sciences* 106 (2009), 1720–24; Coren L. Apicella et al., "Social Networks and Cooperation in Hunter-Gatherers," *Nature* 481 (Jan. 2012), 497–501.

170. Jeffrey Travers and Stanley Milgram, "An Experimental Study of the Small World Problem," *Sociometry* 32 (1969), 425–43. Subjects in Omaha and Wichita were instructed to get packets to target persons they did not know in Boston by sending the packet to the friend or relative they knew personally and who, they believed, were most likely to know the target. Recipients were also told to forward the same packet to someone they believed might know the target and so on.

171. Nicholas A. Christakis and James H. Fowler, *Connected: The Surprising Power of Our Social Networks and How They Shape Our Lives* (New York: Little, Brown, 2009).

172. Adam D. I. Kramer, Jamie E. Guillory, and Jeffrey T. Hancock, "Experimental Evidence of Massive Scale Emotional Contagion Through Social Networks," *Proceedings of the National Academy of Science* 111 (2014) 8788–90.

173. Robert M. Bond et al., "A 61-Million-Person Experiment in Social Influence and Political Mobilization," *Nature* 489 (13 Sep. 2012), 295–98.

The causal dynamics of social networks are not fully understood. Certainly, peer and social pressure, or "norming," has a significant influence, as does homophily, or the tendency of people to befriend and associate with persons they see as similar to themselves. Elaine Hatfield argues that emotional contagion, or the tendency toward emotional convergence, results through automatic mimicry and the subconscious synchronization of one's expressions, vocalizations, postures, and movements with others.[174] An alternative hypothesis holds that people engage in social comparisons to monitor their own emotional reactions for congruence with those of others. In this case, an individual uses others' expressed emotions as "social information" to decide how he or she should be feeling.[175] However, influence within social networks sometimes behaves as if it is independent of emotional contagion as the latter requires the presence of others during arousal, as in mob behavior, whereas networks can exert influence over great distances or times. The three-degree rule does not require that an individual know or make contact with persons beyond an initial friend.

The point of network science, for present purposes, is the way in which relatively small numbers of dedicated avengers can have cascading effects throughout an HSC. Christakis and Fowler estimate mathematically that if one's friend is happy, for example, then, as a consequence of this fact alone, there is a 15% chance that one will be happy as well; if a friend's friend is also happy, add an additional 10% to this effect, and a further 6% if the friend's friend's friend is also happy. This means that the array of three persons, assuming each one knows three other different individuals, has a multiplier effect of 71. For the sake of illustration, if we assume that a population of 1,200 in a small town or urban enclave forms a network, and if an initial 10 people hear of an alleged violation, then, by the three-degree rule, the influence of the initial 10 will eventually result in a total of 710 persons influenced, provided that everyone has at least three "friends." In this way, influence will spread very rapidly to slightly more than 50.8% of the total population of 1,200. Assuming there is no effective counterinfluence, there is no reason to postulate that the cascading influence will stop with that percentage of the population. Given a closely knit community and the excitation and anger about a rumored honor violation, half of the population might eventually know, surely including a sufficiently large cohort of ardent avengers to exert pressures for honor killing on prospective perpetrators.

174. Elaine Hatfield, John T. Cacioppo, and Richard L. Rapson, "Emotional Contagion: Current Directions," *Psychological Science* 2 (1993), 95–99.
175. Gerald Schoenewolf, "Emotional Contagion: Behavioral Induction in Individuals and Groups," *Modern Psychoanalysis* 15 (1990), 49–61.

If the most powerful persons tend to occupy the hubs, or nodes, in social networks, then it is very likely that the multiplier effect will be dramatic. Theoretically, any one individual's influence decays beyond three degrees (beyond the third person affected); however, the effects of influence can be very extensive if there are many arrays of three. Influential power brokers, such as high-status and influential tribal leaders, are likely to have many acquaintances. Suppose for illustrative purposes that in a town of 1,200 there are only 120 dedicated avengers, or 10% of the total population. Nevertheless, given the multiplier effect of 71 in a three-person chain— and possibly longer chains for power brokers—then, assuming that there are 20 power brokers in the village, by the time each has contacted the fourth person, it is very likely that all dedicated avengers will have received news of an alleged honor violation. Most of the community will know of the alleged violation by then, and, even if some oppose killing and others are not willing to go as far as the dedicated avengers, the latter could exert extreme pressure, claiming—as perpetrators often report—that "everyone knows" and that the killing was "fated" or "inevitable."

Social network theory faces a number of difficulties. Here, the concern that the theory treats emotions and attitudes (e.g., happiness) and values quantitatively can be set aside. It is the behavior of dedicated avengers in influencing potential perpetrators that concerns us. Likewise, the possibility of undetected variables (e.g., anti–honor killing influences) is a possible difficulty that I pass over because it is reasonable to assume that in experimental tests involving smoking and obesity, for example, there were similar undetected variables. A more serious concern is that honor killing as a social practice presents a much more complex phenomenon for analysis.

On the other hand, Christakis and Fowler's study of thousands of subjects in the Framingham Heart Study, ongoing since 1948, involved subjects who were being seen by physicians and health care providers.[176] Because the Framingham study looked at numerous contacts with a variety of health care providers over years, as well as subjects' life styles, the study suggests that complexity itself does not impede a social network's influences. In fact, it is possible that the influential effects of social networks will be greater with the number of homogeneous modalities (e.g., shared norms, values, attitudes, and we-acceptances). Members of HSCs are, of course, much more alike in these ways than residents of Framingham, Massachusetts. Moreover, the plausibility of psychologically formidable and negative influences increases when one considers

176. Christakis and Fowler, *Connected*, 105–12.

facilitating background conditions such as extreme gender prejudice, patriarchal expectations about the submissiveness of females, and the legitimation of rage and violence.

Unfortunately, even if the three-degree rule of social networks did not apply, as I predict it does with respect to honor killings, social dynamics might operate to lead a majority to endorse a principle or opinion they do not personally accept. This may occur because people mistakenly think that everyone else endorses it or, alternatively, because people believe they will gain if they conform or suffer a loss if they do not.[177] Although sometimes referred to as "pluralistic ignorance," a better term for this dynamic is the "spiral of silence." Anthony Spencer and Stephen Croucher have argued that the apparent tolerance of Basque terrorism, gay bashing, and even honor killing may be results of spirals of silence.[178]

Sociologists know that the phenomena of "false conformity" and "false enforcement" can reinforce each other, generating a vicious spiral of silence leading to widespread acquiescence with an authoritarian regime that few in the group accept individually.[179] The conformity is false because it is not based on genuine consensus but on mistaken perceptions and misplaced fears about others' beliefs and behaviors; namely, that others enthusiastically support the authoritarian regime and that others are willing to enforce the regime's ideological norms or rules. People may even punish a dissenter who disavows a belief they themselves reject. This is likely, researchers speculate, if individuals feel pressed to demonstrate their own sincerity: "to show other enforcers that they are not endorsing a party line out of expedience but believe it in their hearts. That shields them from punishment by their fellows . . . who may, paradoxically, only be punishing heretics out of fear that they will be punished if they don't."[180]

The influence of the three-degree rule might add to the impetus of spirals of silence, especially when fear of being denounced is strong. Pinker believes that "cycles of preemptive denunciation" can account in part for public hysterias such as purges and witch hunts. When it comes to honor killings, just as some people may be motivated to benefit by outing suspects, many others may be motivated to deflect suspicion away from themselves

177. Pinker, *Better Angels*, 561.

178. Anthony T. Spencer and Stephen M. Croucher, "Basque Nationalism and the Spiral of Silence: An Analysis of Public Perceptions of ETA in Spain and France," *International Communications Gazette* 70 (2008), 137–53.

179. Damon Centola, Robb Willer, and Michael Macy, "The Emperor's Dilemma: A Computational Model of Self-Enforcing Norms," *American Journal of Sociology* 110 (2005), 1009–40.

180. Pinker, *Better Angels*, 562.

and their families, given that suspicion spreads like wildfire and that the consequences of being a suspect are so grave.[181] Pinker says, "Everyone tries to out a hidden heretic before the heretic outs him. Signs of heartfelt conviction become a precious commodity."[182]

Spirals of silence may help explain honor killings that occur when alleged victims have not committed a real infraction. Although it is not possible to know actual numbers, 30.5% of the incidents in the database (Sections 2.1–2.2) involved deaths in which postmortem exams showed that victims did not commit a charged offense or for which confirmatory evidence was otherwise lacking. Of course, whenever gossip spreads quickly, ardent avengers are likely to contribute to the condemnation of falsely accused women. Pressures exerted by ardent avengers, together with the effects of social networks and spirals of silence, can account for the tenacity of honor killing as a social practice even when many in HSCs are open to change.

In closing, my analyses point toward two additional conclusions. First, as discussed at length in Section 5.3, HSCs are burdened with dysfunctional social relations that generate sure-fail mechanisms, and, while these are not scapegoating mechanisms per se, they increase risks that norms will be violated, as well as increase risks that otherwise innocent behavior will be perceived as dishonorable. Given the frailty of the human condition, dysfunctional societies with sure-fail mechanisms will serve up a supply of victims. Second, while there need not be *actual* honor infractions prior to attacks on females, there must be a confluence of several additional conditions: a background of pervasive prejudice against women; the predisposition to behave as warrior masculinity requires; the presumption that others know a family female has behaved dishonorably; the conviction that honor requires family members "must wipe away" the stain; plus pressure producing *fear*, bordering on panic, that the family members will otherwise suffer unbearable shame.[183]

Human behavior, including violence, is complex and multiply determined, and honor killings are certainly no exception. Yet, if there is one point at which we might think to trip a circuit breaker in order to turn off murderous responses to presumed honor violations, then it is at the role of the perpetrator. The complex of presumptively necessary causes all

181. Robb Willer, Ko Kuwubara, and Michael Macy, "The False Enforcement of Unpopular Norms," *American Journal of Sociology* 115 (2009), 451–90.

182. Pinker, *Better Angels*, 532.

183. The panic occurring at such instances is similar to "forward panic." See Randall Collins, *Violence: A Micro-Sociological Theory* (Princeton: Princeton University Press, 2008).

bear on setting the deadly actions of perpetrators in motion and getting them to follow through on their actions. If perpetrators routinely fail, then honor killings do not occur. However, honor killing will remain difficult to eradicate unless potential perpetrators can be adequately influenced *before* they attempt to kill. Increased efficiency at apprehending and prosecuting perpetrators after the fact, combined with harsher sentencing, have not proved to have the expected deterrent effect. While such legal and punitive measures are certainly necessary, as Welchman and Hossain state: "It is abundantly clear that a narrowly legal approach, particularly one focusing on 'state law' and state legal systems as a stand-alone strategy unaccompanied by broader and deeper initiatives and understandings is unlikely to change practice or to combat 'crimes of honour' effectively."[184]

Eradicating honor killing requires appreciating the intricate ways in which the social practice is interwoven with a way of life. As Chapters 4 and 5 demonstrate, reducing violence-proneness, narcissistic tendencies, and the attractions of warrior masculinity are critically important, as is defusing the pressures of ardent avengers. Altogether, this calls for a *moral transformation* because the changes just mentioned implicate a host of other reforms. Creative and innovative change must occur at a multitude of points, including at the many links between harsh socialization, honor, shaming, toxic stress, the construction of femininity and masculinity, the formation of warrior masculinity, the shame-to-power conversion, and sure-fail mechanisms. I explore possibilities for such transformative change in Chapters 7–9. Before then, however, it is necessary to consider the best possible explanation for the rise of honor killing as a social practice, the subject of Chapter 6.

184. Welchman and Hossain, "'Honour' Rights and Wrongs," in Welchman and Hossain (eds.), *'Honour,'* 1–21, 3.

CHAPTER 6
The Cultural Evolution of Honor Killing

Whereas much of Chapters 4 and 5 focus on causal processes at the micro level and reason explanations for honor killing, this chapter develops a causal explanation at the macro level. In this chapter, I examine why honor killing should ever have come into existence in the first place and then why it became a sustained social practice over centuries. While individual agents, singly and collectively, are the units for analysis in Chapter 5, the units for analysis in the present chapter are sociocultural systems and ecological pressures on demographic groups among whom these systems evolved.

Any explanatory theory of honor killing must be consistent with the empirical data analyzed in Chapter 2. Hence, I should expect to assess the adequacy of an explanation by its ability to predict the central tendencies of honor killing identified, given certain noncontroversial assumptions.[1] However, many complex social phenomena can be illuminated by competing explanations. Consequently, in addition to looking at the "fit" between an explanatory theory and data in terms of its ability to predict the central tendencies, I also adopt the criteria for an *argument to the best explanation*.[2]

---

1. To explain, or account, for the central tendencies analyzed in Section 2.2, I understand the explanatory theory to have the following logic: If theory T is true, then the set S of central tendencies C is true as well, or if T, then S {C1, C2, C3 . . . etc.}. As here we reason inductively, we consider the number of central tendencies C a theory T explains, how well it explains them (e.g., without the need for ad hoc hypotheses), whether it does so better than alternatives theories, and so forth.

2. For a helpful discussion of criteria for arguments to the best explanation relating to cultural evolution, see Steven W. Gangestad, "Exploring the Evolutionary Foundations of Culture: An Adaptationist Framework," in Mark Schaller et al. (eds.), *Evolution, Culture, and the Human Mind* (New York: Taylor and Francis, 2010), 83–98. See also

The macrocausal explanation offered here is plausible based on both sets of criteria.

In my research, I did encounter a few published or suggested explanations; however, despite my interest in assessing competing explanatory approaches, none of these alternatives was sufficiently plausible following my assessment in terms of empirical data and the criteria for arguments to the best explanation. Moreover, none of these alternatives offers an explanation that includes cultural evolution and hence illuminates why honor killing developed among certain tribal peoples of the deserts and dry mountain uplands of the Middle East, North Africa, and the northern Indian subcontinent but not among other population groups. Thus, they are presented here only in a footnote.[3]

George C. Williams, *Natural Selection: Domains, Levels and Challenges* (New York: Oxford University Press, 1992).

3. One explanatory approach I call the "mutual dependency explanation." David Ghanim suggests this explanation in *Gender Violence in the Middle East* (Westport, CT: Praeger, 2009), 165–215. This view maintains that there are two systems of domination, each of which causally reproduces the other. The private dominion of men over women is the "pay off" for men's compliance with authoritarianism in the public sphere. A similar account is attractive to some postcolonialists, such as Max Fisher in "The Real Roots of Sexism in the Middle East (It's Not Islam, Race or 'Hate')," *The Atlantic*, 25 Apr. 2012, www.theatlantic.com/archive/2012/04/the-real-roots-of-sexism-in-the-middle-east-its-not-islam-race-or-hate/25632, accessed Jul 1. 2014). Fisher extends Deniz Kandiyoti's concept of the "patriarchal bargain" to what Fisher terms the "gentleman's agreement" between colonial rulers and indigenous men. Fisher also claims that because foreign colonists promoted secular regimes, anticolonists adopted extreme religious interpretations of Islam as a way of opposing them. Fisher also quotes from anthropologist Suad Joseph's *Gender and Citizenship in the Middle East* (Syracuse, NY: Syracuse University Press, 2000) the following as supporting his interpretation: "Women and children were the inevitable chips with which the political and religious leaders bargained."

A second interesting possibility is a "scapegoat explanation" that might be based on applications of René Girard's corpus on mimetic rivalry and scapegoating. Although I am not aware of such efforts, one might consider how the victim of an honor killing is a scapegoat sacrificed as a "solution" to communal hostilities generated by competitive mimetic desires. Antonello Pierpaolo and Paul Gifford combine mimetic theory with a theory of cultural evolution in "Between Animal and Human: The Challenge of Mimetic Theory and the Evolution of Culture," Stanford University, Nov. 15–16, 2010, www.imitatio.org/Papers_files/Thinking%20%the%human.Pdf., accessed Jun. 12, 2014.

Both Amir H. Jafri in *Honour Killing: Dilemma, Ritual, Understanding* (Oxford and New York: 2008) and Tahira S. Khan in *Beyond Honour: A Historical Materialist Explanation of Honour Violence* (Oxford and New York: Oxford University Press, 2006) present explanations for honor killing. Jafri claims that those who commit honor killing are poised between magical and mythical thinking and the rational orientation of modernity. "Perspectival thinking" and rationality is not available to those bound by the hegemony of a mythical-magical worldview. Hence, the practice perpetuates the illogic and irrationalism of the "vast majority of illiterates."

This chapter is divided into four sections. Section 6.1 first briefly discusses the population-level model of cultural evolution, followed by a concise overview of historical and anthropological research on the severe ecological challenges, both physical and human, faced by early ancestors of honor–shame communities (HSCs). Section 6.2 explains how the characteristic features of what I call "consanguine hierarchical patriarchy" (CHP) evolved as certain groups adapted to ecological challenges. Section 6.3 considers the evolution and functions of another cultural system among nomadic and pastoralist peoples known as the *segmentary lineage system* (SLS). It is necessary to understand both CHP and SLS in order to comprehend why honor killing evolved as we encounter it today. Section 6.4 discusses the initial evolutionary formation of honor killing as an explicit social practice. Section 6.5 shows why honor killing persists as an *exaptation*, that is, as a social practice that, although remaining stable in some behavioral components, evolved to serve a purpose different from the purposes the practice initially evolved to fulfill.

6.1 CULTURAL ADAPTATIONS TO ECOLOGICAL CONSTRAINTS

Understanding honor killing at the macro level, as a social practice, requires an explanation that demonstrates how honor killing first arose as a cultural adaptation. I theorize that environmental conditions, both physical and human, imposed severe problems on the early ancestors of HSCs. The resolution of these problems required radical solutions. Insofar as honor killing was functional in contributing to the resolution of certain problems, groups adopting honor killing gained inclusive fitness. They were more successful, given environmental pressures, than similarly pressured groups that did not adapt to honor killing.

We cannot understand what causes some cultural artifacts, including certain social practices, to persist and spread while others, such as infanticide and head-hunting, disappear unless we accept that culture itself is subject to natural selection. I follow Peter Richerson and Robert Boyd in adopting a population-level theory of cultural

Khan situates honor killings within the broad category of "crimes of honor," the vast majority of which are motivated by and committed by men to achieve crass material gains. Khan maintains that notions of honor and ritualistic practices required by honor are perpetuated by structural and cultural violence that permeates and continually circulates throughout all strata of society. Consequently, crimes against women committed for economic gain are abetted by claims that the crime was committed for reasons of honor and the liability of others to regard motives of honor as exculpatory.

evolution.[4] The "human cultural system," a set of organized capabilities for developing and transmitting culture, was itself an adaptation. Humans acquired cultures because groups sharing them were able to adapt to changing environments much more effectively than possible through natural selection on genes alone.[5] Culture is thus an evolving product of groups, or populations, and of human brains "that have been shaped by natural selection to learn and manage culture."[6]

According to Richerson and Boyd, at a basic level, what culture creates is "information"—beliefs, attitudes, values, and behaviors—that can be acquired, stored, and transmitted within a population of individuals and transmitted to descendants. While individuals remain the main locus of genetic variation, differences among individuals are more than the product of interactions between information stored in individuals' genetic codes and influences of the physical environment. Humans create cultures that can, in turn, produce novel evolutionary processes resulting in variations among groups, despite the genetic similarity of individuals across groups inhabiting similar physical environments. As Richerson and Boyd say, "culture is neither nature nor nurture, but some of both. It combines inheritance and learning in a way that cannot be pared into genes or environment."[7] Consequently, it is necessary to consider both how a population of individuals interacts with its physical environment and with its inherited culture.

A population-level model of cultural evolution highlights a number of mechanisms of variation. One of these is "population-level feedback"[8] pertaining to the ways in which an individual's evolving psychology shapes the ideas and behaviors acquired from others, as well as how natural selection affects how an individual thinks and learns from the personal experiences of other individuals. It is possible to speak of "population properties"[9] of various kinds: why some information or artifacts increase in frequency within a population,[10] why some cultures are successfully transmitted and some undergo "inertia,"[11] why a culture can reappear following long suppression,[12] and why cultural change can occur very

4. Peter J. Richerson and Robert Boyd, *Not by Genes Alone: How Culture Transformed Human Evolution* (London and Chicago: The University of Chicago Press, 2005).
5. Richerson and Boyd, *Not by Genes Alone*, 7.
6. Richerson and Boyd, *Not by Genes Alone*, 7.
7. Richerson and Boyd, *Not by Genes Alone*, 11.
8. Richerson and Boyd, *Not by Genes Alone*, 14.
9. Richerson and Boyd, *Not by Genes Alone*, 14.
10. Richerson and Boyd, *Not by Genes Alone*, 11.
11. Richerson and Boyd, *Not by Genes Alone*, 25, 45.
12. Richerson and Boyd, *Not by Genes Alone*, 32.

rapidly.[13] Cultural evolution also can illuminate why certain combinations of information and artifacts become connected over many years and come to form social practices and institutions that are themselves subject to further evolution. Most salient for my purposes, a population-level model illuminates two puzzles about honor killing: first, why the natural selection of culture can often favor behaviors quite different from those favored by selection on genes,[14] and, second, why cultural selection can favor a psychology that causes people to conform to the beliefs and behaviors of a majority even when the initial adaptation has become dysfunctional.[15]

I hypothesize that honor killing as a cultural artifact probably arose because of the coevolution of many cultural artifacts or practices, including honor codes, CHP, patrilineage, patrilocality, endogamy, father–son inheritance, arranged marriages, father's brother's daughter marriages (henceforth FBD marriages), the sequestration of women (e.g., *purdah*), polygamy, and the SLS. The significance of each will be considered herein. The important point is that as these cultural adaptations arose roughly simultaneously within certain population groups, these adaptations constrained alternative possibilities, thus contributing causally to the distinctive lifeworld of early HSCs. In addition, as discussed in Sections 4.4 and 5.1, cultural adaptations of HSCs found fertile "soil" in groups that inculcated in individuals the psychological predispositions needed to act in the ways directed by institutional practices.

For instance, the rigid male–female gender binary, the male drive for domination, and an aggressive male response to loss of honor might have coexisted independently of the cultural adaptation we recognize as honor killing. It is less likely that honor killing could have achieved its initial function without this "politics" of personality and identity. It would be extremely difficult for a group to have adapted honor killing without other coopted and evolved sociopsychological mechanisms—mate guarding, costly signaling, and kin-selected altruism. In a sense, these were probably the primary functional mechanisms for more sophisticated cultural adaptations: CHP, SLS, and, of course, honor killing itself. Thus causal processes at both the micro (individual) and macro (group) levels have been interdependent. Moreover, ways of life continually tied to these cultural adaptations and that replicate these patterns of socialization will continue to regenerate the functional social "needs" that initially gave rise to honor

13. Richerson and Boyd, *Not by Genes Alone*, 43.
14. Richerson and Boyd, *Not by Genes Alone*, 14.
15. Richerson and Boyd, *Not by Genes Alone*, 13.

killing, even though these "needs" are no longer adaptive for groups however strongly individuals continue to feel them.

Honor killing originated in areas consisting, for the most part, of vast desert reaches, arid or semiarid highlands, and rugged mountain ranges that are hot and dry in summers and cold in winters. Only about 14% of the vast land mass stretching from North Africa at the Atlantic and running through the Middle East to north Pakistan and India is suited for cultivation. Most arable land is to be found in desert oases, high mountain valleys, and especially in the plains and deltas of the major rivers: the Nile, Tigris, Euphrates, Indus, Karun, and the Helmand. Made fertile by irrigation, these valleys and plains made it possible for agriculture to originate in the northern regions of the Indian subcontinent, the Middle East, and North Africa long before it developed elsewhere. However, thousands of years of agricultural settlement led to deforestation, salinization, soil erosion, and the silting up of irrigation systems. In particular, the huge and fertile wheat fields of the Tigris–Euphrates delta made Iraq the breadbasket of the ancient world but then returned to desert. Consequently, agricultural productivity in the Middle East continued to decline for centuries, including the later era when Islamic civilization was at its peak.[16]

Ancestors of HSCs were among those inhabiting the least productive hinterlands of the region, although we do not know whether they were indigenous to these areas or were pushed into these extremities by powerful kingdoms and empires which controlled the more fertile plains and valleys. Charles Lindholm remarks on strong continuities between ancient Sumeria and Babylonia and the cultures of the Middle East today,[17] while historians remark that ancient Mesopotamia "was periodically robbed and disrupted by the mountaineers on its east or the nomads on its west."[18]

I follow Lindholm in focusing on three different population groups who succeeded in meeting survival needs based on cultural-ecological adaptations. The first are a nomad group who inhabited deserts and whose way of life centered around domestication of the camel. "Camel nomadism" dates back at least 2,500 years, and within this population group are the

---

16. Jared M. Diamond, *Guns, Germs, and Steel: The Fates of Human Societies* (New York: W. W. Norton, 1997); Nikki R. Keddie, "Material Culture and Geography: Toward a Holistic History of the Middle East," in Juan R. I. Cole (ed.), *Comparing Muslim Societies: Knowledge and the State in a World Civilization* (Anne Arbor: University of Michigan Press, 1992); Charles Lindholm, *The Islamic Middle East: An Historical Anthropology* (Oxford: Blackwell, 1996), 17–18.

17. Lindholm, *The Islamic Middle East*, 41–46.

18. Henri Frankfort, *Kingship and the Gods: A Study of Near Eastern Religion as the Integration of Society and Nature* (Chicago: The University of Chicago Press, 1948), 5.

original Bedouin who were the first to call themselves Arabs, such as the large al-Murrah tribe of Saudi Arabia; the now sedentary Bedouin of Iraq, Palestine, and Jordan; and the Sanusi of Cyrenaica. The present-day Baloch and Brahui in the desert reaches of Iran and Pakistan succeeded in making similar adaptations. A second, more populous group dates from at least 8,500 BC. These are pastoralist tribes of sheep and goat herders living on the desert perimeters and the edges of mountain ranges. Present-day descendants include many of the Berber tribes of the Atlas Mountains in Morocco and Algeria, as well as the Lars, Basseri, Bakhtiari, Qashqai, and some Kurdish and Arab pastoralists herding in the mountains of the Zagros (in Iran, Kurdistan, and eastern Turkey), the Elburz range (in northern Iran), the Hindu Kush (stretching between central Afghanistan and northern Pakistan), and the Kirghiz of the Pamir Mountains of Afghanistan and eastern Iran.

The third group consists of tribal peoples who mostly farm isolated mountain valleys and high, moister plateaus. Among these peoples are the Kabyle Berber of Algeria and the Berbers of the Moroccan highlands, the Kurds of much of Iran and Turkey, and many of the Pashtun of Peshawar, Swat Valley, and other areas of Pakistan and Afghanistan. Although engaging primarily in agriculture or a combination of farming and shepherding, peoples in the third group maintain pastoralist sociocultural elements. Many probably were pastoralist peoples who migrated into more fertile areas, such as the Jats now in the Punjab, Haryana, and Western Uttar Pradesh regions of India.[19]

Domestication of the camel enabled desert nomads to penetrate deeply into inhospitable deserts. Gathering together at oases during dry summer months, nomadic camel herders would and then scatter in winters in search of water and forage for camel herds. Because camels were indispensable for traversing the trade routes crossing deserts, desert nomads subsisted by trading camels for food. The invention of the camel saddle (ca. 500–100 BC) enabled mounted nomads to transform themselves into the mobile warriors of the desert famous in Arabic folklore. In the deserts of Iran and Pakistan, nomadic groups such as the Baloch and Brahui made similar adaptations. As Lindholm notes, "with new mobility, the armed camel riders could not only raid one another, they could also improve their lives by offering 'protection' to trading convoys and extort similar tribute, or *khuwa*, from sedentary villagers."[20] In some cases armed tribes of nomads

19. Lindholm, *The Islamic Middle East*, 17–32.
20. Lindholm, *The Islamic Middle East*, 19.

received payment to guard the boundaries of states, as the al-Murrah tribes have done since being "deputized" by the Saudi monarchy to patrol the Saudi Arabian Empty Quarter.[21]

Certain salient features of the desert nomad's way of life are common across the three population groups. The first concerns the nomads' vaunted courage, self-reliance, and personal independence. These characteristics are believed to be a consequence of the need to range widely during the winter months to take advantage of scattered rainfall and pasturage. Even contemporary al-Murrah Bedouin travel as much as 1,900 kilometers in their search for winter pasturage.[22] Often such searches require division of a tribe into very small units, and those subdivisions into occasional solitary members probing in different directions. "Individuals in this arid country have always had to be willing and able to act on their own, prepared to deal with unforeseen consequences on their long migrations, and ready to stand up bravely to predators and occasional armed opposition."[23]

Ecological constraints imposed by this way of life led to cultural adaptations which eventually gave rise to honor codes and promoted the corresponding personality structure identified in Section 5.1 as "warrior masculinity." Given the absence or ineffectiveness of territorial authorities capable of enforcing impartial or national rules, masculine strength and competitive self-assertion were essential traits. So were courage in "love" and war and a propensity to use violence, especially when prior possession or mediation had little chance of influencing opponents. Not surprisingly, allies were needed, and the desert nomads relied extensively on loyalties based on blood and formed closely knit clans and tribal groups who would gather together at the summer oases. Generosity and hospitality were adapted forms of reciprocity in harsh and unpredictable environments, where wealth gained one day might be stolen or destroyed the next. Even today, the Bedouin are reputed to be careful observers of one's friends and foes and to have a passion for family history and for folklore narratives of the noble and base complexities of human life.[24] Because a man's reputation was the only basis on which to estimate his reliability and to accord him esteem, the warrior's ethos was consolidated as an honor code (see Chapter 3).

21. Lindholm, *The Islamic Middle East*, 19.

22. Donald Cole, *Nomads of the Nomads: The Al Murrah Bedouin of the Empty Quarter* (Arlington Heights, IL: American Museum of Natural History, 1975).

23. Lindholm, *The Islamic Middle East*, 19–20.

24. Lindholm, *The Islamic Middle East*, 20.

Thus conditions for survival in desert wastelands correlate with the deep-seated and continuing "resistance of camel nomads to hierarchy and stratification."[25] According to anthropologists, this ingrained opposition to ranking and limitations on independence was matched by an insistence on equality.[26] The absence of large-scale economic production or distribution, together with low population density and high mobility, made "the division of an institutionalized political hierarchy improbable."[27] Lindholm notes that the Bedouin *shaikh,* or sheik, traditionally organized raids and oversaw defense, but his authority was a matter of voluntary agreement among coequals. As 17th-century Muslim philosopher and historian, Ibn-Khaldun, emphasized: "the leader is obeyed, but he has no power to force others to accept his rulings. . . . There is scarcely one among them who would cede his power to another, even to his father, his brother, or the eldest member of his family."[28]

Following the advent of Islam, Bedouin clans combining to form tribal camel cavalries became irresistible forces, and, through the subjugation of farmers and pastoralists in Egypt, Iran, Iraq, North Africa, and Syria, Bedouin values gained a disproportionate influence in the Middle East.[29] The nomadic value system of Bedouin warriors became a cultural template for ideal life throughout the regions ruled by camel nomads and those into which they migrated.[30] This template included nostalgia for wilderness as the "locus of purity and honor," a distaste for submission, a high valuation of personal strength and fortitude, the pursuit of honor, and self-assertive displays of dominance.[31] Even today, many Bedouin regard themselves as the only true Arabs; until recently, many boys from urban areas were sent to desert camps for hardening and to develop manhood and rectitude.

25. Lindholm, *The Islamic Middle East,* 20.

26. Philip Burnham, "Spatial Mobility and Political Centralization in Pastoral Societies," in L'equip ecologies et anthropologie des societies pastorales (ed.), *Pastoral Production and Society* (New York: Cambridge University Press, 1979), 349–60; William Irons, "Political Stratification Among Pastoral Nomads," in *Pastoral Production and Society,* 361–74.

27. Irons, "Political Stratification," 362.

28. Lindholm, *The Islamic Middle East,* 20, quoting from Ibn Khaldun, *The Muqaddimah* (Princeton: Princeton University Press, 1967), 108, 119.

29. According to Richard Bulliet in *The Camel and the Wheel* (Cambridge: Harvard University Press, 1975), the triumph and prestige of the Bedouin warriors was so complete that use of the camel completely replaced older, wheeled vehicles throughout the Middle East and North Africa.

30. Tribal regions were never capable of supporting all people born there, and many migrated into cultivated or urban areas where, despite frequent impoverishment and low status in cities, they continued to be proud of their heritage.

31. Lindholm, *The Islamic Middle East,* 21.

Despite vast wealth and power, even the King of Saudi Arabia "is addressed by the Bedouin without honorifics, as an equal."[32]

Pastoralists are also nomadic, moving with their herds of sheep or goats from pastures at higher mountain elevations in the summer to lower and warmer pastures in the winter. The need to avoid overgrazing requires pastoralists to spread in low density over large areas, often not exceeding one or two persons per square mile. Herds may include sheep and a smaller proportion of goats, as well as small numbers of camels, donkeys, or horses. Due to their animal husbandry, shepherding groups produce much of their food as meat and dairy products but depend on trade for wheat and other grains, tea and sugar, opium and tobacco, and wood and metal products.[33]

Sheep and goat herding generally requires a more orderly and routinized way of life than desert nomadism. Because pasturage is more reliable if it is not overgrazed, it can continue to be sustainable, but only if there is organization to ensure that herds are rotated and separated to prevent the spread of disease. The movement of great herds, often involving the flocks of numerous herders, across relatively great distances also requires considerable coordination.[34] Consequently, patrilineal clans and tribal associations were especially important for pastoralists. Moving through large stretches of unbounded territory required speedily organized defenses to ward of raiding parties, as well as the ability to protect grazing territories against other migrating bands.[35] Some clans or tribal groups also needed protection to move through territories of unfriendly agriculturalists who might try to impede their migration.[36]

Despite differing from the Bedouin and other camel nomads in certain respects, pastoralist herders also adopted the cultural ideals of independence, equality, resilience, determination, and a propensity for both violence and honor. By means of tribal networks led by powerful leaders, "these shepherds, like their deep desert brothers, managed to resist state power to a large degree, and to assert their own independence as confederacies, while holding dependent peasant farmers in contempt."[37]

32. Lindholm, *The Islamic Middle East*, 20.

33. Allen W. Johnson and Timothy Earle, *The Evolution of Human Societies: From Foraging Group to Agrarian State*, 2nd ed. (Stanford: Stanford University Press, 2000), 233–41.

34. According to estimates, annual sheep migration in the Fars region of southern Iran involved more than a million animals in the late 1950s. See Lindholm, *The Islamic Middle East*, 23.

35. Nikki R. Keddie, *Women in the Middle East: Past and Present* (Princeton and Oxford: Princeton University Press, 2007), 17.

36. Lindholm, *The Islamic Middle East*, 23.

37. Lindholm notes that, historically, most of the states of the eastern half of the Middle East and the Indian subcontinent originated in conquest by herders

When centralized regimes became too strong, pastoralists, following the motto "divide that ye may not be conquered," scattered into more remote and forbidding terrain, "breaking apart into small unruly clans impossible for the center to hold."[38] Persisting for thousands of years, this pattern was evident during the Russian invasion of Afghanistan in 1979, with the opposition first of the Kirghiz in the Pamir Mountains and then of the Pashtuns and other tribal groups. The Russians called them *basmaci*, or bandits, but the Kirghiz they fought called themselves "holy warriors," or *mucahit* and *mujahideen*.[39]

The upland farming tribes are least like the other two populations. Desert nomads and pastoralists share low population density, mobility and migratory lifestyles, variable productivity, and conflicting or avoidant relations with state or regime power. None of these characteristics is prominent among the upland farmers. Sedentary farmers are attached to specific locales through property arrangements (by family, clan, or tribe) in locales that might have high population density.[40] In good years, farming groups produce surplus crops with the aid of irrigation, and, while they resent taxation, they generally have more peaceable relations with central state authorities. However, as Lindholm notes, the routine and diligence required for successful farming and greater social and economic organization has not led to cultural orientations with profoundly different values and norms. On the contrary, upland farmers, as with desert nomads and pastoralists, "unanimously maintain ideologies of egalitarianism and personal independence, . . . [and] claim the honor and respect due to a warrior."[41]

The presence of honor–shame cultures among upland farmers might seem puzzling unless we assume that their ancestral antecedents were nomads and pastoralists. For instance, many Kurds, occupying areas of present Iraq, Iran, Syria, and Turkey, were pastoralists until the end of World

and mounted nomads migrating from the steppes of central Asia; the pre-Islamic Achaemenid, Parthian, and Sasanid regimes were all products of such nomadic invasions, as were the Muslim Seljuk, Qatar, and Ottoman Empires. See Lindholm, *The Islamic Middle East*, 23.

38. Lindholm, *The Islamic Middle East*, 24; Lois Beck, "Tribes and the State in Nineteenth and Twentieth-Century Iran," in Philip Khoury and Joseph Kostiner (eds.), *Tribes and State Formation in the Middle East* (Berkeley: University of California Press, 1990).

39. Johnson and Earle, *The Evolution of Human Societies*, 235.

40. When Lindholm did his research in Swat, northern Pakistan, the population density was about 1,660 per square mile—greater than Bangladesh. See Lindholm, *The Islamic Middle East*, 25.

41. Lindholm, *The Islamic Middle East*, 27.

War I. After 1918, Great Britain's enforcement of colonial borders began to impede the seasonal migration of large flocks. The continued border clashes with the new states of Iran, Iraq, and Turkey required most Kurds to abandon their traditional way of life and settle in villages and cities. Pastoralist cultural values and social practices can endure even where farming has been the main form of sustenance for centuries. In areas of India where honor killings are frequent, such as Bihar state, Haryana, Punjab, Rajasthan, and Utter Pradesh, the Jats and Rajputs are also most numerous. Men in these Indian groups identify with a warrior past, strongly endorse cultural ideals of honor, and appear to have originated as pastoralists in the lower Indus River valley and to have migrated north and east.[42]

Pakistan likewise has a large population of Rajputs and Balochi in Sindh province where honor killings rates are high, and they are high in areas settled predominately by the Pashtun: Punjab, Swat, Waziristan, and the Northwest Frontier. The Pashtun consist of a group of about 60 tribes who settled northern Pakistan and much of Afghanistan more than 1,000 years ago. Their origins are obscure, but it is most likely that they were initially herding people who migrated across large areas and developed the capacity to protect themselves from a long list of marauders, raiders, and erstwhile conquerors.[43] The Pashtun consider themselves a "race of warriors," and they live by a code of honor known as *Pashtunwali*, or "the way of the Pashtun." While it is hardly surprising that a majority of Pashtuns would adopt farming for the greater economic security it provides, many Pasthun continue to engage in herding, and the Pasthun themselves continue to distinguish between the *qalang*, the farming and sedentary Pasthun who cannot evade taxation, and the pastoral *yaghestan*, or *nang*, who regard themselves as "chivalrous."[44] A Landinfo Report (from Oslo, Norway) reviewing research on honor killing in the Islamic Republic of Iran likewise indicates that honor killings occur most frequently in areas in which pastoralists predominate or in which majorities or large minorities were former nomadic or pastoralist peoples.[45]

---

42. Catherine B. Asher and Cynthia Talbot, *India before Europe* (Cambridge: Cambridge University Press, 2006).

43. Anatol Lieven, *Pakistan: A Hard Country* (New York: Public Affairs, 2011), 383.

44. Maleeha Aslam, *Gender-Based Explosions: The Nexus Between Muslim Masculinities, Jihadist Islamism and Terrorism* (Tokyo and New York: United Nations University Press, 2012), 170; Lindholm, *The Islamic Middle East*, 25.

45. Khuzestan province has a majority population of Arab, Lori (from a pastoralist background), and Kurds. According to the Asia Pacific Women's Watch in 2004, a government representative in Khuzestan reported that, in 2001, 565 women in the province lost their lives due to honor killing. Ilam has similar demographics, whereas the pastoralist Lori predominant in Loristan, the Kurds in Kurdistan, and Arabs and

Research by John Davis and Michael Gilsenan corroborates the hypothesis that upland farmers who practice honor killing were initially nomads and pastoralists.[46] In particular, Davis calls attention to the cultural continuities among upland farmers, as with nomads, of what he calls "shifting indeterminacy" and "endemic competitiveness." The first term refers to temporary and shifting alliances, while the second signifies competitive tendencies requiring constant wariness and the readiness of each man to look out for himself. Perpetuation of these endemic cultural patterns has two effects: no overarching power can gain uncontested and lasting domain, and, second, status rankings will be local and subject to rapid fluctuation, or in other words, subject to the two Arabic rules: "the enemy of my enemy is my friend," and "me against my brother, me and my brother against my cousin, me, my brother, and cousin against the world." Davis asserts, "thwarted in their attempts to gain dominance, men settle for the next best—'we are all equal'; at least they can resist others' assertions of dominance."[47] In Davis's view, some compensation for the difficulties of attaining distinctions of status and power is afforded through *sharaf* competitions in demonstrations of bravery, generosity, and loyalty.

Indeed, as Lindholm notes, agrarian Pashtun communities exhibit a high level of violence among close kinsmen who are rivals for the small plots of land left to them by their common ancestors. "In fact," Lindholm adds, "among the Pukhtun [Pashtun], the term of reference for a father's brother's son is *tarbut*, which also means 'enemy.'"[48] Thus, while the level of conflict among nomads is often extensive, the greatest conflict occurs between rival clans. In addition, when herders settle down in agrarian communities such as those of the Pashtun, members of a clan continuously live in proximity. Consequently, it is hardly surprising that the norm has become face-to-face confrontations among close relatives.[49]

Balochi in Sistan, all provinces in which honor killing rates are high. In Iran, honor killings are reported to be lower where Persian Iranians dominate. See Landinfo, *Landinfo Report: Honor Killings in Iran* (Oslo, Norway: 2009), www.landinfo.no/asset/960/1/960_1.pdf, accessed May 22, 2009.

46. John Davis, *People of the Mediterranean* (London: Routledge and Kegan Paul, 1977); and Michael Gilsenan, "Lying, Honor, and Contradiction" in Donna Lee Bowen and Evelyn Early (eds.), *Everyday Life in the Muslim East* (Bloomington, IN: Indiana University Press, 1993).

47. Davis, *People of the Mediterranean*, 99.

48. Lindholm, *The Islamic Middle East*, 59.

49. This may be a result of settling within states and increased protection from attack by large well-organized adversaries, as well as the occasional surpluses produced and fallow periods that enable men to absent themselves from farming to provide a more specialized defense.

The extreme ecological difficulties, both physical and human, faced by early pastoralists, nomads, and agriculturalists cannot be overemphasized. I suspect that struggles between intertribal groups were always waged on a "winner-take-all" basis from the fact that this feature continues today. "The common perception in a tribal society [remains] . . . that any social contest is a zero-sum game in which the gain of one is considered a loss to the other."[50] Even the development of the honor code as a check on the ruthless ambitions of the individual did not soften the warrior's attitude toward an opponent. As important as gratitude and hospitality were, they applied almost exclusively to temporary allies and intratribal relations. As Salzman notes, "There is no honor in 'playing fairly,' 'doing your best,' or 'upholding the rules.' Winning, to paraphrase a famous American football coach, is not the best thing, it is the only thing."[51] Nevertheless, further cultural adaptations would have to reconcile incompatible tendencies between the need for self-assertive, competitive, and self-justifying individualism on the one hand, and, on the other, the cooperation, solidarity, and sociability required for effective group self-help and self-defense.

6.2 THE EMERGENCE OF CONSANGUINE HIERARCHICAL PATRIARCHY

Recent research establishes a very high correlation between the development of wealth through property in herds or flocks, father–son inheritance, and a patrilineal system in which the locus of identity is found in descent through males rather than through the distaff side of the family.[52] CHP is an extreme hierarchical structure based on blood relationships among males, probably the first feature of this system. The wealth and influence of a family head was limited by the manageable size of his herd or flock. Beyond this limit he had to rely on the labor of others, but this was a risky option. Hiring shepherds as laborers was too risky because, given the absence of law enforcement, it would have been more profitable for hired hands to rustle animals than work for wages. Allowing daughters to attend to flocks was even riskier because female mortality was high, and females

50. Alon Ben Meir, "Iraq's Insurgency—A Catch-22," Alon Ben-Meir Blog at http://www.alonben-meir.com/articles/iraqs-insurgency-a-catch22/, accessed Apr. 15, 2014.
51. Philip Carl Salzman, *Culture and Conflict in the Middle East* (Amherst, NY: Humanity Press, 2008), 184.
52. See John Hartung, "Polygamy and the Inheritance of Wealth," *Current Anthropology* 23 (1982), 1–12; Laura L. Betzig, *Despotism and Differential Reproduction; A Darwinian View of History* (Hawthorne, NY: Aldino, 1986).

were liable to be kidnapped either to be sold, kept as slaves, or to increase the kidnapper's own supply of fighting sons. The most effective alternative was for brothers to tend herds together, to arrange first-cousin marriages between their sons and daughters, and then pass care of herds and flocks on to sons expected to be loyal to the family.

The proclivity to celebrate a male birth and to mourn a daughter's birth—still very common—had its origin, I surmise, in the greater labor value and defensive abilities of sons and, hence, the greater net profitability of sons over daughters. This was especially true when female births became more numerous than male births in a family or clan, and dowries were required to dispose of daughters through marriage. Allegedly, female infanticide occurred in some areas of the nomadic-pastoralist domain during the *Jahiliyya*, the "age of ignorance," or time before the coming of Islam. Female infanticide appears clearly paradoxical, but the logic of competitive group advantage can recommend this course when survival is difficult. When scarcity threatens the survival of both male and female children in groups inhabiting a certain region, one group may find it advantageous to allow female infants to die and to invest exclusively in the survival of male children. This strategy will be adaptive if, when older, healthy male offspring of the first group are able to kidnap fertile women from groups weakened by efforts to raise all offspring.[53] Hence, it is likely that where female infanticide had become established, it did not end until the groups from whom women were poached developed the ability to protect themselves.

In harsh living conditions, care had to be exercised over the reproductive assets of one's stock. It was necessary, for instance, to be careful that lambing and kidding occurred in the spring, probably at the end of the migration to summer pastures, where the best forage would be available. It is probable that a similar view was taken of human reproduction; certainly, giving birth and caring for a child would be much more difficult during migratory passages while traveling great distances in the cold, dry winter months in search of sparse fodder. Male efforts to manage female reproduction probably arose analogously with efforts to maximize the reproductive assets of herds and flocks by maximizing the survival of offspring and minimizing costs in time, effort, and the drain on moveable food stocks. Thus what began as self-interested methods of ensuring the

---

53. Steven Pinker, *The Better Angels of Our Nature: Why Violence Has Declined* (New York: Penguin Books, 2011), 421; and Mildred Dickemann, "Female Infanticide and Reproductive Strategies of Stratified Human Societies," in Napoleon A. Chagnon and William Irons (eds.), *Evolutionary Biology and Human Social Behavior* (Scituate, MA: Duxbury Press, 1979), 320–64.

survival of small family groups became over time a sociocultural function necessary for the group's reproduction of itself through the control of female sexuality.

The institution of father–son inheritance appears to have evolved to maintain cohesion within the extended family, clan, and tribe. A son's interests in attending to the herds or flocks of fathers and uncles was likely to be reliable while he remained dependent on patriarchal assets and could expect to receive a bride, have children of his own, and succeed eventually to the status and influence of an elder. The alternative of receiving herding animals as gifts from patriarchs and setting up households on their own was far too risky, as his own animals would require their own pasturage and his family could no longer count on the protection of family or clan. Consequently, we must expect that even younger sons, when a patriarch had many, avoided becoming supernumerary by working with older brothers to increase the size of herds. Given propensities to be egoistic and fiercely independent, frustration, envy, and strife must have clouded relationships among brothers, especially as difficult living conditions favored what psychologists call a "fast living style"—one in which girls become brides as soon as (or before) they reach puberty and thus have extended childbearing years.[54] Yet, because wealth and status lay in the size of a family's herds and would decline if stocks were divided among many sons, the best course for all was to maximize productivity by increasing herds up to the carrying capacity of the locale, thereby increasing wealth and status and sharing honor as a family attribute.

Father–son inheritance was a mainstay of this strategy. With rare exceptions (see Section 8.3), father–daughter inheritance, matrilineal descent, and matrilocal communities were not adaptive advantages. The father–son and patrilineal options had greater adaptive fitness: presuming continual needs to tend grazing animals and for fighting men to defend encampments and the clan or tribe, patrilineal groups could outpace matrilineal groups in the "production" of helping hands, as well as in the conservation of assets such as food stocks to stave off hunger or animals for trade. In addition, more rapid reproductive rates within polygamous patrilineal groups would enhance opportunities for successful raiding. When marriages were endogamous, inheritance as consistent investment in sons would result in the conservation of assets in the patrilineage. By contrast, for an extended family or clan, investment in daughters risked a significant

---

54. Eric J. Pedersen, Daniel E. Foster, and Michael E. McCullough, "Life History, Code of Honor, and Emotional Responses to Inequality in an Economic Game," *Emotion* 15, 5 (Oct. 2014), 920–29.

loss of assets in only a generation or two. A daughter can only bear one child, on average, in nine months; health risks are greatest during pregnancy; and, especially, the father would have a claim on the child born of the union. Not only would father–daughter inheritance reduce the numbers of available herders and warriors, it would result in serious loss if the father's family had a falling out with the mother's family, or if a dispute elsewhere in a complex lineage system required the families to become rivals (see Section 6.3).

Communal interest in the continuing strength in numbers likely brought with it a strong interest in reproduction within the group and group identity. Control over reproduction, and hence female sexuality, intensifies when a group seeks to preserve its identity. Reproduction acquires a normative stature for a community and occurs as a social phenomenon, a public affair rather than one that is private. In addition, initially, some sons' reproductive mates must have been slaves captured in raids or kidnapped from more distant and unrelated clans. Female slaves were highly sought for breeding purposes, and women were frequently captured and made concubines. However, at some point after the formation of a clear identity for a population group as a "people," clan and tribe membership was closed to almost all except those with a full-blooded pedigree; that is, men and women whose ancestry on both sides consisted of tribal members.[55] In fact, the ban on adoptions from outside the family continues today in most Muslim-majority countries, although the Prophet Mohammad had been an orphan and himself adopted a son. As of 2009, of the 23 independent countries in the regions studied here, all but 5 legally prohibited both domestic and intercountry adoptions.[56]

Lindholm and others regard blood relationships among early nomads and pastoralists as largely "ideological,"[57] but it is more logical that the exclusion of slave-born and adopted males was a functional feature of

---

55. Because the Qu'ran and *hadith* of the Prophet and his companions did not forbid slavery or sexual relations between Muslims and female slaves, Muslim jurists struggled to define the status of children borne by a female slave whose father was Muslim. The general solution was to recognize such children as free and legitimate. See Kecia Ali, *Sexual Ethics and Islam* (Oxford: Oneworld, 2006), 46.

56. India, Lebanon, Sudan, Tunisia, and Turkey permit adoptions, but they are not legally accepted in Afghanistan, Algeria, Dijibuti, Egypt, Iran, Iraq, Jordan, Kuwait, Libya, Mauritania, Morocco, Oman, Qatar, Saudi Arabia, Somalia, Syria, United Arab Emirates, and Yemen. See United Nations Department of Economic and Social Affairs, Population Division, "Child Adoption: Trends and Policies" (New York: UN, 2009), www.un.org/esa/population/publications/adoption2010/child_adoption.pdf, accessed Oct. 20, 2015.

57. Lindholm, *The Islamic Middle East*, 53–54.

nomadic and pastoral ancestors of HSCs. Restricting membership to birth within the same clan or tribe makes sense if we postulate that contact between different tribes was limited to trade or hostile circumstances. In addition, reproduction with a female captured in a war or raid was far from ideal. Traumatized and alienated mates could not be counted on to make reliable mothers or tribal members in socializing their children. Moreover, captured mates posed risks of absconding with children or other acts of betrayal unless guarded, and, if unable to escape, might bend their efforts to alienate offspring against the men who sired them. (As noted in Section 5.3, this appears to be a significant problem even for many married couples coming from the same extended family or clan.) Serious alienation of sons from fathers would constitute a severe blow. Even if defection to the mother's tribe was a remote possibility, the lack of extensive kinship would weaken the bonds within the extended family and between it and the larger clan and tribe: offspring of enslaved mates would be less desirable as mates, and they might be unreliable herders or warriors. The cumulative effect of such concerns was an evolved cultural proclivity to reject membership from outside the clan and exogamous unions.[58] And as I discuss in Section 6.4, these changes had significant effects on the development of honor killing.

The danger of relying for reproduction on potentially disloyal or subversive mates could be lessened greatly in the same way that loyal labor could be increased, namely, by marrying "close to the bone." It is possible that the practice of cousin marriages (or between nephew–aunt and uncle–niece) was promoted initially by a shortage of marriageable partners, but, as noted earlier, it was institutionalized as a means of maximizing assets held by a close kinship group as well as ensuring that marital unions would contribute to greater stability for the group because both partners were now subjected to the same family discipline. The ideal arrangement came to be FBD marriages in which a son marries his *bint amin*, or his paternal uncle's daughter. Such FBD marriages became so strongly favored that, among many groups, a young man could exert a marriage claim over his *bint*

58. The male fear of sexual usurpation is very widespread and tenacious. The widespread and culturally promoted male desire for virgin brides appears to derive from concerns that a female's prior experience may signal possible sexual disloyalty (especially if the bride judges performance to be inadequate). As well, Matthew Ridley reports, fear of betrayal may explain what is otherwise bafflingly counterintuitive: namely, that husbands of rape victims are more likely to be traumatized and, despite themselves, resent their raped wives if the wife was not physically hurt during the rape. Presumably, spouses process physical harm (perhaps subconsciously) as evidence of resistance. See Matthew Ridley, *The Red Queen: Sex and the Evolution of Human Nature* (New York: Harper Collins, 1993), 237.

amin, which required his permission before she could marry anyone else.[59] Endogamous FBD unions were accompanied by patrilocality, a system in which the bride leaves her family's home to live with her husband's family, which lives very near other descendants of a common patrilineal ancestor.

As FBD marriages occurred frequently (and they still comprise approximately 40–50% of all marriages within Pakistan and among Pakistani British immigrants), familial relations became denser because of the multiple marriage transactions within the same lineage. Consequently, sociability, common identity, and *asabiyya* developed.[60] The latter refers to "group feeling" and a sense of obligation to one's kin. In addition, individual identity was based on common genealogical descent on the father's side of the family; moreover, over time and through FBD marriages, group identity increased as virtually everyone was descended from the same common ancestor.

At this stage, CHP existed as a fully fledged and complex institution. In a patrilineal and patrilocal group, the system of father–son inheritance and arranged endogamous marriages dramatically increased paternal control over potentially unruly sons.[61] Because women must be protected from raiders and poachers, their activities were restricted to family caretaking and they themselves were valued first and foremost as "vessels" through which the family and clan reproduced itself. Consequently, the husband's dominion over wife and daughters developed in parallel with the *pater familias'* domination of his sons and grandsons.

Nevertheless, adaptive fitness among nomads and pastoralists required finding a way to balance contradictory dynamics. On one side, the independent, self-reliant, self-aggrandizing, jealous, and aggressive traits of individuals needed to be curbed; unless reined-in, these antisocial traits would render impossible the needed prosocial benefits of reciprocity and cooperation, such as managing husbandry to avert the collapse of overgrazed pasturage. Yet, resoluteness, boldness, and fierceness also needed nurturing so that men would be effective as warriors defending encampments and successfully raiding outsiders. Such a combination of

59. Lindholm, *The Islamic Middle East*, 55.
60. Lindholm, *The Islamic Middle East*, 53–55.
61. Lindholm, *The Islamic Middle East*, 58. Kinship alliances were strongly associated with geographical proximity. Brothers live together in the extended household, first cousins are within the same local neighborhood, and second cousins are somewhat farther away. This pattern predominates even today and in urban areas as well as rural villages or encampments. In fact, everywhere it is generally assumed that those physically closest are one's closest kin and thus one's closest allies—or closest enemies, depending on the situation at the moment.

contrary traits produced a volatile "cocktail" prone to frequent irruptions. Despite *asabiyya*, trust was a frequent casualty. For instance, can one expect that aid given today will be reciprocated tomorrow if today's recipients find on the morrow that their self-interests no longer align with those of yesterday's benefactors? The following passage from Lindholm, referring to Frederick Barth's study of Pukhtun [Pashtun] farmers, was true, I suggest, for camel nomads and shepherds generally:

> Each person is acting according to what he understands as his own personal interests against his most salient opponents and will switch sides with alacrity when advantage is perceived. For instance, if one individual is very successful in his political maneuvering, he will find his erstwhile allies joining his enemies to humble him. The zero-sum game leads to a long-term balance of opposition, as Frederick Barth has elegantly shown to exist among the Pukhtun. The same pattern can be seen on a larger scale, and accounts for the perpetuation of shifting dualistic factional struggle that has so prevailed throughout the Middle Eastern history. [62]

6.3 FUNCTIONS OF THE SEGMENTARY LINEAGE SYSTEM

A larger form of communal organization based on kinship and codefensive needs developed among peoples for whom honor killing would become adaptive. This system of organization is known as the SLS. It is likely that when the SLS emerged, population sizes had made it too difficult for simpler forms of patriarchal patrilocality to respond adequately to internecine conflicts. Consequently, to increase adaptive fitness, larger kin networks had to "solve" three problems. First, the loyalty of larger groups of men had to be retained despite becoming increasingly distant from one another. Second, the larger a kin network became, the greater the risk of overtaxing environmental resources. Environmental degradation, as well as conflict over scarce resources, could be mitigated by dispersal but at the possible cost of being overwhelmed by nonrelated tribes. Third, large kin groups coming together for collective defense had to be structured to be flexible: they needed to bend without breaking, especially because of the

---

62. Lindholm, *The Islamic Middle East*, 61, 124; Frederick Barth, "Segmentary Opposition and the Theory of Games: A Study of Pathan Organization," *Journal of the Royal Anthropological Institute* 89 (1959), 5–21, at 15–19; Robert Murphy and Lawrence Kasdan, "The Structure of Parallel Cousin Marriage," *American Anthropologist* 19 (1959), 17–21.

proximity of competing families and clans and the increased likelihood of continuing conflicts within tribes. The SLS was a cultural adaptation in response to these problems. The SLS did not replace CHP, but, as an addition, it enabled CHP to extend over an entire tribe or even a number of distantly related tribes.

On their own, CHP and the FBD marriage system might have increased intragroup conflicts within a larger lineage system. Functionally, CHP would operate to arrange unions, and, while FBD operated to preserve capital within the extended family, stability also required a certain degree of stagnation. Younger sons who inherited less and might not have had cousins to marry were likely to have been restless and to have believed they could do better by leaving the larger collectivity and devoting themselves exclusively to their own immediate families. Self-interest stronger than *asabiyya* and splintering would have posed risks of survival for the larger group, however. Ironically, the defensive needs of the larger collectivity did not diminish with increases in its size, wealth, and power—precisely the conditions that might encourage smaller "denser" cohorts to separate from it. The difficulty was that, given the similar cultural evolution of pastoral and herding peoples, a lineage group increasing in size, wealth, and power would have come into greater contact with and would have been a desirable "prize" for other increasingly powerful lineage groups, either through the greed and ambition of the latter or its own abilities to raid encampments or attack trading caravansaries. Thus, the adaptive advantage for the lineage collectivity as a whole was to resist subdivision and retain the protective services and opportunistic benefits of the maximum of young, fierce, and hardy male warriors.

The survival and cohesion of the lineage group thus required "bridging the gap," as Philip Salzman says, between the short-term interests of individual group members and families versus the long-term interests of the larger group.[63] The adaptive solution was the development of communal emphasis on honor and shame. Salzman rightly emphasizes that a social milieu in which men are the primary agents, and in which a man's honor is the highest good, will be a cultural milieu that creates and imposes *extrinsic* rewards and punishments. In effect, when honor and shame are a matter of *public* approbation or disapprobation, acquiring the highest good cannot be entirely a matter of personal effort or good fortune. As Salzman points out, this makes "actions to support the group in the long run a matter of immediate consequence to the individual."[64]

63. Salzman, *Culture and Conflict*, 104.
64. Salzman, *Culture and Conflict*, 105.

As emphasized at various points (e.g., Sections 1.1, 2.2, and 3.2–3.3), a person who loses honor usually faces (or fears facing) a wide range of imminent and negative consequences. Moreover, among the primary principles of the honor code are loyalty to one's closest kin as well as the obligation to avenge any harm befalling a blood relative. Consequently, because of the demands of honor, "The gap between the individual and the group, and between short-term interest and long-term interest, is bridged. The individual's interest in his honor is manifested in fulfilling his duty for his group, and thus the active commitment of individual members is secured for the group."[65]

Although by no means limited to them, among the peoples of the African and Asian deserts and upland pastures, the SLS evolved to maximize equality and independence among men during times of peace and to maximize unity and power during times of war. These functions were achieved by ensuring that, should there be conflict, individuals would bond through a simple principle: namely, that close patrilineal relatives should unite together when a dispute arose involving more distant relatives. Hence, the SLS operated to maintain a rough power balance and thereby "contain" conflict by ensuring a near parity of force. When groups face off against each other, the system enables each side to complement its fighting forces to prevent being overwhelmed, but only in a manner that balances, or complements, opposition of the other side.

Furthermore, within the SLS, all tribesmen can organize in response to danger without need for a designated military class or leader provided that each "unit" of the SLS is based on CHP, thus enabling leadership roles to devolve on the most senior relevant patriarch. Likewise, the SLS enables effective fighting forces to emerge without time and effort lost in organizing and training provided, of course, that each male is sufficiently socialized as a warrior. Moreover, despite unity and synchronized actions when conflicts arise, the SLS enables individuals to regard themselves as having equally indispensable places, enjoying equal honor, or *sharaf* (see Section 3.4).

As indicated earlier, the SLS can also perform effectively in a seemingly paradoxical way. While able to unite individuals, even formerly bitter adversaries, into a coordinated fighting force, the SLS also serves as a brake on the extent to which potentially divisive conflicts arising from within the system become so destructive as to lead to unregulated violence (and the

---

65. Salzman, *Culture and Conflict*, 105.

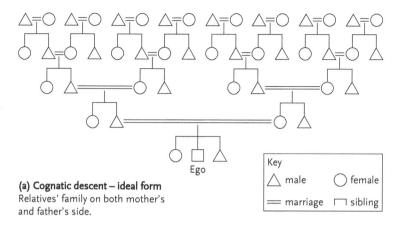

(a) Cognatic descent – ideal form
Relatives' family on both mother's
and father's side.

Ego

Key
△ male ○ female
═ marriage ▢ sibling

Figure 6.1 The European and North American lineage system: cognatic descent—ideal form.
Source: From Charles Lindholm, *The Islamic Middle East: An Historical Anthropology,* Blackwell (c) 1996.
Reprinted with permission from John Wiley & Sons Ltd.

destruction of the system itself). The latter function is achieved through "complimentary opposition,"[66] or balanced opposition.

This complexity of SLS functioning can be elucidated by considering differences between the SLS and the cognatic kinship structure in Europe and North America. For the latter, marriages are predominately exogamous, with partners coming from unrelated families. Partly for this reason, as well as the norm that spouses and their respective families deserve equal consideration, any resulting conflict between the maternal and paternal lines may impose conflicting demands for loyalty. Hence, in the Western system, there is no systematic resolution; rather, family conflicts are settled (if they are) on a case-by-case basis, and resolution may require recourse to agents (e.g., lawyers) outside the families involved.

Figure 6.1 represents the ideal form of cognatic descent for a person (represented by "Ego") of Western European heritage. Note that in this model there is no connection between relatives of the individual's father's side and the individual's mother's side of the family. By contrast, the patterns of relationship in the SLS in Figure 6.2 are unambiguous. (Figures from Lindholm, p. 57.) Rather than standing at the nadir of a large inverted pyramid, the individual is one node of the SLS at the base of a large triangle that reaches its apex with the original patriarch five generations back.[67] As Lindholm indicates, "All individuals in the system know or can discover their exact genealogical distance from every other individual in it

66. Lindholm, *The Islamic Middle East,* 58.
67. Lindholm, *The Islamic Middle East,* 57.

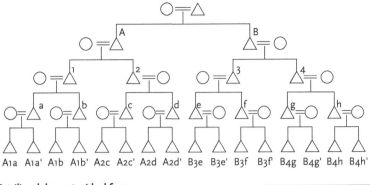

(b) Patrilineal descent – ideal form

Only patrilineal relatives count in terms of inheritance and kinship rights, and blood obligations. Idealy, all A are allied politically against all B, A1 are allied against A2, A1a are allies against A1b. However this simple pattern is cross-cut by alliances on the grounds of "the enemy of my enemy is my friend."

Key
△ male ○ female
═ marriage ⊓ sibling

Figure 6.2 The Middle Eastern segmentary lineage system: partrilineal descent—ideal form. *Source:* From Charles Lindholm, The Islamic Middle East: An Historical Anthropology, Blackwell (c) 1996. Reprinted with permission from John Wiley & Sons Ltd.

by tracing back to the common ancestor and then down again to the person in question."[68] The person in question, is, of course, the person with whom the individual, say A1a, must ally himself or oppose in an ongoing quarrel. For instance, if a serious quarrel between A1 and B3 breaks out, then all the descendants of A1, including A1a (in the furthest generation) must side with A1, as well as all the descendants of A2, A1's brother, right down to A2d'. Similarly, all of B3's descendants and closest blood relatives must side with B3. This pattern of commitment is economically summarized by the common Arabic expression: "I against my brother, my brothers and I against our cousins, my brothers and cousins and I against the world."[69]

All males living within the SLS are supposed to be able to trace their patrilineal line back at least five generations. Thus, when it comes to conflict against a nonrelated group, or "my brothers and cousins and I against the world," then whole clans and tribal units, and even allied tribes, can unite with great rapidity. Likewise, members in any node of the kinship system, if they chance on an opportunity for aggrandizement, can cause the system to expand rapidly, thus defeating, incorporating, or enslaving competing groups that lack the capacity to expand with equal alacrity. The SLS can

68. Lindholm, *The Islamic Middle East*, 57.
69. Salzman, *Culture and Conflict*, 61.

mobilize and put into the field thousands of fighting men, or even hundreds of thousands, depending on the characteristics of the opposition.[70]

At times of relative quiescence, the SLS remains decentralized and clans and individual men and their families pursue their own independent objectives on terms of equality. There is in the SLS no need for permanent leadership, hierarchical organization, class structure, or stratification of any kind. Even clans and tribes living in regions frequently beset by invasion have no need for a permanent and rigid structure. Except in the event of trouble or opportunistic gain, life continues on the "premises of equality, autonomy, and the acquisition of reputation. Thus no man has power over another nor can his authority outstrip his reputation."[71]

Studying rivalries among leaders within the al-Qays tribal confederacy as Islam spread, Welhausen records the many cases of jealous rivalry intended to block the advantage-taking of relatives, but also adds: "although they might play each other ill tricks, they nevertheless held faithfully with each other against foreign clans."[72] Thus segmentary lineages expand and contract in size and weight, permitting flexibility in fluid social groupings while tolerating as much antagonism as cooperation.[73] In addition, the SLS continues to be very much alive, as demonstrated by the studies of Salzman of the Sarhadi Baluch people in Iran,[74] and Kressel's study of segmentary opposition between two urbanized Bedouin tribes, the Barabha and the Shalalfa, in the Israeli town of Rala.[75]

The dynamics of the SLS require that the principle of "collective responsibility" apply throughout the lineage. This means that any person's individual problem, when it might possibly cross lineage lines, becomes the affair of the entire patrilineage.[76] Thus SLS introduces a dynamic that, when it works well, tends to make opposing sides equal in strength, thus promoting stalemate and, consequently, reducing the dangers of unrestrained violence. In addition, by inducing stalemate, the SLS supposedly promotes opportunities for the resolution of the conflict through mediation and arbitration. Consider Figure 6.2 and note that, although all of

---

70. Salzman, *Culture and Conflict*, 79.

71. William Lancaster, *The Rwala Bedouin Today*, 2nd ed. (Prospect Heights, IL: Waveland, 1997), 73.

72. Julius Welhausen, *The Arab Kingdom and Its Fall* (London: Curzon Press, 1927), 27, cited by Lindholm, *The Islamic Middle East*, 58.

73. Elizabeth E. Bacon, *Obok: A Study of Social Structure in Eurasia* (New York: Wenner-Gren Foundation, 1958).

74. Salzman, *Culture and Conflict*, 65–93.

75. Gideon M. Kressel, *Ascendancy Through Aggression: The Anatomy of a Blood Feud Among Urbanized Bedouin* (Weisbaden, Germany: Otto Harrasowitz Verlag, 1996).

76. Kressel, *Ascendancy*, 53; Salzman, *Culture and Conflict*, 108.

those in the fifth generation from the top down have the exact same great-great-grandparents, if a conflict were to occur between A1a (on the far left) and B4h' (on the far right), then, due to complementary opposition, the entire patrilineage would cleave into two equal parts, with all A's siding with A1a and all B's siding with B4h'.

In sociocultural and geopolitical contexts otherwise characterized by a zero-sum, "winner-take-all" ethos, complementary opposition is an important way of keeping tribal groups from internecine bloodshed, which risks resulting either in the wholesale elimination of a group or its subjugation by an aggressor not itself weakened by internal fighting.[77] In relating an individual's obligations to his next of kin, the SLS also fosters what Lindholm refers to as a "band of brothers" mentality abetted by ideals of *asabiyya*.[78] Often grazing rights, farmlands, and timber entitlements are held cooperatively by the lineage as a "corporate" unit.[79] In addition, given this "all for one and one for all" mentality, it is easy to understand how the principle of shared blood debt evolved. Every male in the direct lineage is regarded as equally responsible for a death inflicted on an adversary, and, likewise, all are responsible to avenge a death inflicted on one's blood kin.[80]

Yet, collective responsibility in matters of vengeance illustrates a major weakness of the SLS. If stalemate failed, then blood feuds between opposing tribes or clans could continue interminably—or up to the proverbial last man standing—because, given equal responsibility, it did not matter who in the opposing group was harmed in a reprisal. As Mohandas Gandhi allegedly said, "an eye for an eye eventually leaves the whole world blind," and indeed, revenge, or *badal*, could lead to the decimation of entire

---

77. Salzman maintains that complementary opposition "as part of a 'segmentary model' was the way that Sarhadi tribesmen themselves looked at political alliances and action." See Salzman, *Culture and Conflict*, 94. In addition, Salzman claims that complementary opposition continues to be operative in Middle Eastern towns and cities, citing as an example a case from Gaza in 2006 (98–99). Indeed, the primary form of organization throughout the Middle East even today continues to be tribal and based on the SLS and complementary opposition. See Salzman, *Culture and Conflict*, 131–212. These observations are critical for they demonstrate both that the SLS is not a model imposed by anthropologists on the people studied but instead a feature of reality embraced by the peoples studied and that this millennial cultural adaptation continues today. Salzman at 94 says that the social problem of two or three *brasrend* (minimal lineages) ganging up on a single *brasrend* was "solved by biological—at least conceptually biological—means." For Lindholm, who did his fieldwork among the Pushtans of the Swat in Northern Pakistan, the SLS is a matter of "kinship ideology"; see Lindholm, *The Islamic Middle East*, 53. Thus both Salzman and Lindholm recognize, at least to some degree, the cultural origins of the SLS.

78. Lindholm, *The Islamic Middle East*, 53; Salzman, *Culture and Conflict*, 67.

79. Lindholm, *The Islamic Middle East*, 54.

80. Lindholm, *The Islamic Middle East*, 54.

groups. Complementary opposition was most effective in preventing serious harm; once blood-letting began, it was far more difficult to end. Thus, although collective responsibility for avenging a fallen comrade is a by-product of the SLS, no institutional way of avoiding the destructiveness of vendettas accompanied it.

The limited effectiveness of the SLS in this last instance points to two additional liabilities that bear more closely on honor killing. One concerns the *rapidity* with which hostility can build between solidary groups, even over trivial causes. For instance, one of the tribal conflicts recounted by Salzman began over an incident which involved a stray and "greedy" camel helping itself to dates growing on palms owned by Rashid, a member of the Kamil Hanzai tribe.[81] When Mirad, of the Rahmatzai lineage, eventually came for his camel, Rashid told Mirad he could have the camel back, but only if he paid Rashid for the dates eaten. Within two days, the conflict had escalated into physical fighting among members of the tribes, and only five days after the initial incident, a party of just over 100 men of the Kamil Hanzai and their Soherabazi allies set off to battle the Rahmatzai. This case also illustrates the *persistence* of hostility, as the dispute continued intermittently for three years, sometimes breaking out into violence, before being resolved.

A further liability of the SLS arises from the failure of the SLS to balance and pacify conflicts involving both *males and females*. In discussing the SLS, anthropologists always presuppose that agents in conflict are men. Yet, what is likely to happen if the conflict arises because of a woman's alleged dishonor? As noted earlier, CHP does not count descent on the distaff side: a woman's lineage is the same as her brothers. However, consider the complications of FBD marriages, and especially the most favored double-cousin marriages in which two children of each of two brothers are married: the daughters of one brother marrying the sons of the other brother. When marriages between close kin have been frequent throughout generations, then many wives will share the same male ancestors with their husbands. For instance, if they are children of a double-cousin union, then they will have the same male genealogical descent as will first cousins, and even second cousins will share great-grandparents on at least one side of the family. A conflict between two brothers or male first cousins over allegations of the questionable conduct of a close female relative, possibly the wife of one and the sister of the other, is a conflict that cannot be "balanced" within the SLS. Given that descent is virtually the same, there

81. Salzman, *Culture and Conflict*, 74.

will be no clear lines of demarcation along which subgroups can separate to engage in "counterweight" balancing.

In summary, the SLS developed as a way to rapidly organize *males* according to the principle of kin relationship and to decentralize smoothly into small units when the dangers or opportunities of conflict temporarily fade. However, unless cooler heads could prevail nearer the top of a hierarchy, the SLS was also liable to breakdown by turning localized, potentially isolatable disputes involving few individuals into lethal conflicts between tribes. More serious, the SLS, as a social structure, did not offer a way of resolving conflicts that centered on alleged breaches of honor by women and implicated closely related males in the natal family and among accusers. This second problem must have become increasingly acute among prospering lineage groups and as FBD and double-cousin marriages became more common.

6.4   COSTLY SIGNALING AND THE ADVENT OF HONOR KILLING

Legend says that Qays bin Asim, the ancient leader of the al-Ash-Sheith clan, a major branch of the large Banu Tamine tribe of Arabia, was the first to kill his daughters for honor. He is alleged to have murdered his daughters to avert the possibility that they might have caused him dishonor. However, the Baloch tribes of Iran and Pakistan and the Pashtun of Afghanistan each claim a distinctive origin for the social practice. In truth, scholars have no idea of the place of origin of honor killing or whether it coevolved in different locales or spread through cultural transmission.

However, the most important question is this: *Why* did a social practice as seemingly dysfunctional and wasteful as honor killing arise in the first place? The best explanation, in my view, suggests that honor killing was initially infrequent when hardships, scarcity, and danger to isolated groups did not permit the growth of larger tribal populations with advanced SLS. However, the social practice became adaptive when SLS were instituted virtually everywhere HSCs existed throughout the Middle East, North Africa, and the pastoralist areas of Afghanistan, Pakistan, and northern India. Once SLS were prevalent, and logic required that one's own group adapt SLS provided enemies did, then a new problem arose: how to prevent the destruction of the SLS by irresolvable conflict from within. Honor killing developed, I infer, as a functional means of resolving this problem.

Because honor killing involves complex sets of attitudes, behaviors, and norms, it could not have arisen *sui generis* as a social practice: it must have had some earlier but partial precedents. In fact, we can surmise that honor killing first evolved through the combination of two other culturally evolved sets of behavioral traits known as *mate guarding* and *costly signaling*. There is a biological basis for the behavioral traits of each. I offer an account of how both mate guarding and costly signaling became adapted into the social practice of honor killing. It is important to remember that honor killing as it exists today is the final product of a long process of cultural evolution. I shall argue in Section 6.5 that the practice has become an exaptation; that is, it has evolved further to serve a secondary function that goes beyond its initial function.

Recall that because early ancestors of camel nomads and pastoral shepherds needed to disperse widely to tend to grazing herds or flocks, they confronted a serious and recurrent problem: the theft of reproductively valuable mates. The most common human response to this problem is one shared biologically with animals of many species: various forms of mate guarding. Mate guarding is a practice by which one mate—a male in this case—attempts to secure sole access to the reproductive benefits of the other—the female mate.[82] Mate guarding among humans reaches an extreme form in HSCs and elsewhere throughout the Middle East and adjacent regions. Practices common today likely had their origins in the distant past and consist of the segregation of women from men (except male members of the family), sequestration in the home (e.g., *purdah*), veiling, and chaperonage when the female traveled outside the home.

In addition, if a male needs to be away from his spouse all day, or longer, he can ask his mother and his neighbors to keep an eye out. As indicated in Section 5.4, it is common in HSCs to install the mother-in-law in the home of a married son to serve as a supervisor, a general practice among today's modern descendants of the early nomadic and pastoralist tribes.[83] Evolutionary biologists report that gossip is rife among African pygmies, as it is in HSCs. A husband's best chance of deterring his wife's misadventures is to make sure she knows that he keeps up with gossip.[84]

Where mate guarding achieves a near hysterical degree of extremity, it is reasonable to infer a high degree of suspicion and anxiety about the possible encroachment of male competitors. In addition, as noted in Section 5.4, males facing reproductive failure are likely to take extreme risks to attain reproductive success, using violence if necessary, including rape, to

82. David M. Buss, *The Evolution of Desire: Strategies of Human Mating* (New York: Basic Books, 2003), 264–69.

83. Pinker, *Better Angels*, 421.

84. Ridley, *The Red Queen*, 229.

attain this end. Anxiety and vigilance is likely to be exacerbated (for potential poachers as well as guardians) when the supply of marriageable women declines, as is probable once CHP dominates a society. In CHPs, the supply of available partners is reduced by polygamy among males who are relatively more affluent; arranged marriages between nubile, fertile girls and older, high-status men; steeper bride prices as marriageable girls become scarcer; and higher rates of mortality among female infants as well as pregnant teens and women.

Chapters 4 and 5 considered the development of violence-proneness and warrior masculinity in terms of individual and social psychology. However, in addition to processes such as upbringing, shaming, identification with aggressors, and narcissism, there also may be evolved psychological processes or mechanisms that motivate the hyperdefensive actions of masculine warriors in honor–shame cultures.[85] Indeed, a variety of cultures around the world have been identified in which men behave remarkably similar to men in HSCs "in their quick, certain, and often violent responses to an insult or challenges to their strength and toughness."[86] Individuals in all of these cultures of honor share, with the ancestral groups of HSCs, the need to eke out livings in conditions of extreme uncertainty and vulnerability and where there are no overarching legal authorities able to deter or punish plunder, kidnapping, or murder committed by one clan or tribe against another. Says Shackelford, "The apparent universality of cultures of honor (under the necessary conditions) lends support to the argument that the behavioral manifestations of cultures of honor may be underpinned by universal (albeit sex-specific) evolved psychological mechanisms."[87] If this hypothesis is true, then the evolved and underlying psychological manifestations of those with warrior masculinity match the evolved cultural characteristics leading to honor killing.

Extreme mate guarding also implies heightened anxiety and suspicion about the intentions of wives and female family members. Reasons for fears about unguarded females turning into sexual wantons and unloosing *fitna*, or chaos, were explained in Section 5.1. Likewise, the tradition of blame placed on females for the destructiveness of male desire was explained in Sections 5.1 and 5.3. Here, it can be added that such concerns were abetted by a tenacious (and universal) causal fallacy known as *post hoc, ergo, propter hoc*. In other words, absent males enduring long and arduous efforts to

85. Todd K. Shackelford, "An Evolutionary Psychological Perspective on Cultures of Honor," *Evolutionary Psychology* 3 (2005), 381–91, 386.
86. Shackelford, "An Evolutionary Psychological Perspective," 386.
87. Shackelford, "An Evolutionary Psychological Perspective," 387.

ensure the survival of the family and clan must have helped sustain themselves through abstract and idealized longings. But, once in the physical presence of females, sexual desire supplanted those ideals; consequently, it seemed (fallaciously) that women and their bewitching charms (or wiles) must have caused these sexual urges.

It is likely, too, that there were some ancestral experiences of female infidelity. Evolutionary theories of female sexual desire, colorfully called "sperm competition theories," ascertain that a married woman is most likely to be unfaithful (intentionally or unintentionally) if she perceives her mate to be of low genetic quality in contrast to the genetic value of a willing usurper. In other words, a woman who has to settle for a mate she would not willingly choose—an increasingly likely outcome of arranged cousin marriages—may seek to reap the benefits of his investment in child-rearing, especially if he must remain closely bound to his family, while acquiring a superior male's genes for her offspring.[88] Like most people today, ancient nomads and pastoralists would not know the evolutionary biology behind this "Emma Bovary syndrome"; nevertheless, they might have observed correlations between illegitimate relationships and the perceived attractiveness or status of males.

However, it remains unlikely that men would have been willing to kill unfaithful wives if they could recoup her reproductive assets, unless she was pregnant and there were already too many mouths to feed. Even if honor prohibits taking her back, it is unlikely that patriarchal males would squander valuable resources rather than evolve arrangements for seeking reparations for "damaged goods" or arranging a trade or sale with an out-group. It seems even less likely that a cuckolded husband would insist that men in her natal family kill their daughter or sister, and even less likely that a girl's father or brothers would make this demand—but, of course, this is exactly what does occur in honor killing. Therefore, before honor killing was to emerge as a full-fledged social practice, extreme mate guarding and the psychological processes undergirding it must have combined with another evolved process—costly signaling. The inference drawn is that when risk of serious loss through mate poaching persists despite extreme mate guarding, costly signaling will be adapted as a significant next step.

Evolutionary biologists regard signals as traits, including structures (e.g., the peacock's colorful tail) and behaviors that have evolved specifically because they change the behavior of receivers (either co-specifics or animals

88. Ridley, *The Red Queen*, 218–19; Buss, *The Evolution of Desire*, 234–40.

of different species) in ways that benefit the signaler.[89] One simple example is the warning cry of an alert bird detecting a stalking predator, when the warning cry leads the stalker to abandon the hunt. An interesting example of signaling is the "stotting" or "pronking" of young African springbok and Thompson gazelle; rather than dashing away from predators, springbok and gazelles jump close to a cheetah or lion, signaling that they are fit and fast animals and not worth chasing.[90] In both examples, successful signaling benefits the receivers as well as the senders. Biological signals like warning calls or the peacock's tail feathers are regarded as *honest signaling* because the signaled information also promotes the adaptive fitness of the receiver.[91]

A stable system of honest signaling can generate *dishonest signaling* on the part of individuals who intend to cheat or free-ride. For instance, hunter-gatherers who depend on sharing protein, especially meat, face uncertainty over the success of hunting forays that require a group to go a long time before having meat to eat. A hunter who shares his kill indiscriminately with a large group will have no control over whether his generosity will be reciprocated, and free-riding, or reaping the benefits of group living without contributing to its maintenance, becomes an attractive strategy for some who receive meat.[92] A tribal member signals dishonestly if, when he takes shares of meat, he offers assurances that he will reciprocate but secretly hoards or fails to participate in hunting parties. However, only honest signals increase the inclusive fitness of the group because every increase in dishonest signaling weakens the integrity of the signaling system, and every corresponding case of cheating weakens reciprocity. Consequently, when dishonest signaling and cheating become too great, the signaling system and corresponding reciprocity will collapse.

It is likely that increasing the costs of signaling has the effect of stabilizing the signaling system and simultaneously increasing the adaptive fitness of so-called costly signalers. Evolutionary biologists Amotz and Avishag Zahavi developed the handicap principle by drawing on the metaphor of a sports handicapping system. The point of handicapping is to make

89. Jack W. Bradbury and Sandra L. Vehrencamp, *Principles of Animal Communication*, 2nd ed. (Sunderland, MD: Sinauer, 2011).

90. John Maynard Smith and David Harper, *Animal Signals* (Oxford: Oxford University Press, 2003).

91. Sasha R. X. Dall et al., "Information and Its Use by Animals in Evolutionary Ecology" *Trends in Ecology and Evolution* 20, 4 (Apr. 2005) 187–93.

92. Pauline Wilson Wiessner, "Leveling the Hunter: Constraints on the Status Quest in Forging Societies" in Polly Wiessner and Wulf Schiefenhövel (eds.), *Food and the Status Quest: An Interdisciplinary Perspective* (Providence, RI: Berghanh, 1996), 171–94.

the sporting contest more competitive by reducing disparities between entrants. For instance, in a handicapping horse race, horses known to be faster are given proportionately heavier weights to carry underneath their saddles. Hence, the size of the handicap serves to signal the racehorse's quality. Likewise, the large lustrous tail of a peacock acts as a handicap. According to the Zahavis, peacocks able to "waste" greater resources in the growth of a large and splendid tail engage in costly signaling.[93] The costs for the peacock's display might include intrinsic "production costs" in terms of resources allocated to the tail and "extrinsic costs" in terms of greater challenge and conflict with rivals.[94] Yet, a peahen knowing nothing about rival peacocks except the sizes and qualities of their tails would be strongly attracted by the honest signaling of the peacock with the gaudiest tail. The costly signaling conveys information about the peacock's greater genetic quality.

In human beings, costly signaling also evolved to increase the adaptive fitness of individuals able to provide the best outward displays of (presumably) internal genetic quality. Thus, for instance, extensive research on hunter-gatherer societies has indicated that men often risk extensive losses of energy, time, and caloric intake to supply a group with their favored food (e.g., turtle meat among the Meriam community in Torres Strait of Australia, antelope among the Hadza of Tanzania)[95] or to fish for dog-toothed tuna in a ritualized and aesthetic manner (e.g., men of the Ifaluk Atoll in the Pacific).[96] It is important that, although possibly maladaptive for a particular signaler (e.g., a peacock wounded in a battle), costly signaling functions to stabilize a social signaling system. When honest signaling is costly, it will be more difficult for cheaters or free-riders to fake a signal and fool receivers. Thus honesty increases overall when males who can pay the higher costs of signaling succeed more frequently in attracting genetically superior mates.[97]

93. Amotz Zahavi and Avishag Zahavi *The Handicap Principle: A Missing Piece of Darwin's Puzzle* (New York: Oxford University Press, 1999).
94. William A. Searcy and Stephen Nowicki, *The Evolution of Animal Communication: Reliability and Deception in Signaling Systems* (Princeton: Princeton University Press, 2005).
95. Rebecca Bliege Bird, Douglas W. Bird, and Eric Alden Smith "The Hunting Handicap: Costly Signaling in Human Foraging Strategies," *Behavioral Ecology and Sociobiology* 50, 9 (2001), 9–19; Kristen Hawkes, James Francis O'Connell, and Nicholas G. Burton Jones, "Hadza Meat Sharing," *Evolutionary Human Behavior* 22, 2 (2001), 113–42.
96. Richard Sosis, "Costly Signaling and Torch Fishing on Ifaluk Atoll," *Evolutionary Human Behavior* 21, 4 (2000), 223–44.
97. Amotz Zahavi, "Mate Selection—A Selection for a Handicap," *Journal of Theoretical Biology* 53 (1975), 205–14; Kristen Hawkes and Rebecca Bliege Bird, "Showing Off,

The last point indicates that signaling as a social institution has itself undergone cultural adaptation and that costly signaling was evoked as a way of responding adaptively to the problems posed by dishonest signaling and subsequent threats both to signaling as communication and to reciprocal efforts within a group. Costly signaling continues to evolve as a means of staying ahead of dishonest signaling, free-riding, and cheating. For instance, costly signaling theory explains how organized religions (although arising relatively late in human prehistory) increase and maintain strong intragroup cooperation by requiring religious converts or initiates to engage publicly in elaborate and costly rituals. In these ways co-religionists demonstrate loyalty to the group by signaling their investment in the religious group. Costly signaling theory predicts further that the signaling is costly enough to deter free-riders.[98] Evidence indicates that this may be true: individuals appear more willing to join, participate in, and contribute to a church that makes more stringent and costly demands on its communicants.[99]

The probable evolution of costly signaling as a response to the burdens caused by dishonest signaling suggests a hypothesis about the cultural evolution of honor killing. As noted, it is probable that the initial stage consisted of threats to kill wayward girls and women, made solely for deterrent purposes. Actual killings "for honor" were likely to have been infrequent and isolated cases. However, a second stage probably coincided with the completion of CHP and development of SLS as systems of social control. At this second stage, honor codes had developed and were normatively robust, and patterns of reciprocity and cooperation were well established. In addition, we can expect the population of clans and tribes to have grown and density to have increased, although communities had not resolved problems relating to the artificial shortage of marriageable females, especially for arranged marriages and polygamy.

The more settled and populous a group, the greater the likelihood of illegitimate consorting with females from *within* the clan and tribe, as well as from outside it. A dwindling supply of reproductive mates made kidnapping or clandestine consorting with a girl well worth running the

Handicap Signaling, and the Evolution of Men's Work," *Evolutionary Anthropology* 11, 2 (2002), 56–67.

98. William Irons, "Religion as a Hard-to-Fake Sign of Commitment," in Randolph M. Nesse (ed.), *Evolution and the Capacity for Commitment* (New York: Russell Sage, 2001), 290–30.

99. Laurence R. Iannaccone, "Sacrifice and Stigma: Reducing Free-Riding in Cults, Communes, and Collectivities," *Journal of Political Economy* 100, 2 (Apr. 1992), 271–91.

risk. Prosperous groups with a surplus of females were seen by competitors as possessing "bountiful" resources, thus enticing more frequent but smaller scale attacks or forays intent on securing one or two girls at a time. Some of these attacks may have come from members of tribes which were also becoming increasingly powerful. The presence of cheaters and poachers from among one's band of brothers also posed a new dilemma. The consolidation of SLS significantly reduced the effectiveness of warnings to absconders both within and outside a tribe.

It would not have been adaptively advantageous for a group to seek revenge against a girl's seducer, rapist, or abductor. Revenge killings did occur, and especially when the two were caught *delicto flagrante*, which occurs today. However, as honor killing as a social practice continues to reveal, killing adulterers or paramours was not part of the solution. After the SLS was in place, to kill a man in one's own lineage would be catastrophic because it would set off internecine warfare that would threaten the existence of the tribe itself. Because the principle of collective responsibility formed the backbone of the SLS, reprisals against members of opposing tribes were also far too risky since drawing blood would set off a relentless vendetta; even a weaker neighboring clan might be related by association with a powerful tribe. Revenge could plunge an entire tribe into an unremitting struggle for survival. The gruesome solution, honor killing, was also the one that was least costly, given the nascent gender-based prejudice.

The new situation initiated further adaptations in signaling. Threatening words and gestures must have failed to deter dalliances often enough to require a change in what counted as honest signaling; that is, signaling could count as *honest* only if threatened actions were carried out, but not if verbal threats went unheeded and preventive behavior was unavailing. A draconian but simple message was conveyed by converting honor threats into honor killing. A single man or group seeking to gain an illicit mate could not succeed if honor action reliably followed an honor-killing threat; that is, if a girl or woman was hunted down by male family members and killed. A 17-year-old girl interviewed by Filiz Kardam's team in Batman, Turkey, reported a threat that continues to be common: "If you run away with this boy, even if you go to the end of the world, I will find you and kill you."[100]

Once CHP and SLS are well established, then the descent of genes among very closely related kin is no longer a matter of the survival of any

100. Filiz Kardam, *The Dynamics of Honor Killing in Turkey: Prospects for Action,* with contributions from Zeynep Alpar, Ilknar Yüksel, and Ergül Ergün. Ankara, Turkey (United Nations Population Fund, 2006), www.unfpa.org/sites/defaultfiles/pub-pdf/, 35.

nuclear family, let alone single individuals. It is sufficient that the surviving population group retains sufficient numbers of healthy individuals and a sufficient balance between the sexes to remain a breeding population. At this stage, the sexuality of females of childbearing age becomes a matter of interest for the entire community, as well as whichever individuals might stand to gain or lose in the distribution of mates. With the stabilization of a reproducing community, honest signaling serves to maintain patterns of reciprocity and cooperation within the community. If the social functions of honor killing were related to signaling, as I have argued, then, as a practice, it too served to sustain a network of cooperative and reciprocal relationships in the community as well as to eliminate, as much as possible, individual defections from communally sanctioned mate assignments.

Signaling systems become more ritualized and normatively driven the more critical they are for a group. Honor codes such as *Pashtunwali* might have achieved much of their full normative structure by this time, but even refined signaling invites cheaters to attempt to take advantage of the social benefits of reciprocity by cleverly engaging in dishonest signaling. In a group bound by an honor code such as *Pashtunwali*, the dress, behavior, and comportment of daughters, accompanied by threats against disobedience, signals a family's intention to preserve daughters' virginity. A cheater might signal dishonestly by proclaiming that his daughters and sisters are virgins, adding in his public announcement that he will kill them if they leave home alone or defy his decisions about marital partners. When the message is dishonest, anyone who relies on it could be exposed to loss and severe humiliation if he marries a girl who cannot sustain a reputation for constancy. At worst, the husband and his family might be at risk of supporting offspring who are not his own, not to mention the agony of constant vigilance to prevent future dalliances and endless worry.

The point is not that those signaling dishonestly about the purity of daughters will always try to "peddle" unvirtuous girls or victims of rape or incest. (Although at least one father discovered during research insisted to members of his family—but not neighbors—that a daughter was marriageable as a virgin despite having been raped by him. His excuse was that he and the girl "were one and the same flesh.") In any case, the critical point is that faking, when skillful, cannot be easily distinguished from honest signaling; hence, once cheating occurs, it undermines the entire signaling system and thereby threatens continued reciprocity and cooperation. In addition, as noted in introducing costly signaling theory, costly signalers reap the benefits of greater inclusive fitness.

As shocking as it seems, a family that executes a female alleged to have behaved dishonorably also gains in adaptive fitness. Before an execution, a tainted family risked being consigned to the status of social outcasts; following an execution, the family is redeemed and often celebrated as loyal members of the community. Most important, while some families are reluctant to marry daughters into families that have killed females, honor killings usually make a perpetrator and his sons and daughters (or siblings) *more attractive* as potential mates. Honor killings thus have the net effect of increasing the adaptive fitness of families that kill by increasing the likelihood of passing genes to the next generation. In any event, because of high numbers of cousin marriages, genetic similarity is maximized among surviving offspring. Despite some increase of congenital defects, in fact, inbreeding results in a rapid advance of kin-selected altruism. This raises the "dark" possibility that, over a long time, with the cumulatively strengthening predisposition toward kin-selected altruism, tribal members come to view the sacrifice of female family members as being for the "good of the group."[101]

I have been discussing honor killing as it must have been shaped toward the end of the second stage of cultural evolution and as a requirement for costly signaling. I suggest that a family willing to kill is a family willing to handicap themselves by bearing the costs of losing a daughter and suffering the psychological trauma of being the cause of her death (although most perpetrators continue to *consciously* protest that the female was the cause of her own death). Families thus signal honestly by being willing to carry out threats of death, and they do so in order to restore their honor and to redeem the "market" value of remaining sons and daughters. Social dynamics are yet more complicated, however, and there is one more stage to explicate. An explanation for this third and final stage in the evolution of honor killing opens up when we confront the question: Why must the natal family be the party responsible for executing a "wayward" daughter? In addition, why a penalty as drastic as death, rather than some other means of shaming?

6.5 THE FINAL EXAPTATION OF HONOR KILLING

A cuckolded husband will be deeply grieved, especially if his wife bears another man's child. As all children are identified by male lineage, an illegitimate child cannot be socially his. Moreover, unless he repudiates his wife

---

101. Hbd chick Blog 92: "Inclusive Fitness," posted Feb. 3, 2015, https://hbdchick.
wordpress.com/?s=inclusive+fitness, accessed Oct. 30, 2015.

and the child, he and his family will bear the costs of sustaining the wife and raising the child, while the CHP and SLS will deny them any benefits from these investments. Yet it is far from obvious why a community should expect the natal family of the wife to bear such a grim duty as executing the wayward wife. In addition, it is puzzling that norms governing group reproduction did not distinguish between sexual "dishonor" exclusively among members within the group versus *intrusion from outside the group*. If a cuckolded husband repudiates a wife or group members shame a pregnant girl, then—assuming both biological parents are group members—it is reasonable that communal norms would require a natal family to take the girl or woman back (possibly with a payment to a cuckolded husband). Likewise, honor norms could require that the family of the biological father raise the offspring of an illegitimate liaison. This norm is wholly consistent with CHP and the SLS. Moreover, even if disgraced, an able-bodied female could make a valuable contribution to a household and might yet be married off to a (possibly desperate) bachelor.

Note that, in trying to understand why the responsibility for an honor killings came to fall on natal families, it will not do to say that tradition and honor requires this. This response just pushes the line of questioning further back: Why should an honor code distribute responsibility in this way? It is not difficult to conceive of alternative "solutions," assuming, of course, that honest signaling requires threats be carried out. In the case of married women, executioners might have been drawn from the husband's family. Alternatively, a community member more impartial (not as closely related) might be assigned this grim office, or it might be rotated among males capable of bearing arms.

I believe the most plausible answers to both questions bear on the way costly signaling is combined with the *distribution* of the costs and benefits of reproduction. Let us revisit the scenario in which a wayward wife succeeds in deceiving her husband and his family about both an illicit affair and the paternity of the child she bears. If she succeeds, then the effects will be the same as the worst outcomes of dishonest signaling. That is, it will be her husband and his family who bear all of the costs of maintaining her and raising the child (and possibly other illegitimate children in the future). Suppose that, at some later time, but after parental investment, the husband discovers that he has been deceived. If he does, then he will know that he will not receive the benefits of his past or any continuing investment because the child will not be recognized as his own, and he cannot adopt should he desire to do so.

Instead, the child will be a member of his biological father's lineage. In addition, should the mother and her child survive, her family will enjoy significant gains; first, she will pass on her own genes and those of her family rather than those of her husband's family. Second, if the biological father is himself a close blood relation of the mother, then she and her family might benefit from whatever future security and productivity the grown child might provide. Thus, an unfaithful wife and her close relatives would be free riders, gaining nonreciprocal but costly benefits, for they would have shirked most of the costs of maintaining the wayward wife or of raising the child while increasing their own welfare.

It is not known when or why the cultural prohibition against adoption arose. However, it is reasonable to infer that the ban on adoption arose partly because of the nonreciprocal advantages accruing to a female and her family from an illegitimate pregnancy. After all, in a patrilineal system, the woman's father would also be a member of a lineage and possibly (depending on the date at which cousin marriages began) closely related to the husband's family. In any case, the ban on adoption corroborates my hypothesis about the exaptation of honor killing. As long as a family can be thought to have gained illicitly as a consequence of a daughter's or sister's misbehavior, they will be perceived as cheaters, or free-riders, who have no right to their ill-gotten gains. In being judged deceitful and untrustworthy, they will have lost honor, and the consequences could be extremely costly if not downright damning. Under the circumstances, it will not matter exactly what the facts are (i.e., that the patriarch and his family did not engage in dishonest signaling). Because the outcome is the same as it would have been had dishonest signaling occurred, some members of the community may assume illicit intent or that the patriarch knew all along of his daughter's immodest or rebellious proclivities; indeed, others may regard the patriarch himself as blameworthy for failing to raise a pure and virtuous woman, and deceitful about those failures.

If correct, this analysis shows that, to prevent being regarded as the recipients of an ill-gotten gain or as fostering a woman still prone to stray, the woman's natal family must renounce the possibility of any gain—both actual and prospective—and in a symbolically powerful way. Already, at stage two, we saw that, in addition to costly signaling that is primarily verbal, there is a mode communicated through action, as *performative*.[102] Now, with the exaptation of honor killing, we find that, as performative, the ritualized killing communicates a secondary message. In addition to demonstrating honesty, slaying the female assumed to have gone astray is, tragically enough,

---

102. I claim there are two different acts of costly signaling: one is a declamation of intent, the second is performative and is communicated through the act of execution.

the means by which a family abjures any actual or prospective benefit accruing from her misconduct. The prohibition against adoption would have closed the natal family's option of raising the child as their own and possibly paying an aggrieved husband for his loss of a wife.[103] In addition, because the costly signaling must be addressed to the community as a whole, the signal (action) is sent when it appears to the signaler(s) that the receivers (communal members) have convinced themselves that a female is guilty through "trial by gossip." This explanation thus accounts for a number of heretofore puzzling features: why gossip seems so significant, why the intent to kill for honor is publicly proclaimed and generally (until relatively recent legal sentencing provisions) carried out in public, and why (again until recently) the perpetrator calmly awaits the response of others (now policemen).

As indicated at the end of Section 6.3, SLS is ill-equipped to accommodate conflicts involving charges of women's dishonorable behaviors when gossip and accusations are made by those closely related to males in the female's family. Recall that in the SLS, disputes over honor will generate, as Kressel notes, "two groups of approximately the same size who occupy adjacent positions on the hierarchical ladder."[104] While individuals on each side will try to avoid domination by attempting to strengthen their numbers, this strategy can succeed in averting actual bloodshed. Thus, when lineage groups achieve numerically and hierarchically equivalent strength, the SLS can function to generate a balanced opposition.[105] It is through upward extension and further removal of kinsmen from the immediacy of the conflict that stalemate occurs, as well as the greater reluctance of those with higher status to risk their influence over minor matters.

However, patrilineal clans cannot divide into balancing oppositions in the situation just described. There are three reasons why disputes arising between blood-related men over blood-related women will become increasingly lethal for everyone directly involved. First, if the dispute occurs between more senior cousins nearer the top of the hierarchy, then splitting will extend downward, possibly to the lowest generation, but it cannot extend upward in a manner that will tend to bring cooler heads to prevail and dampen the flames. Second, the principle that, in a conflict, one allies with one's next of kin can hardly apply when allegations might be made,

---

103. Certainly, some families were too poor to take such rectifying measures, but it is unreasonable to assume that the clan or tribe collectively could not have met the obligation. We know today that in cases in which a mediated or arbitrated dispute goes against a family but implicates the entire tribe, then the tribe does collectively make payment when the family cannot do so.

104. Kressel, *Ascendancy*, 105.

105. Salzman, *Culture and Conflict*, 112.

for example, by a male against the sister of his first cousin or by a second cousin against another second cousin. Third, because a single patriarch may have many sons by more than one wife, and many grandsons by more than one wife, it will be difficult to discern who counts as next of kin should a conflict arise among grandsons. (A result that would not occur against "enemies" outside the lineage.) In these cases, conflict could spread lethally across nodes of the tree as well as vertically, as intended.

I present such hypothetical possibilities to suggest that an increase in cousin marriages along with the establishment of the SLS might have had the effect of ensuring that honor killing would continue until it became a "remedy" to the inadequacy of costly signaling and then a "solution" to the inability of the SLS to resolve conflicts involving disputes over the honor of kinswomen who are not at liberty, unlike men, to redeem their honor through action. I conclude that honor killing as a social practice emerged over a long course of time, beginning first with threatened punishment and, in a second stage, with honest signaling to repel would-be poachers and to deter female misbehavior. At the third stage, signaling, to remain honest, required a handicap, and thus became costly signaling plus death. In effect, threats were no longer enough. At this stage, the content of most signals changed from bellicose and exaggerated verbal rituals to stronger communicative gestures requiring performative acts of killing. In addition, the signal "receivers" changed as well. Rather than just the potential internal and out-group poachers and wayward females, major receivers became members of the HSC at large. Assuming the concomitant evolution of CHP, SLS, and the ban on adoption, a female's family was socially committed to performing the execution. The social group as a whole was firmly invested in honest communication about the likelihood that future and present brides would be tractable, self-restrained, and chaste. Finally, honor killing underwent a further exaptation as a way of responding to a major defect within the SLS due to its design and function. This final exaptation of honor killing produced the social practice recognized today.

There are certainly far too many occasions in which women are literally trapped and destroyed due to the ways that men (usually husbands, brothers, or fathers) have sought to take advantage of other men and the ways that the latter have resisted or fought back.[106] In *Women in*

---

106. Tahira Khan writes of cases in which a husband, father, or brother blackmails a comparatively wealthy man in the community by accusing him of having illicit relations with his wife, sister, or daughter; next, "they kill their own woman, declaring her immoral; then they settle the matter with the accused man by extorting a substantial amount of money to spare his life" (67). Such practices, Khan claims, "occur among all economic low classes living in the semi-rural areas of Sindh and Punjab provinces of Pakistan" (67).

the Crossfire, I have used "crossfire" primarily as a metaphor. In earlier chapters, the term designates the ways that social institutions designed by men, populated by men, and benefiting men require the systematic victimization of women. Here, the term refers to processes of cultural evolution that, although they were adaptations for the inclusive fitness of group populations—and groups obviously including women—these adaptations nevertheless functioned to preserve social stability in ways that benefited men far more than women, to say nothing of the women whose lives were sacrificed.

CHAPTER 7

Providing Protection and Leveraged Reform

From the beginning, the important objective has been to bring research on honor killing to bear on questions of prevention and protection. As noted in this study, honor killing is a discrete and long-standing social practice that has proven quite durable. Chapter 3 demonstrates the significance of honor for individual identity and collective solidarity in honor–shame communities (HSCs). Honor killing requires that members of the community support firmly held norms, or "we-acceptances," about proper female behavior as well as honor codes demanding particular male responses to public insinuations about the dishonorable behavior of female family members. Analyses in Chapters 4 and 5 reveal how ongoing child-rearing, socialization, and male initiation rituals contribute to the development of warrior masculinity, a personality structure that primes males to act violently in vindicating the demands of honor. Chapter 6 demonstrates that honor killing evolved socially as one of a closely knit and mutually reinforcing traditional practices. In addition to presenting an analysis of a complex social practice, the proceeding chapters paint an admittedly bleak picture. The practice of honor killing is so ancient, its psychological and sociocultural underpinnings so complex and resilient, and the record of legal-political efforts at prevention so discouraging that one could not be faulted for wondering whether there is, indeed, anything to be done to deter the phenomenon.

Let us consider, first, how we might think about possible responses. An initial distinction can be made, however roughly, between short-term *protection* and long-term *prevention*. Because an honor killing occurs somewhere in the world about every 90 minutes,[1] there is an acute need to protect girls and women at risk. Short-term protective measures such as emergency hotlines, women's shelters, and teen hostels can be thought of as taking place against a background of longer term prevention. The ultimate objective, of course, is the end of honor killing. For the reasons just summarized, this will require very significant and long-term cultural, legal, and social changes. Consequently, the need for protective, safekeeping measures is likely to be acute until that point is reached (and will need to be permanently available because of the then continuing, although lessened, dangers of assault). Section 7.2 discusses possible protective interventions.

In addition to *temporal* differences—short-term emergency responses in contrast to long-range solutions—we can also distinguish between the location of the impetus for change; that is, between changes imposed primarily from *without* a community in contrast to changes undertaken *within* the community. Finally, it is useful to distinguish between differences in the *reasons and motives* for change among both outside agents and among members inside of HSCs. There are thus two quite different "models" for facilitating long-term change. One model, the subject of Section 7.3, involves leveraging by outside agents. Leveraging focuses on changing behaviors within HSCs, especially those of potential perpetrators, and through coercive as well as persuasive means. The primary objective of these measures is to make the continuation of the practice too *costly* for the members of HSCs, to reduce opportunities to commit crimes, and to increase inhibitions within potential perpetrators.

Outside and coercive interventions seek to induce an end to honor killing, whether or not local community members "subjectively" accept this objective and adopt the ideas, attitudes, disposition, norms, and behaviors required for effective prevention. This model thus poses serious risks. Because honor killing is a social practice, integrated with all other practices and belief systems that contribute to the subordination and oppression of women, coercive intervention from outside would have to

---

1. Nicholas Kristof, "Her Father Shot Her in the Head," *The New York Times*, Jan. 31, 2016, 11.

be extensive and would be perceived by HSC members as attacks on their chosen way of life.

Thus this model might result in severe dislocation and possibly greater violence. HSCs might come apart, leaving members psychologically unmoored; or, more likely, local community members might retrench and aggressively reaffirm their identity, possibly insisting that honor killing is itself, like the *hijab* or *burka*, a valued symbol of identity. Consequently, policy strategists and activists must consider carefully whether outside interventions are likely to promote greater harm than the good they might accomplish. Adopting such an approach also raises difficult questions about human rights "tradeoffs"; in particular, the protection of the rights of potential victims versus a flagrant disrespect for the autonomy of those expected to change.[2] Finally, reason suggests that if social reform is to be effective, then it cannot be perceived as a threat that requires a defensive or violent response. And, if reforms are to be sustainable, they cannot be imposed against the will of those who must live with them.

For these reasons, I believe it highly advisable to pursue an alternative model of change. This second model emphasizes noncoercive change from *within* communities resulting in *moral transformations.* This model emphasizes facilitating opportunities to experience and evaluate a range of alternatives in nonthreatening environments, thereby nurturing self-directed change. The long-term objective is to enable those undergoing transformation to become *owners* of these processes and outcomes, insofar as they endorse and participate willingly in them. The concept of a moral transformation I employ is similar in certain ways to what in *The Honor Code* philosopher Kwame Anthony Appiah calls a "moral revolution."[3] However, while the major moral revolutions Appiah considers resulted from a confluence of largely unplanned factors, I emphasize up-front conscious planning, leadership, and direction. Due to their potential significance, I devote all of Chapter 8 to preventative responses that seek to initiate a moral transformation.

Obviously, successful transformative measures should eventually make unnecessary all coercive and externally imposed measures. However, the short-term protective interventions recommended in Section 7.1 must

2. Coercive interventions also may be paternalistic for those they are designed to protect, at least insofar as girls and women share the values and we-acceptances of their communities.

3. Kwame Anthony Appiah, *The Honor Code: How Moral Revolutions Happen* (New York and London: W. W. Norton, 2010).

exist until no longer needed, despite tensions with the objectives of long-term transformation from within. The critical importance of protective interventions increases dramatically if hearts and minds are insufficiently influenced to make the moral transformation from within a reality. Moreover, because transformative measures must be phased in and lasting change occurs slowly, there may be lapses, backlashes, or failures, and women will continue to be victimized. So change agents must be prepared to rely on interventionist methods and especially crisis intervention. There is no logical inconsistency in recommending the simultaneous development of capacities to pursue both transformative and interventionist methods.

A few additional points need to be stressed. First, given the intransigence of long-established customs, as well as the epistemic invisibility of the reasons for honor killing, there will be need for facilitators from the outside. Such facilitators must play critical roles as *knowledge agents* in initiating change, both with respect to shorter term protective measures and long-term solutions. Likewise, initial efforts at safeguarding may need to be initiated by women's organizations and child or family services outside the community. The ideal objective, however, is to have local, on-site *change agents* who are also members of the community, assuming roles and responsibilities as soon as their competence and commitment allows. Moreover, long-term moral transformation requires a context of trust and sympathy. Change agents initiating and facilitating these transformations must respect those they serve, speak the local language or dialect, and, insofar as possible, share significant features of religion, ethnicity, origin, and culture. Developing partnerships will enable the ownership of change to be turned over to respected members of local communities.

To date, studies of efforts to end honor killing have focused only on legal interventions (detection, prosecution, sentencing) and political movements including protests and legislative changes. There have been few reported attempts to bring about systematic efforts to prevent honor killing *from within communities* or to measure the effectiveness of such attempts. The methods suggested here have not been field-tested in HSCs, except, perhaps, in the most rudimentary ways. Moreover, it is not plausible to expect general recommendations to be sensitive to the wide variety of economic and political conditions prevailing in areas in which honor killings occur. Strategies recommended here, when modeled on other programs, are offered as instructive analogies, and tactics are intended only to be feasible as "best bets." In the long run, change agents "on the ground" must accept responsibility for developing their own strategies and tactics, designed to best meet local needs and contingencies. I must echo the words of renowned nonviolent theorist Gene Sharp: "An outsider like me can't tell you what to do, and if I did, you shouldn't believe me. Trust yourselves."[4]

Finally, proposals presented here are "idealistic" in two senses. My emphasis is on *what needs* to be done in terms of moral imperatives: *what ought to be done*. Considering the practicalities of implementing recommendations in terms of political will, the availability of trained personnel, or the financial capacities of states or private parties lie beyond the scope of this work. Second, there is a large literature on grassroots organizing and subjects such as social movement theory and resource mobilization. However, I must leave aside questions about the best ways of implementing particular recommendations or organizing activities. I agree with activists Mark and Paul Engler that it is possible to "bridge the gap" between structure-based organizers and movement mobilizers, and research in the theory and practice of nonviolent activism is providing new insights on "momentum driven organizing."[5]

The objective of this chapter is to extend and broaden the discussion of possible responses. I must leave it to sociologists, political scientists, policy analysts, activists in nongovernmental organizations (NGOs), and state officials who are more attuned to the specific realities in areas in which they may initiate action to give very serious and careful consideration to the possible implementation of the recommendations made here.

7.2 EMERGENCY INTERVENTIONS

This section considers protective procedures to be implemented immediately. The need for emergency interventions is a function of the legitimacy of honor killing in a community and the consequent risk of harm. As noted earlier, a long-term objective of moral transformation as envisioned here will be communal acceptance of protective measures, such as shelters and halfway houses, until danger ceases (Chapter 8). One significant effort

---

4. Gene Sharp as quoted in Mairi Mackay, "A Dictator's Worst Nightmare," CNN, June 25, 2012, http://www.cnn.com/2012/06/23/world/gene-sharp-revolutionary/index.html, accessed Mar. 12, 2016.

5. The quoted phrases are from Mark Engler and Paul Engler, *This Is an Uprising: How Nonviolent Revolt Is Shaping the Twenty-First Century* (New York: Nation Books, 2016), 57, 72. The Englers offer a good overview of the relative strengths of grassroots movements and structured organizations and ways to combine the benefits of both. For studies of nonviolent social change, see Andrew Boyd and David Oswald Mitchell (eds.), *Beautiful Trouble: A Toolbox for Revolution* (New York: OR Books, 2017); Gene Sharp (ed.), *Waging Nonviolent Struggle: 20th Century Practice and 21st Century Potential* (Boston: Porter Sargent, 2005).

toward this end will be the training of local individuals so that staffing of these facilities can eventually pass from state officials and NGO specialists to the local communities. In addition, because agencies, experts, and NGO professionals must be empowered to act, they must have legitimacy conferred by law, as well as necessary resources. Consequently, some of the interventions mentioned here overlap with outside pressures (Section 7.3).

The emergency measures discussed herein are highly interrelated. They are grouped into separate categories for ease of discussion.

Emergency Hotlines, Smartphone Apps, and Information Networks

In connection with shelters and centers discussed later, 24-hour crisis hotlines must be available for first contact as well as for emergency intervention. Hotline specialists will be trained to respond to a range of needs, including suicide, depression, loneliness, and chemical dependency, as well as violent or threatening situations and requests for immediate rescue. Callers may remain anonymous. However, conversations may be "coded" so that, in the event that a caller is overheard, the caller may still be able to signal for help without being stopped by family members. Callers can be asked a question (e.g., "Do you feel safe right now?"), and, depending on the response, hotline respondents will be able to activate a phone number identification service and use a reverse lookup code to find a street address. If contact with a caller is interrupted and broken off for more than 30 seconds, the hotline respondent automatically dispatches a Mobile Crisis Team (see later discussion). Emergency hotline services will be located at protected shelters where persons in need of immediate assistance can also walk in at any time. Counselors at shelters should be available on a 7-day, 24-hour basis.

Michael Lissack and associates at the Institute for the Study of Coherence and Emergence (ISCE) have invented two antiviolence smartphone apps.[6] One, known as the I've-Been-Violated (IBV) App, is the first of its kind to enable a victim of sexual assault to confidentially record evidence (both video and audio) of an incident as soon afterward as possible. When victims have reached a safe place, they can turn the app on and relate what has happened by following on-screen instructions. The app prompts the user about what to include in the narrative while making the video

---

6. Michael Lissack, from Lissack@isce.edu, an email distributed through the Peace and Justice Studies Association listserv, Feb. 10, 2016. See also www.we-consent.org/index.php/41-apps-abcd/103-i-ve-been-violated-app.

and audio recordings. The app also uses geo-coding technology to store information about where the victim was when the video was recorded. The evidence is doubly encrypted and stored offline. As a legal and personal safeguard, only appropriate health or legal authorities first contacted by the victim can retrieve the recorded information, and, subsequently, only by court order.

ISCE also has developed an antibullying app with a number of functions: a child can use it as a panic button, it delivers a clear warning to whomever is threatening or harassing the child, it immediately alerts his or her parents, and it creates evidence of the threatening situation. Both apps were initially offered for free and, in the United States, they remain extremely low in cost ($1.00 or less) at widely available outlets.[7]

A similar app can be created for girls and women at risk in HSCs. It could combine the functions of warning others that an attack is likely to occur and, whenever possible, record evidence of crimes ranging from abduction, rape and sexual assault, physical beatings, confinement, and threats within or outside the family. The app could be especially helpful in providing real-time location of the device via email when the app is interrupted or deactivated. Evidence recorded by the app would demonstrate that what happened was not just the victim's word against others. It would make it more difficult for authorities to do nothing, and it would have the effect of deterring attacks.

Information conveyed over hotlines and a modified I-Need-Help app raises provocative issues about privacy and the rights of the family. Rights can be derogated, however, and the rights of life, freedom, and bodily and psychological security and integrity of the victims and threatened females are accepted here as more basic and therefore as taking precedence over other persons' privacy. One significant practical difficulty is the unavailability of communication technology, whether land lines or smartphones, and the ease with which family members or others could deprive girls and women of the possession and use of the technology. It seems almost certain that family members planning an attack would become more secretive, arrange for a smartphone to be "lost" or "stolen," and hold the girl or women incommunicado.

There are a number of measures that may ameliorate such problems. One measure discussed later relates to crisis perception and mobile crisis teams. This measure is the best one to pursue when no communicative technology is available. Where smartphones are available and mobile crisis

7. http://isce.edu, and http://thenoapp.com, accessed Jul. 15, 2016.

team members suspect a threat, a signal can be sent to an I-Need-Help app turning on a specific signal. This signal would be transmitted whenever the smartphone is in use to a transponder in a designated authority's office, most likely a shelter hotline respondent or a member of a mobile crisis team. When a user's smartphone becomes inactive for an unexpected period, the transponder would immediately generate a text message on its screen plus an address or coordinates for the last known location of the smartphone.

Because individuals engaging in crisis intervention may be threatened or find themselves in risky and tumultuous situations, they, too, must be provided and carry smartphones with I-Need-Help apps. This includes all staff and directors of shelters, youth hostels, and halfway houses, including guards, and all NGO and local volunteers, community observer/informers, mobile crisis teams, the network coordinator, and lawyers, and officers of courts. Obviously, it will be to no avail if a shelter administrator's smartphone simply contacts the hotline where she or he works. It must be possible for the smartphone apps of crisis/emergency personnel to be activated by a vocal "signature" or a single preset keystroke. This message, sent only in distress, will go immediately to the police.

Observer/Informants and Early Warning Signals

Honor killings ordinarily result because of the public perception of dishonor and are typically preceded by gossip. It is critically important, therefore, to enlist an individual who will work to become a trusted member of the community and who will serve as its unofficial "eyes and ears of conscience." An observer/informant (OBI) must reside within the local community and maintain friendly and cordial relationships with all. He or she will make it a point to regularly visit places commonly frequented, such as markets, wells or water fountains, and coffee- or teahouses. The OBI will make a special effort to form an information chain including local individuals likely to hear gossip but possibly unsympathetic to honor killings. Moreover, an OBI should make it a practice to be in regular contact with all specialists who may have information about an impending attack. Such contacts will include doctors and nurses at regional or provincial health clinics or hospitals because girls and teens are often brought in for "virginity tests" and examination during pregnancy. Others will include social workers or psychologists and counselors when available and schoolteachers who observe unusual bruising or note unexcused absences or unusual behavior in a child, such as a girl's anxiety or fearfulness about going home.

The OBI's major responsibilities are two: first, she or he will discreetly convey to a small core emergency network (CEN) information about possible threats to girls and women. CEN members will include the mobile crisis team (see later discussion) and either the director of the emergency hotline or the director of the nearest shelter, hostel, or halfway house. In the event of a rapidly developing crisis, the OBI should contact the police before CEN members. In this way, the OBI serves, like the I-Need-Help app, as an early warning signal. The second responsibility of the OBI is to maintain strict confidentiality about the sources of information shared with the CEN. The OBI must be impartial and should not become directly involved in an intervention. If there are individuals who find honor killing abhorrent, even such persons may be reluctant to pass on information if they fear reprisals from the majority or a powerful family or clan. Consequently, it is necessary to enable community members to maintain plausible deniability.

The purpose of the OBI's role might be easily detected, and, moreover, an OBI can hardly be expected to deny his or her role if directly confronted or to refuse to cooperate with authorities if a case goes to trial. For this reason, any one person's ability to serve as an OBI may be short-lived. In this event, efforts should be made to surreptitiously recruit a subsequent OBI from within the community. If the latter is impossible, and especially if the communal group stoutly resists emergency interventions, then an "exposed" OBI can continue to make an important contribution by serving as an outspoken critic of honor killing and becoming a *moral entrepreneur* (Section 7.3). On the other hand, a community in the process of moral transformation (Chapter 8) will cease to need this form of intervention, in large part because the early warnings of possible attacks will be picked up and registered through the community's own consensual institutions.

Shelters, Hostels, Halfway Houses, and Family Centers

The desperate need for a larger number of protective shelters for women in danger and runaway girls must be addressed at the national level in every country in which honor killings occur. The United Nations, under the auspices of the UN High Commissioner for Extrajudicial Executions, should advocate for and coordinate international funding to address this need. In addition, NGOs should develop fundraising campaigns to fulfill this need.

The number of facilities needed should be based on studies of the frequency of honor killing by country, region, city, town, and locale, as well as the proximity of facilities to one another and the ease of transportation between them. Likewise, facilities must be staffed, and those sheltered must receive the services of health care providers, legal counselors, psychologists, social workers, and security guards, as the need may arise. Larger, more centralized shelters and halfway houses must also include educators and job trainers, although some of these needs can be met through attending other readily accessible schools and training centers. There is no ready-made formula for calculating the number of service personnel per facility, and some experts, such as psychologists and legal counselors, can visit a number of centers as long as caseloads are not too great. Many NGOs can be counted on to train personnel, including some women staying in these facilities for long periods.

Shelters will accept women of legal age on their own recognizance and women with their minor children. Shelters are to be distinguished from youth hostels as the latter are designed for children under 18. Youth hostels are necessary because minors cannot be accepted at shelters, but there is a need for places where battered, threatened, and eloped or runaway minors can be safe before or even after custody cases are heard in court. Government- or NGO-run shelters and youth hostels must be supported by legal provisions, and, just as agencies such as Social Services and Child Protection Services should be given authority to have a child removed from a home, they should be empowered to have minors retained in youth hostels until they are no longer at risk. In order to reach endangered minors in a timely manner, it will be necessary to implement mobile crisis teams. In addition, justices should make determinations based on the "best interests of the child." If necessary, girls should be allowed to remain in youth hostels if endangered and until able to consent as adults to enter shelters.

Halfway houses are facilities in which women and minor children may live together for longer periods; mothers and children will receive education and employment training, counseling, and legal advice as needed, as well as psychological assessment if necessary. Women in halfway houses may plan on reentry into the larger community or seek transfer and release at another location. Alternatively, women who have reason to consider themselves in continuing danger may remain in halfway houses while applying for emigration.

Family centers are facilities that provide shelter for married or eloped couples when both may require safety. Family counseling, along with psychological testing will be available, and if one or both partners become convinced that the union was a mistake, then clients as single individuals can be transported to appropriate facilities. Necessarily, shelters, youth hostels, and halfway houses will be segregated by gender as far as living spaces and internal activities are concerned, although they may be located in the same compound and share adjoining exterior walls. Research indicates that males charged with carrying out honor executions but who subsequently refuse to kill may become victims (Section 3.2). These individuals should receive protection in appropriate shelters.

It is extremely difficult to decide whether clients must remain sheltered for a minimum amount of time and whether parents or other family members should be allowed to visit. These are questions specialists in psychology and social work can best answer. Filiz Kardam notes that victims often are not psychologically free to make their own decisions, and counselors must be sensitive to the particularities of the case.[8] Yet research indicates that seeking assistance outside the home often increases the chance that a girl or women will be harmed. Thus, although no one needing shelter should be turned away, I suggest that women who receive shelter be asked to consent, as soon as appropriate, to remain for at least a minimum period of 72 consecutive hours. In addition, for as long as a woman consents to remain sheltered, visits with family or husbands must require consent of the client and take place within common spaces and under supervision. Under no circumstances during the mandatory waiting period can there be unannounced, unplanned, and unsupervised "off-campus" visits.

Another difficult issue concerns the need for trained and armed guards. Each facility should have guards available on a 24/7 basis, and it should be possible when necessary for the facility to operate on a lock-down basis. An armed guard should accompany staff and a driver in a van to transport clients from one facility to another or to and from court hearings. The same is true should a client be required to leave a facility for hospitalization. The necessity for such measures has been demonstrated repeatedly. Women hospitalized as a consequence of family attacks have been assaulted and killed when left unguarded in hospitals. Women have been attacked even in the offices of their lawyers, sometimes even when guards have been nearby.

For a majority of the population, the idea of a woman away from either her natal family or her husband's home is unthinkable. Consequently, it is

---

8. Filiz Kardam et al., *The Dynamics of Honor Killing in Turkey: Prospects for Action* (Ankara, Turkey: United Nations Population Fund, 2006), 54.

typical for many to regard shelters as poorly disguised brothels. It is critical therefore to convince the public of both the necessity of shelters and of their real function.

Mobile Crisis Teams and Protective Accompaniment

Mobile crisis teams will consist of two-person teams with training in mental health, social work, or developmental psychology through the master's degree level and at least 3–5 years of field experience. Both crisis teams and OBIs will be trained in danger assessment, including the use of a risk assessment tool for predicting a deadly attack.[9] Mobile crisis teams will be called on to respond with the police to family crises, psychiatric emergencies, acts of violence, and other traumatic events in the community, whether in private or public locations. Most important, crisis team members will have the authority to initiate responses to warnings received from OBIs and hotline respondents about a potential attack or one under way. Mobile crisis teams will be empowered to respond by signing petitions requiring police to intervene and to transport an individual to a facility for questioning, evaluation, or protection. Transportation and evaluation may be voluntary or involuntary. If the crisis team judges the individual to be at risk to self, he or she will be transported to a hospital for psychiatric evaluation. If evidence indicates either that harm has been committed against others or is imminent, then actual or potential perpetrators will be transported to a police station, and victims to a hospital, shelter, or youth hostel.

Mobile crisis teams must render a written judgment, or determination, for each petition and allow adequate time for assessment and consultation with doctors, psychiatrists, social workers, or lawyers. The time required may vary (e.g., because a girl is hospitalized or an expert is temporarily unavailable), but determination should ordinarily be rendered within a 5- to 7-day period. If an emergency intervention was made on behalf of an adult, then the determination will indicate whether the person should remain hospitalized or if he or she chooses to move to a shelter or return home if advisable. If on behalf of a minor, then the determination will recommend for the placement of the minor in a hostel, if necessary, or that the family receive the minor back home. Determinations shall be released

---

9. Jacqueline C. Campbell, Daniel W. Webster, and Nancy Glass, "The Danger Assessment: Validation of a Lethality Risk Assessment Instrument for Intimate Partner Violence," *Journal of Interpersonal Violence* 24, no. 4 (April 2009), 653–74.

to the family or married partner and submitted to the judge of an appropriate court. Information or testimony judged by the crisis team as a likely cause of increased danger to a girl or women will be redacted from reports submitted to families or spouses. Determinations will otherwise remain private. Should the crisis team acquire information alleging that a criminal activity has or might occur, this, too, shall be included in the reports to court officials.

When OBIs or hotline respondents receive information of a developing situation but one short of an outright crisis, or when a women or child temporarily removed from a home has returned, then mobile crisis teams may activate a safeguarding team modeled on the work of Peace Brigades International.[10] Safeguarding teams will consist of volunteers trained as nonviolent activists willing to provide safe conduct, shields, or vigils. For instance, safeguarding teams can accompany an at-risk child to and from school or on errands outside the home, provide protective accompaniment for adults with or without traditional and male family guardians, provide protective shields for girls or women recuperating in hospitals, and even provide silent and respectful but watchful vigils outside schools, in markets, or outside homes.

Coordination and Training

The protective and problem-solving measures discussed so far will require coordination among the experts and staffs of different agencies: all involved NGO volunteers, hospital liaisons, court officials, municipal or district officials, and relevant state organizations. The number of OBIs and mobile crisis teams to be deployed should depend on a careful analysis of factors such as the frequencies of honor killings and suspicious suicides, population density, transportation facilities, distances, and so forth. It may be possible for coordination to be overseen in one central office per district with 6–10 recognized HSCs. Depending on projected caseloads and the complexity of interactions (e.g., in urban environs such as Ammon, Birmingham, Cairo, or Istanbul), a full-time network coordinator may be needed; otherwise, responsibility for oversight and coordination might be vested in the senior officer of a shelter or rotate among mobile crisis teams.

The coordinating officer (CO) shall receive reports on all crises and interventions as soon as possible and shall receive weekly or biweekly

10. www.peacebrigades.org, accessed Jul. 15, 2016.

reports from officials in all units. Located at the hub of the network, the CO shall be responsible for (1) ensuring the readiness and efficiency of all units of the emergency protection and intervention system, (2) verifying the accuracy of information received and maintaining records, (3) ensuring completion and distribution of crisis team determinations and communicating all other pertinent information directly to legal and government officials, (4) ensuring that operations are consistently legal and meet the highest professional standards, (5) preparing data for analysis and assessment by state officials and university specialists, and (6) meeting with the media, mayors and officials, NGOs, citizen groups, state agencies, and the like to investigate issues and to engage in collaborative problem-solving.

Training at all levels is critically important. It is expected that, in addition to professional expertise and experience, all staff and respondents in the protection and intervention system will be familiar with honor killing and the characteristics of perpetrators and victims and possess a strong understanding of local cultures and traditions. Whenever possible, staff and respondents should speak the local dialect and share religious, ethnic, and other cultural affinities. They should be tolerant, broad-minded, possess high standards, and be capable of appreciating and respecting the people with whom they work. Moreover, they should understand that there is no one solution that fits for all cases and that they should seek, insofar as possible, resources for mediated solutions already existing within a clan or community (Section 8.4).

Training provided by NGOs should be coordinated with state agencies and professional associations of social workers, physicians and public health professionals, professors and teachers, law enforcement officers, and lawyers and judges, as needed, with an emphasis on knowledge of honor killing as a social practice and of the steps and procedures undertaken to eradicate it. In addition, all persons, whether professionals or volunteers having contact with vulnerable women and youth, must be carefully vetted in advance to ensure that they will not attempt to take advantage of their positions and betray the trust of the vulnerable.

Legal and Official Initiatives

It is expected that states and legal subunits which have honor killing problems will enact and enforce human rights protections and include specific provisions in criminal codes prohibiting honor crimes and severely punish perpetrators. Obviously, a number of additional legal initiatives or reforms will enhance the protection of girls and women, such as legal revisions of the rights of women to divorce and to inherit and own property, and prohibitions of child marriage and forced or nonconsensual marriages. A major objective of moral transformation (Chapters 8–9) is the willing adoption and support of these provisions in local communities. Respect for such changes, when they come, will be gradual. The first objective is ending honor killing as the worst of these human right violations, and it is not clear that such sweeping legal reforms are necessary to end *that* practice. On the contrary, moving too quickly might incite reactionary and frenzied efforts to save "hallowed" traditions, making the situation worse. I make recommendations for more extensive legal reforms to be considered when efforts to end honor killing meet with resistance and thus require the leveraging of change imposed from outside of the HSC (Section 7.3).

Here, I consider only those specific legal initiatives indispensable for successful crisis intervention. One initiative is the legal authority of child welfare or protection agencies to gain protective custody of an endangered child and have her removed from her home. Mobile crisis teams must also have legal authority to sign petitions empowering police to intervene and to transport adults and minors, based on evidence of need, to appropriate facilities for evaluation and shelter. Physicians, psychiatrists, social workers, and counselors working in or with authorized hospitals, shelters, or hostels to which minors have been brought must have the authority to observe and assess possible evidence of abuse and to question and evaluate minors without parental consent. In addition, legal initiatives must prohibit police from ever regarding themselves as fulfilling their responsibilities by tracking down a girl or woman who has eloped or run away and returning her to her family or husband. Likewise, in the event that a girl or woman goes directly to the police for help, they cannot remand her to her family simply on the father's and brothers' assurances that no harm will come to her, even when assurances are committed in writing and witnessed by town officials. Such measures appear useless in providing protection and may actually increase the probability of an attack (Section 2.2). Thus, in such circumstances, legal officials must immediately contact mobile crisis teams, and the latter will be authorized to decide whether or not such persons should be admitted to shelters or hostels.

The law should require mobile crisis teams to complete determinations and establish a binding procedure to ensure both confidentiality and reasonable access by families to information. Court officials who receive determinations must provide families the opportunity to attend a hearing. Judges in juvenile courts should be required to make final decisions about the custody of minors on the basis of the "best interest of the child" standard.[11] In cases in which minors are to return home, justices may stipulate requirements to be met by families, such as writs analogous to those for *habeas corpus* requiring periodic presentation of the child to officials or mobile crisis teams. The appropriate training of police, lawyers, and town officials (elected or appointed) should be mandatory, like the vetting of volunteers in NGOs.

Finally, one important official procedure ought to be undertaken at the beginning of efforts to eradicate honor killing, and renewed on a semi-annual basis until no longer required. Areas in which honor killings are known to occur ought to be designated as a recognizable community for the purpose of a house-to-house census of residents, including the age and sex of children. The objective of semi-annual enumerations is to deter efforts to conceal executions and "honor suicides" and to prevent families from having victims transported to locales where relatives might perform executions. Enumerations that expose irregularities shall be grounds for mobile crisis teams to sign petitions for police investigations. Such surveillance, as well as other interventions, are likely to be resented by communal members, but they can be assured that the need for such measures will end when girls and women are cherished for their development and contributions, and when such care and respect extinguishes the tendency to respond with lethal violence to allegations of dishonor.

Public Relations

Among the most important functions of the network CO will be to provide accurate and unbiased information about efforts to hinder honor killing and successes and difficulties encountered. Information about available services should be distributed through whatever venues will cooperate: schools, health clinics, and hospitals, and through progressive religious and political leaders. Citizens in local communities should be informed about the emergency facilities as they are implemented, except for the role of OBIs. In contacts with media through newspapers, TV programs, and radio talk shows, the CO should discuss the history of the problem and the importance of emergency measures. This should include interviews with knowledgeable persons respected in the region and administrators of shelters,

---

11. This standard was established by the 1989 United Nations Convention on the Rights of the Child; see https:/treaties.un.org, accessed Jul. 17, 2016.

hostels, halfway houses, and mobile crisis teams, who can describe the positive roles available to the community. When incidents do occur, network coordinators should encourage the media to spurn sensational stories and provide objective, in-depth reporting that attempts to present the complicated issues forming the background of the incident.

It is critical to convince the public that shelters are not brothels and that youth hostels do not encourage illicit behavior, which is widely assumed in certain sectors. In addition to media coverage of the necessity for and actual services provided at facilities, open houses and public tours should be held when facilities are first opened. Subsequent tours should be permitted at regular intervals, provided that guards are available and occupants can be adequately and safely shielded from prying and accusatory eyes.

Also critically important is the network CO's interaction with families at hearings about determinations and at court cases. There should be "open mic" sessions with the general public to discuss matters of concern or to respond to questions over new initiatives or changes of procedure. (Such sessions can be conducted in collaborative community-school centers; see Section 9.5.) Because of the high probability of anger and frustration, citizens should be warned in advance that disorderly conduct will not be tolerated, that police will be present at the public sessions, and that civilians who may be carrying weapons or dangerous objects (e.g., hammers or tire irons) will have them confiscated at the door.

Refugee Status and Asylum

In some cases, the best remedy will be to arrange for the removal of a woman from her family and community. She might be securely transported to a halfway house in an urban area where she may look forward to eventual independence and self-sufficiency. However, there are cases in which a woman has migrated to a larger city in the same country, assumed a new identity, and frequently changed addresses, and, despite hiding from the family, has been tracked for years, eventually discovered, and executed. If evidence indicates that a sheltered woman faces such a future, then NGOs and officials of foreign governments should work with shelters and network coordinators to assist her in applying for asylum as a refugee. As applications must be made at the embassies or consulates of prospective host counties or at offices of the UN High Commissioner for Refugees, clients will need safe conduct to these sites, and they may need overnight shelter and maintenance in facilities nearby. Applicants must provide documentation proving the persecution they are facing in their home country, and staff in facilities and mobile crisis teams, as well as local police and legal officials, should provide sworn testimonials, affidavits, and the paperwork documenting such evidence.

US and international asylum law require that, to qualify as a refugee, an applicant must fall within one of several categories who fear persecution based on race, religion, nationality, membership of a particular social group, or political opinion.[12] International and national laws must be reformed to include gender as a recognized category for which one may be persecuted.[13] To date, proposals to add persecution based on gender as a category have received little support because sexism and gender violence have been viewed as cultural norms instead of reasons for granting asylum. This is a specious argument, for historically persecution based on religion has often been a matter of culture, as has persecution based on political opinion. Honor killings occur not just because of women's status in her society, but because she is victimized due to her society's demands for honor. Moreover, a potential victim is in a guarded shelter and applying for asylum because, even where her intended assailants cannot act with impunity, the state cannot assure protection of her person and her rights. In 2011, the US Seventh Circuit Court of Appeals recognized honor killing as a form of gender-based persecution in *Sarhan v. Holder*.[14] This important precedent should lead to appropriate revisions of national and international asylum and refugee laws.

To summarize this section, many emergency interventions will occur in hostile environments. It is therefore important that publicity efforts stress the focus of crisis intervention on specific instances of gender violence and human rights violations. Community residents are likely to protest that, because honor is a critical feature of their culture, emergency responders are undermining their entire culture. In response, it must be stressed that, in addition to responding to very specific "honor" problems, there are alternative conceptions of honor that should guide male behavior and community attitudes and responses when problems arise (Sections 8.1–8.3). Emergency interventions thus are not intended as attacks on a

12. US Citizenship and Immigration Services at htttps://www.us.gov/humanitarianism/refugees-asylum, accessed Jul. 17, 2016.
13. Karen Musalo, "Personal Violence, Public Matter: Evolving Standards in Gender-Based Asylum Law," *Harvard International Review*, Fall 2014/Winter 2015, 45–48. See also the Center for Refugee Studies, University of California, Hastings College of Law at www.cgrs.uchastings.edu/our-work/honor-killing-and-other-violence, accessed Jul. 17, 2016.
14. 658 F. 3d 349 (7th Cir. 2011).

way of life; rather, they are a needed response to an archaic, dysfunctional, and murderous social practice and, like surgical interventions against a cancer, are designed to promote the positive and inclusive functioning of the community.

In addition, citizens unhappy with emergency interventions can be assured that there is an open pathway toward the end of "interventions" from what might be perceived as the "outside." This path requires their willingness to undertake a moral transformation, to make the safeguarding of the lives of all community members a matter of honor and based on revised social practices which members own and regard with pride (Chapters 8–9). Those who remain intransigent, holding on to dysfunctional social practices, can be told that emergency interventions will continue unabated and that efforts to conceal honor killings as accidents or suicides cannot succeed, nor can efforts to send girls or disgraced wives to locales where attacks may be made with impunity. In fact, intransigent citizens can be given information that the alternative to noncompliance will be more drastic interventions, including some of the strategies and tactics for leveraging change.

7.3 LEVERAGING OUTSIDE INFLUENCES

The discussion in this section is guided by three hypotheses: (1) either emergency intervention and a moral transformation as discussed in Chapters 8–9 have not or cannot prevail, or (2) the risks to life and health are so immediate and widespread that minimally coercive and gradual transformation is ill advised, or (3) alternatively, for one reason or another, strategies for a moral transformation are too costly or not politically feasible. Strategies and tactics discussed in this section are either explicitly coercive or otherwise do not presuppose the cooperation of members of HSCs. They have the objective of creating *leverage*; that is, of making continuing honor killing *too costly* for perpetrators or the community, or otherwise increasing the difficulties of perpetrating the crime.[15] These strategies and tactics include reducing the aggression of perpetrators, enlarging the role of moral entrepreneurs, increasing media

15. Understood here as a verb, to leverage or leveraging involves the employment of external resources in such a way as to produce the desired effect with minimum effort. See David M. Anderson, "Introduction," in David M. Anderson (ed.), *Leveraging: A Political, Economic and Societal Framework* (Heidelberg and New York: Springer, 2015), 3–34.

and public pressure against the "backwardness" of communal beliefs and practices, and expanding revisions of legal codes well beyond the criminalization of honor killing.

Two additional points need to be made. First, many of the strategic measures discussed in this section, and especially new legal codes and provisions, are desirable given the ultimate objectives of gender equality and vindicating human rights. However, I limit my consideration only to their role in ending honor killing. Second, whatever mix of strategic measures is both possible and effective, residents of communities should be given explicit assurances that, with the cessation of honor killing and gender violence, many outside coercive pressures can end.

Legal Reforms

Often one's first reaction is to call for tougher legal measures: if only the practice were banned and properly punished, it would cease. However, measures imposed by state legal and criminal justice systems have met with very limited success. There are several reasons for this. In the first place, many legal systems compete against greater loyalty given to tribal, caste, and communal "legal" systems such as the directives of *khap panchayats* in India or *jirgas* in Pakistan. Second, given strong clan, tribal, or ethnic identifications, and weak identification with the national state, many community members refuse to cooperate with law enforcement efforts. Third, for complex reasons, the rule of law has not penetrated very deeply into the social consciousness in HSCs. Finally, given the identification of male honor with "cleansing" the family's reputations, HSCs prefer to retain traditional practices while devising devious means to get around harsh sentences: killings occur more frequently in private than in public, evidence is destroyed (e.g., by immolating the victim's body in a shed in which execution occurred), "accidents" or "suicides" are staged, or juvenile males are selected to commit executions.

Turkey, until recently, was more progressive in responding to gender violence than many states in the Middle East or Asia. Nevertheless, it provides an informative study. During the early 2000s, as Turkey sought to join the European Union, legislation was passed to crack down on violence against women in general and on honor killings in particular, at least on paper. In 2004, as part of extensive reforms to the Turkish Penal Code, laws once used to grant leniency to honor killers were revised. First, a provision referencing "unjust provocations" was amended so that it was no longer applicable to honor killings. Second, "homicides by motivation of custom"[16] were included in a list of aggravated homicide circumstances.[17] In 2005, Turkey passed a piece of legislation urging cities with more than 50,000 people to create a women's shelter; but because the legislation was noncompulsory, compliance has been incredibly slow. In 2010, there were only 58 women's shelters in Turkey, with a combined capacity of 1,354 women, despite the fact that 1,400 Turkish cities are at or above the threshold of 50,000 inhabitants.[18]

Despite its forward-looking legislative changes, rather than a reduction in its number of honor killings, Turkey experienced a tremendous spike between 2002 and 2011. Based on figures reported by Turkish officials, murders of women appear to have increased 14-fold between 2002 and 2009.[19] In 2006, *The New York Times* reported that many Turkish families were using forced suicides to avoid prosecution for honor killings. Reporter Dan Bilefsky shares a particularly chilling story, in which Derya, a 17-year-old Turkish girl who had a "love affair" with a boy she met at school, received a text from her uncle: "You have blackened our name. . . . Kill yourself and clean our shame or we will kill you first."[20] Derya's hometown of Batman, Turkey, has been nicknamed "Suicide City." A woman commits 3 out of every 4 suicides in Batman; this is noteworthy because just about everywhere else male suicides outnumber female suicides 3 to 1—and most of the suicides in Batman are forced.[21] Because of the difficulties previously identified, in 2009, Batman's chief prosecutor described these cases as "almost impossible to investigate."[22]

In some Muslim-majority countries, legislative bodies and public opinion still struggle to disentangle traditional religious principles and customary practices from the need to protect women's human rights. In 2009, for example, a Law on the Elimination of Violence Against Women

16. The term "honor killing" is often replaced with "customary killing" in Turkish law. Hence, "motivation of custom" is roughly analogous to "motivation of honor."

17. Pinar Ilkkaracan and Liz Ercevik Amado, "Good Practices in Legislation on Violence Against Women in Turkey and Problems of Implementation," in Moha Ennaji and Fatima Sadiqi (eds.), *Gender and Violence in the Middle East* (London and New York: Routledge, 2011), 189–99.

18. Cagla Diner and Sule Toktas, "Women's Shelters in Turkey: A Qualitative Study on Shortcoming of Policy Making and Implementation," *Violence Against Women* 19, no. 3 (2013), 338–55.

19. Alexander Christie-Miller, "Turkey Grapples with Spike in 'Honor' Killings," *Christian Science Monitor*, Apr. 14, 2011.

20. Dan Bilefsky, "How to Avoid Honor Killing in Turkey? Honor Suicide," *New York Times*, Jul. 16, 2006.

21. Ramita Navai, "Women Told: 'You Have Dishonoured Your Family, Please Kill Yourself,'" *Independent*, Mar. 27, 2009.

22. Quoted in Navai, "Women Told."

(EVAW) was enacted in Afghanistan by presidential decree. However, the law has not been ratified by parliament because of conservative resistance, and hence, there is no firmly established legal framework to defend women's rights.[23] Today, Afghan prisons are filled with women who have been rejected by their families because they have been raped, fled abuse or forced marriages, have been accused of adultery, or become pregnant with partners their families do not accept.[24]

In Pakistan, with its long and troubling history of honor killing, one effect of the Law of *Qisas* (revenge) and *Diyat* (payment), introduced in 1989, was that punishments for murder and bodily harm, including honor killing, were to be determined not by the severity of the crime but by the perpetrator–victim relationship and available proof. In addition, victims of bodily harm and family members of victims of murder were given the right to forgive or compromise with an accused perpetrator.[25] Consequently, honor killings were generally treated by the state as private matters to be settled for the "good of the family," which involved very little deterrence when a woman's parents were responsible for deciding she should die. Honor killers thus were punished lightly, if at all,[26] and courts continued to endorse the use of pleas of "grave and sudden provocation."

However, the legal tides are starting to shift in Pakistan. The 2001 case *Muhammad Akram Khan v. The State* marked the first time the Supreme Court referenced the rights of a victim of honor killing. The court held: "Legally and morally speaking, nobody has any right nor can anybody be allowed to take law in his own hands to take the life of anybody in the name of '*Ghairat*.'"[27] Subsequent rulings have been in a similar vein. Until 2015, these legal precedents and minor statutory reforms made little if any difference, but finally Pakistan has taken serious steps in addressing its honor killing problem. In late 2014, four men in Lahore were sentenced to death for killing their pregnant 25-year-old female family member, Farzana Parveen, after she married a man of her choosing.[28] In early 2015, Pakistan

23. Fawazia Koofi, "It's Time to Act for Afghan Women: Pass EVAW," *Foreign Policy*, Jan. 13, 2015, www.foreignpolicy.com/2015/01/13/its-time-to-act-for-afghan-women-pass-the-evaw, accessed Jul. 16, 2016.

24. Gabriela Maj, "Afghan Women Imprisoned by Their Culture," *Washington Post*, Aug. 14, 2015, A17.

25. Sohail Akbar Warraich, "'Honour Killings' and the Law in Pakistan," in Lynn Welchman and Sara Hossain (eds.), *"Honour": Crimes, Paradigms, and Violence Against Women* (London and New York: Zed Books, 2005), 78–110, 86.

26. Warraich, "'Honour Killings,'" 86.

27. PLD 2001 SC 96, 100, quoted in Warraich, "'Honour Killings,'" 97.

28. Waqar Gillani, "Four Pakistani Men Sentenced to Death for 'Honor Killing,'" *New York Times*, Nov. 19, 2014.

passed legislation recognizing honor killing as criminal and equivalent to murder.[29] It is too early to know to what extent or how consistently these new laws will be enforced and whether or not they will reduce the number of honor killings that occur each year.[30]

In addition to continuing to respond to honor killing as murder, and as requiring leverage to end it, each of the following provisions should also be considered in addition to those specified in connection with emergency prevention measures (Section 7.2):[31]

- Protect the same range of human rights for women that men enjoy as specified in the Convention on the End of All Forms of Discrimination Against Women (CEDAW) adopted by the UN General Assembly in 1977 and entering into force as international law in 1981.[32] Reservations adopted by some signatories must be judged to express only the preferences of government officials and therefore lack legal effect. Special attention should be given to control over one's own body, movement, liberty and freedom of expression, and the right to choose one's own marriage partner, the right to receive education, the right to work, the right to own and inherit property, and rights to due process and equal treatment before the law, including matters pertaining to divorce and the custody of children. Denial of these rights should be criminalized.
- Increase punishment for rape and kidnapping.
- Criminalize and punish incest, spousal abuse, and child abuse.
- Study the harmful effects of certain practices relating to honor violence with a view to recommendations about criminalization, including imprisoning a female in the home or depriving her of outside contacts, forcing her to travel against her will, interrupting her education, denying her the receipt of health care, or refusing visits by child welfare agents.

29. Irfan Haider, "Senate Passes Bills Against Rape, Honour Killing," *Dawn*, Mar. 2, 2015.

30. One positive sign is the recent willingness of Pakistani Prime Minister Nawaz Sharif and his PML-N party to pursue some women's rights, such as ending child marriage, even against stiff conservative opposition. See Tim Craig, "Business-Focused Pakistani Chief Willing to Step on Clerics' Toes," *Washington Post*, Mar. 10, 2016.

31. Compare the draft bill proposed in India in 2010 by Dr. Girija Vyas, "Prevention of Crimes in the Name of 'Honour' and Tradition Bill," www.vicw.nic.in/PDFiles/Bill_against_honour_killing_crimes.pdf, accessed Jan. 25, 2016.

32. CEDAW, www.un.org/womenwatch/daw/cedaw, accessed Oct. 17, 2017.

- Hold all members of a family, clan, *khap panchayat, jirga*, or community guilty for a collective decision to execute a girl or women or for initiating plans to do so.[33]
- Increase to life sentence without parole the punishments for family members who are convicted of honor killing that occurs following their execution of a bond or surety with a magistrate, police officer, mobile crisis team, or other official declaring that they will keep the peace and not harm a girl or woman remanded to their custody.
- Recognize hate crimes as a category of criminal offense and include as a hate crime engaging in malicious slander about an "honor" violation when harm is foreseeable, with the said offense to be punishable by a 3- to 6-month sentence.
- Enact as a crime for "harassment" with penalties of 1 to 10 years, any of the following:
  - Declaring publicly that a person, male or female, should be put to death or inciting a riot or disturbance, public or private, leading to death or injury.
  - Requiring through physical force or intimidation that any person or organization sheltering or harboring a person accused of an honor crime turn that person over to you.
  - Ordering, enticing, or paying juveniles to participate in honor crimes.
  - Imposing deprivations or hardships on a couple who contract a marriage or on a family that shelters a female when these deprivations are intended as a form of shaming or shunning. Hardships include dismissal from a job or loss of wages, nullifying a contract or sale, or imposing an economic or social boycott.
  - Attempting to have a marriage annulled or dissolved against the wishes of both parties.
  - Insisting that a girl or woman undergo a "virginity test" before marriage or requiring that she submit to hymenoplasty.
  - Requiring or causing a newly married couple to submit to proof of virginity by presenting a blood-stained sheet or clothing.

---

33. The honor killing of Ghazala Khan and the conviction of nine members of her family by the High Court of Eastern Denmark on June 27, 2006, set an important precedent in Europe. The arrest of 14 members of a *jirga* in Abbottabad, Pakistan, in May 2016 for the burning to death of Ambreen Riasat is among a number of similar initiatives in Pakistan and India. See, respectively, Filip van Laenen, "Danes Sentence Entire Clan for Honour Killing," *Brussels Journal*, www.brusselsjournal.com/node/1143, accessed Apr. 18, 2014; Amir Iqbal and Tim Craig, "In Pakistan, 14 Are Held in Girl's Death," *Washington Post*, May 6, 2016, A13.

- Causing any other harm or other acts of mental or physical intimidation in connection with allegations of dishonor and which result in suicide.

While all of these legal provisions are critically important, if outside pressure is the only means of ending the practice, then by using leverage we should propose reforms "across the board"; that is, against all major patriarchal pillars that support honor killing. Hence, in addition, each of the following ought to be considered:

1. Raise the age for legal marriage and require that only authorities licensed by the state be permitted to perform marriages.
2. Prohibit polygamy and punish its practice.
3. Enable women to initiate divorce proceedings and eliminate the "right" of men to divorce a wife without legal proceedings.
4. Enact spousal rape legislation and make spousal rape, along with domestic abuse and cruelty, grounds for divorce.
5. Ensure that women have rights equal to men in owning and inheriting property.
6. Change adoption laws so that adoption is legal, and so that a mother can adopt a child born out of wedlock or, if she marries or remarries, her parents or her spouse could adopt the child.

These recommended legal changes, and especially 1–6, certainly will be regarded as radical in many areas and are likely to incite considerable resistance to enabling women to enjoy their full human rights. From the narrow perspective of ending honor killing, however, this perception of alarm is not undesirable if change agents do not overplay their hand, so to speak. Pushing for social reforms that simultaneously address a number of problems can be seen as attacks on a whole way of life and thus generate reactionary, radical, and even violent responses. Of course, if the objective is to get sanctimonious but unyielding conservatives to realize that it is far better to surrender on the issue of honor killing than to risk more radical and far-reaching changes, then even the knowledge that such legal reforms have been introduced as bills in parliament, or news of such possibilities, may be enough to make retaining honor killing too costly an option. This is a very risky gambit to take, however, and very careful and sensitive political calculations are required before embarking on such a course.[34]

34. Much might be learned from the relative success of Sharif and PML-N party progressives in Pakistan. Even more important, there is much to learn from the burgeoning

One approach that can be combined with aspects of legal reform, but that may be less threatening overall, is a social movement analyzed and named by Howard S. Becker.[35] *Moral entrepreneurs* (MEs) are individuals who usually join together in a group to define and construct an understanding of reality. In effect, MEs are either norm creators or rule enforcers, and I focus primarily on norm creators. Some examples of MEs familiar from recent US history include the anti-tobacco lobby, Mothers Against Drunk Driving (MADD), the LGBT social movement, the anti–date rape and anti–child abuse movements, and pro-life and pro-choice groups in the abortion controversy.

Norm-creating MEs are involved in four critical activities, each of which is important for present purposes: (1) they take the role of moral crusaders and, through labeling or "typifying," publicize the conviction that a social evil is a problem not only for members of some group or subculture, but for all members of society; (2) they expend great energy on successfully persuading and enlisting followers; (3) they define the problem in a way that suggests what appropriate social policy is needed to solve it; and (4) they seek to influence those in power and, through public protest and legislation, to put an end to the threatening social evil.[36]

Theorists note that MEs are often very successful in revising social norms and even creating new norms. By articulating and publicizing the best perspective from which a problem should be understood (e.g., medical, moral, criminal, political, etc.), MEs often reframe problems so that they are no longer seen as tolerable variations but as critical time-sensitive problems and as matters for which the advice of experts and professionals is welcome (Section 8.2).

In addition, one consequence of the actions of MEs is the definition of a practice as *deviant* (e.g., drunken driving), which signifies blameworthiness on the part of those engaging in it.[37] Of course, labeling norms

literature on nonviolent social change. See, for example, Engler and Engler, *This Is an Uprising*.

35. Howard S. Becker, *Outsiders: Studies in the Sociology of Deviance* (New York: Free Press, 1963), 147–53.

36. Joel E. Best, "'Typification' and Social Problems Construction," in Joel E. Best (ed.), *Image and Issues: Typifying Contemporary Social Problems* (New York: Aldine Press, 1995); Martha Finnemore and Kathryn Sikkink, "International Norm Dynamics and Political Change," *International Organization* 52 (1998), 887–917.

37. Anne L. Schneider and Helen M. Ingram, *Deserving and Entitled: Social Constructions and Public Policy* (Albany: State University of New York Press, 2005).

as deviant runs the risk of producing considerable resistance and, consequently, possibly posing increased risks for women. The effectiveness of moral entrepreneurship might depend, then, not just on the extent of public protest from outside, but also on how costly members of the community perceive this external disapproval. If moral disapproval from the outside leads to perceived losses of employment opportunities, state benefits, or, most important, honor, then the effect could be significant. In this context, reference can be made to the common perception among outsiders that men commit honor killings for personal and materialistic motives and use honor as a cloak for their mendacity (Section 8.2). Because this association is antithetical to conceptions of male honor in HSCs, awareness of this public impression may incline truly honorable men to avoid the social practice.

Influence of Media and National Elites

Some interviewees claim that the media is a major cause of "the problem" of honor killing. In the minds of traditionalists, this typically means that, by communicating Western and globalizing trends, the media have too strong an influence on impressionable females. However, media and prominent, nationally known figures can also exert leverage in a number of ways. These respected and well-known figures, especially sports stars, movie actors, famous writers and artists, and religious leaders can be featured in media spots in which they share their commitment to end honor killing. Spokespersons in such media campaigns should *personalize the issue* by expressing their personal dismay and opposition and speaking of the practice as a blot on the honor of all members of their national group (e.g., Afghans, Indians, Iraqis, Saudis, Turks). Spokespersons should add that they do not want people in other countries to associate them and their countrymen with this cruel, archaic, and unjustified practice.

Major TV networks should air documentaries about honor killing, such as the Oscar-winning story about Saba's survival of an attack in Pakistan in 2016, depicted in *A Girl in the River: The Price of Forgiveness*.[38] There are remarkable and true stories of cultural change, such as *What Tomorrow Brings*, a 2016 documentary about the success, against terrific odds, of

---

38. www.hbo.com/documentaries/a-girl-in-the-river-the-price-of-forgiveness, accessed Mar. 28, 2017.

Razia Jan in founding the Zabuli Education Center for girls in the Afghan village of Deh'Subz.[39] The airing of such documentaries should be followed by broadcast interviews with public figures offering commentaries.

The UN-sponsored program undertaken by Kardam and her colleagues in Turkey revealed that a sizable proportion of interviewees were aggrieved by the sensational journalistic reporting of honor killings and the negative light it cast on their communities and culture.[40] In addition, many Muslims were insulted and upset by the use of an alleged honor killing as the vehicle for anti-Islamic political tracts, the most notorious being Norma Khouri's best-selling *Honor Lost* of 2003, a piece of politicized fiction masquerading as a "memoir" about the alleged honor killing of her best friend, Dali, in Jordan.[41] It is critically important that media campaigns not become politicized, and therefore, partisan politicians should not be involved. In addition, extreme care must be taken to ensure that programing and media coverage is factual and accurate. Appeals for a change of attitude and behavior should be as honest and straightforward as possible.

Influencing Potential Perpetrators

Successful implementation of the programs for moral transformation will provide the best way to decrease the probabilities that men will become perpetrators (Sections 8.2–8.4). The emphasis must be placed on the formative years for, according to criminologist Jeffrey Goldstein, efforts to introduce behavioral interventions "leave untouched the basic core of aggression, that is, the acquisition of aggressive and antisocial values, attitudes, and behaviors."[42] It is not surprising that Goldstein emphasizes the *opposite* of what typically takes place during socialization in HSCs (Chapter 4). Goldstein points to three ways that we might move toward the elimination of violence: removal of incentives for violence, reduction of institutionalized modeling of aggression, and social problem-solving.

---

39. www.pbs.org/pov/pressroom/2016/girls-school-in-rural-afghanistan-defie-the-odds-and-uncertain-future-in-what-tomorrow-brings/pov, accessed Mar. 28, 2017.

40. Kardam et al., *The Dynamics of Honor Killing,* 48.

41. The book's publisher withdrew it when fraud was discovered, but it had already been a commercial success. The real author, Norma Bagain Toliopoulos, gained asylum on the basis of false events described in the book although she had not lived in Jordan since she was three years old and had grown up in Chicago. Jordanian journalist Rana Husseini uncovered the fraud. See Rana Husseini, *Murder in the Name of Honor* (Oxford: Oneworld, 2009), 90–100.

42. Jeffrey H. Goldstein, *Aggression and Crimes of Violence*, 2nd ed. (New York: Oxford University Press, 1986), 165.

In eliminating incentives, it is necessary to revise normative behavior, which must begin very early in the lives of children. Positive reinforcement by parents of nonaggressive behaviors is critical. Goldstein writes, "It is during childhood that the underlying core of aggressive behavior and related attitudes, values, and norms are acquired. Parental behavior is the greatest influence on this learning."[43] Thus, encouraging parents not to reward violent behavior, to show affection appropriately and frequently, to give children reasons or explanations for what they are required to do, and to react without aggression even in the face of their child's most frustrating behaviors—all should have pronounced effects on reducing aggression.

Goldstein also points out that respect for the law and for civic virtues can be useful tactics for reducing violence. "The more tolerant a society is of various kinds of acceptable violence, as in child-rearing, play, humor, sports, politics, entertainment, and daily social intercourse, the more likely it will be to have high rates of criminal violence since the former serve largely as training grounds for the latter."[44] In addition, Goldstein writes briefly on attitudes and social problem-solving norms: "attitude change is most effective when it is immediate, a result of personal experience and face-to-face encounter."[45] Obviously, "widespread attitude change" and changing social norms are critical for the abolition of honor killings. Likewise, problem-solving is among the most important skills children should acquire as it enables potential perpetrators to exercise self-control and conceive of alternative, nonharmful options. Efforts of this kind are explored more fully in Chapter 9.

Here, the concern is with prospects for influencing potential perpetrators if the changes sought through moral transformation do not occur or during difficult periods while a transformation is in process. An intelligent estimate requires some model of aggression. For this purpose, I adopt the "general theory of aggression," or "integrative model," proposed by Goldstein.[46] The model presents aggressive or nonaggressive behavior as the result of a conflict occurring within the agent.

43. Goldstein, *Aggression and Crimes of Violence*, 167.
44. Goldstein, *Aggression and Crimes of Violence*, 177.
45. Goldstein, *Aggression and Crimes of Violence*, 187.
46. Goldstein, *Aggression and Crimes of Violence*, 24–29, 107–09. Subsequent research seems to corroborate Goldstein's model. See C. Nathan DeWall, Craig A. Anderson, and Brad J. Bushman, "The General Model of Aggression: Theoretical Extensions to Violence," *Psychology of Violence* 1, no. 3 (2011), 245–58; Wilhelm Hoffman, Malte Friese, and Fritz Stroch, "Impulse and Self-Control from a Dual-Systems Perspective," *Perspectives on Psychological Science* 4, no. 2 (Feb. 2009), 162–76.

Whether an agent behaves aggressively or nonaggressively depends on the number and relative strength of a number of opposing pro- and anti-aggressive factors or tendencies. The behavioral outcome is a consequence of the combined product of these opposing tendencies. Thus Goldstein holds that there is "cognitive arithmetic" that occurs with extreme rapidity within the mind of agents, and the more prone to aggression (or alternatively, nonaggression) an agent, the more rapid this "arithmetic" calculation occurs. Of course, individuals are rarely aware of all of the factors, of their relative weights, or even of the decision-making process itself. The objective is to enable agents to understand and exercise control over this conflict process, and to avoid the resolution of tension through aggression, as well as aggression by default as occurs on "automatic pilot" or in patterns of "mindless choosing."

There can be up to six pro-aggression factors involved in this mental arithmetic, and I turn to a brief explanation of them.[47] The point to emphasize is that inducing a conflict between factors correlates with a *decrease* in the likelihood of aggression. For instance, doubt or uncertainty, emotional stress, hesitation, and resistance are among signs of conflict within an agent. Thus to decrease the probability of deadly violence, the conflict situation needs to be ratcheted up. By increasing various inputs (factors), low-conflict mental situations, in which there is too little effective resistance to honor killing, need to be turned into high-conflict mental situations in which anti-aggression factors will outweigh pro-aggression factors.

Of the six factors, two are primarily dispositional and internal to the agent, namely (1) *personal predispositions to aggress*, that is, personality traits such as defensiveness, narcissism, and hostility. I include as especially relevant for our purposes the formation of narcissistic and violence-prone personalities (N-VPP) and warrior masculinity, and the shame-to-power conversion. Closely related is (2) the *impetus to aggress*, also referring to certain internal states in the agent, namely, arousal (including activation of brain pathways for revenge); affect, including anger or frustration; and the presence or absence of impulsiveness.

Two factors are primarily situational or environmental, including (3) the *opportunity* and *ability to aggress* (e.g., presence of intended target; strength or skill of the potential aggressor; availability of weapons; support of accomplices; absence of effective restraints or deterrents, risks of harm, or apprehension). The other factor in this category involves (4) *situational*

---

47. Goldstein, *Aggression and Crimes of Violence*, 24–29; although indebted to Goldstein, my identification and discussion of the six factors differs significantly from his.

triggers: physical or verbal behavior of others (especially of the victim) perceived and interpreted as having a particular meaning (e.g., as an insult, as a threat, as a violation, etc.), as well as the behavior of bystanders who may be supportive or, alternatively, intervene or call authorities. Other situational factors typically include place or location and consumption of alcohol or use of drugs.

The remaining two factors represent the agent's socialization and internalization of norms and thus reflect an agent's social identity. They include (5) the *appropriateness of targets*, such as stereotypical denigration of the victim, norms and we-acceptances about justifiable aggression, and norms and we-acceptances about masculinity and femininity. Finally, there is (6), the *presence or absence of inhibitions against aggression*: these may be various but examples include norms and we-acceptances opposing aggression, feelings of affection and compassion, presence of disapproving peers, fear of the consequences, and the availability of alternatives to aggression.

Elements of each of these six factors may be involved in the cognitive calculus that occurs within an agent and before he acts violently or non-violently. The difficulty, as noted, is that such a calculus occurs almost automatically and often without self-conscious awareness of any but a few factors (e.g., one's perception of a violation, one's felt rage, and the approval of bystanders). It is precisely a successful process of transformation as outlined in Sections 8.2–8.4 that would greatly "open up" this decision process to conscious self-reflection and, therefore, to greater self-control; that is, as long as the transformation included appropriate problem-solving, sensitizing educational processes, and reconstructed models of masculinity and femininity (Chapter 9).

Unfortunately, if the conflict model I am assuming is correct, then this exercise exposes the poverty of attempting to leverage change without broader normative and cultural transformation. The difficulty is that purely external influence can be brought to bear only on the environmental or situational factors (categories 3 and 4 in the preceding list). In this connection, increasing both the effectiveness of enforcement and the certainty of punishment is recommended, as well, of course, as emergency measures that will reduce the likelihood of apprehending and harming intended victims. There is little else that affords opportunities for leverage; for instance, despite the increasing reliance of perpetrators on gunshot wounds, deaths are also caused by stabbings, drowning, poisoning, hanging, burning, acid attacks, staged accidents, and more, which indicate that a specific weapon is hardly necessary. Consequently, an effort at "gun control," while advisable for other reasons, might have little effect, if any, on the incidence of honor killing. Moreover, as this and other studies indicate, even increased criminalization has not had the intended effect.

This review demonstrates beyond question the desirability, if at all possible, of a comprehensive and transformative approach to honor killing as a social practice. Approaches that depend on external leveraging minimize opportunities for members of HSCs to consent to and own the changes. Moreover, they run the risk of encouraging resistance and backlash and therefore of playing into "us versus them" scenarios that risk supporting radical and fundamentalist defenses of "culture."

In concluding this chapter, I again stress the necessity for emergency intervention programs (Section 7.1). Whatever coercive impositions they require, these measures are more than justified by the willingness to tolerate, if not actually impose, risks of death and grievous human rights violations. Yet, it is in the nature of such emergency programs that the need for them should be self-limiting; that is, the need for external intervention becomes less significant the more communities adopt them as their own and honor killing, as a social practice, becomes increasingly rare.

CHAPTER 8

Moral Transformation

Taking Honor Out of Honor Killing

This is the first of two chapters focused on ending honor killing through *moral transformations* made *within* communities, rather than leveraged changes from without. In addition to moral transformation, the emphasis is on facilitating and *curating*[1] reforms that community members should come to adopt as their own. I have found it helpful to rely on a rough distinction between ends and means, or between *what the future might look like* and *how we might get there*. Of course, means are ends in the making; what must change is a complex of beliefs, attitudes, and dispositions, tightly woven together with norms of the concept of honor and behavioral scripts for male and female performances and indispensable for social practices, including honor killing. Nevertheless, it is possible to conceive of the intended end—one in which no one can see *an honor killing as an honorable deed*—independently of the multifaceted and incremental reforms necessary to reach that point. In this chapter, I focus on ways of achieving this revolutionary outcome. Even if genuine transformation is destined to be a long-term, incremental process, for which Chapter 9 provides recommended steps, taking honor out of honor killing must be a necessary part.

1. The concept of "peer mentors" who "curate" social reform is suggested to me by Carrie McManus and Andrea Silverstone in their paper "Peer Support: Curating Environments to Heal," presented at the conference on "The Global Status of Women and Girls," Christopher Newport University, March 24–26, 2017.

My concept of moral transformation shares similarities with Kwame Anthony Appiah's notion of "moral revolution" in *The Honor Code.*[2] In Section 8.1, I refer briefly to Appiah's historical examples of moral revolutions; however, most of Section 8.1 discusses a remarkable moral transformation Appiah does *not* discuss, but one especially appropriate for our purposes, especially as it concerns a fierce people variously known as the Pukhtun, Pashtun, or Pathan, who live by an exacting code of honor known as *Pukhtunwali* (see Chapters 3 and 5) This case study provides a plausible response to those inclined to think that moral transformations within honor–shame communities (HSCs) are impossible.

Section 8.2 discusses the psychological processes involved in moral transformation. I argue for isolating and demarcating one element of honor. I suggest that this objective is best achieved by reframing and recentering honor so that one cannot be a *real* man of honor and also engage in honor killing. Section 8.3 provides examples of real honor–shame cultures similar in important ways to HSCs, except that they do not practice honor killing. Finally, Section 8.4 explores possible substitutes for the functions that honor killing fulfill (Sections 6.4–6.5). These consist, first, of traditional methods of dispute resolution not heretofore extended to cover cases involving the alleged dishonor of females, and second, alternative ways of engaging in costly signaling.

Achieving the outcomes discussed in Chapter 8 would end the normative expectation that honor killing is ever appropriate. Of course, making these outcomes *sustainable* will require a wide range of incremental and step-by-step reforms. While set within the context of improving communal life overall and building ownership of the changes, these must focus cumulatively on three agent-centric "revolutions." First, eliminating or reducing punitive authoritarianism, socialization through shaming, toxic stress, and negative attachment, hence reducing the likelihood of violence-prone personality (VPP) and narcissism. Second, redirecting masculine identity away from warrior masculinity and breaking the connection to the shame-to-power conversion. Third, developing recognition of sure-fail mechanisms and introducing constructive efforts to overcome the sociocultural contradictions that give rise to these mechanisms. These elements for a holistic and sustainable moral revolution are addressed in Chapter 9.

2. Kwame Anthony Appiah, *The Honor Code: How Moral Revolutions Happen* (New York and London: W. W. Norton, 2010).

8.1 MAKING A MORAL REVOLUTION: THE KHUDAI KIDHMATGAR

A moral revolution is a major sociocultural change of life based primarily on a group's growing conviction that what had once been regarded as morally acceptable, or honorable, is now morally wrong. In *The Moral Code*, Appiah discusses moral revolutions that have special relevance for the ending of honor killing. Appiah examines the end of dueling with pistols in Great Britain, the Quaker-led prohibition against the slave trade in Great Britain, and the demise of foot-binding in early 20th-century China. In each instance, a long-standing cultural interpretation of honor began to be replaced by a newer conception incompatible with the social practice. Reformers mobilized shame and contempt, so that those in a position to vote or otherwise influence laws saw themselves as dishonored by belonging to a class or society in which previously accepted practices occurred. In addition, older conceptions of honor came to be regarded, not just as compromising morality, but also as "an accessory to the crime rather than a defense against it."[3]

A convergence of events dealt a decisive blow to the custom of pistol dueling in Great Britain. One was increased access to mass-manufactured and less expensive pistols, thus permitting men who lacked aristocratic bearing to engage in dueling. More devastating was the press's increasing portrayal of dueling as archaic and foolishly laughable; this rebuke was particularly effective when combined with the growing popularity of the view that gentlemanly refinement was inconsistent with dueling. As Cardinal Newman insisted, a gentleman should be defined as "one who never inflicts pain."[4] The man who refused to contemplate dueling henceforth might be honorable; the man insisting on it hardly a gentleman.

The Quaker-inspired antislavery movement in Great Britain confronted vested interests in the economic benefits of slave-trading and, consequently, the movement initially lacked support in Parliament. Advocating the principle of universal equality among humans, reformers continued to mobilize shame and contempt for slave-trading as well as the vicious degradation of captured men and women. What eventually prevailed, however, was not an abstract principle of universal humanity, but, as Appiah observes, the "honor of the workingman."[5] That is, the antislavery movement eventually

---

3. Simon Blackburn, "Review of *The Honor Code*," *The Guardian*, www.theguardian.com/books/2010/oct/so/simon-blackburn-honor-code-review accessed Apr. 19, 2011.
4. Quoted in Appiah, *Honor Code*, 49.
5. Appiah, *Honor Code*, 134.

prevailed when tradesmen and workers in Great Britain came to regard the toleration of slavery as an affront to their own dignity as laborers.

In the case of binding women's feet in China, honor became of pivotal importance in a different way. Foot binding was a customary practice among families of higher social status, and for ages an honorable man could not consider marrying a maiden whose feet had not been unnaturally constricted by foot binding. Yet elite attitudes about foot binding underwent a complete reversal within a generation as Chinese elites, mostly educated abroad, saw that their foreign counterparts regarded foot binding as exemplifying a backward and repressive society. For Chinese elites seeking to be regarded as the equals of European intellectuals, ending foot binding became a matter of national honor.

Responses from abroad were strongly influential in the case of foot binding, unlike in the other two moral revolutions. However, each revolution pivoted around the identification of a practice, reassessment of it as shameful and dishonorable, and the emergence of a new way of thinking about honor. The gripping question, therefore, is this: Is it possible to contemplate a similar moral revolution from within HSCs aimed at eradicating honor killing? The entrenchment of honor killing as a social practice and its evolutionary history seem to strain against this possibility. Yet each case discussed by Appiah is remarkably unlike the others, apart from the significance of honor. Perhaps a contemporaneous observer of each practice might have regarded its demise as improbable, just as a skeptic today might conclude about honor killing. Nothing we learn from Appiah's case studies suggests that a similar moral revolution *cannot occur* within HSCs.

On the contrary, realities about honor–shame cultures present other possibilities found in the accounts of another remarkable moral transformation, but one not discussed by Appiah. This history involves the transformation of a most unlikely group, the Pathans—infamous for their feuding, vengefulness, and violence upheld by their code of honor, *Pukhtunwali*. Nevertheless, tens of thousands of Pathans were able to become disciplined, to renounce vengeance, and become nonviolent activists against British rule in Pakistan. Given the Pathans' proclivities for violence, the ability of tens of thousands to adopt nonviolence provides an important and encouraging historical lesson. In addition, the way in which Badshah Khan and his followers effected change provides several useful illustrations worthy of attention. I rely extensively on the work of Mukulika Banerjee who, in addition to extensive archival research, interviewed 75 veterans of the nonviolent movement.[6]

___

6. Mukulika Banerjee, *The Pathan Unarmed: Opposition and Memory in the Northwest Frontier* (Karachi and New Delhi: Oxford University Press, 2000). See also Eknath

Between 1930 and 1947, a steadily growing number of Pathans known as the Khudai Kidhmatgar, or "Servants of God" (also known as Red Shirts for their distinctive uniforms), rejected their rifles and guerrilla tactics and relied on nonviolent civil disobedience. Khan Abdul Gaffar Khan, known honorifically as Badshah Khan, began this process of transformation in 1921, when he and a small group of activists launched the Anjuman i Islah ul Afghani, the Society for the Reform of Afghans. Khan envisioned the Khudai Kidhmatgar as a nonviolent "army" in the struggle for independence from British rule and the defense of social reforms against conservative reactionaries.

Khan's success is especially remarkable considering the rapidity with which volunteers for this nonviolent vanguard were enlisted and trained. By 1929, Khan concluded that the need for selfless service among the Pathans could best be met by instilling in them a sense of self-sacrifice.[7] By 1931, an estimated 25,000 volunteers were able and willing to risk injury or death in the nonviolent cause, and those numbers grew to an estimated 50,000 Red Shirts in 1938. In the 1940s, the Khudai Kidhmatgar were also recruiting large numbers of women although they had to break *purdah* to do so.[8]

Many of the changes Badshah Khan and his followers brought about suggest important possibilities for moral reform. Among these is formal education. A small group of Society activists toured villages to discuss the importance of education and communal support for local schools. For example, in the Peshawar district, for every 10 to 12 villages, a site was selected for the foundation of a middle school for children 10–14 years of age. Khan also opened Azah Islamia high schools all over the province. Attendance was free and open to students of all religions, classes, and castes, while finances for education came from the *izakat*, or 10% property tax expected of every Muslim, and from funds donated by Society members, many of whom also taught. Rather than having conservative *mullahs* collect the taxes designated for schools, Khan had schoolchildren collect and submit them.[9]

Schooling focused on the development of skills necessary for independent thinking; while literacy and numeracy were emphasized, so,

Easwaran, *A Man to Match His Mountains: Badshah Khan, Nonviolent Soldier of Islam* (Petaluma, CA: Nilgiri Press, 1984); and M. S. Korejo, *The Frontier Gandhi: His Place in History* (Karachi and Oxford: Oxford University Press, 1993).

7. Banerjee, *The Pathan Unarmed*, 52–53.
8. Banerjee, *The Pathan Unarmed*, 100.
9. Banerjee, *The Pathan Unarmed*, 51–52.

too, were discussions of verses of the Qur'an. Badshah Khan wanted students to question the passive and fatalist interpretation of Islam that the *mullahs* purveyed and that Khan blamed for discouraging change and self-improvement. Notably, schooling sought to separate aspects of Pathan heritage to be retained and celebrated from those targeted for reform. Hence, the intrinsic beauty of the Pashto language, poetry, and drama were stressed as well as traditions such as *melmastia*, or generous hospitality, and *nanawati*, or refuge and sanctuary. However, Khan spoke out against extravagant bride prices, wasteful and corrupt practices, infighting between clans and tribes, and especially *badal*, or the custom of redressing perceived injuries by seeking blood revenge.

In addition to schooling, Khan and Society members emphasized communal self-improvement projects. A special emphasis was placed on sanitary village life, including basic preventative measures against illness, the digging of latrines, and the construction of drainage ditches. As the cohort of Khudai Kidhmatgar increased, trained detachments would march from campsites to villages to undertake repairs, clean up, and initiate civic improvements. At the core of the sanitation and self-help projects was Khan's reformulation, in part, of Pathan pride and honor. Khan and his followers emphasized that these projects were declarations of independence and self-assertion: they were "a defiant refusal to continue to submit meekly" to continual neglect under the heel of colonialists, corrupt lackeys of the foreigners, and conservative and self-seeking *mullahs*.[10]

In the camps, recruits also received political education, including information about the colonial situation and the independence movement; they underwent physical training to prepare them to be volunteers for the physical demands of lengthy marches, rigorous self-control, and a Spartan existence.[11] Especially important was training in the strategies and tactics of nonviolent civil disobedience and resistance. New recruits were required to understand that membership could entail hardships, injury, and imprisonment. Recruits were required to take vows of service and, whether wealthy or poor, all dressed alike in the same red uniform; in addition, when not engaged in political campaigns or service, all spent time spinning raw cotton on the *charkha*, grinding wheat to make flour, or grinding grape-seed to make cooking oil.

Training for nonviolence required two major transformations for Pathans. One was a major psychological adjustment in the recruits' typically explosive reaction to provocation. The recruits' vows stressed service,

10. Banerjee, *The Pathan Unarmed*, 53.
11. Banerjee, *The Pathan Unarmed*, 53–57.

sacrifice, nonviolence, tolerance, and nonretaliation.[12] Shrewdly, Badshah Khan stressed both the need for *biraderi,* or fellow feeling, among Pathans, and the notion that *melmastia,* generous hospitality, consisted of *khidmat,* or humble, selfless service for one's people. The Khudai Kidhmatgar were taught to serve others without asking for anything in return. Most important, Badshah Khan's message to recruits and to Pathans generally was that response for insult or an injury did not require violence in return. As Banerjee points out, Badshah Khan appealed to the Pathans' demands for bravery and honor by proclaiming that the greatest bravery was to confront the British in a determined and unflinching manner, but always courteously and unarmed.[13] For instance, in training for nonviolence, the Red Shirts were taught to respond to *lathi* attacks by grasping the cane when possible and saying, "We are ashamed to hit back."[14] The Pathans' "volatile bravado of violence" was thus replaced by the willpower and steadfastness to calmly await approaching and armed soldiers and defy them to strike.[15]

Khan frequently claimed that the best way for the Pathans to avenge themselves on the British would be to "show them up as the unprincipled villains they were and eject them from India with their reputation in tatters."[16] Khan insisted that violent colonial retaliation to nonviolence demonstrated the Pathans' moral superiority; in addition, nonviolent tactics were "intensely satisfying in so far as they undermined colonial claims about both the Pathans' inherent violence and anarchy and their [the colonists'] own civility and civilization."[17] The Khudai Kidhmatgar were told that if they could persevere in being nonviolent in the face of oppression they would win honor in the eyes of people all over the world.[18]

In addressing the Pathans more generally, Badshah Khan alternated between shaming men outright and appealing to them for a reformulation of their conception of honor. How could men of true honor have allowed themselves to be subjugated both to corrupt indigenous leaders and to the British?[19] The following was a common refrain: "Have some shame! You call yourself Puktuns. Do not be so shameless. . . . Your heads are full of slavery. . . . Feel a little *gherat* for your mothers, sisters and children who are dressed in rags . . . get up and throw the yoke off your country."[20] Khan

---

12. Banerjee, *The Pathan Unarmed,* 73.
13. Banerjee, *The Pathan Unarmed,* 155.
14. Banerjee, *The Pathan Unarmed,* 79.
15. Banerjee, *The Pathan Unarmed,* 157.
16. Banerjee, *The Pathan Unarmed,* 155–56.
17. Banerjee, *The Pathan Unarmed,* 156.
18. Banerjee, *The Pathan Unarmed,* 156.
19. Banerjee, *The Pathan Unarmed,* 154.
20. Khan quoted in Banerjee, *The Pathan Unarmed,* 154.

used a similar approach to persuade the Pathans to end their vendettas. As he berated them: "You cut the flesh of your own brother yet you are afraid of him who has taken the country of your forefathers."[21]

In his speeches, Khan repeated that the ranks of the Khudai Kidhmatgar were open to everyone but cowards. However, since men who were still engaging in vendettas or revenge could not join, there was a clear implication that those who continued feuding were cowardly for continuing to evade the true enemy. In addition, Khan often presented himself as representing the voiceless—namely, women and children who were appealing to men of honor to give them refuge and sanctuary from the British enemy.[22] Khan also appealed to notions of *meran*, or manliness. He accused the British of lacking manliness for adopting tactics of stealth and subterfuge, including the use of agents and provocateurs, not to mention their willingness to beat unarmed men and women. By contrast, Khan extolled the Khudai Kidhmatgar for demonstrating true *meran*. In this way, manhood was redefined: a steely will and proclivity to respond stalwartly to danger were retained, but capacities for self-control, the ability to suffer, and nonviolence replaced the proclivity for violence and winning by any means.

A veteran Khudai Kidhmatgar interviewed by Baneerjee offered an especially compelling example of Badshah Khan's imaginative recreation of traditional concepts and traditions. This veteran's father had been engaged in an unrelenting blood feud for 10 years with a relative named Musahib Khan. "He [Badshah Khan] told us that one way to settle disputes was to put a knife and rifle in the hands of your enemy and ask him to kill you. If he spares you then he can become a Khudai Kidhmatgar." The veteran reported that his father was moved to follow Badshah Khan's advice, and continued: "When my father made this appeal, Musahib Khan fell to his knees and kissed my father's feet."[23] As Charles Lindholm notes, among the Pathans, "Great value is placed on courage, which is not in the act of killing so much as in the willingness to take ruinous consequences for the sake of cleansing one's honour."[24] Banerjee concludes that Badshah Khan successfully "negotiated a conceptual and cultural space for the virtue of non-violence and implied to his audiences that it was not as great a departure from their previous practice as it at first seemed. In this way, the key terms of *Pukhtunwali*—such as shame, honour, refuge and hospitality—were subtly redefined."[25]

21. Khan quoted in Banerjee, *The Pathan Unarmed*, 155.
22. Banerjee, *The Pathan Unarmed*, 155.
23. Quoted in Banerjee, *The Pathan Unarmed*, 82.
24. Lindholm quoted in Banerjee, *The Pathan Unarmed*, 52.
25. Banerjee, *The Pathan Unarmed*, 166.

The Khudai Kidhmatgar movement lasted for 17 years, and, despite the end of colonial rule, the moral revolution among Pathans might have lasted longer had it received political support. Instead, after the partition of India and Pakistan, conservative Islamists and authoritarian politicians gained ascendance. Badshah Khan's subsequent efforts to create a Pathan autonomous region were crushed, and Khan spent most of the remainder of his life in jails. It must be noted, however, that Khan's primary objective was the independence of Afghanis and Pakistanis from colonialism. Neither Khan nor the progressive Pathan intelligentsia and lesser *khans*, or community leaders, were able to make the moral revolution sustainable and thus complete it. Both stages—reconceiving of honor and achieving sustainability—must be successful. Moreover, support and resources from the larger political unity must continue; for Khan and his progressive allies, political support and resources for continuing the transformation were cut off or coopted by conservative and dictatorial political forces.

In summary, himself a Pathan of charismatic stature, and given his nascent Pathan constituency, Badshah Khan was able to deploy strategies that, in the context of honor killing, lie partly in the category of transformative change and partly in the category of outside, leveraging pressure (Section 7.3). In effect, Khan succeeded at least temporarily in transforming conceptions of honor and shame among his fellow Pathans, both by insisting that honor required the opposite of central traditional practices and also by demonstrating how other principles of *Pukhtunwali* were consistent with these new reconfigurations. Khan's work demonstrates as well how rapidly new conceptions of honor can spread. The Khudai Kidhmatgar movement was open to Pathans of all ranks, and, once those of comparatively lower status had signed on, men of higher status who held out risked being doubly embarrassed. After the 1930 British-led massacre of more than 200 at the Kissa Khani bazaar, it increasingly became a question of honor for a family to have at least one member in the Khudai Kidhmatgar.[26] This was an obligation of honor among the Pathan not seen again until the anti-Soviet resistance in Afghanistan some 50 years later.

While aspects of Badshah Khan's partial moral revolution might not be compatible with transformations best designed to end honor killing, there are a number of intriguing possibilities. Perhaps the best aspect is Khan's suggestion that an honorable man end a blood feud by confronting his

---

26. Arthur Bonner, *Among the Afghans* (Durham, NC: Duke University Press, 1987), 45.

enemy unarmed and declaring, in effect, "accept the conclusion of our feud or make me and my family suffer."[27] Any man who sees himself as honorable and values the ideal of refuge cannot help but accept. This possibility compels us to ask, could it fulfill the same costly signaling function that honor killing evolved to fulfill? I consider possible answers toward the end of Section 8.3.

8.2 EFFECTING COGNITIVE DISSONANCE AND REFRAMING HONOR

Ending honor killing requires accepting that the social practice is not just archaic and unnecessary but also shameful: an activity to which a truly honorable person could not conceive of lending his support. Respect for autonomy requires that change agents use persuasion and minimize manipulation. Hence, reaching the desired objective will require argumentation, but not just arguments that appeal to cognition. We cannot expect people to give up a social practice simply by explaining or giving an account of why their ancestors developed the practice and then completing this account with "and now you can see that there is no need for this outdated, cruel practice in today's world." Some in HSCs may reject the explanation of cultural evolution (Chapter 6) outright; they may claim they *know* that without the fear of honor killing girls cannot be deterred from sinning and bringing *fitna*, or chaos, into being; others will claim to *know* that honor killing is required by religion, or that it is necessary to maintain the natural order of life, and so forth. Still others will resist because the social practice fits within a way of life, and an attack on honor killing might seem to call into question a whole lifeworld.

Consequently, sensible strategy recommends a *transcendental* approach; appeals must be made to individuals' realization of the value of changes in their orientation *through lived experiences*, without depending on their explicit understanding of the phenomenon—the social practice—that is to be changed. In other words, initiatives and innovations can be offered that, if accepted, will change agents' beliefs, attitudes, and dispositions, including a reevaluation of honor killing as shameful. Candor and respect for autonomy require that we be open about the objectives of recommended innovations, but there is no inconsistency in our respecting agents'

27. This interpretation of Badshah Khan's meaning has been influenced by my reading of Barry L. Gan, *Violence and Nonviolence: An Introduction* (Lanham, MD: Rowman & Littlefield, 2013), 85–113.

self-directed choices and designing or curating experiences that change their views *as long as agents voluntarily participate* in the processes and programs that offer life-changing experiences.[28]

Two additional points must be made. First, interviews conducted by Filiz Kardam's team in Turkey reveal a pervasive sense of hopelessness among many opposed to honor killing. These feelings were most intense in Batman and Şanlıurfa, where honor killing occurs frequently. Feelings of hopelessness reflected acceptance of honor killing as a "matter of fact" and were accompanied by a "sense of powerlessness and despair."[29] Only university students expressed optimism about overcoming the problem. Obviously, if a moral transformation is to occur, then Kardam's team is correct: there can be "no room for hopelessness."[30]

Second, research on major life changes indicates that the external direction of change (the "Path") must come to be aligned with all three components of persons: the rational element (nicknamed the "Rider") and both the intuitive and emotional sides (the "Elephant").[31] What Chip and Dan Heath call "see-feel" change refers to the engagement of the emotions and intuitions to accompany the "analyze-think" cognitive changes. The point is that "see-feel" intuitive and emotional adjustment is more important than intellectual "analyze-think," although this is commonly overlooked. Opportunities for emotional connection, and especially for positive emotions such as curiosity, wonder, and joy, broaden minds and increase a willingness to accept new possibilities.

Overcoming hopelessness and making change holistic—and appealing to the whole person—is the subject of Chapter 9. I mention the significance of these objectives here, however, to underline the importance of introducing a complement of bottom-up and incremental reforms at the same time that an effort is made to reconceive of and reframe honor. The latter also poses the difficulty of gaining entry or getting a foothold without exciting overwhelming anxiety about attacks on an HSC's way of life. An

28. The objective is not to design "choice architecture" that constrains free choice, but rather to design opportunities for experiences that will change voluntary choices. For the concept of choice architecture, see Richard H. Thaler and Cass R. Sunstein, *Nudge: Improving Decisions About Health, Wealth, and Happiness* (New York: Penguin Books, 2009).

29. Filiz Kardam, *The Dynamics of Honor Killing in Turkey: Prospects for Action*, with contributions from Zeynep Alpar, Ilknar Yüksel, and Ergül Ergün. Ankara, Turkey, United Nations Population Fund, 2006. www.unfpa.org/sites/defaultfiles/pub-pdf/, 50.

30. Kardam et al., *The Dynamics of Honor Killing*, 54.

31. Chip Heath and Dan Heath, *Switch: How to Change Things When Change Is Hard* (New York: Crown Publishing, 2010).

initial step is to *separate* honor from honor killing and to make it clear that only the association between killing females and honor is the subject of negative criticism. Hence the *link* between honor and killing dishonored females is *decoupled*, allowing honor killing to be *isolated* as dishonorable and to be eliminated. At the same time, the community can be reassured that it is not pressured to abandon the centrality of honor. Quite the contrary: curating mentors help community members understand that there is (initially) just *this one* social practice that must be eliminated because it is not only archaic and dysfunctional, but it is based on an immoral error— that is, that being an honorable person could ever require the killing of daughters, sisters, or wives.

Maintaining the initial valence of honor is critical for a moral revolution requires effective *cognitive dissonance*. Here, cognitive dissonance will pivot on the inconsistency between needing to see one's self as an honorable, virtuous, and good person in the eyes of others (see Chapter 3) and continue to regard honor killing as acceptable. Yet, in order for cognitive dissonance to be truly transformative, additional conditions must be fulfilled. First, one cannot ignore the dissonance; pressures for a cognitive and affective change must remain unrelieved. Second, the easiest course must be to resolve dissonance through accepting change rather than redoubling one's commitment to traditional belief or behavior. Attempts to revert to tradition must increase cognitive discomfort and doubt.

Third, the *cognitive dissonance must have centrality for life*; a moral revolution does not concern trivial or passing matters, but what is central to an individual's identity and self-understanding. Honor concerns one's fundamental social reality and hence, in close-knit groups, one's identity (Sections 3.4–3.5). The cognitive dissonance must be such that it cannot be ignored, dismissed, or suppressed. For honor–shame cultures, what is isolated and selected for elimination must be positioned as wholly inconsistent with honor.

The way a problem is *framed* can affect the onset of cognitive dissonance. Framing can heighten perceptions of a problem as requiring *resolution*, as well as whether it is a problem a group can *own* and see themselves as resolving.[32] When honor killing is thought of as a tradition existing since the origins of time and mystically preordained for communal well-being, then it will be extremely difficult to perceive the problem as changeable.

---

32. Drawing on research in cognitive science, George Lakoff understands a frame as "a word or set of words that activates a whole network of cognitive, affective, emotional, and moral associations." See George Lakoff, *The Political Mind: A Cognitive Scientist's Guide to Your Brain and Its Politics* (New York: Penguin Books, 2009), 12–13, 233, 25.

However, if members of HSCs come to *speak* of honor killing as a man-made crisis and one they can end, they will come to *think* of the social practice in this way and share the we-acceptance that together they possess the skills and competences to implement alternatives.[33] Obviously then, it is necessary that there be simultaneous programs to enhance independent, critical thinking and self-efficacy (Chapter 9).

An important lesson about reframing comes from Selen A. Ercan's study of the unique challenges between host countries and members of immigrant communities who believe it is sometimes acceptable to kill to restore honor.[34] Ercan compares the honor killing debates in the United Kingdom and Germany and highlights key differences in framing and outcomes. Ercan finds that, initially in the United Kingdom, change agents and police officials adopted a cultural frame in responding to honor killings. However, feminist groups such as the Southall Black Sisters successfully challenged the cultural frame because it suggested irreconcilable differences between traditional British culture and immigrant subcultures, such as those of the Kurds and Pakistanis. Moreover, the initial cultural frame was rejected in the United Kingdom because of its tendency to "normalize" gender violence within the subgroups in which it occurred and because it served to mitigate punishments. The problem of honor killing was successfully reframed in the United Kingdom by adopting a gender-based lens, whereas efforts to respond effectively in Germany remain hampered by a culture-based frame.[35]

By adopting a gender frame, activists aligned opposition to honor killing with long-standing political pressures to end gender violence in the United Kingdom. Immigrants in honor subcultures rejecting honor killing thus saw themselves as good British citizens and allied with compatriots in a similar cause. In Germany, by contrast, a culture frame persists due to

33. The connections between speaking, believing, and doing are far from fanciful. Because, as Lakoff notes, "language is a matter of neural connections," frequent encounters with certain terms and images develop "neural pathways" and can thus evoke whole structures, or "neural bindings," without having to pass through conscious thought. Lakoff, *The Political Mind*, 25.

34. Selen A. Ercan, "Same Problem, Different Solutions: The Case of 'Honour Killing' in Germany and Britain," in Aisha K. Gill, Carolyn Strange, and Karl Roberts (eds.), *'Honour' Killing and Violence: Theory, Policy and Practice* (New York: Palgrave Macmillan, 2014), 199–217.

35. This example of the significance of the gender frame for efforts to end honor killing in immigrant communities and in non-Muslim majority countries is not meant to suggest that a gender frame should be advocated for HSCs. As it might be interpreted as an attack simultaneously against all features of patriarchal domination, it might arouse great opposition. Hence, I recommend an initial frame that remains focused on honor.

the prevailing narrative of "parallel societies" surrounding honor killing, in which immigrant values are seen as fundamentally at odds with traditional German values. Despite the efforts of feminist groups such as Terre des Femmes and Papatya, politics in Germany make it more difficult to adopt a gender frame.[36] Not surprisingly, as Ercan notes, the prospects for combating honor killing are presently more favorable in the United Kingdom than in Germany.[37]

Questions arise about how to induce cognitive dissonance and a shift away from the *honor sometimes requires killing women* framing to a more appropriate *honor forbids killing women* frame. As noted earlier, the cognitive dissonance required for a moral transformation pivots on the inconsistency between seeing one's self and associates as honorable and accepting honor killing. Hence, one way to induce cognitive dissonance is not to challenge the presumption that members of HSCs are honorable, but rather, to offer factual evidence that many perpetrators of honor killing and their supporters—tens to hundreds of thousands of them—*cannot* be considered honorable even by members of HSCs. The objective is thus to invite an HSC member to consider: "Whereas I was accustomed to believing honor killing was sometimes necessary, is it possible that I and others have been mistaken, and do we risk derision as dishonorable if we continue to cling to this old belief?" An effective way of communicating doubts is through sponsoring information programs and discussions of the global reality of honor killing and femicide, highlighting stories about men who claim honor justifies their killing of women when, in fact, they obviously murdered for profit or other self-interested reasons. Tahira Khan has complied cases that demonstrate the "role of increasing material greed by using women's bodies as sources of financial benefits through the exploitation of honor."[38]

Although Tahira Khan relies on cases primarily from Pakistan, instances based on despicable and shameful motives can be found everywhere claims of honor are given as motives for killing. Now, those insisting that they are honorable must be asked: *Can truly honorable men allow themselves to be seen as brothers of selfish cowards who kill women for reasons having nothing to do with honor?* Certainly it will be objected: "It is different for us; we do not murder for money or for personal benefit." One rebuts this response by retorting: *How can anyone really believe you? Even in your community, authorities who examine*

36. Ercan, "Same Problem," 204.
37. Ercan, "Same Problem," 210.
38. Tahira S. Khan, *Beyond Honour: A Historical Materialist Explanation of Honour-Related Violence* (Karachi and Oxford: Oxford University Press, 2006), 168–69.

past incidents will bring to light facts showing that some girls were killed who did not behave dishonorably, possibly even in your community and tribe, and, moreover, they will show that some perpetrators kill without regard for honor. Let us uncover the secrets. If you are right, what do you have to lose? This response appeals to the value of courage but also aligns being honorable with behaving rightly and out of respect for the truth, that is, in conformity with a higher moral ideal of honor. As Badshah Khan had found, the man who claims to be exemplary and above suspicion must conform his behavior to the facts when they can no longer be ignored. Moreover, the same strategy can employ empirical data to demonstrate the falsity of popular beliefs that honor killing deters female misbehavior, while scholarly research can be marshaled to rebut false claims that religion requires honor killing.

Inciting the desire to distance one's self from negative perceptions can be bolstered by pointing out that, as Amir Jafri's research indicates, those who commit honor killings are widely regarded as ignorant, unable to control themselves, and dominated by irrational and mythical ways of thinking.[39] Thus members of HSCs can be confronted with two additional challenges. One is to point out that persons chained to "mythical mentalities," as Jafri puts it, will be derided by employers and government officials as inappropriate for the workforce required by the 21st century. Can an individual who clings to old-fashioned notions about killing women for honor really work successfully in a diverse group that includes women and in a job that may require cooperating with and trusting strangers? A related point is to emphasize preserving essential honor and letting false honor go for, as Badshah Khan exhorted among the Pathans, can a man be regarded as *truly honorable* if he does not adjust his behavior to the requirements for supporting his family?

Other efforts to incite dissonance involve issues of character. How can truly independent, self-reliant, and resourceful men be so like children in lacking impulse control, or so unimaginative or ignorant in being unable even to conceive of other, more resourceful ways of responding to the perception of dishonor? And again, how can an honorable man be so slavishly dominated by other's rumor-mongering as to be rendered unable to think independently and critically for himself?

In addition to self-reliance, independence, and high-mindedness, elements of gratitude and hospitality already present in honor codes can be enlisted for the reframing and recentering of honor. As "moral

---

39. Amir H. Jafri, *Honour Killing: Dilemma, Ritual, Understanding* (Oxford: Oxford University Press, 2014), 13, 139–40.

entrepreneurs," curators can emphasize the absence of inconsistency between recognition respect, or *sharaf,* familiar in the honor subculture and respect as moral appraisal, that is, honor regarded as a matter of character or inherent worth. Agents can emphasize that honor requires assisting the weak and defending and shielding sisters, mothers, and daughters against the taunts and recriminations of others, as well as warding off *all harm.* To be honorable requires good will and unrequited kindness, while forgiveness is valiant. An ideal model of manliness can be promoted, compounded in parts from Aristotle's discussion of *megalopsychia,* or "greatness of soul" and Marcus Aurelius's stoicism.[40] The true man casts off desires for vengeance; he has no need for violence as he will never strive for an unjust end and he will never give another man a just cause for grievance. A great man will fear no one, and he is of such a stature that nothing can diminish him; he lowers himself should he respond to an insult with violence. Thus those who do wrong are to be pitied, not punished, for their going astray is evidence of weakness, pain, or error.

 I stress how change agent curators might induce cognitive dissonance. This process is entirely conversational, persuasive, and tolerant; although persistently transformative, it is never coercive. As previously noted, individuals can insulate themselves from the effects of cognitive dissonance unless other experiences cause dissonance to be acute and virtually inescapable. In addition, alternative experiences must make it relatively easy to resolve dissonance in the desired direction, in contrast to retrenching. Fulfilling these conditions means that individuals asked to change must have opportunities for awakening—to see familiar aspects of life in new ways or connected with new experiences—opening worldviews, trying new attitudes, and seeking new possibilities.

This will be a difficult, uneven, and probably a long process, especially when starting from such a traditional culture. It must begin with training boys to be empathetic and parents to support and reason with children. Community members must be shown how to work together with girls in solving problems: redirecting competitive efforts away from personal gambits to gain status and patterns of male domination and toward activities that promote team spirit (e.g., sports and community development) and that are beneficial for the whole community. There is, I believe, no alternative to a constructive strategy—a comprehensive combination of programs such as those discussed in Chapter 9. In addition, because the

---

40. Aristotle, *The Nicomachean Ethics,* trans. by H. Rackham (Cambridge, MA: Harvard University Press, 1968), Book IV, 213–30; and Marcus Aurelius, *Meditations,* trans. George Long and Alice Zimmerman (London: Dover, 1997).

moral transformation will require a transitional period fraught with continuing dangers, preparations for emergency interventions (Section 7.2) must remain in place until the community recognizes their value and owns them, including taking on responsibilities for staffing and management.

8.3 HONOR–SHAME CULTURES WITHOUT HONOR KILLING

I begin with imaginative possibilities for ways of living honorably that do not revolve around social practices of honor killing, vendetta, and the systemic oppression of women. The red-shirted Pathan Khudai Kidhmatgar (Section 8.1) provide one real example of this kind, but there are also other cultural groups very like HSCs in important ways, but in which honor killing does not exist. Each group is similar in origins, ancestral prehistory, ethnicity, religion, and the emphases on the centrality of honor and shame. Critically significant differences in the way honor is understood, as well as cultural emphases on male and female behavior, offer the most plausible reasons for the absence of honor killing. Here are concise overviews of three groups, the Turkic and Kurdish Alevis of eastern Turkey, the Arabic Sohari of Oman, and the Berber-related Taureg of the Sahel and Sahara in North Africa. Each group offers a notable model for living honorably, and richer, more detailed exploration through film, presentation, and discussion, should be explored in HSCs via methods discussed in Chapter 9.

With a population of 15–20 million, nearly 50% of the Alevis live in modern Turkey where they represent about 15% of the population. The Alevi are ethnically and linguistically of Turkmen descent from Central and Eastern Anatolia. The homeland for many is the Taurus Mountain valleys, especially the Munzur Valley in eastern Turkey. The most conspicuous feature of Alevi culture, for our purposes, is their adaptation of a syncretic religious orientation. Thus, although outwardly conforming Shi'a Muslims, the Alevi were strongly influenced by the Sufi spiritual strain of Islam and elements of Turkic shamanism, Anatolian folk culture, and the veneration of a 13th-century Sufi and Alevi saint, Haji Becktash Velie.[41]

Alevi identity is centrally focused on internal spirituality and virtuous perfection. The Alevi ideal is the *Al-insān al-Kāmil*, or the Perfect Human Being. The ideal human task is to achieve this state of perfection, present in true and pure consciousness, while embodied as particular human beings.

---

41. See David Shankland, *The Alevis in Turkey: The Emergence of a Secular Islamic Tradition* (Richmond, UK: Curzon Press, 2003); and John Shindeldecker, *Turkish Alevis Today* (Istanbul: Sahkulu, 1996).

This necessitates full control of one's hands, tongue, and loins, as well as treating all people equally and serving the needs of others. This focus on inner perfection appears to have resulted in the reorientation of honor away from outward performance and toward character as determined by inner motives, feelings, and principles. For this reason, as Sevgi Kilic notes, "covering women's hair or concealing the female body cannot, by themselves, legitimate a family's moral, social, or political worth. Thus an unveiled Alevi woman cannot impugn her honor or that of her community."[42] As John Shindeldecker adds, "Alevis are proud to point out that they are monogamous, Alevi women worship together with men, Alevi women are encouraged to get the best education they can, and Alevi women are free to go into any occupation they choose."[43]

Honor and shame still have great significance for Alevis. Despite the "neutral" status of female bodies and the absence of gender segregation in both private and public domains, Kilic notes that male and female gender are constructed "within the honor/shame paradigm."[44] Central to Alevi morality is being free of major offenses that can cause an Alevi to be declared *dūṣkūn*, or to be shunned. These crimes cause shame and include homicide, adultery, stealing, and, interestingly, divorcing one's wife and backbiting or gossiping. In addition, Alevi men enter a complex extrafamilial brotherhood, or companionship (*mūsahiplik*), that dramatizes the integration and unity of the community. "Companions" enter a covenant relationship in the presence of the *dede*, or spiritual leader, often along with their wives. In this central ritual they make a lifelong commitment to care for the spiritual, emotional, and physical needs of each other and their respective children. These ties are regarded as being as strong as blood relations, so much so that the children of covenanted couples may not marry.

Turning next to the Sohari of Oman, I depend on the research of Unni Wikan who made two field trips to Oman in the 1970s.[45] Sohari, an ancient trading center on the coast of Oman, consisted of about 22,000 people, included Baluch, Ajam (Persians), and Zidgalis, as well as Arabs. Wikan focuses her research on the Sohari Arabs. The Sohari, like the majority of Omani, belong by descent to one or another tribes of ancient Arabia, the most prominent being the ruling Al Ba Said. Sohari had long been subject to

---

42. This passage is attributed to Sevgi Kilic in "Alevi," IslamWiki islam.wikia.com/wiki/Alevi, accessed Jul. 12, 2016.

43. Shindeldecker, *Turkish Alevis Today*, www.alevi.dk/ENGELSK/Turkish_Alevis_Today, 23, accessed Jul. 12, 2016.

44. Kilic, "Alevi," IslamWiki.

45. Unni Wikan, *Behind the Veil: Women in Oman* (Baltimore and London: Johns Hopkins University Press, 1982)

raids by the less sedentary Bedouin (*Bedu*) from the interior of the Arabian Peninsula. On her first visit in the early 1970s, Wikan reported on the "all too vivid memories of present-day Soharis: the *Bedu* (Bedouin) raiding, looting, and abducting hundreds of Sohari citizens, mainly young children, to the slave markets of Burainmi. From where only two ever returned."[46]

Wikan's study of the Sohari is important both because of the close analog between Sohari life and HSCs and because of Wikan's persistence in seeking reasons for the absence of honor killing despite a prominent case of adultery that occurred during her fieldwork. The adulterous affair of Sheikha was widely known and discussed among the Sohari. Wikan was perplexed by the calm and tolerant response of Sohari women concerning the adulterous Sheikha. Evidence indicated that even Sheikha's husband knew of her illicit liaisons but chose to look the other way. Sheikha's friends did admit to Wikan that Sheikha's behavior was *'aid*, or shameful, but they also offered excuses for Sheikha such as, "But she is very kind and hospitable."[47] Under Wikan's prodding, women explained that it would not be right to intervene. Sheikha's friends even apologized for her husband's failure to act as honor demanded, yet respondents steadfastly insisted that it would be immoral to publicly embarrass Sheikha's husband by expressing disapproval.

Wikan asserts that the Soharis placed no less emphasis on honor and shame than did others with Arab subcultures. The apparent paradox was resolved, according to Wikan, by Sohari reordering of the attributes of honor or dishonor attached to various behaviors. The Sohari had modified their honor norms so that what was *most dishonorable* was an open break with an acquaintance; that is, it was *more shameful* to impose shaming behaviors, including public exposure, disparagement, ridicule, and shunning, than to put up with an acquaintance's shameful behavior. Thus, for the Sohari's, being honorable required *not accusing* Sheikha, but instead looking past her adulterous behavior and continuing to accept her for her positive qualities.

Wikan, who earlier had studied residents of Cairo, says, "Whereas among the poor in Cairo, life seems to center on the shaming of others so as to gain value for oneself by contrast, in Oman the concern is to build merit within oneself by *honouring* others. In Egypt the focus is always on other people's faults and weaknesses . . . but in Oman the emphasis in on positive characteristics."[48] Wikan adds, "The person's honor requires that he or she honors others. What seems the only feasible way to achieve value in one's own

46. Wikan, *Behind the Veil*, 43.
47. Wikan, *Behind the Veil*, 166.
48. Wikan, *Behind the Veil*, 166.

eyes in Egypt—to aggrandize oneself while denigrating others—would be below every person's dignity in Oman."[49]

The third model of an honor-centric way of life concerns a people descended from North African Berbers known widely as the Taureg, although many refer to themselves as *Kel Tamacheq*, people of the Tamacheq (Berber) language, or *Kel Tagelmust*, people of the veil, or just *imashahen*, or "free men." The Taureg are a semi-nomadic people of 1–1.5 million who live primarily in the Sahel and Saharan regions of the present-day states of Niger, Mali, Algeria, and Libya. According to Taureg cultural legends, seven clans of nobles descend from daughters of the same mother, Queen Tin Hinan. During the third or fourth century, Tin Hinan allegedly led an exodus of her people into the wilderness to evade subjugation by Arab conquerors of the Maghreb. According to tradition, Takamet, the queen's handmaiden, was the progenitor of the peasant caste.[50]

Taureg society remains highly stratified, and although many must now practice subsistence herding or oasis gardening, such occupations are regarded as servile; nomadic stockbreeding confers greater privilege. Before French colonization, the Taureg nobility gained prominence as warrior-raiders and breeders of camels, donkeys, and goats. Nobles also guided caravans across the Sahara for the lucrative trade in salt, spices, ivory, gold, and slaves, as well as collected tariffs and offered protection services. The Taureg assimilated outsiders who formed a slave caste. Vestiges of this highly stratified society and slave caste remain today.

According to Susan Rasmussen, "The introduction of Islam in the seventh century had the long-term effect of superimposing patrilineal institutions upon traditional matriliny."[51] Although each of the original matrilineal clans remains an important corporate body and descent-group, and allegiance is through the mother, social-stratum affiliation is through the father, and political office, in most subgroups, passes from fathers to sons. Islamic influences have affected inheritance patterns as well. Although women may own animal herds, two-thirds of property is left to sons and one-third to daughters, unless there are written and witnessed "wills" indicating otherwise, but the matriarchal tradition of reserving "living milk herds" for sisters, daughters, and nieces is maintained.

49. Wikan, *Behind the Veil*, 166.
50. Susan J. Rasmussen, "Taureg," *Encyclopedia of World Cultures*. Encyclopedia.com, 1996, http://www.encyclopedia.com, accessed Jun. 20, 2016.
51. Rasmussen, "Taureg."

Despite the influence of Islam, a woman's social standing in Taureg society remains significant. Taureg communities are based on the nuclear household, with each sheltered by a tent or compound named for the married woman who owns it. Tents are usually made by elderly relatives and given as a dowry, and women retain ownership and dominance over the microspace of the tent. Traditionally monogamous, Taureg women may initiate divorce and eject an ex-husband from the tent. Ideal unions are close-cousin unions within the same social stratum and endogamous, as in much of the Arabic world, but commonly matrilocal, as indicated by female dominance of the tent. Matrilineal traditions did not require female chastity before marriage, and although Qur'anic scholarship has made chastity a matter of greater concern, young women are still allowed to take lovers as long as they abide by strict rules of propriety: the utmost discretion and respect must be observed. Women's faces and bodies are not veiled or covered, and they are not secluded; rather, relations between the sexes are characterized by freedom of social interaction. One consequence of this more open, relaxed relationship between the sexes is the scarcity of child betrothal among the Taureg, with marriage in most castes occurring typically around age 20 for brides.

The Taureg distinction between masculine and feminine conceives of the genders as different sides of the same whole, thus offering a more familiar and relaxed view of their relationship. The maternal side, known as *tedis*, or "stomach," is associated with emotional and affective support, while the paternal side, known as *arum*, or "back," is associated with fulfilling bodily needs and authority over the ego. Although differing in form and function, feminine and masculine are far more complementary than oppositional. The relative insignificance of gender is particularly prominent in Taureg appreciation of the arts. There is a large body of poetry, music, song, artistry, and craftsmanship. Men and women both create art works, dance, sing, and perform instrumental music.

A frequently remarked feature of Taureg society is the veiling of men but not of women, although both sexes wear headscarves. The male veil covers the entire face and head except for the eyes. Initial face veiling takes place around 18 years of age, and the wrapping is central to the male's gender role and cultural values of reserve and modesty.[52] The veil is very rarely removed, remaining in place in front of family members and even while drinking and eating. A traditional veil, or *tajel*, is cotton and dyed indigo, although black, white, and lighter blues are also worn. One obvious function

---

52. Rasmussen, "Taureg."

of veiling is protection from sandstorms and the searing sun, although loosely fitting headscarves also worn by women can be pulled over the face. It has also been suggested that veiling protects men from *Kel Esuf*, or evil spirits, a prominent feature of Taureg belief.[53]

Honorable Taureg go to great lengths to maintain personal dignity and to avoid shame. An honorable man must not complain or feel sorry for himself, nor ask for food or water that are not offered, yet he must be hospitable in turn. He will not risk showing his face to anyone whose social standing could be superior to his own. A noble Taureg male is ashamed to eat in front of elders, his mother-in-law, or in front of any woman with whom it is taboo to have sex. Wearing the veil shows one's reserve and dignity and is a sign of piety and self-control. Yet, why this curious but puzzling connection between honor and hiding of the face? Why is it shockingly indecent, as Rasmussen says, for a man to let his mouth be seen by anyone to whom he owes respect?[54]

Robert Murphy offers the most plausible explanation by pointing to the symbolic distance between self and social others.[55] The veil functions to maintain social relationships by ensuring a needed degree of distance, aloofness, and reserve. Murphy refers to this as an "idiom of privacy," but it is not difficult to understand how this symbolic shield also provides a cover that enables a man to maintain his demeanor. The mouth and teeth in many cultures are associated closely with sex and aggression as well as with eating.[56] For the Taureg, only if a man is improper in his speech or virility is he dangerous to his family or tribe. Hence, respectability is closely tied to a man's ability to keep hidden facial expressions others might regard as threatening or disgraceful.

Thus the Taureg, like the Sohari and Alevi, maintain the centrality of honor in their respective cultures while inventing ways of expressing its requirements without honor killing or the in-group aggression common in HSCs. Thus these models demonstrate the viability of retaining an honor-centric culture but one in which honor killing has been isolated, renounced, and abandoned. Such alternative models will offer mind-opening possibilities for those who need to become "unstuck"—that is, able to envision opportunities for renewing social life while not undermining honor.

53. Dominique Casajus, "Why Do the Taureg Veil Their Faces?" www.anthro.08.ac.uk/filename/ISCA/JASO/Occasional_Papers_1985/4_Casajus.pdf, accessed Jun. 11, 2016.
54. Rasmussen, "Taureg."
55. Robert Murphy "Social Distance and the Veil," *American Anthropology* 66 (1964), 1257–74.
56. Casajus, "Why Do the Taureg Veil Their Faces?"

8.4 NONVIOLENT CONFLICT RESOLUTION AND ALTERNATIVE COSTLY SIGNALING TECHNIQUES

It is very important for HSC members to appreciate that conflicts revolving around female dishonor can be settled in ways that do not require attacks on her person. These consist of methods of nonviolent conflict resolution, as well as alternative costly signaling techniques, should the latter still be thought necessary for the HSC despite transformative changes. Combining these methods with the reframing and recentering of honor will be most effective; however, even if cognitive dissonance does not occur and reframing stalls, these methods are still valuable as alternatives since they would blunt the lethality and violence of communal action.

A method of dispute resolution known as the *sulha*, or negotiated settlement, is sometimes used to settle conflicts between two families or tribes to avoid bloodshed. The *sulha* is based on mediation through the offices of sheiks or other mediators and judges recognized as impartial. Joseph Ginat provides examples of *sulhas* or other mediated negotiations successfully resolving charges of murder when committed by men;[57] disputes between different tribes, or *hamulas*,[58] and between Christians and Bedouin;[59] within a variety of ethnic groups (e.g., among Druze as well as Bedouin and rural Arabs);[60] to determine settlement by *dyyat* (payment); and even to settle blood feuds.[61]

Methods of arbitration and mediation exist not only among the Bedouin in the Middle East, but similar mechanisms also exist among the Berbers of the Atlas Mountains in Morocco, the Pashtuns of Afghanistan and Pakistan, the Sansusi Arabs of Cyrenaica in Libya, and elsewhere.[62] In addition, there are long-established traditions of arbitration and mediation conducted by special mediators, and each tribe is expected to have a *wasita* (or *wasta*), or intermediary go-between, or arbitrator.[63] The most renowned arbitrators or

---

57. Joseph Ginat, *Blood Revenge: Family Honor, Mediation and Outcasting*, 2nd rev. ed. (Brighton, UK: Sussex Academic Press, 1997), 37–42, 162–63.

58. Ginat, *Blood Revenge*, 155.

59. Ginat, *Blood Revenge*, 98–99.

60. Ginat, *Blood Revenge*, 38–39.

61. Ginat, *Blood Revenge*, xiv–xvi, 18, 21, 41, 55, 38–39, 191–92.

62. See, for example, Edward Evans Pritchard, *The Sansui of the Cyrenaic* (Oxford: Oxford University Press, 1949); Ernest Gellner, *Saints of the Atlas* (Chicago: University of Chicago Press, 1969); and Jacob Michaud-Black, *Cohesive Force: Feud in the Mediterranean and the Middle East* (Oxford: Basil Blackwell, 1975).

63. Layish Aharon and Avshalom Shumeli, "Custom and Shari'a in the Bedouin Family According to Legal Documents from the Jordan Desert," *Bulletin of the School of Oriental and African Studies* 42 (1979), 21–45.

judges are generally known as "saints."[64] The Berbers and Taureg in particular rely on carefully selected and trusted "saints," or *marabouts*, as judges; the latter often possess charisma, widely thought to derive from *baraka*, or God's grace. Because these arbitrators do not belong to disputing clans or tribes, they are "strangers" and can be expected to be impartial. Ginat asserts that the value of mediation cannot be overemphasized especially because daily life is so "highly politicized" and because of daily concerns about "intrigues."[65]

It is not possible to tell how many girls or women have been saved from honor killing attacks because of alternative methods—through the skills of "saints" or through a *sulha*. The media rarely give attention to such "successes." However, Kardam does note that in 2005 the *Milliyet* ran a story about a remarkable man from Diyarbakir, Turkey, who had spent 30 years as a mediator and managed to reach a peaceful outcome in some 300 cases, of which 87 involved kidnapped girls.[66] Kardam is certainly right that such anecdotal reports highlight the critical need for fieldwork on mediation to identify the conditions most likely to result in peace. Based on my review of case studies, *sulhas* or other methods of nonviolent conflict resolution are rarely employed when females are charged with dishonorable behavior.

Why gender should be a major factor in accepting or spurning nonviolent dispute resolution cannot be considered further here, although I venture that it relates to the primary function of honor killing as costly signaling. In disputes among males, dishonor arises from giving in or losing; there is the opportunity to save face when a disinterested third party brokers an outcome. I hypothesize in Chapter 6 that, over time, a family accused of dishonor could not dramatically demonstrate the restoration of its standing without the violent elimination of whatever prospects the "soiled" daughter might have brought home. The charged female was, in effect, the instrument through which a disgraced family was required to cleanse its honor. Thus, while at present I am not able to say how methods of dispute resolution might be remolded to address allegations of sexual and gender misconduct, reframing honor is a critical step. Because attacking females would become dishonorable, questions about resolving a family's standing in the community would be separated from responses to females' behaviors.

64. Gellner, *Saints of the Atlas*.
65. Ginat, *Blood Revenge*, 89.
66. Kardam et al., *The Dynamics of Honor Killing*, 58.

Given the ongoing discussion of moral transformation, we should consider what proportion of the community must be persuaded and how well they must be convinced. For obvious reasons, no exact answer can be given. As indicated in connection with the Heaths' research, usually the "rider" part of the human mind cognitively accepts change only after the "elephant," or intuitive and affective, parts have already decided that the new "path" is a good one. Dan Sperber and Hugo Mercier argue that reasoning is basically a social activity; people present reasons and arguments primarily to defend commitments publicly and to persuade others, rather than to engage in impartial assessment of the truth.[67] Hence, while HSC groups must engage in consensus-making that requires defensible reasons for claims that a transformation is going in the right direction and that life is getting better, an emerging consensus must be underwritten by positive emotions arising from new and rewarding experiences. Still, the question about numbers does not disappear since it is necessary to have a committed core willing to seek a new consensus.

Perpetrators sometimes express regret over having been "forced" to kill, asserting that the community left them without a choice. Some even attempt to evade killing altogether. Hence it is highly likely that most HSCs harbor a core of members ready, with proper support, to become vocal advocates for alternative solutions. It is helpful in this context to recall the research of Nicholas Christarkis and James Fowler on social networks (Section 5.4). This research demonstrates the ability of a small number of dedicated and well-connected individuals, perhaps as small as 15%, to have a powerful effect. The higher the degree of commitment, the greater the effect of small numbers. Research published in 2011 by scientists at Rensselaer Polytechnic Institute showed that "when just 10% of the population holds an unshakeable belief, their belief will always be adopted by the majority of the society."[68] Finally, Erica Chenoweth and Marcia Stephan, who have made extensive studies of nonviolent changes, speak of the "3.5% rule," and they claim: "no campaign failed once they'd achieved the active and sustained participation of just 3.5% of the population."[69]

67. Dan Sperber and Hugo Mercier, "Why Do Humans Reason?" *Behavioral and Brain Sciences* 34 (Apr. 2011), 57–74.

68. Rensselaer Polytechnic Institute, 2011, "Minority Rules: Scientists Discover Tipping Point for the Spread of Ideas," http://news.rpi.edu/luwakkey/2902, accessed Aug. 25, 2015. See also Jia-Rong Xie, Sameet Sreenivasan, Gyorgy Korniss, Wei Zhang, Chjan Lim, and Boleslaw K. Szymanski, "Social Consensus Through the Influence of Committed Minorities," *Physical Review E* 84, (Jul. 22, 2011), 1–9.

69. Erica Chenoweth and Marcia J. Stephan, *Why Civil Resistance Works: The Strategic Logic of Nonviolent Conflict* (New York: Columbia University Press, 2011), 30; see also Erica Chenoweth, "My Talk at TEDx Boulder. "Civil Resistance and the 3.5% Rule,"

Chenoweth and Stephan's 3.5% refers to people in civil resistance campaigns who are actually motivated to take a stand and thus would be comparable in their opposition to honor killing to "dedicated avengers" (Section 5.4). But even if the higher figures are more realistic than the 3.5% rule, the point helps to put an admittedly daunting task in perspective. A committed minority unshakeable in its condemnation of honor killing might be able to tip the scales away from continuation of the practice and toward new ways of accommodating demands for honor. The outsized influence of small numbers might coalesce and exert influence sooner if change agents adroitly enlist the support of community leaders and moral entrepreneurs (Section. 7.3).

Some stout resistance may be rooted in men's anxieties over their manliness when they can no longer sequester women, engage in mate-guarding, or punish sexual indiscretions. Given the long evolution of honor killing as costly signaling and the inability to say why one might be fearful of change, it is understandable why some might be reluctant to abandon the view that an honorable man takes drastic action at the first sign of a sexual catastrophe. For this reason, the reframing and recentering of honor needs to go hand in hand with the innovations discussed in Chapter 9, which should short circuit the effects of gossip and innuendo by building trust in the results of careful inquiries modeled on legal and forensic methods, including, perhaps, applications such as the I've-Been-Violated app discussed in Section 7.1.

Insofar as honor as personal integrity comes to replace the emphasis on communal face-saving, then one can encourage the corresponding development of personal qualities and resources presently too weak in the masculine warrior construct. Reliance on dramatic, outrageous, and public performances as tests of trustworthiness arise in part because, when interpersonal skills are underdeveloped, lowest common denominators provide the surest tests. Greater competency in social skills, such as "reading people" as described in Chapter 9, will go a long way toward replacing dependence on public perceptions and dramatic demonstrations. Yet because transformation may move slowly and the need for some sort of costly signaling technique may linger, change agents must consider less violent ways of signaling that honor has been "cleansed." Much as William James suggested in 1910 that humankind find a "moral equivalent for war,"[70]

Rational Insurgent, Nov. 4, 2013, http://rationalinsurgent.com/?s=My+Talk+at+TED Boulder&submit=search, accessed Jul. 20, 2016.

70. William James, "The Moral Equivalent of War," in Robert L. Holmes and Barry L. Gan (eds.), *Nonviolence in Theory and Practice*, 2nd ed. (Long Grove, IL: Waveland Press, 2005), 176–85.

I recommend that those living in HSCs find a moral equivalent to deadly costly signaling.

Note that, because the *willingness* to kill supposedly distinguishes honorable men from cheaters and free-riders, it will hardly do to recommend as substitute techniques the public forms of shaming frequently associated with the Puritans: public confessions and penitential acts, the stocks, or pillories. Public whipping of the female charged with an offense will not suffice either, even if violence were to be countenanced—which it should not—because it is not *her* trustworthiness that must be vouchsafed. Flogging of the male (father or brother, etc.) regarded as responsible for failing to control the female might seem more fitting, if we were—contrary to intention—to accept a violent solution. Yet, flogging will not suffice because honor and masculinity prohibit men defamed to be passive recipients of punishment; rather, they must make amends—*actively do something* to reinstate their trustworthiness.

Whatever alternative measure is suggested must be sufficiently costly. Overly easy remedies might allow potential cheaters to pass the test. That is, whatever one must do to make amends and reestablish his standing must be such that those tempted to mimic this sincerity will be deterred; the ordeal must be such that no one would undertake it with a cheating heart—that is, still intending to betray other members of the extended family or community if his interests depart from communal needs (see Section 6.5). So how can making amends be sufficiently costly?

It might be suggested that if a tribunal finds the allegations true beyond a reasonable doubt, a family can, if it believes it must, declare the girl or woman lost to them, thereby severing all family relationships with her. No one would be permitted to harm the girl or woman or violate her freedom; indeed, we must presuppose that services described in Section 7.1 will be available. However, the family would forego any benefit accruing to them from her birth into the family, just as they would if she were dead; this might include a bride price that would not be realized or one to be repaid, the loss of her reproductive assets and her domestic services, and (possibly most embittering for the family) greatly reduced opportunities for arranged marriages for her siblings or marriages of high status.

The option just described is not optimal, in my judgment, although it is a plausible candidate as a substitute technique. My own recommended alternative reflects the spirit of Badshah Khan's account of a truly honorable way of ending a blood feud. This alternative draws on the way gift-giving generates obligations of reciprocity, it engages the entire community in responding constructively to the problem, and it also resonates with the older notion that honor should be a matter subject to communal participation. Again, suppose a tribunal finds the allegations true; then, this time, a solemn communal ceremony is held at which HSC members swear that the life and health of the offending girl or woman is to be preserved as a *gift* from the community to the family in exchange for the family's binding itself to be honorable by performing designated service projects for the community.

The amount, kind, and period of family service to restore honor could be set in advance or at the communal ceremony when the girl or woman becomes a ward of the community. During this time, the disgraced woman could also be required to perform service in exchange for her keep. A communal feast could be held to mark the reintegration of the family into the community when it has cleansed its honor. At this point, the family may reassume responsibility for raising a daughter or taking a divorced wife back into the home, but only with her consent if she is of age or with the supervision of child welfare officials in the case of minors. This option may meet the community's need to identify and publicly condemn infractions; certainly, a public ceremony of this kind would be the occasion for shame.

In addition, given that in HSCs *sharaf* honor is associated with freedom from *required* service to others (in contrast to voluntary hospitality), community service would be perceived as quite onerous, especially as it cannot be finished all at once. Consequently, such an alternative would satisfy the need for making amends and, moreover, a man with a proclivity for dishonest signaling is unlikely to be willing to undergo this process of humiliating restitution. Whatever alternative signaling technique is selected, in the long run, the incremental changes discussed in Chapter 9 should eventually result in the elimination of public shaming and restitution for honor infractions, thus changing all sexual misadventures other than rape and violations of basic human rights into private matters rather than public affairs.

As noted at the outset of this section, we cannot expect members of HSCs to understand and accept explanations for the cultural evolution of honor killing. However, once measures for a bottom-up transformative process such as those recommended in Chapter 9 are well under way, there ought to be explicit and demystifying discussions of honor killing. One important point to stress is that honor killing persisted in part because of *scarcities of both time and trust*. If members of HSCs still think and feel that their honor and identity are threatened, they should be helped to see that a large part of this perception results from self-inflicted wounds based on the segmentary lineage system (Section 6.3) and contradictory interpersonal relations which produce sure-fail mechanisms (Section 5.3). Self-imposed dangers can be ameliorated through the efforts of increasing knowledge, skills, and competency within the group. In addition, despite the persistence of poverty, unemployment, and stress, the greatest dangers to HSCs from outside the group come not from progressive changes that remove archaic and dysfunctional practices, but rather from sectarian discord and violence, repressive authoritarian governments, continuing discrimination against women, and the ideology and terrorism of extremists such as those of ISIS, al-Qaeda, and the Taliban. Clinging to dysfunctional traditions will increase a HSC's vulnerability to ideological extremism, just as it will hamper its efforts to succeed in the 21st century. This point has to be brought home to members of HSCs.

CHAPTER 9

Moral Transformation

Sustainability and Community Ownership

Chapter 8 focused on grand strategy—the necessity of reframing and recentering honor—directed at demonstrating the incompatibility of honor killing with a truly honorable way of life. I recommend innovative programs and structures to build sustainable transformation with community ownership. This chapter emphasizes *how we might get there*, that is, achieving a sustainable future without honor killing, with the emphasis on grassroots, bottom-up, incremental changes that will break the cycles (Chapters 4–6) that continue to produce perpetrators and victims.

The focus here is on *processes* in terms of *specific procedures, programs, and institutions,* with expectations that these measures will facilitate moral transformation. After considering effective diffusion of change in Section 9.1, with the success of Tostan as a model for honor–shame communities (HSCs), each subsequent section is on a type of recommended program or set of incremental steps. Emergency interventions that I recommended in Section 7.1 must be assumed to be in effect until particular HSCs have adopted them as their own. The programs and institutional innovations that I recommend here must be introduced in connection with the grand strategy of Chapter 8 for they serve as indispensable support in keeping the so-called elephant and rider together on the right path (Section 8.2).

Recalling the formation of violence-proneness (Section 4.5) and warrior masculinity (Section 5.1), we can appreciate the need for grassroots changes in child-rearing, interpersonal relationships, and socialization. Far fewer males will develop violent-prone personalities (VPPs) if punitive authoritarianism, toxic shaming, and negative attachments are greatly reduced.

Likewise, with fewer VPPs, less social antagonism, less intrapersonal splitting of nurturing elements from masculine identity, the attractions of warrior masculinity will be weaker; and when fewer men are socialized to adapt shame-to-power defenses, then fewer women will be victimized, provided that social contradictions giving rise to sure-fail mechanisms are simultaneously addressed.

To ensure that communities themselves acquire ownership of these innovations, programs must be inclusive—that is, they must include entire families as well as single men and women; they must be comprehensive, offering education, training, and counseling appropriate for each of the life stages; they must present opportunities addressing the most important aspects of life; and they must be mind-opening, unlocking opportunities for individual discoveries of personal interests and capabilities, as well as providing experiences of joy and wonder. And because the explicit objective of sustainable transformation is to end honor killing and dismantle its sociocultural scaffolding, all programs must have a focus, even if subtle, on gender equality and scrutiny of cultural practices and stereotypes. Finally, innovations should be modified by ongoing monitoring and evaluation, assessments that change agents and community members can undertake in concert with nongovernmental organization (NGO) specialists and faculty expertise in area or state universities.[1]

9.1 EFFECTIVE DIFFUSION AND THE TOSTAN MODEL

Everett Rogers has discovered that the use of technology and incentive programs are not enough for the effective diffusion of new ideas. As a social process, successful diffusion requires repeated personal contact; Everett claims that people follow the lead of those they know and trust when deciding whether or not to follow an innovation.[2] Peer mentoring is critical, as is scalability, with one-on-one instruction or mentoring most successful when "playing it forward" is included; that is, when new "recruits" teach others what they have learned. Atul Gawande, studying the effects of concerted person-by-person efforts to change norms in medicine, reports on the stunning success of oral rehydration therapy in Bangladesh.[3]

1. Filiz Kardam et al., *The Dynamics of Honor Killing in Turkey: Prospects for Action* (Ankara, Turkey: United Nations Population Fund, 2006), 54.

2. Everett M. Rogers, *Diffusion of Innovations*, 5th ed. (New York: Free Press, 2003).

3. Atul Gawande, "Slow Ideas: Why Some Innovations Don't Always Catch On," *New Yorker*, Jul. 29, 2013, 34–46. The Bangladeshi nonprofit BRAC sponsored the rehydration therapy program, sending thousands of workers throughout the country door

Emphasizing that contact must initially be frequent or intensive, Gawande claims that peer mentors must also apply the "rule of seven touches," where a "touch" is a personal interaction.[4]

Reviewing the success of a unique program in Africa—Tostan—offers one concrete and compelling example of the way respectful peer-mentored innovations can spread quickly and lead to community ownership and empowerment. Following this review, I organize the remainder of this chapter roughly according to the main functions of the recommended processes and institutional changes. There is successive discussion of school-based programs; public health and domestic violence initiatives; public service, sports, and boys' and men's groups; women's circles and collaborative community school programs; and empowerment of women and men through microfinance. The emphasis throughout is on creative and imaginative processes, rather than on a rigorous assessment of the effectiveness of programs identified.

Tostan was founded in 1991 by Molly Melching to combat female genital mutilation (FGM). However, Melching and Tostan's directors decided they could most successfully meet the organization's objectives by connecting the ending of FGM with sustainable development and positive social transformations in African towns and villages. Tostan uses both a Community Empowerment Program (CEP) and Community Management Committees (CMCs) to achieve these goals in a way that preserves the dignity of all involved:[5]

> When Tostan is invited into a village to begin the [CEP], we assign a trained facilitator to the village. The facilitator is fluent in the local language and is of the same ethnic group as the community members. Facilitators live in the village during the three-year program, getting to know community members both in and out of the classroom. Tostan pays the facilitator and provides the curriculum, and community members house the facilitator and provide classroom space. These mutual commitments encourage everyone to be engaged with the

to door through more than 75,000 villages and showed 12 million families how to save children with diarrhea from death.

4. Gawande, "Slow Ideas," 42. The rule was allegedly formulated in pharmaceutical sales and is as follows: "Personally 'touch' the doctors seven times, and they will come to know you; if they know you, they might trust you; and, if they trust you, they will change."

5. Tostan, "About Us: Mission and History," http://www.tostan.org/about-us/mission-history, accessed Sept. 26, 2015. See also Aimee Molloy, *However Long the Night: Molly Melching's Journey to Help Millions of African Women and Girls Triumph* (New York: HarperCollins, 2013).

program even if they cannot participate in classes. . . . In addition to the CEP classes, communities establish a CMC that is responsible for implementing development projects designed by the community. Trained by Tostan, these are democratically-selected 17 member committees, of which nine members are women.[6]

Tostan reported in 2015 that, since 1991, more than 200,000 people have participated in their three-year program, and more than 2 million people have been indirectly touched by the program. Tostan does not hide the fact that its explicit agenda is to end FGM, but it has found that its success depends on helping African villagers understand how FGM depends on questionable assumptions hidden behind its "customary" status. In addition, Tostan initiatives have shown how living in better and more empowered ways offers villagers alternatives that make FGM irrelevant. For instance, by arranging to have young men pledge to marry "uncut" girls in companion villages, Tostan has undercut the widely cited claim that FGM is necessary to make girls "marriageable."[7] As well as ending FGM in many towns and villages, Tostan's CEPs have led to unforeseen but positive outcomes, including the election of a peace committee to resolve community conflicts in the Senegalese town of Niaming and the successful mayoral campaign of Abdoulaye Mamadou Dia, a Tostan alumna from Mauritania.[8]

Tostan's mission does not include honor killings, and it focuses only on communities in Africa. Nonetheless, important elements of the Tostan model are worth emulating. One is the way efforts to end FGM have been embedded in broader community development and empowerment programs. A similar holistic, or comprehensive, approach involving the entire community is recommended here. A second is Tostan's commitment to enabling community members to become self-directing and to manage improvements. Again, the emphasis here is on the sustainability of moral transformation.

Third, Tostan is committed to entering only those communities that invite the change agents in. Given its record of success and "client"

6. Tostan, "Community Empowerment Program: Program Structure," http://www.tostan.org/tostan-model/community-empowerment-program/program-structure, accessed Sept. 26, 2015.

7. Nicholas D. Kristof and Sheryl WuDunn, *Half the Sky: Turning Oppression into Opportunity for Women Worldwide* (New York: Alfred A. Knopf, 2009), 226–27.

8. Tostan, "Community Empowerment Program: Maximizing Impact," http://www.tostan.org/tostan-model/community-empowerment-program/maximizing-impact; and Tostan, "Success Stories," http://www.tostan.org/success-stories?country=All&impact area=All, accessed Sept. 26, 2015.

satisfaction, Tostan has had no difficulty in extending its services to other villages. Entry-by-invitation raises a significant question in the case of honor killing. Although extremely tempting to focus first on HSCs where honor killings are most frequent, such HSCs are also likely to be least open to transformative efforts. It is certainly critical to focus emergency interventions (Section 7.1) where honor killing occurs frequently and resistance is staunch. However, for the purposes of owning moral transformations, the best practice is to work with communities in which there has already been some noticeable success with the reframing and recentering of honor. These HSCs are more likely to welcome opportunities for change. Change agents and peer mentors in other HSCs might assess community opposition to honor killing and other signs of readiness for change even when the reframing of honor is not yet complete. One objective of moral transformation is a chain reaction of sorts: when benefits are significant and sufficiently well-publicized, other groups should seek similar attention and service. Ideally, with communal consensus that everyone benefits from an improved quality of life, successful peer mentors will be invited into other HSCs. Eventually, communities continuing to practice honor killing will become so few and far between that nearby towns and villages will voluntarily pressure them to end the practice.

Tostan assigns a trained facilitator who speaks the local language and is of the same ethnic group as those in the community, a practice very similar to the one recommended in connection with the staffing of emergency facilities (Section 7.1). Coming to own their own changing way of life necessarily entails the ongoing education and training of local residents to assume responsible roles. A leading figure at the center of the programs (discussed later in connection with collaborative community schools) will be a properly trained and local *Mukhtar,* or community leader, a person selected for his or her appropriateness in overseeing local transformation, rather than a person in authority through religious or political means. Other community members can take part early on, under the supervision of facilitators from official offices, universities, or NGOs, until a community is able to direct its own sustainable efforts and a movement toward gender equality is under way.

Tostan's creation of CMCs is also a model to be adapted; it is a structure that enables local community members to gain a stake in the project, establish on-site and communal responsibility, and solicit buy-in from greater numbers in the town or village. The *Mukhtar* should be a member of the CMC, although its decisions must be made democratically. Ensuring that 9 out of the 17 committee members are women keeps issues affecting girls and women at the forefront. Even if efforts to reframe and recenter norms of honor move slowly, the inclusion of women on the CMC should provide HSC members with evidence that female leadership does not result in mythical chaos, or *fitna*, as well as provide valuable educational examples of women's capabilities. In addition, the 17 member CMC can be the nucleus for what will become the dedicated 10–15% of the population exercising a major influence on the majority, as network theory suggests.

9.2 EDUCATIONAL AND SCHOOL-BASED PROGRAMS

Whether or not the main features of Tostan are replicated, a comprehensive, large-scale transformative program must include a number of multifaceted and first-step innovations to engage community members through a range of activities. Among these innovations are a number of educational and school-based programs and collaborative community school facilities (CCSFs) (Section 9.5). Despite critical similarities, HSCs are otherwise heterogeneous and, as Kardam's team emphasizes, even specific cases offer different constraints and opportunities for response.[9] Hence, general recommendations must be tailored to meet the specific needs of distinct communities.

Reforming Elementary and Secondary Education

Free and universal education is traditionally the provision and prerogative of the secular state, and it has been shown historically to be indispensable for the sustainable development of a state's economy, the welfare of its citizens, and their sense of national loyalty and belonging. Research suggests that, across most cultures, openness to change is highest during an individual's adolescence and early childhood.[10] Moreover, respect for diversity, toleration, nonviolence, and social problem-solving can be taught to very young children and can become the foundation for lifelong learning. Consequently, in every region in which honor killing and gender-based violence are problematic, proper education is likely to be the single most important variable in promoting community ownership of prevention.

9. Kardam et al., *The Dynamics of Honor Killing*, 54.
10. See, e.g., Sara Bullard, *Teaching Tolerance: Raising Open-Minded, Empathetic Children* (Lafayette, IN: Main Street Books, 1997); Olga Silverstein and Beth Rashbaum, *The Courage to Raise Good Men* (New York: Viking, 1994); Nikolas Westerhoff, "Set in Our Ways: Why Change Is So Hard," *Scientific American*, Dec. 1, 2008, http: www.scientificamerican.com/article/set-in-our-ways, accessed Oct. 3, 2015.

In HSCs, many girls are not allowed to continue their education beyond certain elementary levels even when advanced education is available. Families generally require girls to end their schooling with the onset of puberty. Given the significance of education for widening cultural horizons, developing self-efficacy, and preparing youth to participate in the economy, schooling must be mandatory for youth of both genders and through completion of secondary education. In addition, governments serious about ending honor killing and discrimination against women must invest in the legal enforcement of educational requirements. Low-interest loans or grants-in-aid ought to be earmarked for families whose economic straits would otherwise keep older children out of school, either to work or to provide childcare while adults work. The international community should see such financial assistance as a significant investment in human capital, and states in North America and the European Union as well as the World Bank and International Monetary Fund (IMF) should study the feasibility of foreign aid designated for this purpose.

One of the most effective ways of accelerating normative changes is through the ways children are taught to interact with each other, their parents, and with authority figures, as well as by increasing their abilities to solve problems and to think independently. Children are especially vulnerable to the effects of punitive, authoritarian parenting, family violence, and toxic stress (Chapter 4). At no point in the educational process should instructors rely on shaming or punitive techniques. Early education, occurring five days a week and presented as supportive and authoritative (emphasizing reason-giving) can buffer young children from the worse effects of a toxic and violent environment (although not entirely, and hence the need for additional interventions).

In addition to laying the groundwork for literacy and numeracy, children should be encouraged to think about gender, violence, and honor in the larger context of community life. While still very young, children should engage in comparative studies of art, literature, languages, history, music, and more, as well as in opportunities to express themselves in activities such as drawing and music. Such activities enable children to exercise imaginative and creative abilities and to become acquainted with alternative attitudes and values and use artistic expression and story-telling to depict or describe their own experiences.

Education for Problem-Solving and Social Skills

Beginning as young as ages 3–5, boys and girls will benefit from early instruction in positive and nonviolent conflict resolution. Myrna Shure's research demonstrates a correlation between fewer occurrences of violence and well-developed social problem-solving skills among children.[11] Very young children learn through imitation and therefore should be given opportunities to observe simple scenarios in which conflicts are successfully resolved, often as simple as taking turns in sharing a toy, book, or tool; role-playing scenarios in classroom; and being allowed extra time at recess when a group successfully solves a problem. Newly learned skills need to be practiced repeatedly in the presence of helpful models (trained adults) in safe, emotionally supportive environments. Obviously, innovations in early education would be relegated to single-sex schools, but, if at all possible, education should be sex and gender neutral, with both boys and girls receiving exactly the same opportunities. Needless to say, where schools for girls do not exist, the government must provide them. In addition, where school districts do not offer nursery school or kindergarten programs, such innovations may have to take place in collaborative community school centers (see later discussion), where childcare is provided to enable mothers to engage in a variety of activities.

Turning to problem-solving education for older children, the Social Decision Making/Problem Solving (SDM) program offers a very useful model for boys and girls. Initially designed for youth between the ages of 9 and 11 and "designed to prevent violence, substance abuse, and related problem behaviors," the SDM program can be modified for children younger than 9 or somewhat older than 11. The key to the SDM program is that "it teaches social, emotional, and decision-making skills that students would utilize throughout their lives."[12] The SDM program relies heavily on interpersonal, cooperative learning and problem-solving methods involving self-control, listening, communicating respectfully, giving and receiving help, role playing, and sharing cooperatively and fairly in group work.[13] The program also emphasizes "means-end thinking" in an effort to improve children's abilities to understand that actions involve choices,

11. Myrna B. Shure, "Preventing Violence the Problem-Solving Way," US Department of Justice, *Juvenile Justice Bulletin* 8 (April 1999); see also, Myrna B. Shure, *Raising a Thinking Child Workbook* (New York: Henry Holt, 1996).

12. National Institute of Justice, "Program Profile: Social Decision Making/Problem Solving Program," https://www.crimesolutions.gov/ProgramDetails.aspx?ID=343, accessed Aug. 25, 2015.

13. Linda Bruene Butler, Tanya Romasz-McDonald, and Maurice J. Elias, *Social Decision Making/Social Problem Solving: A Curriculum for Academic, Social, and Emotional Learning, Grades K-12* (Champaign, IL: Research Press, 2011). See also Mary Karapetian Alvord, Bonnie Zucker, and Judy Johnson Grados, *Resilience Builder Program for Children and Adolescents: Enhancing Social Competence and Self-Regulation* (Champaign, IL: Research Press, 2009).

choices have consequences, and choices and their consequences need to be understood in terms of long-term goals. Young people progress through three stages: (1) a Readiness Phase focusing on students' basic self-control and social awareness, (2) an Instructional Phase including 20 scripted lessons on various aspects of problem-solving, and (3) an Application Phase providing students the opportunity to put their new skills to use in a controlled environment.

A study of early SDM programs in US middle schools identifies some success,[14] and a 2011 meta-analysis of closely related Social and Emotional Learning (SEL) programs showed that such programs are effective at managing juvenile problem behaviors and mental and behavioral health issues.[15] SEL is very much like SDM, as the SEL program is "the process through which students acquire and apply the knowledge, attitudes, and skills associated with five interrelated sets of cognitive, affective, and behavioral competencies: (1) self-awareness, (2) self-management, (3) social awareness, (4) relationship skills, and (5) responsible decision-making."[16]

School-based programs designed to increase social skills and thereby improve conflict resolution are not a strictly American (or even Western) phenomenon. In 2011, the office of the Special Representative of the Secretary-General of the United Nations for Violence Against Children reported a specialists' review of three international programs intended to reduce violence in schools. They praised the Learn Without Fear campaign by Plan International, which "addresses a range of violence issues, including sexual abuse, neglect, verbal and emotional abuse, corporal punishment, bullying, peer-to-peer violence, youth gangs, harassment on the way to and from school, and the use of weapons in and around schools."[17] More than 60% of the 44 countries that participate in the Learn Without Fear campaign have seen improvements in perpetrator accountability and student reporting mechanisms. In the first two years after its inception, the Learn

14. Maurice J. Elias et al., "Impact of a Preventative Social Problem Solving Intervention on Children's Coping with Middle-School Stressors," *American Journal of Community Psychology* 14, 3 (1986), 259–75.

15. Joseph A. Durlak et al., "The Impact of Enhancing Students' Social and Emotional Learning: a Meta-Analysis of School-Based Universal Interventions," *Child Development* 82, 1 (2011), 405–32.

16. National Institute of Justice, "Practice Profile: School-Based Social and Emotional Learning (SEL) Programs," https://www.crimesolutions.gov/PracticeDetails.aspx?ID=39, accessed Aug. 25, 2015.

17. UN Special Representative to the Secretary-General (SRSG) on Violence Against Children, "Tackling Violence in Schools: A Global Perspective," Prepared for the High-Level Expert Meeting on "Tackling Violence in Schools," Oslo, Norway, June 27–28, 2011, 21, srsg.violenceagainsthchildren.org/sites/default/files/publications_final/Tackling_Violence_in_Schools_final.pdf, accessed Aug. 27, 2015.

Without Fear campaign "reach[ed] 94 million adults and children through radio and television shows, leaflets, training sessions and workshops."[18]

Reducing Gender Discrimination and Increasing Respect for Diversity

The 2011 UN report provides anecdotal evidence that the Violence Free Schools project, initiated in 2008 by Save the Children in Afghanistan, also made some headway toward its goals of "address[ing] physical and humiliating punishment and prevent[ing] sexual abuse and gender discrimination in schools." The Violence Free Schools project is somewhat more formal than other campaigns of its kind. Schools participating in the project have three special committees designed to tackle the difficult issues of punishment, abuse, and discrimination: (1) "a child protection committee," which responds to specific problems in the school; (2) "a parent, teacher, and student association" designed to improve communication between these groups; and (3) "a students' council" designed to improve communications among students.[19]

The Violence Free Schools project is based in Afghanistan's Balkh Province, a multiethnic region in Northern Afghanistan, where most inhabitants speak Persian; it serves more than 2,000 students in government schools.[20] Save the Children has operated in Afghanistan since 1976, and their years of experience in the area surely give them an advantage when it comes to implementing programs like Violence Free Schools.[21] Programs such as this one would be difficult to implement without intimate knowledge of a given community, local buy-in, and the support of local government officials. However, Save the Children offers a valuable manual with ideas for potential activists regarding topics such as the ideal program length, the importance of a clear phase-out or transition strategy when responsibility for the program passes to local residents, and how activists can effectively and productively communicate with local teachers.[22]

---

18. SRSG Report, "Tackling Violence in Schools," 21.
19. SRSG Report, "Tackling Violence in Schools," 20.
20. Save the Children, 2011 Report, "Violence Free Schools in Afghanistan," http://resourcecentre.savethechildren.se/sites/default/files/documents/4422.pdf, accessed Oct. 3, 2015.
21. Save the Children, 2011 Report, "Learning Without Fear: A Violence Free School Project Manual," http://www.researchgate.net/publication/271327429_Save_the_Children_Afghanistan_Learning_Without_Fear_-_A_Violence_Free_School_Project_Manual, accessed Oct. 3, 2015.
22. Save the Children, "Learning Without Fear."

Finally, the UN report suggests that UNICEF's Child Friendly Schools initiative, which works to manage not just violence but also a litany of other problems that plague schools, can help students feel safe and happy while learning. These schools promote education for girls and young women and encourage adults in families and the community at large to buy into the project's mission.[23]

Another school-based program is the Gender Equity Movement in Schools (GEMS) program, spearheaded by the International Center for Research on Women (ICRW), Committee of Resource Organizations for Literacy (CORO), and the Tata Institute for Social Sciences (TISS) with funding from the MacArthur and Nike Foundations. The earliest GEMS programs were implemented in India between 2008 and 2014 and centered on a curriculum designed "to engage young girls and boys, age 12–14 years, to discuss and critically reflect on the issues related to inequitable gender norms and violence."[24] ICRW reports that the GEMS pilot programs were promising and showed "attitudinal change to support equitable norms."[25]

Gordon Brown, former British Prime Minister and UN Special Envoy for Global Education, reported a very encouraging educational innovation in Lebanon.[26] In 2015, leaders of all major religious groups in Lebanon signed a National Charter for Education on Living Together. The Charter establishes a common school curriculum on shared values to be taught in primary and secondary schools throughout Lebanon for Shiite, Sunni, and Christian students. Although developed explicitly in response to sectarian violence in Lebanon, the Charter curriculum offers a model appropriate for schools in HSCs as well.

The program is for students beginning at age 9 and includes four modules: one is on the global family, emphasizing equal dignity of all persons; a second focuses on the common rights and duties of citizenship, irrespective of ethnic or religious background; the third concentrates on religious diversity and emphasizes the "refusal of any radicalism and religious or sectarian exclusion";[27] and the fourth returns again to the global level with emphasis on cultural diversity. Because this focus on peace and

23. Save the Children, "Learning Without Fear," 22.
24. International Center for Research on Women (ICRW), 2015 Report, "Gender Equity Movement in Schools (GEMS)," http://www.icrw.org/where-we-work/gender-equity-movement-schools-gems, accessed Sept. 6, 2015.
25. ICRW 2015 Report, "Gender Equity Movement in Schools (GEMS)."
26. Gordon Brown, "The Antidote to ISIS: School for Refugee Children," *Washington Post*, Nov. 30, 2015, A15.
27. Brown, "The Antidote to ISIS," A15.

reconciliation between religious and ethnic differences is seen as an antidote to extremist propaganda and radicalism, in 2015, Lebanese officials decided to include almost 200,000 Syrian refugee children in the Charter curriculum in Lebanon's public schools.

In sum, programs such as Learn Without Fear, Violence Free Schools, Child Friendly Schools, GEMS, and the Lebanese Charter program should be given very careful attention; appropriately adapted, they could significantly reduce the formation of VPP, warrior masculinity, and gender discrimination. Of course, care must be taken to design and implement tailored solutions intended to work despite the unique challenges of HSCs. Even US-style projects like the SDM model or SEL might be usefully adapted for a number of HSCs. It is pertinent and highly desirable to ask private and well-funded charitable organizations such as the Bill and Melinda Gates Foundation to finance the adaptation of such (or similar) programs for use in Muslim-majority societies and to train teachers in their use.

9.3 PUBLIC HEALTH AND DOMESTIC VIOLENCE INITIATIVES

Violence is increasingly understood as a public health problem, and it is helpful to address honor killing and gender violence through this lens. Apart from the obvious deaths suffered by specific victims, it is hardly surprising that, where it exists, honor killing as a social practice and continuous threat contribute to morbidity and increased mortality.[28] When extreme violence is an ever-present possibility, large numbers of women will be at risk for the effects of chronic stress: depression, generalized anxiety, chemical dependency, substance abuse, hypertension, and a host of other stress-related disorders, whether or not they personally experience direct violence.[29] The World Health Organization (WHO), UN Office on Drugs and Crime (UNODC), and UN Development Programme (UNDP) report that nonfatal physical, sexual, and psychological abuse all contribute to long-term health problems and premature death.[30] The WHO 2014 Global Status Report on Violence Prevention reports:

28. Muazzam Nasrullah, Sobia Haqqi, and Kristin J. Cummings, "The Epidemiological Patterns of Honour Killing of Women in Pakistan," *European Journal of Public Health* 19, 2 (2009), 193–97.
29. Nasrullah et al., "The Epidemiological Patterns of Honour Killing."
30. World Health Organization (WHO), UNODC, and UNDP 2014 Report, "Global Status Report on Violence Prevention," http://www.who.int/violence_injury_prevention/violence/status_report/2014/en/, accessed Sept. 7, 2015.

Many leading causes of death such as heart disease, stroke, cancer and HIV/AIDS are the result of victims of violence adopting behaviors such as smoking, alcohol and drug misuse, and unsafe sex in an effort to cope with the psychological impact of violence. Violence also places a heavy strain on health and criminal justice systems, social and welfare services and the economic fabric of communities.

In a 2012 report, the WHO and the Pan American Health Organization (PAHO) considered various forms of femicide, including honor killing, and made several general recommendations for its prevention.[31] They called for (1) better collection and analysis of death- and violence-related data; (2) training and sensitization of various health care workers and police, enabling professionals to identify and respond more adequately; (3) further research on prevention and intervention practices; (4) stronger gun laws; and (5) further research on honor killing and other honor crimes.[32]

A 2001 *Preventative Medicine* article analyzing a large study of intimate partner violence in 11 US cities concludes that health care providers can help prevent femicide. The authors note that, "early identification, supportive education, effective referral, and ongoing support can eventually reduce the prevalence of abusive injury by up to 75%."[33] One important predictive instrument—the Danger Assessment—is discussed in Section 7.1. Additional research points to the value of on-site and on-the job training for appropriate responses to possible intimate partner violence, as well as professional and specialist education.[34] "Providers have an important role in stopping and ultimately preventing intimate partner violence, but they are not alone in this effort. They need to know how to access the growing network of assistance including women's advocates, the criminal justice system, and other members of increasingly dynamic community coalitions."[35]

Still other research finds that women who are murdered by a lover in a domestic violence homicide often visit an emergency room prior to their

31. WHO, PAHO, 2012 Report, "Femicide: Understanding and Addressing Violence Against Women," http://www.who.int/reproductivehealth/publications/violence/rhr12_38/en/, accessed Sept. 7, 2015.

32. WHO, PAHO 2012 Report, "Femicide."

33. Phyllis W. Sharps et al, "Health Care Providers' Missed Opportunities for Preventing Femicide," *Preventative Medicine* 33, 5 (2001), 373–80, 378.

34. Lynn M. Short, Denise Johnson, and Alison Osattin, "Recommended Components of Health Care Provider Training Programs on Intimate Partner Violence," *American Journal of Preventative Medicine* 14, 4 (1998), 283–88.

35. Short et al., "Recommended Components," 283.

death.[36] This finding suggests that emergency room personnel are in a particularly strong position to identify patterns of escalating gender violence and alert social case workers who can intervene. It is logical, therefore, to expect that health care providers—from admitting nurses through physicians—can be trained to recognize patterns of abuse in girls and women who are at high risk of becoming victims of honor killing or continuing gender violence. Health practitioners should be equipped by social workers with tools enabling them to respond to these situations in safe, productive ways. "Universal screening of [emergency room] patients as well as timely interventions using available community resources may provide for optimal treatment of these patients."[37]

These are all US-based studies, but there is no a priori reason for supposing that the similar techniques and interventions will not be effective in HSCs, given sensitivity to adaptations. Obviously, the rights of abused and battered women to health care and psychological assistance cannot be less as a consequence of cultural difference, and the conditions of women and girls in HSCs, where their access to health care will frequently be inadequate, justifies demands for increased state and international public health investment in these locales.

When compiling data for the Churchill-Holmes dataset (Chapter 2), we observed that many eventual honor killing victims did seek medical attention or other community resources (such as counseling services or aid in women's shelters, or the intervention of a *sheik*) in the weeks or months before their death. The act of seeking such help greatly increased her family's experience of shame, thus aggravating the situation and increasing risks of attack. Note that there is another risk in making emergency rooms, physicians' offices, or counseling agencies or women's aid offices the first stop for girls and women who fear that they will soon die in the name of honor. Namely, if health care providers in those places are known to be equipped with the tools to help the frightened females, then fathers and husbands might simply forbid their daughters and wives from seeking medical advice and attention altogether, even for physical or mental health issues unrelated to suspicion of an honor violation.

Preventive measures must include the training of community observers (observer/informants [OBIs]) and mobile crisis teams in assessing the risks that identified girls and women may suffer violence,

---

36. Michael C. Wadman and Robert L. Muelleman, "Domestic Violence Homicides: ED Use Before Victimization," *The American Journal of Emergency Medicine* 17, 7 (1999), 689–91.
37. Wadman and Muelleman, "Domestic Violence Homicides," 691.

include caretaking "brigades" and working with the police and local authorities to prevent reprisals against those seeking help (Section 7.1). To be successful, these protective measures must fit into a comprehensive program. Concern for health and women's welfare must be worked into the tapestry of revived communal life. Boys, girls, and adults need to receive basic educational training in hygiene and in shame-free education of human anatomy and biology, as well as family life and sexual relations. In addition to an emphasis on gender equality in schools, community programs for adults must emphasize that girls possess, on average, mental capabilities equal to boys and that families and partnerships are happier overall when women can develop their own capacities and interests. Women and girls need to have access to *women's discussion rooms*—nearby safe places reserved for women— where women can discuss together, with the participation of trained nurses, counselors, and other experts, their concerns relating to sexuality, family planning, family violence, and child-rearing.

In addition, discussion sessions on women's sexuality and health, as well as male–female relationships, should be made available for men in *men's discussion rooms*. Men's and women's discussion groups, as well as health care clinics, should be located in or adjacent to CCSFs, described more fully later. A holistic view of public health and communal well-being is necessary because there are no firm boundaries between physical and mental health, on one hand, and a peaceful, sustainable community on the other. Ideally, CCSFs would encompass boys' and girls' schools or be adjacent to them; for instance, CCSFs could house health/dental care clinics and serve as places where schoolchildren can be immunized and screened on a regular basis. As for preventative and acute care, patients of all ages could be seen by internists and dentists and referred to specialized facilities in the district, region, or nearest urban area. It is unquestionable that in many rural areas (e.g., in Afghanistan and Pakistan) and war-torn countries (e.g., Iraq and Syria) as well as in refugee camps, adequate personnel, medical facilities, and medicines are absent or in short supply. Thus I encourage all parties concerned, including international organizations like the WHO, to research how, in working with local experts and representatives, practical solutions to these problems can be financed and implemented.

9.4 PROGRAMING FOR BOYS AND MEN

As Chapters 4–6 make clear, the rearing and socialization of boys and young men has been critical in perpetuating the capacity for honor killing.

Ending the cyclical generation of violence-proneness and warrior masculinity will require the cumulative influence of the entire transformative program. Here I focus on a critical element: achieving the active involvement of boys and men. Most critical at the beginning will be winning over, via person-to-person contact (and the "rule of 7 touches"), a cohort who will be proselytizers for changing assumptions, attitudes, and expectations for masculinity. In addition, new attitudes and behavioral scripts must be connected with reframed conceptions of honor and buttressed by rewarding experiences that hold out the promise of a more fulfilling way of life.

Organized Sports, Boys' Groups, and Service Programs

Sustainable transformation should begin by reducing boys' tendencies to identify with models of aggression and domineering masculinity. In CCSFs, along with sex education and coming-of-age classes or sessions, boys can be encouraged to learn more about male anatomy and male and female gender differences, to discuss their own experiences of growing up, and especially how to recognize and discuss emotions, including how it *feels* when one is shamed. Boys will hear about the experiences of others, be asked to put themselves in their shoes, and thereby develop greater empathy. It is critical that such learning sessions be directed by males already identified as self-confident, friendly, nonauthoritarian, and nonshaming role models. In addition, there should be organized activities in which boys play or work with older boys or men who provide alternative, positive models of masculinity. These activities can give boys opportunities to bond with others constructively. Some activities can be designed specifically to develop male support for the equality and empowerment of girls, such as HeForShe and Sharaf Heroes (discussed later). There is also a great need for activities which assist boys in forming efficacious, confident, and tolerant identities through close association with males who embody the ideals of honor as a matter of personal *character* and not public perception.

Organized sporting activities provide obvious and well-known occasions for enjoying fellowship, learning new skills, developing teamwork, and learning to abide by rules, both for the sake of the team and the sport. As noted by some researchers, sporting activities or organized games of any sort are notoriously absent in many HSCs.[38] In addition,

---

38. Susan Schaefer Davis and Douglas A. Davis, *Adolescence in a Moroccan Town: Making Social Sense* (New Brunswick, NJ: Rutgers University Press, 1989).

boys and teens could be organized on models similar to the Boy Scouts and 4-H Clubs to engage in community service activities under the leadership of competent adult men. Service activities would be especially valuable in impoverished areas, but, as demonstrated among the Khudai Kidhmatgar (Section 8.1), they also instill pride and a sense of belonging, as well as impart valuable life skills. Service projects could range from clearing streets of refuse and litter, to planting gardens and trees, restoring pathways, raising chickens or rabbits, caring for lambs and kids, working on irrigation projects, building shelters and homes, recording and preserving oral history and art, and even learning about the local ecosystem and working to maintain or restore it by identifying and preserving endangered plants and animals.

Initial leadership for such service programs might come from qualified volunteers such as those in the US Peace Corps. However, rather than relatively "exotic" facilitators and teachers from abroad, wherever possible, program leaders should be postgraduates who speak the same language and share the same religion and ethnicity. In addition, rather than directing two-year-never-to return programs, project leaders should commit to returning to the local communities in which they served for periodic brief visits to renew old ties. An indigenous Peace Corps program of this kind would be a very powerful way of modeling successful examples of adult, competent masculinity, especially as these leaders would embody skills at solving problems, openness and toleration, and nondominant self-assurance. A community with a successful service program could take pride in a refined sense of *asabiyya*, or group fellow feeling, as well as in its increasing ability to solve common problems.

Initially, such service programs might be derided by those who regard labor as servile and lacking in dignity; however, service programs would operate in tandem with other transformative processes that would develop the view of service—when *voluntarily offered* rather than compelled and for the benefit of others rather than personal gain—as highly honorable and not disrespectable (as in the case of the Khudai Kidhmatgar). In addition, as community members enjoy success in owning the transformation, and as the public–private gender divide decreases along with gender discrimination, there would be no reason to exclude girls and women from such service activities. In supervising cadres of boys and girls (sex segregated or with male/female co-leaders), women in this national service corps would provide valuable models of skill, knowledge, competence, independence, and strength—very empowering models, indeed.

A number of specific pilot programs engage males—both youth and mature men—as active partners in working for gender equality. HeForShe is a campaign created by the UN Women Solidarity Movement for Gender Equality in 2014. Speaking before the UN General Assembly as the campaign was launched, UN Goodwill Ambassador and film star Emma Watson said, "Men—I would like to take this opportunity to extend you a formal invitation. Gender equality is your issue, too."[39] Within months, a video of Watson's remarks had been viewed more than 1 million times on YouTube, and the UN Women Solidarity Movement claims that hundreds of thousands of men have pledged to work in their own institutions for gender equality.[40]

The HeForShe campaign outlines a three-part strategy: (1) heightened awareness through education and sensitization, (2) advocacy to affect policy and programming, and (3) fundraising and related actions.[41] While HeForShe does not explicitly aim to tackle honor killings, its efforts to build a global audience may serve as a leveraged resource against honor killing (Section 7.3). Boys and young men can be invited to join local chapters, to pledge to work for gender equality, and to discuss examples of HeForShe activities as ways of identifying projects for their group to undertake.[42] Another networking and advocacy organization, MenEngage Alliance, with Joni de Sand as Global Coordinator and Advocacy Manager, has online resources for such discussions and projects.[43]

Already by 2007 the WHO had published a report on engaging men and boys in group education to think critically about gender norms and masculinity, to reflect personally about how these norms affected their lives and the lives of others, and to take time to apply new lessons to real life.[44] In

39. Emma Watson, "Comments Before the UN General Assembly at the Launch of the HeForShe Campaign," 2014, https://www.youtube.com/watch?v=gkjW9PZBRfk, accessed Sept. 7, 2015.

40. UN Women, http://www.heforseh.org/en/newsroom/IMPACT10X10X10, accessed Oct. 17, 2015.

41. UN Women, HeForShe Strategy Overview, 2014, http://www.heforshe.org/impact, accessed Sept. 7, 2015.

42. For instance, boys could discuss the decision of a chief in Malawi to annul 330 child marriages, as reported by HeForShe, and use that as a springboard for the investigation of different traditions. See http://www.heforshe.org/en/newsroom/politics/malawi-chief-annuls-child-marriage, accessed Jul. 15, 2016.

43. MenEngage Alliance, www.menengage.org/resources, accessed Jul. 15, 2016.

44. Gary Barker, Christine Ricardo, and Marcos Nascimento, "Engaging Men and Boys in Changing Gender-Based Inequality in Health: Evidence from Programme Interventions" (Geneva: WHO, 2007), http://www.who.int/gender/documents/Engaging_men_boys.pdf, accessed Sept. 7, 2015; see also Christine Ricardo, Gary

order to be successful within HSCs, men's programs must begin, as with boys, with a proselytizing cohort as a nucleus. In general, there should be three types of *men's initiatives* connected with CCSFs. First, men should be assisted in responding to the shocks and stress of unemployment, underemployment, and chronic poverty, as well as health problems that may require medical consultations. Second, *fatherhood interventions* should offer practical training ranging from changing diapers and bathing infants to conversing and playing with small children and providing growing children with authoritative (reason-giving) instruction. Fatherhood skills should be provided in a context in which men are encouraged to take pride in fathering with competence and sympathy.

Third, men's interventions must focus on anger management and on recognizing and expressing surprise, dismay, and a range of other emotions in open but nonviolent and constructive ways. Training to enhance self-control could be extended to include communicative skills and practicums, in which men share skills with wives and relatives and exercise them together. Such activities, when successfully established, could do much to engage fathers and fathers-to-be in positive child rearing, to diminish their remoteness as authoritarian figures and their perceived need to rely on force and punishment, and to improve the overall quality of family life. Ideally, given available resources, men should be encouraged to continue their own education, but even men seeking education to enhance "marketable" skills (e.g., in auto repair, computers, etc.) should be required to complete a curriculum that increases reflectivity and self-awareness, in a supportive environment. The objective is to enliven moral imagination, enhance empathy, and encourage critical thinking with the hope of weakening or ameliorating connections between difficult life experiences and violence-proneness, and between the latter and warrior masculinity (Sections 4.4 and 5.1).

The 2007 WHO report found that community outreach, mobilization, and mass media campaigns could be effective but worked best when combined with other programs, such as counseling, group education, and telephone hotlines.[45] All of these are activities that could be connected through CCSFs. Finally, the WHO report discusses various service-based programs for men, analogous to those for women in crisis, that offer health services, counseling, home visits, and other services. While the report

Barker, and Marci Eads, "Engaging Boys and Men in the Prevention of Sexual Violence: A Systematic and Global Review of Evaluated Interventions" (Sexual Violence and Research Initiative and ProMundo, 2011), www.svri.org/menandboys/pdf, accessed Sept. 9, 2015.

45. Barker et al., "Engaging Men and Boys."

found that these programs could be very costly, they could positively affect men's beliefs and behaviors. One less expensive program—hotlines for men—is generally promising: "One fairly unique programme offered a telephone hotline and counseling for men who felt they might use violence against their female partners, as a preventative way to reach men and to encourage them to participate in group or individual counseling sessions."[46] The same might be true of males who feel at risk of acting violently for reasons of honor.

Sharaf Heroes—Men Who Fight for Women's Rights—is an anti–honor violence project launched in 2003 by the Swedish feminist and antiracist organization Electra.[47] The impetus for its founding was the honor killing of Fadime Sahindal in Sweden (Section 1.1). Based on research findings indicating that young people are often influenced as much by peers as their families, Sharaf Heroes seeks to change old patterns of patriarchal thinking among the younger generations. The name of the organization signifies Electra's interest in reclaiming the word *sharaf* from negative associations with patriarchal oppression and violence. It seeks to educate young men from different backgrounds and religions on human rights and equality.

The organization offers educational workshops and spaces for dialogue where men can discuss issues of honor and violence with each other, as well as explore contentious issues through theatrical productions. Enrolled young men are taught to understand their attitudes, perspectives, and actions in relation to equality and human rights. In addition, Sharaf Heroes acts as a support group for males who have rejected sexist attitudes, but then find themselves criticized or even threatened by their families or other males. After completing a 10-week course, men receive their first diploma and then may move on to more advanced courses, including training to become a discussion leader or a lecturer. "Qualified" Heroes may be asked to give presentations in schools or for immigrant groups in Norway, Sweden, and Germany.[48]

In 2006, the sister project, Sharaf Heroines, was launched to offer education for young women on the issue of honor violence, to act as a support network for girls who have been threatened or are victims of honor-related

46. Barker et al., "Engaging Men and Boys."
47. Moa Keskikangar, "Sharaf Heroes: Violence Is Not Our Culture," www.violenceisnotourclture.org/sites/default/files/Sharaf%20Heroes.pdf, accessed Apr. 2, 2016.
48. Young men trained in programs like Sharaf Heroes might also join an organization such as Love Commandos, a voluntary nonprofit set up by Sanjoy Sachdev in India in 2010 to assist couples seeking to marry for love. See www.lovecommandos.org, accessed Aug. 10, 2015.

violence, and to offer training designed to strengthen girls' self-confidence and independence. More than 100 Heroes and Heroines have received diplomas at the programs' centers in Stockholm, Gothenburg, and Malmö. Sharaf Heroes also has inspired the organization of TransAct in the Netherlands and liaison with Ni Putes Ni Soumises (Neither Whore Nor Submissive; NPNS) in France, first founded in 2003.[49] A 2012 research study of Sharaf Heroes found evidence of attitude change among men in the program but stresses the need for education and socialization to simultaneously pursue two tracks: "one is focused on the equal value of human-beings in the sense that girls have the same capacities and abilities as boys, so that [old-fashioned] honour norms confine girls to an inhuman life. The other track is focused on the conditions of boys in the honour culture, where it is urgent to unquestionably show how [old-fashioned] honour norms circumscribe and restrict their freedom and life conditions, in as much as it is expected of them to oppress and punish closely related women's 'improper behavior.'"[50]

9.5 COLLABORATIVE COMMUNITY-SCHOOL FACILITIES AND EMPOWERING WOMEN

Collaborative Community-School Facilities

Given the necessity for close collaborative efforts among schools, health care providers, and emergency facilities (Chapter 7), I recommend the establishment of collaborative CCSFs. CCSF would not be schools per se, but rather centers available for the community, where educational activities could be extended more broadly to adult members of the community and where critically important women's services can be planned, coordinated, and undertaken. Given the likelihood of continued segregation of education in most Muslim majority countries, CCSF spaces optimally would be located in all-weather structures close to and between a designated boy's school and one for girls. Ideally, CCSFs would occupy the center of a compound that contains an adjacent health clinic and nearby sports and recreation facilities.

49. TransAct—Dutch Centre for Gender Issues in Health Care and Prevention, http://www.transact.n/, accessed Jul. 15, 2016; Ni Putes Ni Soumises, www.npns.fr, Accessed Jul. 15, 2016.
50. David Rexvid and Astrid Schytter, "Heroes, Hymens and Honour: A Study of the Character of Attitude Change Among Male Youth with Their Roots in an Honour-Based Context," *Review of European Studies* 4, 3 (Jun. 2012), 22–32, 32.

These CCSFs would be designated as community-run and -managed, although initial assistance from NGO professionals, state officials, and volunteers might be required. In addition, they would be collaborative to reflect the need for a section of the center to be set aside for the organization and coordination of a multitude of simultaneous activities. There should be coordination with emergency intervention specialists, the network supervisor (Section 7.1), and personnel staffing shelters, although shelters would not be located physically in the center or in the same compound. Following the model of Tostan in Africa, I advocate that CCSFs be administered by a 17-member Community Action Committee (CAC), consisting of nine women and eight men drawn from the local community. As noted earlier, each CAC would include a recognized secular leader, or *Mukhtar*, as a member, and all executive decisions about CCSFs and related programs would be made by majority vote. CACs could request advice from trained experts, and they would be assisted as needed by trained monitors who could supervise many of the activities of the CCSFs.

CCSFs would be designated as public spaces, but spaces in which girls and women are welcome for specific programs and activities and where they need not be supervised by family guardians due to the continual presence of trained monitors, members of the CAC, and (when possible) the *Mukhtar*. These authorities could provide assurances of the propriety of girls' and women's behavior while in CCSFs. In addition, because male members of the community also would be welcome at these centers, they could also verify the propriety of behavior, such as the segregation of boys and girls in different rooms or the seating of boys and girls on opposite sides of a common hall. CCSFs would have specially designated discussion rooms for males and females.

Women's and Family Services

Because CCSFs would be safe places for girls and would include areas open only for girls or women, including one-on-one counseling rooms, they should also serve as sites where girls could seek help and advice from psychological and legal counselors and health practitioners. Screening programs related to health care, such as immunizations, vision and hearing testing, dental care, and testing for learning difficulties could take place, as well as unobtrusive screening for signs of physical abuse or emotional or mental difficulty. In addition, in supervisory offices at CCSFs, school counselors and health practitioners could confer with legal officials about girls and women who might be at risk and together devise preventive plans.

Planning might involve a number of entities, such as OBIs and mobile crisis teams (Section 7.1).

One critically important function of CCSFs is to serve as venues for women's ongoing education, self-awareness, and self-expression, as well as provide services especially designed to improve the quality of women's lives by reducing structural violence. One program to emulate is the highly successful Indashyikirwa ("Champions of Change") Couples Curriculum implemented in 2014 among highly paternalistic groups in Rwanda. Implemented by CARE Rwanda, Rwanda Women's Network (RWN), and Rwanda Men's Resource Centre (RWMAREC) across three provinces of rural Rwanda, the Indashyikirwa program was designed to reduce intimate partner violence (IPV) and to "transform the attitudes, norms and practices that underpin violence and power imbalances in relationships."[51] To date, more than 800 heterosexual couples have completed a 20-session curriculum, and approximately 25% of individuals completing the program have received further training and mentoring to become community activists who will demonstrate and diffuse nonviolent techniques for building more equitable relationships.

Facilitators for the Couples Curriculum live within the village community, and the program requires that small groups of couples meet together in the presence of both male and female facilitators and on neutral ground away from their private residences. Facilitators help couples directly address types of power imbalance using concepts that can readily be understood (e.g., power over, power to, power with, and power within). They also address triggers of violence so that these can be identified and either avoided or managed. A range of skills pertaining to joint decision-making, conflict resolution, finance management, gender roles, and the consequences of intimate partner violence are also taught.

Early results from the Indashyikirwa Couples Curriculum look very promising. Among the results are couples' reported changes in attitudes, knowledge, and skills, as well as participants' appreciation for being trained together, increased quality time together, closer bonds among couples, and a willingness to use new skills to help others.[52] Of course, it is too early to tell how deep and lasting these reforms will be or how widely reforms will

51. Erin Stern, "The *Indashyikirwa* Couples Curriculum to Prevent Intimate Partner Violence and to Support Healthy, Equitable Relationships in Rwanda," International Conference on the Global Status of Women and Girls, Christopher Newport University, March 24–26, 2017. See also www.care.org.rw/our-work/programs/vulnerable-women/rw-projects/item/232-indashyikirwa-project, accessed Mar. 31, 2017.
52. Stern, "*Indashyikirwa* Couples Curriculum."

diffuse through larger communities. However, the promising direction of these effects indicate that this is the kind of program that ought to be seriously considered for HSCs.

CCSFs also will be ideal venues for the production and presentation of a range of cultural and artistic activities initiated by school students as well as by members of the larger community and as a place to host events brought in to the community. One striking example of new and unexpected self-expression, self-understanding, and cross-gender dialogue is the story of Ummiye Koçak, a 43-year-old illiterate women from the village of Arslanköy, in the Taurus Mountains of Turkey. Inspired by her own viewing of a play about Turkish history, Ummiye Koçak learned to read and write and began a career as a playwright which subsequently led to her fame. Unmiye first organized a woman's theatrical group in 2003 and persuaded a rural school principal to allow her to use his school to stage *Women's Outcry*, a play about the women's life experiences, including kidnapping, forced marriage, and domestic abuse. The play was performed successfully and drew large crowds, including husbands, men, and village officials.[53]

CCSFs should be available for the performance of folkdances, poetry readings, art exhibitions, plays, and a range of school-sponsored cultural activities. One idea is to include a photographic exhibition of women throughout much of the Middle East and other areas of the globe; another would be an exhibition of art objects created by women.[54] CCSFs are also spaces for viewing of films or TV productions selected for the depiction of a rich variety of life and worldviews. Although subjects likely to suggest threats to the communal way of life should be avoided, controversial subjects about communal life are to be added as capacity for tolerance increases, including pointed films and documentaries about gender violence. One good example is *A Girl in the River: The Price of Forgiveness,* an Oscar-winning documentary about Saba Qaiser, an 18-year-old Pakistani women who survived an attempted honor killing (Section 8.2).

---

53. In 2006, *The Play*, a documentary about Ummiye Koçak and the Arslanköy Women's Theatre won international acclaim, winning prizes at the Trieste and Tribeca film festivals. In 2009, Ummiye Koçak played the title role in an all-female cast in her adaptation of *Hamlet*. See Elif Batuman, "Stage Mothers: A Women's Theatre in Rural Turkey," *The New Yorker,* Dec. 24, 2012, www newyorker.com/magazine/2012/12/24/stage-mothers.

54. An example might be the Shamama Contemporary Arts Gallery run by Munera Yousefzada in Kabul, Afghanistan. See Peter Holley, "The Art of Fighting Extremism," *Washington Post,* Sept. 13, 2015.

It is highly desirable that residents share pride in the CCSF, offer it their support, and see in the CCSF possibilities for extending positive community solidarity and building a common sense of communal well-being. In addition to partnership with district and regional authorities, community members should be permitted to take part in additional activities in these spaces. Possibilities might include after-school recreation programs organized within the community or by teachers, as well as participatory child care programs either while mothers attend events or simply as common and protected places where caregivers can meet together outside homes. Other activities might include music lessons, storytelling, foreign language lessons, handicraft and job training, and history and cultural seminars, as well as scholarship programs for students.[55] Moveable "idea boxes" equipped with a satellite Internet connection, 20 laptops and tablets, electronic books, and a "built-in cinema" would help make activities at a CCSF flexible and easy to set up.[56] Centers also should be available for communal celebrations of special holidays, ceremonies, and festivals.

The local *imam* (leader of community prayers) and *mullah* (religious leader) should be welcome in these spaces and, with CAC agreement, conduct weekly worship, as well as offer prayers on holy days or for special celebrations. Other activities usually associated with religion may also take place at CCSFs, such as preparations for marriages or for funerals and burials. However, it must be insisted that, as public and secular spaces, CCSFs cannot be commandeered for religious purposes or dominated by religious directives. Achieving this objective might require severely limiting the number of religious personnel permitted to sit on the CAC at the same time.

It is critically important that men and women have access to different discussion rooms in which issues relating to women's experiences and human rights norms can be explored. There are a variety of materials to assist peer mentors, or curators, develop the abilities of community members to serve as discussion facilitators and problem solvers. Handbooks such as Julie Mertus, Mallika Dutt, and Nancy Flowers, *Local Action/Global Change* provide excellent modules for introducing group learning activities; in addition, online resources on professional development, raising awareness, and a range

55. One example is Banaa: Empowering Sudanese Peacemakers, http://Banaa.org, an international organization that brings students from Sudan and South Sudan to the United States for university educations. Students must be committed to returning to their home country after graduation to work as peacemakers.
56. Used successfully by children in refugee camps, the "Ideas Box" is described in Nick Anderson, "First Lady Urges Men to Foster Gender Equity in Education," *Washington Post*, Nov. 5, 2015, A12.

of issues are available at Teaching Tolerance.[57] CCSFs could house groups such as local chapters of Sharaf Heroes and community service programs, as well as training facilities for boys (e.g., in woodworking, electronics repairs, bicycle maintenance, or emergency life-saving) pertinent to the safety and maintenance of the community. Finally, CCSFs could also be venues where confidential problem-solving could take place; for instance, a *wasita*, or go-between, might conduct negotiations between families at a CCSF, or a modified version of a *sulha* could be held there. The local *Mukhtar* and CAC would take a major step toward ending rumors and gossiping by stressing the privacy of important affairs at the CCSF.

Empowering Women and Men Through Microfinance

Certainly, many of the preceding examples seek to empower women, whether through stronger legal protections, increased access to education, or through better healthcare to enable them to live safer, happier lives. In addition, because honor killing is the result of complex sociocultural phenomena, I have stressed as indispensable those programs that address social norms and male behaviors. In this last subsection, I touch on the role microcredit could play in empowering women and in possibly decreasing the likelihood of honor killings and family violence. Although I know of no studies examining the effects of microfinance in HSCs per se, I consider first whether or not microcredit might possibly have a positive effect on lessening gender violence.

Many researchers find microfinance to be a promising tool for empowering women; it gives them a start at owning a business, generating income, and controlling their own finances. Others worry that the practice is essentially extortion and might actually worsen the plight of women by adding to social pressures.[58] Using evidence from Tanzania, Mushumbusi Paul Kato and Jan Kratzer found that women who receive microloans "have more control over savings and income generated from the business, greater role in decision-making, greater self-efficacy and self-esteem, and greater freedom of mobility and increased activities outside home."[59] Sylvain Dessy

57. Julie Mertus, Mallika Dutt, and Nancy Flowers, Local Action *Global Change: Learning About the Human Rights of Women and Girls* (New Brunswick, NJ: UNIFEM and the Center for Women's Global Leadership, 1999); for Teaching Tolerance, see https://www.tolerance.org/about.

58. Kentaro Toyama, "Lies, Hype, and Profit: The Truth About Microfinance," *Atlantic*, Jan. 28, 2011.

59. Mushumbusi Paul Kato and Jan Kratzer, "Empowering Women Through Microfinance: Evidence from Tanzania," *Journal of Entrepreneurship Perspectives* 2, 1 (2013), 31–59.

and Jacques Ewoudou use a game theory model "to argue that conditioning well-trained women's access to credit to the adoption of high-productivity activities may enable [microfinance institutions] to induce the emergence of networks of female entrepreneurs large enough to mitigate patriarchal practices that raise the costs of operating such activities in the informal economy."[60]

Other research shows that microfinance can have mixed results for women and that, even when it does lead to self-empowerment, it may still reinforce traditional norms about "women's work" and "men's work."[61] However, such objections are not decisive as training programs for women can reduce traditional norm reinforcement as women enter new businesses, especially when training is combined with microfinance targeted to support women's entrepreneurship in what had been exclusively "men's work." One might wonder about the advisability of female competition for jobs where male unemployment rates are already staggering. Today, 47% of Middle Eastern and North African youth are either unemployed or underemployed. By 2025, the region will have 250 million people under age 25.[62] However scarce and badly needed employment is, there is no ethical or rights-based argument for *unequal access* based on gender. Moreover, along with the increasing recognition of the necessity for women to work, empowering women to enter the labor force helps advance an appreciation of positions or roles based on skill or ability rather than traditional, patriarchal allocations.

One model to emulate is the comprehensive approach offered by the Kashf Foundation, a Pakistani group that, since 1999, has provided not just microloans but also wealth management and financial literacy training to low-income women.[63] In November, 2014, Roshaneh Zafar, the founder of Kashf, blogged that the organization had given almost 6,000 training sessions to nearly 69,000 male and female participants. The Kashf Foundation has been successful, in part, because it increases the employment prospects of both *women and men*. Zafar notes that domestic violence

60. Sylvain Dessy and Jacques Ewoudou, "Microfinance and Female Empowerment," 2006 Report of the Centre Interuniversitaire sur le Risque, les Politiques Économiques et l'Emploi (CIRPEE), http://www.cirpee.org/fileadmin/documents/Cahiers_2006/CIRPEE06-03.pdf, accessed Sept. 7, 2015.

61. Hirut Bekele Haile, Bettina Bock, and Henk Folmer, "Microfinance and Female Empowerment: Do Institutions Matter?" *Women's Studies International Forum* 35, 4 (2012), 256–65.

62. Brown, "The Antidote to ISIS."

63. Kashf Foundation, "What We Do," http://kashf.org/?page_id=16, accessed Sept. 26, 2015.

falls when women contribute financially to their household and also highlighted results from a survey of the husbands of Kashf clients: "[We] found that more than 50% stated that they respect their wives more since they have started contributing to family income."[64] Perhaps most impressively, she indicated that almost 60% of Kashf clients report an improvement in their husbands' perception of the role of women.[65]

That Kashf has enjoyed this success in Pakistan, a country with numerous HSCs and a record of relatively frequent honor killings, makes the work of the foundation even more promising. Research on microfinance in other countries suggests that the holistic Kashf approach might be useful elsewhere, such as in Turkey, where microcredit has been described as a life preserver for women.[66] For example, in 2012, Cisem Dincer reported that, in Turkey, when women there "gain power by earning 'like a man,' even when buying groceries and paying the bills, their level of confidence increases enormously."[67] She also notes that traditional gender roles and social norms are incompatible with Turkey's need for economic growth and productivity: "Strong cultural beliefs which keep women at home for better family life [are] not sustainable any more. Women's participation in the workforce is the only way to achieve long term prosperity and growth since the future of the economy does not look promising at all due to a high current account deficit and high unemployment rate."[68]

As the work of the Kashf Foundation shows, such efforts help women directly by allowing them to be more independent and a more vital part of the household and indirectly by elevating their esteem in their husbands' eyes. As men start to see their wives differently, as well as women more generally, it can be hoped that there will be a galvanizing network effect throughout a community. Consequently, microfinance opportunities modeled on those of the Kashf Foundation should be available for men and women comprising a community in transformation.

This concludes my overview of five types of programs intended to make moral transformation sustainable. These are, of course, just some examples, and change agents, NGOs, and others will know of addition

64. Roshaneh Zafar, "16 Days of Activism," *Vital Voices Global Partnership*, Nov. 16, 2014, http://www.vitalvoices.org/blog/2014/11/16-days-activism-empowering-women-pakistan, accessed Sept. 26, 2015.

65. Zafar, "16 Days of Activism."

66. Cisem Dincer, "The Role of Microfinance in Women's Empowerment in Turkey," (Boston, MA: Boston University, 2012), 1–23, http://www.bu.edu/bucflp/files/2012/04/24-08-2014-Microfinance-in-Turkey.pdf, accessed Oct. 3, 2015.

67. Dincer, "The Role of Microfinance," 16.

68. Dincer, "The Role of Microfinance," 18–19.

incremental, bottom-up, and increasingly community-owned means of effecting positive, nonviolent progress toward ending honor killing and establishing greater equality between men and women in HSCs. The long-term objectives are to unloose the ties that bind human beings to dysfunctional social structures, enable women to move forward as equals with men, and also convince those accepting these changes that they must not be reversed, for everyone concerned—men as well as women—will know and agree that life is now far more meaningful and rewarding than their forefathers ever could have dreamed.

SUBJECT INDEX

Abu Ghraib prison, 153–154
abuse
  physical, 15–17, 63, 72, 117–119, 124,
    130–131, 158–159, 164, 230, 232,
    244, 292, 294, 298, 306
  psychological, 117–118, 130–131, 293,
    296 (*see also* shame)
  sexual, 118, 118n75, 119, 122, 158,
    169, 244, 292, 294, 298
  spousal, 247, 294, 298, 308 (*see also*
    gender violence)
  substance, 127–128, 292, 296
  and traumatic bonding, 130–131
acculturation. *See* child-rearing
adoption
  prohibition of, 219–220 (*see also*
    segmentary lineage system)
Afghanistan
  abused women and, 118
  Anjuman i Islah al Afghani (Society for
    the Reform of Afghans), 259
    (*see also* Khan, Badshah)
  arbitration and mediation in, 277
  Balkh Province, 294
  Baloch (Balochi) tribes, 192, 208
  honor and, 86, 103
  honor killing in, 4, 19, 22–23, 25–26,
    31, 42, 58, 86, 161, 192, 208,
    244–245
  honor-shame communities in, 92–93
  immigrants from, 24
  Kashf Foundation and, 311–312
  Kirghiz resistance, 191
  Law on Elimination of Violence
    against Women, 243–244

  mujahideen (holy warriors), 191
  origins of honor killing, 31
  Pashtun (Pukhtun) and, 31, 140, 187,
    192, 208, 260 (*see also* Pashtun)
  Pastoralists and, 24, 208
  Pew Survey and, 26
  public health and, 299
  public opinion and, 25–26
  rape and, 9
  Russian invasion, 191
  Save the Children in Afghanistan,
    294, 296
  Shamama Contemporary Arts Gallery,
    308, 308n54
  Taliban and, 28 (*see also* terrorism)
  upland farmers and, 187, 191
  women's human rights
    and, 244
  Zabuli Education Center, 250
Africa, Saharan and sub-Saharan
  honor crimes in, 16
  political rape in, 16
  Rwanda, 307–308 (*see also*
    Indashyikirwa)
  Sahel, 271–277 (*see also* Taureg)
  Tostan in, 287–290, 306 (*see also*
    Tostan Program in Africa)
aggression
  adaptive fitness and, 194, 199
  adolescence and, 124–125 (*see also*
    male adolescence)
  anti-aggression factors, 251–252
  as armor, 144 (*see also* warrior
    masculinity)
  automatic pilot, 252–253

aggression (*cont.*)
    behavioral intervention and,
        250 (*see also* honor-killing
        perpetrators: influencing
        potential perpetrators)
    brain architecture and, 252
    children and, 251
    chronic stress and, 128–130
    cognitive arithmetic and, 252
    cognitive conflict and, 252
    devaluation of victim and, 143,
        161–166, 168
    frustration-aggression hypotheses,
        124–125, 147
    general theory of, 251–253
    inhibition and, 253
    internalization of, 125–126, 251
    legitimate targets of, 124, 253
    narcissism and, 142–144
    parental behavior and, 251 (*see also*
        child-rearing: punitive)
    personal predispositions and, *see*
        violence-prone personality
    shame-to-violence conversion and,
        252, 256 (*see also* shame:
        shame-to-violence conversion)
    shaming and, 96, 113, 113, 117, 129,
        133–134, 138 (*see also* shame)
    situational triggers and, 104, 252–253
    social learning theory and, 119
    traumatic bonding and (*see* violence-
        prone personality: traumatic
        bonding)
    us versus them and, 19, 254
    and violence-prone personality,
        252 (*see also* violence-prone
        personality)
    and warrior masculinity, 252 (*see also*
        warrior masculinity)
agnatic patrilineal. *See* consanguine
    hierarchical patriarchy
Alevis
    absence of honor killing, 271–274
    Alevi saint, 271
    companionship ceremony, 272
    honor as character, 272 (*see also*
        honor: modifications of)
    ideal person and, 271
    Munzur Valley in Turkey, 271
    neutrality of female body, 272

religious orientation and, 271
    shunning and, 272
    Turkmen descent and, 271
Ali, Mohammad (The Prophet), 87, 197
Al-insān al Kámil, ideal person, 271. *See
    also* Alevis
Al-Qays tribe, 205
altruism: kin-selected, 185, 217
America. *See* United States
anthropology
    etic and emic distinction, 11–12
    human universals, 105–106
antislavery movement, 257–258
argument to the best explanation. *See*
    methodology
attachment theory, 131–133
    care-givers and, 131
    and dove profile, 132
    forms of, 131
    and hawk profile, 132
    motivation and, 131–32
    as negative, 131–133, 256 (*see also*
        violence-prone personality)
Australia
    Merriam in Torres Strait, 213 (*see also*
        honor killing: costly signaling)
autonomy, 264
ayb (shameful behavior). *See* shame
Azah Islamia high schools, 259. *See also*
    Khan, Badshah

Balkans, 16
Batman (Turkey), as "Suicide City," 243
Bedouins
    camel nomadism and, 186–188
    first Arabs, 189
    heritage of, 140, 189–190
    sheik (shaikh) and, 189
    Sohari Arabs, 272, 273
behavioral scripts. *See* performative
    scripts
Berbers of the Atlas Mountains, 277
best interest of the child (standard
    of), 232, 238
Bosnia, 153
boys' groups
    Banaa model, 309
    Boy Scouts model, 301
    empathy and emotional training,
        300–301

4–H Clubs model, 301
  masculinity and, 301
  moral transformation and, 300–309
  National Service Corps, 301
  organized sports and, 300–301
  service activities and, 301
  tolerance and, 301
brain architecture
  anxiety and fear, 129–130
  attachment schema and, 131–132
  definition of, 103–104n12
  and impulse control, 129–130
  interpersonal neurobiology, 132
  prefrontal cortex, 129–130
  toxic stress and, 128–130, 132 (see also
    toxic stress)
Brazil, 17

cads versus dads, 169. See also
    males: mating strategies
CARE Rwanda, 307. See also
    Indashyikirwa Couples
    Curriculum
CEDAW. See UN Convention on the
    Elimination of All Forms of
    Discrimination against Women
change agents, 266, 289
  curating reform, 255, 270, 309
  feminist activists and (see feminist
    activists)
  from within, 255
  idealism and, 227
  knowledge agents, 226
  leveraging and, 224–225
  moral entrepreneurs and (see moral
    entrepreneurs)
  peer mentors, 289, 309
  policy strategists and, 225
  transformative (see also leveraging;
    transformative change)
child-rearing
  abusive, 117–119, 124, 130–131, 285
    (see also abuse)
  adverse conditions and, 127–128
  boys and (see male children)
  effects of stress and, 128
  girls and (see female children)
  homosexuality and (see male children)
  honor and, 112–113
  incest and (see female children)

parenting and (see
    parenting: parenting styles)
  physical abuse in, 117–118, 128–129,
    130–131, 285
  rape and (see female children)
  sexual abuse and, 118–119
  shaming and, 103, 113–114, 117–118,
    129–130, 256 (see also shame)
  violence-prone personality and, 107,
    108–109, 285
Churchill-Holmes Study. See also honor-
    killing studies
  central tendencies, 34, 35n3, 56,
    58–68, 72
  compared with Chesler and WikiIslam
    studies, 35, 55, 58–65
  figures and tables, 38, 43, 45, 46–47,
    48–49, 50–51, 53
  honor-killing characteristics
    central tendencies and, 65–67
    statistics, 59, 62–63
  honor offenses, 59–60, 91
  immigrants, 38, 52–55 (see also
    immigrant communities)
  limitations of study, 57–58
  means of execution, 50–51, 60
  methodology of (see methodology)
  other hypotheses to explore,
    68–70
  perpetrator characteristics, 38, 45–47,
    49, 61–62, 64
  principal indicators, 35, 35n3, 44,
    55–56, 70
  role of gossip, 60–61
  torture and excessive force, 64–65
  victim characteristics, 47–49,
    61–62, 64
co-dependency, 147–154, 158. See also
    warrior masculinity
coercive intervention. See
    leveraging change
cognitive dissonance
  effecting dissonance, 264–267
  moral transformation and,
    255–256 (see also moral
    transformation)
  and reframing, 164, 256, 266 (see also
    reframing: honor)
  results of, 266, 268, 277
  sustainable change and, 256

collaborative community-school centers (CCSCs)
after-school activities, 309
arts and culture, 308–309
child-care programs; 309
community-action committee (CAC), 306, 309
community managed, 306
community management committees (CMCs), 306
counseling in, 306
educational activities in, 299, 303, 306
emergency intervention and, 306
facilitators and, 300, 303
fatherhood interventions, 303
gender equality and, 299, 305
handbooks and guides for, 309–310
health care clinics, 299, 306
hotlines for men, 303–304
idea boxes and, 309
men's discussion rooms, 299
mobile crisis teams and, 306
mukhtar and, 289, 306
network supervisor and, 306
observer-informants and, 306
religious activities in, 309
scholarship programs and, 309
sulhas in, 310
wasita in, 310
women's discussion rooms, 299
women's shelters and, 298, 306
colonialism, 260–261, 263. See also Khudai Kidhmatgar
Committee of Resource Organizations for Literacy (CORO), 295
communication: high and low context, 96–97
community empowerment program (CEP). See moral transformations; Tostan Program
community management committees (CMCs). See collaborative community-school programs; Tostan Program
community school programs. See collaborative community-school programs

consanguine hierarchical patriarch, 185, 194–199, 201
adoptions, 197, 197n56 (see also cultural evolution)
agnatic patrilineal system, 194
animal husbandry and reproduction, 195
asabiyya (group feeling), 199–201, 206
and control of female sexuality, 195–196, 197
definition of, 194
fast living style (females), 196
father-son inheritance, 185, 196
first-cousin (FBD) marriages, 185
segmentary lineage system (see also segmentary lineage system)
crimes of passion. See Brazil; violence
cultural evolution, 184–185
and contrary dynamics, 199
control of female sexuality and, 195–196, 197, 216–217
cultural-ecological adaptations, 186–188, 200–201
culture as information, 184
desert nomads and, 186, 187–188, 189
ecological pressures and, 194
female infanticide and, 170, 195
of honest signalers, 212–213 (see also signaling system)
honor killing and (see honor killing: inclusive fitness)
and honor-shame communities, 208 (see also honor-shame communities)
honor-shame cultures and, 210 (see also honor-shame cultures)
mate guarding and, 209–210, 211
matrilineal descent and, 196–197
and pastoralists, 187, 190–191
patriarchy and (see consanguine hierarchical patriarchy)
population model of, 183–184
and segmentary lineage system, 200 (see also segmentary lineage system)
and upland farmers, 191–193
and warrior masculinity, 210 (see also warrior masculinity)

definition by limiting conditions, 73
Denmark
    conspiracy to commit honor killing, 4
    first taped honor killing, 4
    honor killing in, 4, 23, 42
desert nomads. *See* cultural
    evolution: desert nomads and
devshirme system, 149. *See also* warrior
    masculinity
diffusion of ideas
    effectiveness of, 286
    oral rehydration therapy in
        Bangladesh, 286–287
    person-by person, 286–287, 300
    playing it forward, 286
    rule of seven touches, 287, 300
dueling, 257

education
    as antidote to extremism, 295–296
    in arts and culture, 291
    critical thinking, 302
    cultural diversity and, 295
    decision-making, 292–293
    emotional expression and control,
        293, 296
    for empathy, 292–293, 296
    equal dignity for all, 295, 302 (*see also*
        gender: gender equality)
    and foreign aid, 291
    foundations and, 295–296
    gender equality, 290, 292, 294–295
    girls' programs and, 291, 295–296
    grants-in-aid and, 295–296
    human biology and anatomy, 299
    independent and critical
        thinking, 291
    means-end thinking, 292
    nonviolent conflict resolution, 291–292
    reducing emotional abuse, 293, 294, 295
    reducing sexual and physical abuse,
        293, 294, 295
    religious diversity and toleration,
        290, 295
    rights and duties of citizenship, 295
    self-control, 292
    shame-free, 299
    social problem-solving skills, 290,
        291, 292

    social skills, 290–292
    UN Women's Solidarity Movement for
        Gender Equality, 302
    as universal, 290
Egypt, 104, 105, 115, 141, 142
    abused children and, 117 118
    abused women and, 118
    contrast with Sohari of Oman, 273
    Guhā (Jūhā) and folklore, 142
    honor and, 90
    honor killing and, 16–17, 21, 23, 42, 58
    National Council for Social
        Research, 119
    public opinion survey, 24
    rape and, 119
    unemployment and, 127
Electra, 304. *See also* feminist activists
emergency interventions, 228–241,
        285, 306
    best interests of the child, 232, 238
    child protection services, 232
    early warning signals, 230–231
    emergency hotlines, 228, 229–230
    emergency network (CEN), 231
    family centers, 232, 233
    guards and, 233
    halfway houses, 232, 233
    information networks, 228–230
    legal reforms and, 236–237
    mobile crisis teams, 230–232, 234,
        238, 240, 246, 306
        legal authority of, 237
        and legal obligations, 237
        training and, 298
        written determinations and, 234–235
    network coordinator, 230, 235–236, 306
        duties of, 236
        and public relations, 238–239
    observer/informants (OBIs), 230–231,
        234, 235, 298, 306
    refugee status and asylum, 239–240
    safeguarding teams, 234–235, 299
    semi-annual enumerations, 238
    smartphone apps, 228–230
        anti-bullying app, 229
        I've-Been-Violated app, 228, 280
        I-Need-Help app, 229–230
    women's shelters, 231–232, 233, 243
    youth hostels, 232, 233

honor-shame communities and,
101–102
masculine identity, 101–103, 107,
280, 286 (see also warrior
masculinity)
as performative, 102–103, 107
role expectations, 107, 108
sex and, 101–102
sworn virgin (virgjinesha), 101n4
third gender (xanith), 101n4
Gender Development Index, 26
Gender Equity Movement in Schools
(GEMS), 295–296. See also moral
transformation; school based
programs
genital cutting. See Tostan Program
Germany
honor killing in, 23, 42, 58
Papatya and, 268
reframing honor and, 267–268
Sharaf Heroes and, 304
Terre des Femmes and, 268
ghairat. See honor: as sharaf
gherat. See honor: as sharaf
gift-giving
preserving life and, 282
reciprocity and, 281
A Girl in the River, 249, 308. See also
moral transformations
Give Mom Back Her Name, 114
gossip and rumors, 11, 60–61, 80, 84, 86,
90, 114, 122, 171, 280
and African pygmies, 209
mate guarding and, 209–210, 211
and mobbing, 166
in segmentary lineage system, 220
trial by gossip, 220
Great Britain
antislavery movement and, 257–258
colonialism and, 192, 257
dueling in, 257
first honor killing in, 3–4
honor killings in, 4, 20–24, 26, 42, 58
London Metropolitan Police Service
review, 22
mobilizing shame in, 257
reframing honor in, 267–268
Scotland Yard investigation, 22
Southall Black Sisters, 267
Gurkhas, 103. See also warrior masculinity

Hadza of Tanzania. See costly signaling
Haryana State, India. See India
health care. See public health
HeForShe, 300, 302. See also engaging men
Hezbollah, 30
homoeroticism. See warrior masculinity
homosexuality, 42, 58, 67, 68
abuse and, 119, 121–122
homoeroticism and, 148–149
homophobia, 19, 152
humiliation and, 19, 119
male children and, 119, 121–122
male-on-male sex, 121
as rape, 16, 153
third gender (xanith) (see gender)
honor. See also honor-shame
communities
antebellum South and, 19, 81,
109, 126
Bedouin heritage and, 140
character and, 256, 261, 269–270,
272, 280
child-rearing and, 112–113
co-liability and, 90 (see also honor
codes: collective responsibility)
concepts of, 12–13, 78–82
cultural defense of, 12, 17, 254
dishonor and (see shame)
external and internal, 78–79, 85–86
eyes of beholder and, 79–80, 82, 85,
91, 114, 123, 144, 201, 282
face (wajh) and, 80–81, 85–86, 90,
123, 139, 140, 168, 169, 278
and fear of contamination, 146–147,
149, 165
gender and, 86–89, 90–91, 113
honor-based violence (see
violence: gender violence)
horizontal v. vertical, 88
identity and, 80, 86–87, 90, 95,
97, 101–02
as 'ird, 71, 87–88, 89–91
Kabyle and, 82
modifications of, 269, 273, 281
morality integrity and, 78–79, 280
and narcissism, 143–144
(see also narcissism)
and presumption of guilt, 92
purification and, 84–86, 126, 165
rape and, 91

honor (*cont.*)
  as reframed, 273
  as reflexive, 89
  revenge and, 86, 141, 152
  as *sharaf*, 71, 86–88, 90, 97, 149, 202,
    270, 282, 304
  sharaf honor competitions, 87,
    125, 166
  and social death, 103
  stakeholders in, 87
  vagina and, 90–91
  vigilance and, 85–86, 91, 126, 144–145
  violence and, 31 (*see also* violence)
  and zero-sum ethos, 166, 194, 200, 206
honor codes, 15–16, 76–77, 81, 88, 216
  Bedouin and (*see* Bedouin)
  check on aggression and, 194
  collective responsibility and,
    205–206, 215
  cultural adaptation and, 188, 194
    (*see also* cultural evolution)
  ecological constraints and, 194
  gratitude and hospitality, 194
  Khudai Kidhmatgar and (*see* Khudai
    Kidhmatgar)
  loyalty and, 202
  manliness and, 140 (*see also* warrior
    masculinity)
  pastoralists and, 191–193
  Pukhtunwali and, 140–141, 192,
    216, 256
  revenge and vengeance, 6, 202, 206,
    215, 252
  warrior code and, 103
honor crimes, 12–13, 16. *See also*
  violence: gender violence
honor cultures. *See* honor-shame culture
honor killing
  alleged honor offenses, 38, 42, 91
  cases (incidents), 2–4, 26–27, 84–85,
    96–97, 173, 244, 246n33
  characteristics of, 59, 62–63, 65–67
    (*see also* honor-killing studies)
  co-liable accusation and, 40, 52
  communicative aspects of, 52,
    219–220
  conspiracy to commit, 4
  costly signaling and, 278, 280–281
    (*see also* signaling systems: costly
    signaling)

and crimes of honor (*see* gender
  violence; honor crimes)
cultural evolution of, 11, 91, 280, 282
dedicated avengers, 138, 172–173,
  176–177
definition of, 4–5, 4n13
deterrence and, 159, 165, 264
distinctiveness of, 1, 5–6, 8–19, 29
double-standards and
  (*see* honor-shame
  communities: double-standards)
dysfunctional practice, 282–283, 313
ending honor killing, 180, 290, 313
  (*see also* transformative changes)
as exaptation, 217–221
family council and, 52
formal and material conditions, 73
function of, 11, 91, 183, 185
as gender violence, 2 (*see also*
  violence: gender violence)
geographical extent, 19, 20–24, 77
gossip and, 11, 39–40, 60–61, 220
  (*see also* gossip and rumors)
historical occurrences, 29, 31
immigrants and (*see* immigrant
  communities)
inclusive fitness and, 183, 200, 208,
  214, 216–217, 221
kinship and, 198
and Landinfo report, 192
legal system responses, 37, 180 (*see
  also* leveraging change; legal
  reforms)
mass media and, 1, 4, 301
modernization and, 26
motives for (*see* honor-killing
  perpetrators: motives)
as Muslim problem, 27–31
non-Muslim religions and, 29
obligation of natal family, 174,
  218, 278
offenses and, 59–60, 91, 146–147
origins of, 31, 208
patriarchy and, 24, 26, 162 (*see
  also* consanguine hierarchical
  patriarchy)
perpetrator-victim relationships,
  45–47, 49–50
popular support for (*see* honor-killing
  studies; surveys)

International Center of Research on
Women (ICRW), 295. *See also*
school based programs
International Monetary Fund, 291
Iran (Islamic Republic of)
honor killing and, 21
Landinfo report and, 192
Iranian and Kurdish Women's
Organization (IKWRO), 20
Iraq
Bedouin and, 187, 197
honor killing and, 4, 21, 25–26, 42,
57, 58, 59
honor-shame communities in, 93
immigrants from, 24
pastoralists and, 153, 186, 187,
191–192
poverty and unemployment, 127
public health and, 299
Islam. *See* religions: Islam
Islamic Law Council of North
America, 30
Islamic Society of America, Office for
Interfaith and Community
Alliance, 30
Islamic State in Syria (ISIS). *See*
terrorism: ISIL
izzat. *See* honor: as *sharaf*

Jahiliyya (Age of Ignorance), 195
Jats, 192. *See also* warrior masculinity
jirgas, 5–6, 6n17, 45–47, 56, 242
Jordan
Bedouin and, 187
feminist activism in, 2
honor killing and, 1, 2, 22–24, 25, 27,
29, 42, 58
legal reforms in, 2, 24
Mediterranean Women and, 23
unemployment in, 127
just world thinking, 158

Kabyle, 62, 187
Kardam (Filiz) UN Qualitative Study. *See*
honor-killing studies
Khan, Badshah. *See also* Khudai
Kidhmatgar
advocacy of nonviolent resistance,
259–264
Azah Islamia high schools, 259

honor code redefined
courage, 261
hospitality (*melmastia*), 260, 261
Pukhtunwali and, 262
refuge and sanctuary
(*nanawati*), 260
revenge (*badal*), 260, 261
vendettas, 261–262
Islam and, 260
manliness (*meran*) redefined, 262
shaming of Pathan men, 261–262
Society for the Reform of
Afghans, 259
khap panchayats, 5–6, 6n17, 45–47, 56,
151, 242
Khudai Kidhmatgar, 259–264, 271.
See also Khan, Badshah
capacity for suffering, 261–262
and community improvement, 260
education and, 259
fellow feeling (*biraderi*) and, 261
Kissa Khani bazaar massacre, 263
nonviolent resistance and, 259–260,
261, 263
and Pathans, 258–259
self-discipline and, 260–262
selfless service (*khidmat*) and, 261
Kosovo
castration in, 153
homosexual rape, 153
Kressel (Gideon) Quantitative Study. *See*
honor-killing studies
Kurds, 58, 187, 191–192, 267. *See also*
pastoralist peoples
Kvinnofoum, 94, 97. *See also* honor-
shame communities

law. *See* legal reforms; shari'a
Law of *Qisas* and *Diyat*. *See* Pakistan
Law on the Elimination of Violence
against Women. *See* Afghanistan
Lebanon
brothers and sisters, 120–121
Committee of Resource Organizations
for Literacy, 295
National Charter on Education on
Living Together, 295–296
Syrian refugees and, 296
UN Special Envoy for Global
Education, 295

New Testament: Matthew, 1, 18–19
Nike Foundation, 295
Ni Putes Ni Soumises, 30
nonviolent conflict resolution, 94, 235,
    253, 291, 303, 307–308, 313
  alternatives to honor killing, 277–278
  arbitrator (*wasita*), 63, 278, 310
  costly signaling and, 281
  education and, 219, 291–292
  interpersonal skills and, 280
  Khudai Kidhmatgar and, 259–260,
    261, 263
  negotiated settlement (*sulha*), 277, 310
  payment (*dyyat*), 277–278
  saving face and, 278
  tribunal's decisions and, 281
  Turkish mediator's success, 278
Norway, 304

Old Testament
  Deuteronomy, 13–14, 22
  Numbers, 3
Oman. *See* Sohari of
omertā. *See* honor: as *sharaf*
onore. *See* honor: as *sharaf*
Ottoman Empire, 149

Pakistan
  abuse of women in, 118, 119
  child-rearing and, 108–109
  desert nomads, 187
  FBD marriages and, 199
  honor concept and, 86
  honor killing in, 2–3, 5, 19, 22–23, 24,
    31, 36, 42, 45, 58, 244–245, 249,
    268, 308
  honor-shame communities and, 81, 93
  Human Rights Commission, 3
  immigrants and, 267
  jirgas in, 5–6, 45, 242 (see also *jirgas*)
  Kashf Foundation and, 311
  Khan (Badshah) and, 258 (*see also*
    Khan, Badshah)
  khap panchayats in, 5–6 (*see also* khap
    panchayats)
  Law of *Qisas* and *Diyat*, 244
  legal and social reforms, 97, 149, 186,
    208, 244–245, 308
  masculinity and, 153, 162 (*see also*
    masculinity)

Mohammad Akram Khan v. The
  State, 244
  origins of honor killing and, 31
  parliament, 3
  Pashtuns, 31, 103, 140, 192, 277
    (*see also* Pashtuns)
  pastoralists, 187, 192–193
  shari'a law and, 3, 21, 244–247, 249
  Taliban and, 16, 28
  upland farmers, 187, 191–192, 193
Palestine (Gaza and the West Bank)
  abuse of women and, 118
  child-rearing and, 92–93
  disproportionate births and, 170
  honor killing in, 8, 23
  honor-shame communities, 93
  immigrants and, 23
  Syrian Women's Observatory
    (SWO), 24
Palestinian-Israeli conflict, 28
Pan American Health
    Organization (PAHO)
Papatya, 268
parenting
  in Arabic world, 116–117
  authoritarian parenting, 116, 256,
    285, 291, 303
  authoritative, 313
  child-rearing and (*see* child-rearing)
  fathering, 285, 303, 313
  inconsistent parenting, 117
  parenting styles, 115–117
  violence-prone personality and, 118–119
Pashtun, 3, 31, 103, 140, 187, 192, 197,
    208, 227, 260
pastoralists, 24, 153, 186, 187,
    191–192, 208
Pathan. *See* Pashtun
patriarchy, 24, 26, 162, 201, 304. *See*
    also consanguine hierarchical
    patriarchy
penis. *See* male children
performative scripts, 84, 102, 134,
    138–139, 145, 219, 221, 255, 300
perpetrators. *See* honor-killing
    perpetrators
personality. *See* *fahlawi* personality;
    violence-prone personality
peshmerga, 103. *See also* warrior
    masculinity

school based programs (*cont.*)
  Social and Emotional Learning (SEL),
    293, 296
  UNICEF's Child Friendly Schools
    initiative, 295–296
  Violence Free Schools project,
    294, 296
segmentary lineage system
  as adaptation to problems, 200–202
  asabiyya (group feeling) and, 201–202
  and balanced opposition, 202–205
  and band of brothers, 206
  Banu Tamim tribes of Arabia, 208
  and Barabha-Shalalfa conflict, 205
  case of the greedy camel, 207
  and cognatic kinship structure,
    203–204
  collective responsibility in, 205–206
    (*see also* honor culture; honor
    codes: collective responsibility)
  defects of, 206–208, 220–221, 282
  and defensive needs, 200–201,
    202–203
  dynamics of, 205–206
  FBD marriages and, 185, 201 (*see also*
    marriages)
  Kamil Hanzai-Rahmatzai conflict, 207
  and Sarhadi Baluch pastoralists, 205
Servants of God. *See* Khudai Kidhmatgar
shame
  behavioral scripts and, 83, 135, 139, 145
  communal service and, 282
  as cultural adaptation, 201, 206 (*see
    also* segmentary lineage system)
  different from guilt, 82–84, 138
  dishonor and, 81, 86, 89–90, 91, 98
  dissolution of self and, 138, 155
  double-standards and, 6
    (*see also* honor-shame
    communities: double standards)
  as embodied, 138–139
  in eyes of beholders, 80
  as feeling like a woman, 153–154
  gossip and (*see* gossip and rumors)
  honor killing and, 6–7 (*see also* honor
    killing)
  and man-making process, 148–149
  peer pressure (*see* social perceptions)
  production of, 105
  public ceremony and, 282

and rage, 144–145 (*see also* violence)
and regression, 155
scenes of shame, 134
seppuku and, 83
shame cultures, 85–86 (*see also* honor-
  shame cultures)
shame-proneness and
  aggression, 155
shame-to-violence conversion, 84,
  100, 104–105, 134–135, 137–138,
  147, 154–155, 252, 285 (*see also*
  violence)
shaming behaviors, 84–85, 96, 114,
  118–119, 122, 133–134, 138, 159,
  173, 180, 210, 217, 246, 256, 261,
  273, 281–282, 285, 291
social pain and, 139
social perceptions and, 84–85
toxic stress and, 133–134, 256
vigilance and shame, 144–145
and vulnerability, 154
washing away (cleansing), 6, 18, 83–84,
  105, 282
Sharaf Heroes, 300, 304–305, 310
Sharaf Heroines, 304–305
shari'a, 3, 21, 29, 243, 244-247, 249
shelters. *See* emergency interventions
signaling systems
  adaptive fitness of honest signalers,
    212–213
  alternatives to honor killing as
    signaling, 277–278
  costly signaling, 209, 211–213, 221
  dishonest signaling, 212,
    216–217, 219
  Hadza of Tanzania, 213
  and handicap principle, 212–213,
    219–221
  honest signaling, 212–213, 215–216
  honor killing and, 219–221
  Ifaluk Atoll in Pacific, 213
  Meriam community of Torres
    Strait, 213
  peacock and, 213
smartphone apps. *See* emergency
  interventions
Social and Emotional Learning (SEL)
  Programs. *See* school-based
  programs
social death. *See* shame

Social Decision Making/Problem Solving
  Program (SDM). *See* school-based
  programs
social identity. *See* honor: identity
social learning theory, 19
social networks
  agents in networks, 174
  automatic mimicry in, 176
  behavioral contagion in, 175
  cascading effects within, 176–177
  collective intelligence and, 175
  emotional convergence in, 176
  network effect, 312
  network theory, 174, 176–178
  nonviolence and, 279–280
  properties of, 174–175
  rule of three degrees of influence,
    175–177, 178
  rule of 3.5 percent, 279–280
  small world experiment, 175
  social comparisons, 176
social practice
  cognitive certainty and, 76–77,
    165, 264
  defining characteristics, 73–77
  distinctiveness of, 72–73
  honor killing as, 167, 183, 203
  moral dumbfounding and, 77, 165, 264
  non-elective participation, 75–76
socialization. *See* child-rearing; male
  adolescents
Southall Black Sisters, 267
Sohari of Oman
  absence of honor killing, 272–273
  Al Ba Said tribe of Arabia, 272
  contrast with Cairo, Egypt, 273
  modified honor norms, 273
  Sheikha's adultery, 273
sorocide-filiacide, 5. *See also* honor killing
South Africa
  gender violence in, 9
  rapes, 9
Spartans, 49, 103, 149. *See also* warrior
  masculinity
spirals of silence, 178–179
  Basque terrorism and, 178
  cycles of preventive denunciation,
    178–179
  false conformity and, 178
  pluralistic ignorance and, 178

Stockholm syndrome. *See* traumatic
  bonding
stoicism, 270
sulha, 277, 310. *See also* nonviolent
  conflict resolution
sure-fail mechanisms
  honor-shame communities and (*see*
    honor shame communities)
  moral transformation and, 256
surveys on honor killing. *See* honor:
  identity and
Sweden
  Electra and, 304
  honor killings in, 4, 23, 28, 42, 304
  Kvinnofoum, 94, 97
  parliament and, 4
  Sharaf Heroes and, 304
  Sharaf Heroines and, 304
  Terrafam, 26
symbolic violence. *See* violence
Syria
  honor killing in, 8
  public health, in, 299
Syrian Women's Observatory (SW0), 24

tahara, state of, 123
Tata Institution for Social Sciences
  (TISS), 295. *See also* school-based
  programs
Taureg
  absence of honor killing, 274–277
  Berbers and, 274
  gender and, 275
  Islam and, 274–275
  Kel Esuf (evil spirits) and, 276
  male veiling (wearing a *tajel*), 275–276
  matriarchy and, 275
  shame and, 276
Terrafam (Sewden), 26
terrorism
  al-Qaeda and, 28, 283
  Basque terrorism, 178
  feminizing men as, 153
  honor killing as, 296
  ideological extremism and, 283
  Islamic State in the Levant (ISIL) and,
    28, 283
  militant-jihadists Islamism, 147
  Taliban and, 16, 28, 283
  war on terror, 9

three-degrees rule. *See* social networks
torture
  Abu Ghraib and, 153–154
  castration and, 153
  homosexual rape, 16, 153
  honor killing as, 64–65
  Islamic State in the Levant (ISIL), 28
  rape as, 16, 28, 153
  Saddam Hussain and, 154
  sexual, 16, 28, 153
Tostan Program in Africa
  community empowerment
    program, 287
  community management committees
    (CACs), 287, 289, 290 (*see also*
    collaborative community-school
    centers)
  empowering women and, 288–290
  facilitators and, 287, 289
  female genital mutilation (FGM),
    287–288
  holistic and comprehensive, 288
  model for moral transformation,
    287–290, 306
  peer mentors and, 289
toxic stress, 127, 128–130, 133–134, 256,
  285, 291
TransAct, 305
transformative change, 285. *See also*
  moral transformations
traumatic bonding, 130-133, 137
Turkey
  Alevis (*see* Alevis)
  Batman (city), 93, 215, 216,
    242–243, 265
  Diyarbakir (city) and, 278
  European Union and, 242
  gender violence and, 242, 308
  honor killing and, 2–23, 24, 30, 42,
    58, 146, 160, 242, 243, 278
  honor-shame communities and, 93
  hopelessness and, 265
  Human Rights Directorate, 22
  media and, 250
  microfinance and, 312
  pastoralists and, 187
  revisions (2004) of Turkish Penal
    Code, 271
  Taurus Mountains, 271
  Turkish Penal Code, 242

  Turkmen, 271
  upland farmers and, 191–192
  Women's Center for Legal Aid and
    Counseling (WCLAC), 23
  women's shelters and, 243

United Nations, 231
UNICEF, 108, 128, 293
UNICEF: Child Friendly Schools
  Initiative, 295. *See also* school-
  based programs
UN Convention on the Elimination of All
  Forms of Discrimination Against
  Women (CEDAW), 245
UN Convention on the Rights of the
  Child, 238
UN Development Fund for Women
  (UNIFEM)
UN Development Programme
  (UNDP), 296
UN Goodwill Ambassador, 302
UN High Commissioner for Extrajudicial
  Executions, 231
UN High Commissioner for Refugees,
  239. *See also* refugees and asylum
UN Office on Drugs and Crime
  (UNODC), 296
UN Population Fund (UNFP), 22, 56
UN Special Envoy for Global
  Education, 295
UN Special Rapporteur on religious
  freedom, 22
UN Special Rapporteur on violence
  against women, 2
UN Special Representative of the
  Secretary-General for Violence
  Against Children, 293
UN Women's Solidarity Movement for
  Gender Equality, 302
United States
  gender violence and, 9
  homosexual murders as "honor"
    based, 19
  honor killings in, 4, 23, 42
  lynching and, 11, 19, 161
  racial segregation, 19
upland farmers, 187, 191–192, 193

vagina, 90–91, 110, 121
victimization. *See* women

victimology, 158

Vikings, 103. *See also* warrior masculinity

violence. *See also* shame: shame-to-violence conversion

child-rearing and, 107, 108–109

crimes of passion, 12–13, 16, 17

cultural, 26, 119

danger assessment and, 297, 307

everyday violence, 9

gender violence

domestic violence, 12–13, 15, 291, 296–303

children and, 117–118 (*see also* abuse)

dowry murders, 10, 14

female genital mutilation, 10, 287–288

femicide (gendercide), 8–9, 279

honor crimes and, 2, 12–13, 16

honor-based violence, 12–13, 16, 290

hymenoplasty, 246

physical and psychological, 161, 118

rage and, 143–144, 146

rape, 9, 10, 119, 282

sexual slave trade, 10

spousal rape, 15, 171

and statistics on missing women, 8–9

triggers of, 307

virginity tests, 16–17, 230, 246

institutional, 10, 26

intimate partner, 12, 15, 297

physical, 170–172, 296 (*see also* abuse: physical)

and primal honor, 126

psychological, 26, 170–172, 296

public health responses, 296–303

as redemptive, 105, 147, 149–150

sexual, 16, 28, 118, 296 (*see also* abuse: sexual)

structural violence, 10, 26

symbolic violence, 162–163

Violence Free Schools Project, 294 (*see also* school based programs)

violence-prone personality, 99, 252

adverse life conditions and, 126–127

child-rearing and, 107, 108–109

co-dependency and, 147, 148, 149, 154, 158

cultural adaptation and, 210

egocentrism and, 133

fahlawi personality and (see *fahlawi* personality)

moral transformations, 285–286, 300, 303

narcissism and, 138, 141 143

negative attachment and, 131–133, 285

parenting and, 118–119 (*see also* parenting)

punishment and, 115–119, 129

shaming and, 84, 100, 104–105, 134–135

toxic stress and, 127, 133 (*see also* brain architecture)

traumatic bonding and, 130–131

virginity tests. *See* gender violence

wajh. See honor: face

warrior masculinity

aggression as armor, 144, 156

and aim of violence, 153

band of brothers and, 144, 148, 206

behavioral scripts and, 135, 145

boundary maintenance and, 149–150, 151, 154

can-do body and, 139–140, 144, 148, 151, 153

child-rearing and, 117, (*see also* child-rearing)

as construct, 138, 172

contempt for feminine, 150, 152, 153–154

and cultural adaptation, 188, 210

grandiose fantasies, 146

historical examples, 103, 148

holy warriors (*mujahideen*), 191

homoerotic bonding, 148–149

homophobia and homosexual panic, 152

honor and, 143, 144, 303

impoverished empathy, 125, 128, 130, 133, 210

moral transformations and, 280, 285–286, 300

narcissism and, 143–144, 146

need to control women, 156, 170

need to humiliate, 143–144

neurotoxic glucocorticoids, 130